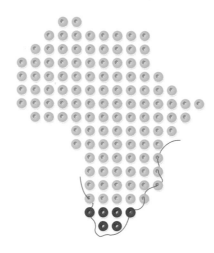

south africa
THE GOOD NEWS

Printed by CTP Cape Town South Africa
First Edition: October 2002
Designed by TerraNova

ISBN (Hardcover) 0-620-296-72-0
ISBN (Softcover) 0-620-296-41-0

Books are available in bulk to government, corporations and institutions. For more information contact the publishers.

Published by SOUTH AFRICA - The Good News (Pty) Ltd.
1 Saxon Road
Hyde Park
South Africa
P.O.Box 5796
Rivonia 2128
Phone (+27-11) 537 4700
Fax (+27-11) 327 2787

www.sagoodnews.co.za
sagoodnews@hls.co.za

Dedication

To Nelson Mandela:
Your vision of peace, democracy and prosperity in 1994 made this book possible in 2002.

To our children:
may the South Africa you inherit
be the land of your dreams
the community of your heart
the passion of your spirit
and the pride of your future.

Nkosi sikelel' iAfrika

The National Anthem

Nkosi sikelel' iAfrika
Maluphakanyisw' uphondo lwayo,
Yizwa imithandazo yethu,
Nkosi sikelela, thina lusapho lwayo.

Morena boloka setjhaba sa heso,
O fedise dintwa la matshwenyeho,
O se boloke, O se boloke setjhaba sa heso,
Setjhaba sa South Afrika - South Afrika.

Uit die blou van onse hemel,
Uit die diepte van ons see,
Oor ons ewige gebergtes,
Waar die kranse antwoord gee.

Sounds the call to come together,
And united we shall stand,
Let us live and strive for freedom,
In South Africa our land.

i

Acknowledgements

Endorsement
SOUTH AFRICA - The Good News has been endorsed by the President's International Marketing Council. Yvonne Johnston, CEO, has been unfailing in her support and has assisted greatly with both production and distribution.

Contribution Acknowledgments
Many people have assisted with the compilation of this book and their contribution is gratefully acknowledged.

To the authors, whose names appear in the Index, a very special thanks. Without your time, contribution and assistance this book would not have been possible.

To those who contributed to the writing of the chapters: Christopher Malan (Financial Stability - The next eight years); Gavin Lewis (International Trade - A Future perspective); Steven Budlender, Siva Kalay Pather, Nasreen Rajab (The Constitution and Constitutional Court); Mandla Matabula (Housing Infrastructure - From Shanties to Suburbia); Liz Sheridan (Tourism - Changing Attitudes, Changing Numbers, Improving Participation); JJ Thabane (Environmental Management - Sustainability Initiatives); Cindy August (Tax Collection - Spreading the Net); Shaun Matisonn (Medical Facilities - Terminal, Curable or on the Mend?) Sare Grobler, Hans van den Groenendal, Amanda Singleton (Global Connectedness); Richard Carter (Exports and Labour Productivity - Re-tooling the Myth); Marius Luyt (Transport Infrastructure - Moving Forward or Going Backwards); Tatjana Von Bormann (From Poverty to Paying it Forward); Angela Bull (The CIDA story); Thaninga Shope-Linney (NEPAD - Positive Change in Africa), Peter De Ionno and Lloyd Coutts and their team (Anecdotes).

A special thanks to Geoff Hill for sub-editing; to Ria Krafft and Terra Nova for design and art direction; the production team of Rozelle Clark, Philanie Jooste, Ronelle Jwalapersad, Marette Koorts, Debbie Liebenberg, Rex Pennington, Maria Saunders, Justine Teiwers, to Dov Fedler for his cartoons, to Desklink, Gallo Images, Shack Chic, Sunday Times, The Star, Touchlife Pictures, and many other photographers for pictures as acknowledged in the References.

Sponsors
Our Sponsors: Barloworld, Dimension Data, Hollard, Business Report, SABMiller plc and The South African Breweries Ltd are gratefully acknowledged for providing the seed capital to enable this project.

Note from the Editors
There are many ideas expressed in the book and some authors differ widely in their views. It is through this very diversity that the richness of the South African fabric is created. The opinions are not necessarily those of the editors or the sponsors. Where editorial comment is made, it is clearly indicated.

For this reason, the reader is encouraged to read all the chapters. It is as a collection that they provide their real value in enabling an informed view of the future.

Brett Bowes   Steuart Pennington

Foreword

South Africa is in the process of developing a branding strategy, "South Africa - Alive with Possibilities" is the slogan. A brand is a promise. Reputation is built on the sustained ability to deliver the promise.

Do many South Africans both at home and abroad sell their country as one that is "Alive with Possibilities"? We think not.

Too often we hear of fellow South Africans slagging the country off, be it at dinner parties, in business, or in general conversation with their children.

We felt that we could no longer stand by. We wanted to do something about it. So we decided to compile this book.

In July 2002 we brainstormed our approach and by October we had gone to print.

Obviously we could not do it alone. We needed providers of seed capital, on the basis that they would be repaid from sales. We reckoned on five corporate sponsors. We found four (having approached seven), the fifth found us. Gratitude to our sponsors is heartfelt, particularly because their passion for the subject really fits with the adage; "put your money where your mouth is".

Given our timeframe, we could not have written it ourselves, nor did we want to. We wanted a range of prominent South Africans to contribute. So we approached 50 people who really know their subjects, politicians, civil servants, business people, academics, NGOs, researchers, journalists and regular citizens.

Not one person refused. Our heartfelt thanks to them too.

We planned on 20 chapters, but had so many unsolicited submissions from people with whom the purpose of the project resonated (and that we simply had to include), that we ended up with 27.

We believe there is no other example, in the history of mankind, that rivals the humility and the bravery, the forgiveness and the honesty, or the sheer boldness of our transition. For us, the journey of learning about the staggering progress we have made since 1994 has made the project a life-changing experience. We hope this book will do that for you, the reader.

Brett Bowes   Steuart Pennington

Building, developing and managing reputation has become increasingly important in recent years, both for corporations and countries.

The consultancy firm, McKinsey and Co., recently conducted a series of surveys to discover how shareholders value corporate governance in both developed and emerging markets.

A key finding was that 80 per cent of investors said they would pay more for the shares of a well-governed company than for those of a poorly-managed one with comparable financial performance.

Clearly, having a positive reputation encourages investor confidence and access to capital, the foodstuff of transformation.

Reputation is not the 'brand' or the 'identity' or the 'image' of a company/country. Rather, it signals the overall attractiveness of the entity to all of its stakeholders, both internal and external. A positive reputation has value because it represents the standing you hold relative to your competitors.

Davis Young, author of **Building Your Company's Good Name**, writes: "You build your reputation inch by inch and day by day. And you lose it in an instant when you stop focusing on its importance."

Countries that fail to manage their reputation will find themselves at a competitive disadvantage when it comes to attracting tourists and, more critically, capital to finance growth or social change.

A good reputation is essential to attracting and retaining investors in rapidly-globalising capital markets, while a failed reputation is likely to hinder the country's global ambitions.

Reputation is a function of perception. It is well known that 'the truth is not what the facts are, but rather what they are perceived to be'.

South Africa's reputation is tarnished by a wide-ranging number of factors; not least of which is the general view of the country by its own citizens; being part of Africa; and, perhaps, an over critical media.

Right now, South Africans, both local and abroad, do not demonstrate the kind of passionate patriotism we see in many other countries. We are a proud people but we are in the habit of focussing on the negative and saying little about the positive. The impact this has on us, and people interested in South Africa, particularly investors and tourists, is damaging.

Being part of Africa - and in particular having Zimbabwe as a neighbour - currently casts a shadow over the many achievements that have taken place under the current government since 1994.

The media has a special role to play in building the reputation of our nation. As Chief Anyaoku of Nigeria said (when receiving a Doctor of Laws, honoris causa at Rhodes University) on the topic of South Africa and the Challenge of Divisive Pluralism: "The media has time and again proved to be a facilitator of integration and healing in divided and traumatised societies. Under apartheid, the media had served the cause of division. Now, as South Africa grapples with the challenges of developing a plural democracy, experience in different regions of the world has shown that the media can become instruments for intensifying the sense of otherness, and hence, impede the process of integration and cooperation in divided societies. In the attempts of the government to gain the confidence of the citizenry and build a new social order where a common humanity is accepted, the media could become a critical factor. The outreach capacity of the media is enormous and it can affect respect for and appreciation of the diversity of the country."

This book, SOUTH AFRICA - The Good News, is an attempt to put the record straight, to highlight the significant number of positive developments in many walks of South African life that are not generally appreciated.

It is true that good news happens slowly and incrementally for the most part and that bad news happens fast and with quantum. We have every confidence that the readers of this book will form a significantly more positive impression of this wonderful land and its people.

Hopefully, as the information contained herein spreads, South Africa's reputation as a land of possibility, of learning and of hope will spread in earnest.

Brett Bowes   Steuart Pennington

Index

It has been said that mankind's ability to learn from history is what sets him apart from other animals. The purpose of our prologue is to ask you, the reader, if you will accompany us on a short but critical journey of history. We challenge you to open your mind to the lesson of what has gone before us. You may find that the facts revealed make a bigger difference than you think.

Prologue
Change Starts in Africa
Dr Lee R Berger

Part 1: The State of the Nation

The Hostilities End

It is eight years post what could only be called a civil war in this country. Granted the bloodshed could have been far worse. However, thousands died on both sides of the conflict. In many areas, the hardest hit were the least expendable, the cream of our youth, the young leadership willing to place their lives in harm's way pursuing the cause of freedom. But at the end of the conflict freedom emerged and the country, and indeed the world, would never be the same. For the first time in this country's history, black Africans were free, at least in law, from the yoke of oppression that had been imposed upon them by more than a hundred years of slavery by peoples of European descent. People whose ancestors had themselves only been on this continent for a few hundred years. Yet in that short time these European colonists had, in the course of building magnificent and rich cities and elite agricultural societies, been able to squash effectively the rebellions of the indigenous populations and enslave poor immigrants. Just a few decades before our civil war, there had been a revolution in that a change of government had occurred. For some, this was seen as a great moment in history, since for all intents and purposes, a great colonial power had been ruling our country from afar and government had finally fallen solely into the hands of people who lived and worked on the land. But there were hard lessons to be learned. Government cannot be by a few people, for just a few people, and thus the events of eight years ago occurred.

The Cry of Freedom

When conflict had ended, we stood staggered by the violence but in awe of the peace. There was jubilation which erupted into spontaneous celebrations in the streets of our cities. We were fortunate at that moment to have great leadership. Men who rose up and proclaimed that we would not punish our former enemies, but embrace them. Although they had fought to stop what most of us saw as inevitable change, they too would be allowed to vote for a representative government. Fortunately and with great foresight a strange peace came over the land, punitive cries were not heeded by the leadership as the process of nation-building began. There were of course moments so low that we often felt that the experiment would fail. When one of our greatest leaders was assassinated by a white man, all thought wholesale retributive bloodshed would follow; yet it did not. When white farmers, who, some say, benefited most under the old system, packed their belongings and left for other countries, famine was predicted, and yet we still held the country together. Famine did not occur. New ways were found to gain the most from many smaller landowners tilling the soil of our fertile country.

Reality

But all is clearly not well in this land of ours. The people who were freed by the struggle, particularly the poorest of the black Africans, the people who, burdened by apartheid style education of the previous regime, and who had not had access to literacy programmes, still suffer greatly. They have few skills, and thus there are no jobs. They have no houses and many wander this country aimlessly looking for the promises that freedom had made. Land is an enormous issue. The conflict with indigenous peoples over who owns the land continues. A conflict that now pits the wealthy, and in many cases the government, against the very poorest. How can people with no access to government, through illiteracy and poor or no representation, challenge armies and established systems? And so, in parts of our continent bloodshed and warfare over land remains, and in some cases threatens to re-ignite hostilities. Racism is still present. Faction groups of the far right still hold to the old ways.

Old Habits Die Hard

The spectre of xenophobia is ever-present. As individuals from more disadvantaged countries flee to our country seeking refuge from famine, warfare, poverty and dictators, we frequently reject them. They are, after all, mostly illiterate, poor and bring apparently little to our country and yet they seem to take so much. They live in our cities like squatters and take jobs at cheaper wages than even our poorest will accept , thus taking food from our mouths. There have been disturbing and frequent incidences of violence against immigrants. Yet, some say that immigrants are a good thing. They bring diversity and work hard to uplift themselves, having taken the risk of leaving their homelands for our shores.

★　★　★　★

We were fortunate at that moment to have great leadership. Men who rose up and proclaimed that we would not punish our former enemies, but embrace them.

But, on the Horizon ...

As we look at our potential at this moment in history, we are a country and continent of vast resources. Of all the habitable continents, we are arguably the least populated, bringing us the potential for expansion and growth that countries in Europe envy beyond almost anything else that we possess. The last hundred years of exploration into this land shows a mineral and ecological wealth that is unsurpassed in the known world - even with the massive amounts of stripping of these resources that has already occurred. If approached correctly and distributed fairly, there is more than enough in this great country and continent for all to live prosperously and free. And at that point, when we have learned to live together there will be no limits to what we can do. We will, as Abraham Lincoln once said, never be destroyed from the outside. If we falter and lose our freedoms, it will be because we destroyed ourselves. We are blessed with a leadership committed to democracy and constructive debate. We have a strong constitution that, even as we struggle to apply its ideals, we recognise as one of the greatest written documents of humankind.

Does the above sound like the history of South Africa?
It's not. I have been writing, not of South Africa in the 21st century, but of the history of the United States of America in the year 1873.

Part 2: South Africa - Our Present Reality

I beg the forgiveness of the reader for the subterfuge of the above. It is not my wish to oversimplify the comparison of the situation of late 19th century America to that of early twenty-first century South Africa.

Africa and America: Apples and?

There are many complex social and technological differences that make such a comparison on one hand naïve, but on the other hand, it does prove useful in removing some of the smothering blankets of day-to-day life and place the situation here in South Africa, and Africa as a whole, into a more historical perspective.

Does History Repeat?

As a historian (some might call me a "pre-" historian) there are, in my opinion, some inescapable realities of this moment in Africa's history that parallel the moment that America experienced eight years post its Civil War. This is not to imply that Africa should aspire to be the powerful nation that America became fifty years after the events of my hypothetical essay. It is, however, an undeniable fact that America is held up as a story of success and affluence - at least for its own people. At a time when South Africans, and Africans often look at our country and continent with despair - the poverty, the war, the famine, the racism and the corruption always seem to overshadow the good, it is important to remember how few years it has been since countries like the United States and continents like North America were in exactly the same situation.

If you are over 45 years of age, it is almost certain that you knew of someone who was alive in 1873. If you are younger, you are almost certainly less than two generations from that moment in time. Just two individual life spans separate the youngest of us from a situation in North America where the Native American Indian wars were still being fought - 1873 was still three years before the battle of the Little Bighorn. The allusions I made to social strife, . xenophobia, economic hardship and famine were very real at the time. The Union, and preservation of democracy, was by no means assured. Black African Americans, while free, were for the most part landless, disenfranchised and poor.

Much like a third force, by the late 1860s, the Klu-Klux-Klan had evolved as an anti-government, and anti-black empowerment movement, and were active in small cells throughout the South, and other parts of the USA. There was rampant dissatisfaction amongst African Americans with the way in which reparations had been made. The former slaves had been promised land and little or none was forthcoming.

In the early 1870s crime and lawlessness were in many parts of the country the order of the day. The great immigration boom loomed on the horizon as the war-era factories shifted to peace-time industry. Along with this emerged early industrial revolution-aged xenophobia - foreigners were taking jobs. Language was an extreme issue. But the world had fundamentally changed. Transport and communication were faster. The oceans of the world were moving from being barriers of weeks and months to days, and even minutes with the successful laying of the second transatlantic telegraph cable. That was the America of the late 19th century.

Not Always, but there are Lessons

All of us who live in South Africa have experienced, at functions or dinner parties, people who dwell on the negatives of life here today. Crime, poverty, the declining rand, neighbouring countries on the brink of chaos. As an historian I have learnt the danger of over-emphasising the moment against the need to examine our existence in the context of time. Our ability to examine history is what sets us apart from all other animals. It is probably our defining trait. We do not need to experience an event directly to understand its implications. We can learn from the successes and mistakes of others and move forward. We are defined as individuals, societies and cultures by our history. Our ability to observe, analyse and learn from history is our single greatest weapon in our arsenal of behaviours and the key to our success. Notwithstanding our individual needs, fears, worries and ambitions we must face this dichotomy as we examine the South Africa of today with an eye to predicting its future.

50 years after 1873 America had emerged as a global superpower. How long will it take South Africa in the age of the super-conductor, the internet and bio-technology?

So, what will our Future be?

How, as an anthropologist and historian, do I see the future of South Africa and Africa as a whole at this moment in time? Before answering this question, I would like to place Africa in a context beyond the socio-political implications one may derive from my essay.

Africa Leads Change in the World - Really?

Africa is the mother continent of humankind. Not only is it the largest habitable land mass with over one-third of all habitable land on this planet within its borders (in practical terms, this means that one may place the habitable land masses of North America, South America and Europe into Africa and have room left over), but it is also a fact that every single critical event in our long history has emerged from this continent. From our physical adaptations - the adoption of an upright stance, reduced canine size, a big brain, acquiring human stature and limb proportions, the fining of our hair, the acquisition of sweat glands, our child-like features - to the very organisation of our brains, are all African inventions. Even more practical adaptations - the first tools and then the first complex tools, the harnessing of energy in the controlled use of fire, the acquisition of more complex tool kits that would eventually lead to the infinite tool kits that define modern human behaviour, and even the first interactions with the marine environment. The more spiritual aspects of humankind are also of African origins - our human language, recognition of our own mortality as indicated by burial of the dead, art and artwork and make-up. As one readily notes, the above are lists of what define us as humans and they are all African in their origin. What is the message from this human history lesson? Africa will continue to drive humankind, and if it is true that history does have a habit of repeating itself, then it is not a question of if, but of when.

And what Lessons do Repeat?

Lets try to look at South Africa and Africa from a more distant perspective. Here we sit, eight years after a relatively peaceful transition to a democratic government. Yes there are very real problems. Land and poverty are probably the biggest issues, but there are others. Many of the previously disenfranchised remain so - not through lack of empowerment efforts, but through illiteracy brought on by having grown up in a disadvantaged education system. Many are simply not qualified for the jobs that are available. Illegal, and sometimes even legal immigration,

is seen as a problem by some. Foreigners take jobs, but it must be remembered that it was largely immigrants who made America in the late 19th and early 20th century. They bring diversity and diversity breeds change. We are an under-populated continent. With the exception of Antarctica and Australia, there is no other continent with so few people and so much land and probably no other with so much habitable land. It is land rich in resources. We have advantages over other continents in that in many ways humankind in Africa has developed in a sustainable way with its environment, despite the many conservation horrors that we are all aware of. After all, humans are an indigenous African animal, over six million years of evolutionary evidence proves that, and thus the ecosystems of Africa are as much a product of us as we are of them. Where we have done damage, we show the capabilities to reverse it. Look to the Lowveld and the expansion of reserves and habitats in the last decade. Look at the population rebound of indicator species like elephants and white rhinos.

And what Lessons Cannot be Ignored?

Africa is busy teaching humans that to ignore history, even our evolutionary history, will be at our peril. By invading and chopping down tropical evergreen forests which our ancestors abandoned more than 5 million years ago, we encounter tropical diseases for which we have no evolutionary resistance - AIDS being possibly one of the best known, but there are many others. We learn in Africa about human overpopulation in urbanised environments and the aberrant behaviours of genocide and other negative intra-species interactions that occur in these situations. Because of its diversity of habitats we see humans in Africa living in every conceivable ecological situation. From arid deserts to lush coastal environments. We see today the first true interactions of the first and third worlds. Who cannot marvel at a twenty-first century city like Johannesburg, with its digital cellphones and economic wealth, that contrasts so vividly with individuals living on its outskirts who are effectively existing in the Iron-Age? Where else will the future of humankind's interactions on racial, economic and social issues be tested in an age of near-instantaneous communication?

So, is this Our Defining Moment?

I would put to you that the future of South Africa and Africa is no less bright than was America's in the late 19th century. We are experiencing teething pains, but these are, I would argue, possibly less than those of other countries and continents even 100 years ago, because we have the advantage of hindsight. We are experiencing almost eerily similar social, economic and political issues, yet our playing field is bigger and indeed richer, and our sense of history is keen, thus our potential is greater. As a historian of Africa, I would argue that success for Africa in the future is assured. As the mother continent of humankind, it is our manifest destiny to lead human change. When it will happen is really more the question. But the world is a very fast place these days. Fifty years after 1873 America had emerged as a global superpower, a largely unified country, with many of the issues raised in my essay largely forgotten. How long will it take for Africa to achieve the same level of unity and growth in the age of the super-conductor, satellite, internet, bio-technology and micro-chip? From a historical perspective this is Africa's moment and one that will happen more quickly than we all realise. How quickly? None of us have the ability to see truly into the future. However, the pace has accelerated from that of a 100 and 125 years ago. We can all sense this and it is certainly my perception as a historian that Africa's and particularly South Africa's, time is right.

I would put to you that the future of South Africa and Africa is no less bright than was America's in the late 19th century. Our time has come.

In this chapter we have presented three different sets of benchmarks to measure the health and the progress we have made as a nation. The chapters that follow deal mostly with topics that influence these benchmarks and our "reputation". While objectivity is our watchword, the remarkable achievements that have been documented will, we hope, enable an appreciation that the tide has turned, and that there is an overwhelming body of Good News.

1

Benchmarking South Africa's Progress

The South African Investment Scorecard
10 Key Investment Criteria - Getting Better all the Time

Part 1
Using the books 'South Africa - How are you?' and 'Hoe lyk dit, Suid-Afrika?'
written by Louis Fourie and JP Landman.

Editorial Comment

"If you can't measure it you can't manage it", is a statement often used in organisations as they wrestle with performance. Also heard in the corridors: "what's important should be measured, and what is measured becomes important."

As the standards of quality and price become ubiquitous, organisations are increasingly concerned about managing their reputations. It is now well documented that a firm with a good reputation can command a premium on its share price of between 15 and 25 per cent, attract the best people, secure customer loyalty, raise capital more easily, and ride periods of economic uncertainty better than those with questionable credentials.

The same may be said of countries. At the time of writing, the United States of America's corporate sector is in turmoil.

A number of significant corporate failures had occurred with severe implications for the New York Stock Exchange and the wealth of many Americans.

Add to that the war-mongering of President George W Bush and you have a nation worried about its reputation and about why the rest of the world is becoming so disaffected, so quickly. As is often said, "Reputation takes decades to build, and can be destroyed in an instant." In South Africa's case, the question may be asked: is our reputation improving or deteriorating? Are things getting better or are they getting worse?

Judged by investor confidence, the brain drain and world opinion, the answer is mostly negative.

Back in 1985, challenged by the lack of empirical data, a team of economic researchers belonging to Citadel, with political analyst J P Landman, investigated the topics used by international rating agencies and economic analysts as measures of investment stability.

According to Louis Fourie, chairman of Citadel, this would, "help us guide people to an unemotional, objective and big-picture evaluation of South Africa."

These were consolidated into 10 criteria and scored by a research team made up of highly rated and respected economists, actuaries, chartered accountants and legal experts from many different parts of the world.

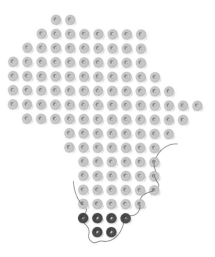

Our objective is to guide people to an unemotional, objective and big picture evaluation of South Africa

What is remarkable about their work (reported below) is the considerable progress that has been made since 1985. Table 1 shows the 10 criteria that were measured and South Africa's score at that time.

1985

•	Democracy and Free Speech?	⦾ ⦾	20%
•	Policy Makers?	⦾ ⦾ ⦾ ⦾	40%
•	Open Economy	⦾ ⦾ ⦾	30%
•	Education System?	⦾ ⦾ ⦾ ⦾	40%
•	Property Rights?	⦾ ⦾ ⦾ ⦾	40%
•	Law Enforcement?	⦾ ⦾ ⦾ ⦾ ⦾	50%
•	Financial System?	⦾ ⦾ ⦾ ⦾ ⦾	50%
•	Our People?	⦾ ⦾ ⦾ ⦾	40%
•	South Africa Incorporated?	⦾ ⦾ ⦾ ⦾ ⦾	50%
•	Our Goal?	⦾ ⦾ ⦾	30%

CITADEL

Table 1: South Africa in 1985

Using the conventional symbols attributed to percentages achieved in end-of-school examinations, the results were:
3 Ds   4 Es   2 Fs   1 G

As a headmaster once remarked to parents who were concerned about their son's exam results, "I didn't know that a G-symbol was possible."

In 1985, South Africa scraped borderline Ds in three subjects and failed the remaining seven dismally.

2002

By 2002, South Africa was working considerably harder at improving her results and, thankfully, it has begun to show.

Louis Fourie says, "South Africans, like citizens of any other country, get wrapped up in emotion when asked about the state of affairs in their beloved land. Whatever has top-of-mind awareness at any particular time dominates their perception and, thus, their response to any such questions.

"Objectivity and an assessment, without emotion, is how we at Citadel approach all decisions made on behalf of our clients. We regularly assess countries, as well as the situation at home, to evaluate what possibilities they hold for our clients' investments. It is this same approach we used in the compilation of the SA Scorecard on which the books were based."

QUICKLY! BEFORE HE GETS ON HIS FEET

South Africa has been transformed from a country engaged in a low level civil war into one of the most politically stable countries on the planet.

To re-appraise the SA situation in 2002, Louis Fourie and JP Landman, with Citadel, considered the same 10 criteria:

1. Do we enjoy democracy and freedom of speech?

The question here is not whether we have reached a perfect situation but whether we have improved and what the future holds.

"Democracy is a culture, not an election. A culture of participation, rights, justice and opportunities for all individuals.

"It is a complex system, but one with the ability to unlock human potential and energy - offering long-term economic progress. We are radically different in terms of the application of democracy compared with 15 years ago."

In the big picture, South Africa is regarded as a radical innovator and a global case study for its conversion to democracy, supported by a cutting edge constitution. The debate is still open as to why we were spared bloodshed and revenge in the process of conversion from apartheid to democracy. In the past 40 years, Africa has seen more than 80 violent or unconstitutional changes of government. SA did not have that. Most people believe quality of leadership was the decisive factor in our miraculous transformation. In all, we get top marks for the progress we have made in this area. South Africa has been transformed from a country engaged in a low level civil war into one of the most politically stable countries on the planet. Ten years ago, nobody predicted such a result. To sustain this we need to ensure the following;

- Our democratic culture has to be embraced and lived at the most basic levels of society.
- Our politicians have to prove to the world that we can fight close elections without bloodshed or without Zimbabwe-style manipulation.
- The ANC, given its dominant position, will need to remain the servant of the people and stay on the moral high ground.

Freedom of speech is rare in Africa and, even in the developed world, some countries have questionable records on that score. In South Africa it is included in the Constitution and, as we have seen recently, is openly and vigorously debated in the context of its relationship with government.

Rating 8/10

2. Are our macro-economic policy makers doing the right things?

"The goal of macro-economic policy is to create a facilitating, not a participating government. In terms of the economy, enforcing democratically decided-upon rules, creating a stable economic playground and being sympathetic to an open market is the role of Government. In the past, macro-economic policy was predominantly used as a political lever. Today we have an environment where our macro-economic policy makers are regarded as leading figures in the international community."

There have been a number of remarkable achievements:

- Between 1997 and 2002 the South African Government has given R38 billion back to taxpayers.
- A portion of the national budget set aside to serve government debt declined from 20 per cent in 1997 to 16 per cent in 2002.
- Government's budget deficit declined from around nine per cent of GDP in 1993 to 2.1 per cent in 2002 - the globally accepted norm is three per cent.
- The number of people employed in the civil service declined by some 15 per cent between 1993 and 2002 - made possible by rapidly managing South Africa out of the 10 "independent" homelands and enforcing financial discipline at all levels.
- Tax collection in South Africa has become dramatically more efficient - collections are regularly exceeding the budgeted expectation.
- Inflation has declined from 19 per cent in 1986 to six per cent in 2001. At time of writing in 2002, it is 10.4 per cent and under temporary pressure from the exchange rate. In chapter 2 Rudolf Gouws believes that, in the longer term, our efforts to control inflation are on target.

Costing SA points on this score is the lack of results on issues like delivery to the poor, privatisation and tax relief.

Rating 8/10

3. Do we live in an open economy?

"Openness is economic democracy. It has been proven, the world over, that globally-integrated economies grow much faster than non-integrated ones. The sudden opening up of the SA economy has resulted in dramatic changes in the span of 10 short years and this has rubbed off on the exchange rate of the rand, currently trying to establish its true natural value in world markets."

Coming from an era of debt moratoriums, sanctions, two exchange rates, travel restrictions and a policy of inward industrialisation, we have transformed quickly to an economy embracing the global market.

Many challenges remain. The first is to attract sustainable foreign direct investment. This has been as absent in the New South Africa as it was in the old. The competitive rand may well trigger such interest and we should do whatever it takes to remain an attractive destination to those investors.

The second is to penetrate the markets of developed countries still suffering from protectionism. The prolonged but promising negotiations with the European Union and the USA have underlined the patience needed and, recently, during the World Summit on Sustainable Development, both the EU and the USA agreed to a process of lifting trade tariffs on agricultural goods.

The third is to get rid of remaining exchange controls. Although progress has been made since 1995, we are still sending a message to the world that we need "confidence protection." As a result, the world is reluctant to invest here.

Rating 8/10

4. Does our education system produce relevant people?

"The ultimate test for an education system is the demand for the people it produces. If only seven per cent of matriculants find formal jobs there is not necessarily a problem with the economy but with the quality of people created for that economy.

"An economy is people, nothing more, nothing less. It is a myth to argue that there is a lack of jobs in SA. The jobs and the skills do not match, that is the problem."

Perhaps the obsession to manage education centrally is the main stumbling block in creating a solution.

"Problems with education are not unique to South Africa or the Third World. It is a global challenge to change from an industrial-age education system to one that is adapted to the needs of the modern era."

As Fourie and Landman point out: "Our education system has three major challenges."

First: "The system has become much bigger than its cause. It has a deep-rooted history, an embedded tradition and powerful vested interests. It is a system driven predominantly by central decision-making and paternalistic values. The consequences are inefficiency, slowness and insensitivity to the economic needs of the future."

They argue that the education system needs to make itself more relevant to the job requirements of the future.

"We do not believe that South Africa is suffering from a lack of jobs. We are suffering form a lack of skills."

Second: the world has become a much faster place since the original design of our education system.

"We need to move away from the practice of preparing people in an isolated, academic environment and prepare them for the fast changing world in which they are expected to be valuable."

Third: "The industrial economy has all but died in so far as the future involvement of mass labour is concerned. It has become a highly automated, efficient production process in which people have very little to contribute in terms of labour. The information economy is about a new set of skills and new ways of being relevant." They conclude: "We have entered an era where people will have to cope with more than one economic cycle in a lifetime. Education simply cannot afford to reflect industrial society anymore; it needs to shape the information society and what will follow after it."

They propose that the involvement of private initiative and enterprise will make a significant contribution to improving the education system and that economic growth, employment and sustainable long-term poverty relief will follow.

Footnote: The reader might like to see chapter 10 on education which offers a contrasting view on the health of our education system.

Rating 5/10   ● ● ● ● ●

5. Are our property rights under threat?

Property rights are protected in our constitution, but the events in Zimbabwe and the Mineral Rights legislation have caused some nervousness.

As Fourie says: "The issue must also include consideration for people who do not have property or a safe place to live in dignity. We cannot afford to keep the homeless... homeless. It requires a radical solution."

According to the globally-recognised definition of property rights, South Africa has displayed a sound track record since 1994 while making huge progress towards correcting the injustices of the past.

The country's legal system today recognises and protects legitimate rights of ownership, and government has been solid in its support, both politically and in execution.

In September 2002, Delingwe Mayende, the Director-General in the Department of Land Affairs, said that there was encouraging enthusiasm and cooperation from white commercial farmers on the issue of land redistribution. In answer to the question, "What would government do if landless people invaded farms as has happened in other parts of Africa?" he said: "Illegal land grabs will not be tolerated... if it is an illegal land grab, the state has to respond by enforcing the law."

Footnote: Later in this book, in chapter 9 on housing, we present the dynamic progress of housing in South Africa. And, in chapter 11 on agriculture, Minister Derek Hannekom looks at the remarkable progress in the area of land redistribution.

Rating 7/10   ● ● ● ● ● ● ●

"To mobilise the energy and spirit of the nation we need a simple, wise, national goal. Only the President can do it."

> "In the World Competitiveness Report, SA is rated Number One in its ability to get poverty relief to the poor."

already unfolding. We expect the South African financial sector to be included. As a result, smaller players, and financial companies with obsolete business models, will disappear or be absorbed by bigger institutions."

6. Do you experience a friend in our system of law enforcement?

"Few other issues attract as much emotion as this one. South Africa suffers from the law of no consequences. The people in SA are no better or worse than those in any other country. What we have is people engaging in criminal activity because there are no consequences.

"Like education, this issue requires massive private initiative to improve."

Statistics show that, in 17 of the 20 major crime categories, incidents have decreased or stabilised during 2002, indicating that the tide is beginning to turn.

There was, for example, not a single mugging in downtown Johannesburg during the World Summit on Sustainable Development.

Footnote: In chapter 16, The War Against Crime, the facts indicate that, slowly but surely, this war, being waged on many fronts, is being won.

Rating 4/10

7. Do we have a reliable financial system?

"South Africa's financial services infrastructure and services are regarded as some of the most sophisticated in the world.

"There is efficient supervision and efficient flow of money but the continuing exploitation of the poor and the so-called "under-banked" is a worrying trend.

"The poor were savers, but now have access to credit through micro-lending and there is also serious insurance overselling in that market."

Fourie concludes by noting that: "Globally, a huge consolidation process awaits financial services. It is, in fact,

Rating 8/10

8. How well are our people?

"A country with a life expectancy of 47 years is not doing well in terms of the well-being of its people. The fact that it is expected that seven million people could die of AIDS before 2010 is a clear indication that a huge human intervention is required in SA.

"Furthermore, due to our recent history, our communities still suffer from physical, moral and mental neglect. The miracle of our political transition and the advent of the Truth and Reconciliation Commission cannot heal these legacies in the short time of 10 years.

"In the World Competitiveness Report, SA is rated number one in its ability to get poverty relief to the poor. Clearly we have made a start and we are doing something right. We need massive human-centred investment in South Africa to restore the humanity of people - in our capacity to trust, care and feel for those with whom we share our country."

Fourie and Landman conclude: "Dignity is the basis for economic usefulness. The miracle has not happened in South Africa yet; it still needs to happen; the miracle of healing people's internal scars and gradually making them well!"

Rating 4/10

9. Is South Africa Incorporated healthy?

Despite South Africa's rather grim corruption rating, Fourie and Landman have confidence in corporate South Africa.

"South African companies have survived a demanding series of issues - sanctions, political instability and tough labour forces, to name a few - and have proven their skill in dealing with such challenges. But we need more participants in private enterprise and we need robust skill-retention strategies."

14

They conclude that five major challenges remain.
- "We need to strengthen our spirit of free enterprise. It should be easy and attractive to start a business in South Africa, even more so a small enterprise. This remains the seedbed of strong economies.
- We need to improve our people's skills. The world is rapidly moving away from the cheap labour and resource-based economic models. Employment is a function of 'being prepared'.
- We need to absorb more labour in the informal economy. One way of doing this is to equip people with relevant skills. Another is less regulation in the labour market. A third is to keep the exchange rate as competitive as possible - sooner or later, the industries flourishing on exports will employ more workers.
- Corporate Governance needs to comply with globally-accepted standards.
- Deregulation should be taken all the way to its logical conclusions, from ending unnecessary government participation in the economy to abolition of remaining exchange controls."

Rating 8/10   ●●●●●●●●

10. Do we have a national goal?

"In a land of diversity, a very firm national goal is essential. We need something that every citizen, every level of worker or executive can work towards. Currently the goals are too fragmented to deliver any significant success."
They conclude: "A national vision is integrated with, and dependent on, inspirational leadership. Although the intellectual design of such a vision is extremely important, it needs to be communicated in an uncomplicated and straightforward manner; specifically its benefits; it must be clear and simple to understand. Many good things do happen in South Africa, but to mobilise the energy and spirit of the nation we need to create a simple, wise, national goal.

"We need to accelerate progress and we need to focus the minds of all the participants in the economy. Only the President of the country can do it."

NEPAD, Proudly South African and the President's International Marketing Council are new efforts to mobilise and consolidate resources in this regard.

Rating 3/10   ●●●

"The goal of macro-economic policy is to create a facilitating, not a participating, government.

Table 2 : South Africa in 2002

2002

	score in 1985
	score in 2002

•	Democracy and Free Speech?	● ●	20%
		● ● ● ● ● ● ● ●	80%
•	Policy Makers?	● ● ● ●	40%
		● ● ● ● ● ● ● ●	80%
•	Open Economy	● ● ●	30%
		● ● ● ● ● ● ● ●	80%
•	Education System?	● ● ● ●	40%
		● ● ● ● ●	50%
•	Property Rights?	● ● ● ●	40%
		● ● ● ● ● ● ●	70%
•	Law Enforcement?	● ● ● ● ●	50%
		● ● ● ●	40%
•	Financial System?	● ● ● ● ●	50%
		● ● ● ● ● ● ● ●	80%
•	Our People?	● ● ● ●	40%
		● ● ● ●	40%
•	SA Incorporated?	● ● ● ● ●	50%
		● ● ● ● ● ● ● ●	80%
•	Our Goal?	● ● ●	30%
		● ● ●	30%

Conclusion

In Table 1, our average score, only 15 years ago was 39 per cent, an F symbol and a dismal failure.

Today, in 2002, our average score is 63 per cent and a C symbol, good enough for a healthy pass. After all, we achieved five distinctions even though we failed three compulsory subjects. So, we are eligible only for a school-leaving certificate and won't gain university entrance (to use the education metaphor).

Is this overwhelmingly bad news? No! But is there room for improvement? Yes! And lots of it.

Hopefully, the chapters that follow will begin to map out where that improvement is required and how it will be achieved.

As Fourie and Landman conclude:
"We have come a long way in the relatively short time of 15 years and we can become a respected and successful country in the next ten.

"We can become an A student and transform South Africa from delivering a so-so-fine performance to a blockbuster attracting world attention. But we need vision, inspirational leadership, massive private participation and radical innovation for solutions to the issues we are struggling with - education, law enforcement, the wellness of our people and a national vision."

The authors provide updates about South Africa's progress on a website - www.howzitsa.co.za - which also provides details about the availability of the book.

Reference:

The study used in this chapter can be found in the book, **South Africa - How are you?** and **Hoe lyk dit, Suid-Afrika?** By Louis Fourie and J P Landman, printed by Paarl Print, 2002.

We have transformed quickly to an economy embracing the global market.

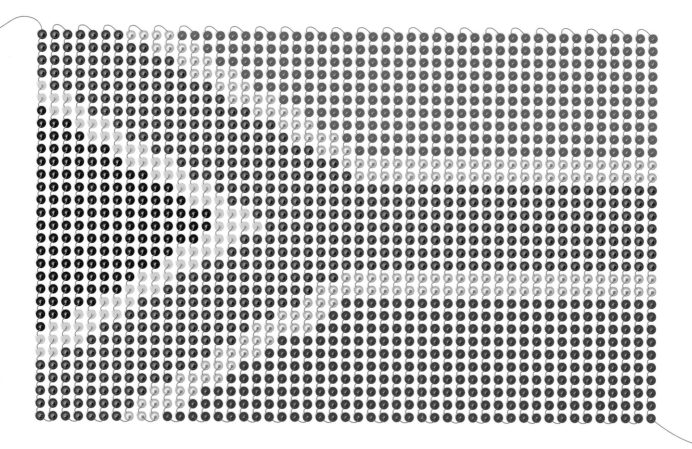

The SA balance sheet
Growing assets - diminishing liabilities

Part 2
Anna Starcke 1994 - 2002

The New South Africa (NSA) was born eight years ago with an unusual, though not unique, mix of excellent and abominable genes, mirrored by first-class assets and frightening liabilities.

If NSA was a firm, a report card today might read "This company has made terrific progress, but needs watching for lingering problems. In global context its potential is exceptionally promising."

This is close to how Mark Mobius, president of the Templeton Emerging Markets Fund, describes SA Inc. Mobius focuses on corporate governance and quality of management in the stocks selection for a $6 bn emerging markets fund that has, since its inception in 1987, outperformed the Dow Jones Industrial Index ... and the biggest investment slice (13 per cent) is in SA. He recently pronounced that South Africa is "on the right track" on corporate governance and that the quality of management in its leading companies is to be consistent with "world class."

South Africa's ugly/beautiful, cowed/triumphant, murderous/forgiving heritage gave birth to what international experts acknowledge as the most progressive Constitution on Earth.

Unpacking a Miracle

South Africa's genes were the subject of President Thabo Mbeki's most celebrated Parliamentary speech to date when, on adopting the country's new constitution, he declared, "I am an African." The African of whom he spoke has both the sins and the glory of ancestors of African, Far Eastern and European origin in his/her veins. An African shaped by wars through centuries, most recently less than 10 years ago, and with the genes of a people who humiliated and killed in the name of racial superiority. Whose notion of self-worth had been pulverised and whose negative influence still spooks the current generation. But, ultimately, an African who overcame both natural and man-made obstacles.

Assets to be Proud of

South Africa's ugly/beautiful, cowed/triumphant, murderous/forgiving heritage gave birth to what international experts acknowledge as the most progressive Constitution on Earth. It underpins a democracy that has its problems, but is conceded by even the most strident critics as being "better than what went before". And well they might: they too enjoy Africa's only fully-functioning constitutional state. One in which basic rights and freedoms are enshrined and ordinary citizens can take their government to court and, if their case is constitutional and Government's is not, expect to win.

Some of us balk at a legislative labour framework that seeks to redress three centuries of disadvantage topped by 40 years of ruthless discrimination; but it has bedded down well with the majority of big-company employers and was amended to afford flexibility to the small firms most in need of it.

Transparency became a concept we learned to appreciate, even as we cringe at revelations of corruption that, in Old SA, remained out of sight. As SA Inc prepared for globalisation, tariffs tumbled, large chunks of exchange control (all of it for foreigners) were scrapped, much of the airwaves were privatised and the media was freed from constraints.

"If South Africa had not democratised when it did, Mark Shuttleworth would not have travelled in space, the country's ports would be derelict and its exports would amount to nothing, with the world and the majority of SA's people united in wanting to overturn the situation. Therefore I say, the new SA with all its problems ... is a much better place than it would have been".

Former state president, F W de Klerk, Tim Modise Show, 8 May 2002

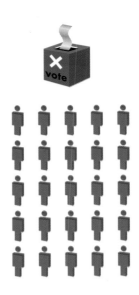

Assets inherited

South Africa has the continent's most powerful industrial base and a run-down but extensive transport infrastructure (15 times the African average in paved roads per land mass, 10 times the average of railway tracks); an electricity grid producing more than half of the continent's power more landline telephones than in the rest of sub-Saharan Africa put together; a network of shopping malls even Americans gawk at and food self-sufficiency with surplus agricultural production.

We also have teaching hospitals of world standard, a range of internationally renowned universities, an awesome defence force, a mature trade union movement unequalled elsewhere in Africa and a cadre of mostly white professional managers second to none.

Inherited Liabilities

The worst wasn't the country's debt, although that turned out higher than anything the ANC in exile had imagined. It wasn't that most rural households had neither water nor electricity, that healthcare for blacks beyond the big cities was scarce, nor that the physical education infrastructure for blacks was either in tatters or non-existent. The incoming Government already knew that.

More of a shock was that the state apparatus was nothing like the well-oiled machine it thought to take over and that the kitty was empty. The worst liability might have been AIDS but, in 1994, few inside Government or society at large took it seriously. But, no. The worst was the un-ready state of mind of its citizens, black and white, those "products of our immoral and amoral past", as Mbeki called them. And he had more to say: "It wasn't just that the majority was badly or not at all educated, the result of the ravages of both apartheid and the freedom struggle. It was that most New South Africans remained emotionally living in the old apartheid country: blacks frozen in victim mentality, whites hankering after an artificially sheltered world gone forever. The freedom dividend was slow in coming."

Eight years on.

The real South African miracle is still in the making but, considering the handicap at birth, it is making remarkable progress and is full of good news.

The world's 20th largest economy out of 230 countries (according to GDP measured in US dollars purchasing-

power parity) has, in the past eight years, provided access to clean water to seven million more of its citizens, made 3.5 million new electricity connections, built more than 1.2 million new houses, redistributed 440 000 hectares of land and settled 29 000 land claims.

That translates to 77 per cent of South Africans who now own their homes, up from 66 per cent, despite an additional 1.5 million households in the 8-year period; 76 per cent of households with water, up from 68 per cent; 80 per cent of homes electrified, up from 58 – in rural areas a staggering 264 per cent improvement.

According to the SA Advertising Research Foundation (from whose AMPS-based Development Index all but the land figures have been extracted), electrification led to a buying spree in electrical appliances from hot plates to stoves and microwaves; fridges, hi-fis and music centres; with TV sets now in almost 45 per cent of rural households and 84 per cent of urban homes.

As U2 rockstar Bono, travelling with the world's most powerful finance minister through Africa has just reminded us, transformation on the ground first and foremost means water where there was none. In NSA the consequence is hundreds of thousands of rural women whose quality of life - including their health, earning capacity and life expectancy - has been enhanced; and tens of thousands of prematurely-old rural men, whose self-esteem and dignity have been restored because they are able, for the first time, to provide for their families by growing fruit and vegetables and raising chickens.

Where they have electricity and telephones as well - apart from water, essential prerequisites for commercial activity, self-improvement and communication - new sources of income have become a reality for millions of South Africans. That probably helps explain why, with an estimated unemployment rate of 29.5 per cent, more people appear to cope than these horrific figures would seem to indicate.

With some 10 million cell (mobile) phones (21 per cent of South Africans, up from four per cent in 1994), SA is among the top 20 out of 170 countries with mobile networks.

Income distribution

While still one of the most skewed internationally, the distribution of income has improved. In 2001, 18 per cent of households earned monthly incomes of R6 000 and above, up from 10 per cent in 1994; those earning R2500 - R5999 constituted 20 per cent; the category of households earning R2499 or less decreased from 74 to 62 per cent; within that last group, those classified as "the poorest of the poor" decreased from just under 20 per cent in 1994 to five per cent in 2001. Among those in the top 10 per cent of earners, non-blacks were last year, for the first time, in the minority.

Along the way we notched up one of the most stable real GDP growth records (an average 2.7 per cent a year) among emerging markets and one of only a few whose growth never went negative in that eight-year period.

The Johannesburg Securities Exchange (JSE) is among the world's top 15 by size and, in the year to date, has been the fourth best performing among 27 emerging markets, 33 per cent up in US dollar terms.

NSA's financial management, with a budget deficit firmly below three per cent of GDP, is held up for emulation elsewhere by the International Monetary Fund and World Bank. Labour productivity has exploded, with only China, Sri Lanka, Taiwan and Korea still rated as more productive by the International Labour Organisation.

According to a 29-country study by the US Bureau of Labour Statistics, SA's manufacturing labour costs, which, 20 years ago, were 260 per cent that of the average Asian emerging economy, are now down to half the costs in those countries. Likewise, as Tradek economist Mike Schüssler has reported, "SA hourly labour costs in dollars have seen the biggest fall of any country in the 29-country survey, having declined by around 40 per cent since 1995.

"This", says Schüssler, "gives clearer evidence of an extremely flexible labour market."

The contribution to GDP of different sectors of the economy.

This is also changing towards the profile of a rapidly-industrialising nation, with two-thirds of contribution shifting from primary to tertiary sectors and the exports mix from primary to manufactured goods, reflected in a 330 per cent increase in earnings from merchandise export earnings since 1994, rose from R60 bn to R240 bn.

The first quarter of 2002 saw an increase of 45 per cent in vehicle exports and a 51 per cent surge in that of clothing and textiles. One of the biggest changes took place in deregulated agriculture, run by a new breed of entrepreneurs, white, black and increasingly female.

Right now, the tourism sector is the star turn and SA is the only tourism destination in the world to have expanded markets after 9/11, the country viewed as a safe tourist haven by international tour operators and their clients. In the first quarter of 2002, total hotel income was up an average 18.6 per cent, that of 5-star hotels by 38.4 per cent. There's also medical tourism: apart from glamour tours for cosmetic surgery with a game reserve thrown in, the British government is now sending us its heart patients, generating funds for better health care for poor South Africans.

Overall, Black Economic Empowerment (BEE) has been a disappointment to Government and emerging business alike, not least because the early efforts were fundamentally flawed in structure and selection.

This is predicted to change, partly due to lessons learnt, partly because of upcoming legislation, mostly perhaps because a new generation of Afro-South Africans is coming into its own.

Already BEE gained 60 per cent last year on deals in 2000 and empowerment mining company, ARMgold, recently became the first new gold mining entrant on the JSE in 15 years. Elsewhere, empowerment has proceeded steadily: 23 per cent of senior management in the private sector and above 50 per cent in the public sector, including the Defence Force (which is now nearly 75 per cent black overall) is Afro-South African. The only brake to faster growth in black participation is too few skills on offer. And there's the rub.

The downside.

Topping international lists is AIDS. As matters stand, anti-retrovirals are not widely used except in mother-to-child transmission. There is no vaccine. South Africans' life expectancy at birth has fallen from 65 to 47.8 years according to UNAIDS.

This outlook could change again within five years or so. While a widely-usable vaccine is estimated to be at best seven to 10 years away, massive use of anti-retrovirals (which, it must be said, is controversial way beyond the views expressed by President Mbeki) and, importantly, a large-scale change in behaviour, may reduce new infections.

Topping the domestic list of grievances are crime and unemployment. Along with other societies repressed for generations - think Russia and all its previous satellites, several of the latter having erupted into civil wars - liberation in NSA saw the violence, previously confined to the vast urban ghettos, spilling over the whole country.

A generation abused by perverted law had bred, in Mbeki's words in 1996, "killers who have no sense of the worth of human life; rapists who have absolute disdain for the women of our country; animals who would seek to benefit from the vulnerability of the children, the disabled and the old; the rapacious who brook no obstacle in their quest for self-enrichment."

The vast majority of victims then, and now, are black. But it was and is Euro-South Africans, the previously sheltered, on whom the effect was devastating. Many, too many, emigrated, and still emigrate ironically, now that the most serious types of crime, including murder, are stabilising or reducing. Crime tops the list of grievances in electorates from Scandinavia to the Mediterranean.

Crime and unemployment are related to the other major handicap of NSA - lack of capacity, a fancy term for too few people with the right skills to do what needs to be done. Lack of skills is, in fact, the single biggest constraint on the economy, on job creation and not least, on the delivery of services to people crying out for them.

These were in short supply to start with but emigration, coupled with throttled immigration, together with a dramatic shift in the skills composition of production and, according to Government, a reluctance to train by the private sector, have resulted in vacancies of between 200 000 and half-a-million skilled to highly-skilled positions right now, depending on whose figures one believes.

With the Minister of Trade and Industry calling for "clear state interventions" as a matter of urgency, there's hope that a newly-botched immigration bill will be fixed. Here are great possibilities for business and government.

For the longer term, education intervention is required. We can't rely on incremental change. In the past eight years South Africans with matric have increased from 14 to 23 per cent overall, 29 per cent in urban areas (up from 20). Literacy improved from 87 to 92 per cent. Not good enough to make the miracle stick.

And yet, there are sufficient signals from a plethora of sources, big and small, that most of us have "emigrated home" into the NSA. Portents of new mindsets, they may advance us faster on the road towards realisation of a country like no other - SA Inc, African by geography, global in outlook, rich in human diversity, a happy marriage between ubuntu and patriotic capitalism. For a country that has produced Mark Shuttleworth, the world's first Afronaut, and discovered in its midst the world's oldest art object - an engraved stone dating from 77 000 years ago - it's certainly within the possibilities.

In any case, however long it takes, even the run-up will be pregnant with opportunities.

"I believe business has a good future in Africa ... rates of return can be 20 to 25 per cent. In Australia you will get about half that. You have an entire continent in which to do business. If you want a little excitement in life, you should stay in SA." Former Australian High Commissioner, David Connolly.

Confidence Indices
Expectations, Perceptions and Reality

Part 3
by Peter Scott-Wilson

There is a well-known expression, "perception is reality".

Marketers know that consumers often have misperceptions about the products or services they promote and, as part of managing it, are required to create a communication strategy that addresses these misperceptions.

Likewise, freely elected governments have to deal with the expectations of the population they serve.

Both these axioms are at play in South Africa today. The question is - What is the reality of the situation? What has happened since the first free elections in 1994? Has the quality of life improved? How confident is the population about the future and the government's ability to deliver on their promises. Using internationally-recognised benchmarks, these issues are examined in terms of perceptions, the reality of rising expectations, and confidence in the future.

Confidence in the Future - Expectations

In the period leading up to South Africa's first free elections in 1994, the population, particularly the whites, were anxious about what lay ahead. They knew the ANC was going to win, but then what?

The elections ran smoothly and exceeded all expectations. Under the guiding hand of Nelson Mandela, people's expectations rose dramatically. South Africa was welcomed back into the world arena. Export of locally produced goods to countries previously closed began to increase. The press was positive about the outlook and the polls reflected this change in the country's mood.

Markinor, a local research house, has been tracking the expectations of South Africans since 1976 and the results can be summarised as follows:

- At the end of 1993 South Africans were apprehensive about the future and this was reflected in a decline in the "Optimism Index" from 116 in 1991 to 91 in 1993.
- The elections came and went and confidence in the future rose dramatically jumping to 131 in 1994 and 144 in 1995.
- 1996 remained positive but, since then, there has been a steady decline; the value of the rand, high unemployment, crime, HIV/Aids and the contagion effect of Argentina and Zimbabwe have led to a steady deterioration in the Optimism Index.

It is interesting to note that the older generation is more negative about the future: 16-24 year olds (who, interestingly, have lived their entire adult lives in the new dispensation) are the only age group that is more positive than negative about the future. In terms of regions, KwaZulu-Natal and Gauteng are the least positive.

Optimism Index

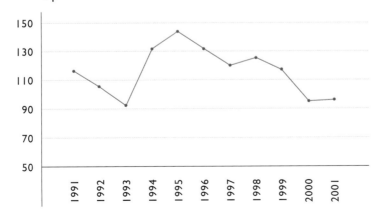

The facts are that the building blocks of a great nation are being laid ... The indices, after all, tell us that.

While confidence in the future has declined as measured by the Optimism Index, have the lives of South Africans improved over the same period? Are South Africans better off than they were before the change of government? Do South Africans reflect a global deterioration of confidence?

The South African Reality for the "man in the street": 1994 - 2001

When the ANC government came to power, they committed themselves to a programme of building houses, electrification, providing running water, sanitation, more accessible medical support, education and a greater role for blacks in mainstream business.

All these goals were encapsulated in the Reconstruction and Development Programme or RDP. The RDP was ambitious by any standards and its overall objective was to improve access to these services by the previously disadvantaged population.

As this book illustrates, the improvement in most areas has been impressive. There were problems with regard to delivery in some regions: for example, it was claimed that new houses were not always allocated on a fair basis and that there was corruption and favouritism. The press exposed this and the relevant authorities got their act together.

Water and Electrification - Up!
A more appropriate measure of the impact the RDP has had on the lives of South Africans is found in SAARF Research. SAARF (South African Advertising Research Foundation) is an independent body financed by a levy on advertising.

The main focus of the research, undertaken annually since 1974, is to establish media consumption and this data is then linked to the ownership and usage of a wide range of products and services.

If we track the movement in these figures, they give us an insight to the changing lifestyle of South Africans. The research study is very large (28 915 interviews in 2001) and the results can therefore be considered an accurate reflection. The survey covers the whole country, including deep rural areas that had been overlooked by

the previous government and where living standards have been particularly tough.

Electricity and water are essential elements in daily living and are accepted without question by most people. In rural areas this was not the case back in 1994, but significant changes have taken place since then.

The electrification of rural houses has resulted in the increased use of electrical goods like hotplates/stoves and refrigerators. In 2001, four out of five households had an appliance for cooking and just over half had a refrigerator in the home.

Water Laid on

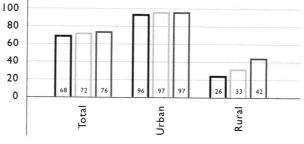

- 1994
- 1997
- 2001

Electrification

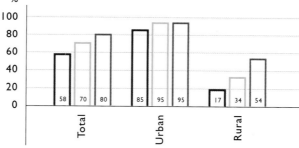

Education - Up!

Another commitment by the ANC government was in the area of education and there have been significant gains, with the number of matriculants in rural areas increasing by 63 per cent compared with 43 per cent in urban areas. Functional literacy among rural people is fast approaching that of their urban counterparts.

Employment - Down!

A result of improved education must be an expectation of employment. Here the figures are down, posting a steady decline over the past seven years.

Figures on employment vary significantly, depending on the criteria used to define unemployment. There is, however, consensus that there has been a steady decline in employment and the economy has lost 500 000 jobs since 1994. Confidence in the future is fundamentally impacted by employment prospects for school leavers.

The Business Confidence Index

Up until now we have focussed on the man in the street but there is another index which looks at the confidence of business (BCI). This includes measures of production, imports, exports and inflation among a wide cross-section of sub-indices. Comparing the Business Confidence Index with the Optimism Index, there are some interesting observations.

Before the first free election, business confidence was below 100, increasing after the election in line with consumer optimism. While consumer confidence declined up until 2001, the BCI has been edging steadily higher to the extent that it is above the consumer trend line.

It would appear that the improvements in business confidence are more significant than those of the man in the street and probable reasons for this are multiple:
- Improved macro-economic policy and fiscal discipline
- Considerable export opportunities
- Business opportunities in Africa
- Well considered initiatives by the Department of Trade and Industry
- Improved labour flexibility
- Growing confidence in Government.

In many respects, the issues for the man in the street are the "in your face" type: price hikes, crime, etc., and they tend to cause greater fluctuations in confidence.

Home Ownership - Up!

There has been a corresponding increase in the number of people owning their own homes. Rural households are more likely to own their dwelling compared with their urban counterparts. The government has built 1.3 million homes in the past seven years and sold 500 000 state owned properties. Eight million people (20 per cent of the population) have been housed.

All the above measures are incorporated in a single scale called the Living Standard Measure or LSM which takes into account the ownership and usage of 13 items to determine which LSM group a person falls into. This scale is generally regarded as more meaningful than just looking at household income.

Living Standards - Up!

The proportion of people falling into LSM 1 and 2 (the groups with the lowest living standard) has dropped. These two groups are predominantly drawn from rural communities where, typically, ownership of the 13 items had been low. However, the marked increase in numbers has been in LSM 3 to 7, effectively creating a new middle class.

There has therefore been a clear improvement in the living standards of South Africans.

Home Owned

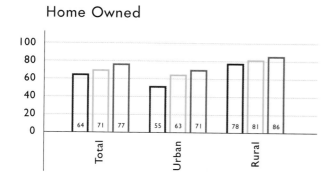

Employment

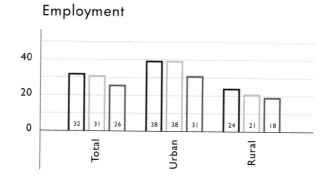

Matric

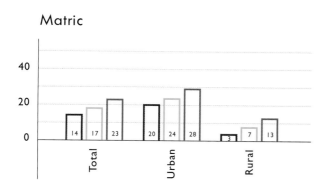

Literacy

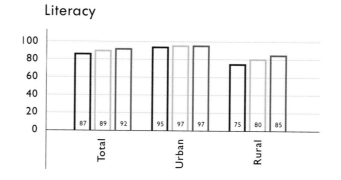

Trends in LSM Levels

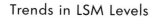
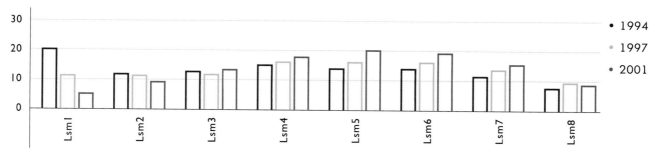

• 1994
• 1997
• 2001

Since 1994 we have reduced
the numbers of very poor,
and created a substantial
middle class.

Consumer Confidence • Business Confidence Index •

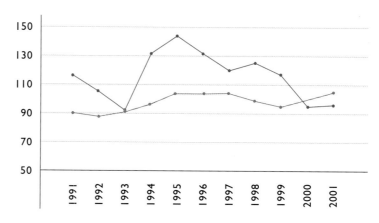

Business tends to have a longer term view and a greater appetite for opportunity, with more measured fluctuation.

When the evidence contained in the chapters of this book is taken into account, it is not surprising that the business index has improved ahead of that of consumers. What is important is that the Optimism Index will catch up, and soon.

South African confidence levels versus the rest of the world.
A second frame of reference on the confidence of South Africans comes from other countries.

Despite the events of 11 September 2001 in the USA and the war against terrorism, corporate failures in America (and South Africa), and fears of global recession, the Optimism Index reveals an interesting range of national perspectives. If the South African Optimism Index is measured against 70 other countries (November/December 2001) South Africa stands at a score of 96. In other words, more people were slightly more pessimistic than optimistic. The most optimistic countries were Kosovo followed by Nigeria. At the other extreme were Zimbabwe and Turkey. In 1993, we scored 91, so the score of 96 shows a small measure of improvement and that the trend is upwards.

Conclusion

South Africa has made good progress on a wide range of fronts since 1994, despite some of the larger ills facing the world. It is true that the ANC manifesto of "A Better Life for All" has impacted the lives of millions of people. So, why are we not more positive about the future?

There are many possible reasons for this, and they do relate to expectation, perception and reality.

In the big picture, our confidence levels are affected by the day-to-day bad news served up by the media. We hear of bus crashes in Stellenbosch and Santiago, murders in Polokwane and Paris, we see jets flying into tall buildings and peoples ravaged by civil war and we feel the effect of the deteriorating rand and the rising cost of living.

As mentioned elsewhere in this book, bad news happens quickly and with quantum whereas good news happens quietly and incrementally. The facts are that the building blocks of a great nation are being laid, the foundations of stability are being secured and the structure of a strong community is being built.

The indices, after all, tell us that.

> The facts are that the foundations of stability are being secured and the structure of a strong community is being built.

International Confidence in the Future

Country	Score
Kosovo	180
Nigeria	170
Denmark	146
USA	142
Russia	132
Canada	130
South Africa	~98
Ireland	~92
Japan	~72
Zimbabwe	~35
Turkey	~45

Political risk
Not so bad after all

By Sven Lünsche

South Africa's political risk profile is improving rapidly despite the continued strife in Zimbabwe and the food crisis in the region.

A recent survey by United Kingdom investment bank, Lehman Bros, and political risk analysis group Eurasia, shows SA among the most stable emerging economies, behind Hungary, Mexico and Poland.

SA is included for the first time in the survey which seeks to measure a country's ability to withstand crisis and to avoid generating one. Political factors have a heavy 60 per cent weighting, economic factors the remaining 40 per cent.

The country's relative political stability is confirmed by another risk analysis firm, London-based Control Risks Group. CRG has rated SA a low political risk since 1994, implying that business can operate in the country with few problems.

"Political institutions are stable, but there is some possibility of negative policy change, while some regulatory or judicial insecurity is overshadowed by strong legal guarantees," is how CRG defines low political risk.

The only other African country to be rated a low risk is Botswana. Other emerging economies on a similar rating include Brazil, Malaysia and the Czech Republic. Nigeria, Kenya and Ghana are rated medium risk, with Zimbabwe and Congo being assessed as a high political risk. CRG's Tara O'Conner downplays the impact of the Zimbabwe crisis on perceptions of SA. "The fact that Zimbabwe happens to share a border with SA, and that there will be consequences for SA, won't destabilise the SA political system," she says.

O'Conner says there have not been many inquiries at her company about investing in SA recently, but this could be "because SA is doing a good job of promoting itself".

A recent survey shows South Africa among the most stable emerging economies

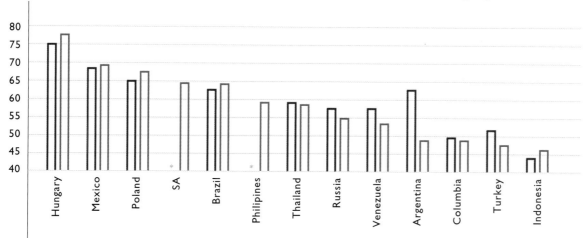

- July 2001
- July 2002
- not available

100=maximum stability

Source: Lehman Brothers: Eurasia Group

There can be little doubt that the team managing our economic health are the finest ever to have done so for South Africa. They are hailed locally, and their council is sought increasingly in various international forums. Having inherited a set of books that would have rendered any company bankrupt, they have made tough choices and have stood by them. The payback for South Africans will be by way of reduced taxes, increased social and infrastructural investment and welfare spending.

The State of the Economy

Our economic journey - is there light at the end of the tunnel?

Part 1
Rudolf Gouws - Chief Economist, Rand Merchant Bank

" THAT'S TOO FAR ! "

Recent changes in economic thinking have been no less impressive than the country's political transition. - International Monetary Fund.

Tough Decisions

Light started to appear in South Africa's tunnel of economic isolation when the country peacefully and successfully became a democracy in 1994.

The light started to shine brighter when it became clear that the new government was not going to opt for politically popular (but economically and fiscally unsustainable) quick fixes for the dire social and economic situation it inherited. Before 1994, there did not seem to be a full appreciation on the part of the ANC of how poor the situation in government finances had become under the previous administration. This included very large budget deficits, a rapidly rising debt-to-GDP ratio, internationally uncompetitive corporate and personal tax rates, inefficient and inappropriate expenditure, and the like.

As a consequence, on taking power, the new government faced the difficult task of finding a balance between early and rapid delivery of needs (and election promises) on the one hand, and addressing major fiscal imbalances (inherited from the National Party government) on the other. A strong political support base and the prospect of being in power for a long time mean that the government is able to take a long-term view of economic policy and can choose sustainability over quick fixes or populist policies. The economic and social goals of the ANC and the critics on its "left" remain the same - employment creation, delivery of basic services to the disadvantaged, and the narrowing of the income and wealth gaps - but the means now differ greatly.

President Mbeki has often made it clear that, for the sake of longer term results, his government will not shy away from politically difficult choices. It has not, and the results have, in most cases, been remarkable.

Economi

WORLD ECONOMIC FORUM

The Government's Early Achievements

- The Government almost immediately reversed the rising trend in real government expenditure of the previous three decades, simultaneously shifting the emphasis of spending towards social delivery. It also put in place systems for improving the efficiency of and accountability for expenditure.
- It set itself the target of holding the ratio of tax revenue to GDP at 25 per cent and removed disincentives to investment, such as non-resident shareholders' tax. It later started a process of gradual reduction in corporate and personal tax rates.
- It started the phased reduction of the budget deficit and elimination of government "dissaving" (the pre-1994 practice of borrowing to fund a portion of recurrent expenditure).
- It committed itself to the simplification and phased reduction of import tariffs with the specific goal of opening up the economy to international competition to make South African industry more internationally competitive, and to reduce the costs of imported foreign capital goods.
- It abolished exchange controls over non-residents, started to ease controls over residents and committed itself to the phased (but eventually total) removal of remaining controls.
- It successfully re-entered the international bond markets, with the aim of raising relatively modest amounts of foreign loan capital and of setting sovereign benchmarks.
- It ensured, through constitutional principles, that the Reserve Bank remained operationally independent and free of political interference, and gave public support to the Bank's anti-inflationary policy stance.

- Despite strong opposition from within the labour movement, government committed itself to a process of privatisation of state-owned enterprises (though it could be criticised for the relatively slow pace). The extent of the early policy shifts was remarkable. The IMF, for example, noted quite early that: "Recent changes in economic thinking in South Africa have been no less impressive than the country's political transformation. Whereas the African National Congress or ANC's earlier economic ideas were perceived as socialist ideology, its policies since coming to power have proved to be a study in moderation."

By early 1996, two years after the political transition, the various strands of economic policy were put into a coherent and internally consistent framework called "Growth, Employment and Redistribution", or GEAR. The chart illustrates the broad outlines of the government's success in implementing the fiscal aspects of the strategy (it also shows the National Treasury's most recent forecast for spending, tax revenue, and budget deficits). A positive development is the fact that the rising tax-to-GDP ratio (shown in the chart) has not been the result of higher tax rates (these have, in fact, been reduced), but of greatly improved revenue collection. The benefits of the fiscal consolidation have been seen in, at first, the halting of the strong upward trend in the government debt-to-GDP ratio and, since 1996, a decline in the ratio from 49.5 per cent to 42.9 per cent (with a projected fall to 37.4 per cent by 2004/05).

● Expenditure as % of GDP

● Revenue as % of GDP

● Deficit as % of GDP

RMB Economics

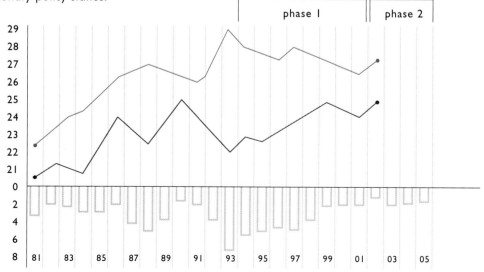

Since 1994 the ANC government has consistently reduced the inflation rate. The long-term trend in South African inflation remains downward.

Positive Results from Difficult Policy Choices

The positive results for the economy of the difficult post-1994 decisions have been apparent for some time. In the 1970s and 1980s, South African business cycles owed their boom/bust nature to stop/start fiscal and monetary policies, which amplified the impact of swings in the terms of trade and other shocks. Now, because government finances are in better shape, the economy does not have to endure fiscal shocks on top of any externally induced shocks that may again occur. Moreover, though many problems remain, the approach to a range of other economic policy issues has improved the prospects for a better overall economic performance over the longer term.

Most importantly, for a relatively small open economy, South Africa has become more resilient in the face of adverse international economic problems. In the 1997/98 emerging market crisis, South Africa's growth rate did slow down, which was not surprising, considering that interest rates were raised sharply to counter downward pressure on the currency. But it did not slow to nearly the same extent as that of other emerging markets where, in many cases, severe declines in GDP occurred.

Similarly, in the current global economic slowdown, South Africa's economy has continued to expand. This is due to the fact that the economy has been made a great deal less vulnerable to external shocks through the improvement of its macroeconomic imbalances, in particular the reduction of the budget deficit and the consequent improvement in the overall savings/investment balance of the economy.

A better savings/investment balance is also reflected in a better external current account balance. As a result, for the first time, South Africa is running a current account surplus after three years of economic upswing. This is, in part, also the result of the fact that the Reserve Bank has not allowed episodes of rand weakness to trigger sustained increases in inflation, which would have eroded the competitive benefits to exporters and import-competing industries of exchange rate depreciation. The nominal exchange rate of the rand, in common with currencies of many other emerging markets, will remain vulnerable to external shocks and swings in investor sentiment.

Government's policy approach and resolve, and the country's consequent reduced risk profile, have been recognised by the international rating agencies. In February 2001, Standard and Poors affirmed South Africa's BBB investment grade rating, and in November, Moody's upgraded South Africa to Baa2. Since February 2000 South Africa has enjoyed investment grade status from all three major rating agencies (in August 2002, Fitch upgraded its BBB-rating for South Africa from "stable" to "positive"). While international sovereign debt spreads in Latin America have recently risen, South African spreads have been falling, despite major current global uncertainties. A major benefit of the opening up of the economy to international competition (through the scrapping of the import surcharge in 1994 and the phased reduction since then in import duties) has been an improvement in industrial productivity and international competitiveness.

There is no doubt that the broad
policy direction taken by
government has put the economy
on a new and stronger growth path.

The value of exports has risen sharply in relation to GDP, and exports of manufactured goods, as a percentage of total exports, have risen from one tenth to nearly one third. An inevitable consequence of having to become competitive after decades of protectionist policies aimed at economic self-sufficiency, was large-scale retrenchments of workers. This, together with staff reductions at (now also much more efficient) state-owned enterprises, as well as in the public service, contributed to a serious rise in unemployment in recent years.

The situation was not helped by some aspects of new labour market legislation, which were viewed by business as onerous and may have contributed to labour-saving investment. It does, however, appear that the largest part of the adjustment is over, and the employment situation may be stabilising.

Fixed Investment - on the Rise

South Africa would have liked a stronger flow of foreign direct investment, but there has been an expansion of fixed investment by South African business. This grew, in real terms, by more than 60 per cent between 1994 and 2002, and a number of private-sector projects across mining and manufacturing are under way.

Also, after years of decline, public sector investment spending has started to rise. Several state-owned entities are planning large projects including Transnet and Eskom, which is spending heavily on electrification and may also be upgrading power stations ahead of partial privatisation next year.

The rise in the public sector's fixed investment is helped by the increasing use of public-private partnerships. The government recognised early on that fiscal constraints as well as its lack of project management capacity required a changing role for the state in the provision of public infrastructure and services. The private sector is now encouraged to engage in the design, construction, financing, operation, maintenance and rehabilitation of a range of activities once regarded as the exclusive domain of the state.

Stance on Inflation Maintained

In 1994, the new government decided to keep on as central bank governor Dr Stals, who had already started South Africa's successful fight against inflation in 1989. Through this and the affirmation of the central bank's autonomy as well as public support for the anti-inflation stance of the present governor, Tito Mboweni, government accepted that there would be no long-term trade off to be made between inflation and economic growth. More specifically (as noted above) it recognised that, when there was a bout of rand weakness, the consequent price pressures should not be allowed to set off an inflationary spiral.

If such a spiral was allowed to take hold, South Africa would suffer all the negative aspects of currency depreciation, but none of the benefits. For instance, because of this year's monetary policy tightening that followed the weakening of the rand late last year, we now have the prospect that the real (inflation-adjusted) effective exchange rate will not be dragged to higher (less-competitive) levels because of domestic inflation.

The lower real exchange rate of recent years has already benefited South African exporters and companies competing against imports. In fact, since the early 90s, exports have risen sharply in relation to the gross domestic product and, as a percentage of total exports, manufactured products have risen from about 10 per cent to more than 30 per cent.

In February 2000, inflation targeting became the formal mechanism of monetary policy and a target of three to six per cent for consumer price inflation was set for 2002. In October last year it was announced that the target was to remain unchanged for 2003, but for 2004 and 2005 a range of three to five per cent was set.

Unfortunately, because of the feed-through of the sharp currency decline of 2001, the 2002 targets will not be met. It may also be difficult for inflation in 2003 to average less than six per cent, but the tightening of monetary policy this year should at least ensure that it falls through 2003. Also, because it is anchored by fiscal discipline and trade liberalisation, the long-term trend in South African inflation remains downward.

Work in Progress

Despite a successful political transition, South African society is still marked by a severely unequal distribution of personal income, wealth and land ownership, as well as the unequal provision of health and welfare services, education, water, electricity, sewerage, roads, transport and access to telecommunication between traditionally "white" and "black" areas, and between rural and urban zones.

Before the political transition, income inequalities between races began to narrow, with the share of personal income accruing to blacks rising from 30 per cent in 1985 to 38 per cent in 1994, and to 41.2 per cent in 2001 (Bureau for Market Research, University of South Africa). The disappearance of legal barriers to black participation in business, the rapid rise of black entrepreneurship, and affirmative action in the private and public sectors have expanded the black middle class. The government's efforts at more rapid "delivery" of social services and social infrastructure to the previously disadvantaged are also yielding results. By December 2001, the cumulative total of low-income houses completed or under construction was 1.2 million, seven million more people had access to clean water and 3.5 million more households had received electricity. The government's willingness to face up to hard realities improved South Africa's chances of raising its growth potential. This, in turn, should boost the capacity to deliver on social demands over the longer term.

Much progress has been made in improving the effectiveness of government spending. Along with a comprehensive Budget Review, the government has published over the past four years a National Expenditure Survey (NES) that gives a detailed account of expenditure and service delivery. The aim of the NES is to assist in identifying wasteful and unproductive expenditure. The government remains resolute about "right-sizing" (reducing the size of) the civil service while improving service delivery. The budget of February 2002 could be described as the second instalment in "phase two" of fiscal policy. Because of the success in consolidating government finances during "phase one" (1994 to 2000), the government could, from 2001, turn the emphasis to underpinning growth through substantial tax-rate reductions and the (mild) acceleration of government spending. This can be seen as payback for seven years of fiscally orthodox policies, where some "gain" could be shown for earlier "pain".

Way Forward

In the 10 years before 1994, economic growth averaged only one per cent, but since then it has averaged 2.7 per cent, and this, despite the emerging-market crisis and the global slowdown that started last year.

This year the economy should grow by about 2.5 per cent (which will be right at the high end of global growth rates), and we expect growth to accelerate to above three per cent in 2003, global developments permitting. While South Africa's growth potential remains constrained by a number of factors (among them the impact of HIV/Aids, skills shortages, and the knock-on effect of developments in Zimbabwe on investor perceptions), there is no doubt that the broad policy direction taken by government has put the country on a new and stronger growth path.

Fully aware that South Africa's prospects are closely tied to those of the African continent, President Mbeki, along with the leaders of Algeria and Nigeria, put forward a programme for the economic regeneration of Africa. Instead of relying primarily on foreign aid and blaming the rest of the world for all the continent's political and economic woes, Nepad (the New Partnership for Africa's Development) sets out to ensure the development of democratic forms of government, better governance, and better and more appropriate economic policies. South Africa has, since 1994, differentiated itself from much of Africa through the adoption of a world-class constitution, the maintenance of a free press, and the implementation of sensible economic policies. Despite the unfortunate developments in neighbouring Zimbabwe, the adoption of Nepad does hold out the promise of a better continental backdrop for South Africa's progress.

There has been a remarkable expansion of fixed investment by South African business enterprises - up 60% in real terms between 1994 and 2002.

Hamburgers and Economic Health

Part 2
Mike Schussler of Tradek

South Africa has just become the only country in the world where a Big Mac costs less than a dollar.

A Big Mac in South Africa costs R9.95 and the rand is more than 10 to the greenback so a burger here costs less than a dollar. And that, according to the Big Mac index, makes us the cheapest country in the world.

In fact we are 13 per cent cheaper than the Philippines (the next best country on the list) and one per cent below the cost in China.

As for the United States, a Big Mac in South Africa costs less than 40 per cent of price over there. This shows that the internal purchasing power of the rand is holding up quite well as the external value falls like a stone. Sooner or later the two must meet with either inflation or the rand recovering. More likely it will be a combination because exports are more likely to perform since productivity in South Africa is higher than in most other countries.

A Big Mac in South Africa costs a third of the price in Denmark and, with bulk airfreight, we could probably make the burgers here and fly them to Copenhagen and feed cheap cholesterol to the Danes.

In fact, the Big Mac index shows that the rand is about 61 per cent undervalued when compared with the dollar, 66 per cent against the Danish krona and 65 per cent against the British pound.

And it's More than Just Burgers

The average house in the UK measures 106 square metres and costs around R1.4 million while the average South African home, at 120 square metres, still costs less than R300 000. That puts our houses at about one fifth the cost of those in Britain.

When it comes to labour, manufacturing in South African costs around $3 per hour compared to $4.25 in Argentina, and more than $34 in Denmark. Our dollar-unit labour costs have fallen by more than 28 per cent in the past four years and, if you combine this with increases in productivity, the drop in price comes close to 50 per cent, making us the fifth most productive labour force in the world.

South Africa has the cheapest electricity in the world and petrol costs 60 per cent less than in the UK and bread is 66 per cent cheaper than in some European Union countries. Rents in Johannesburg Central average less than $5 per square metre, a dollar below those in Bangkok, while average rents in developed counties are often more than $25 per square metre.

No wonder then that a company like the Chinese TV screen maker, Hi Sense, is planning to build a new factory in South Africa.

So, why is the rand falling?

Well, firstly, the rand is one of only four free-floating emerging-market currencies. And, South Africa has liquid exchange, bond and equity markets so we have borne the brunt of international hedging. The sins, from Argentina to Zimbabwe, have been ploughed straight into the rand. If we had high inflation then our burger prices would be shooting up, but they have only increased by about 2.5 per cent in eight months, so inflation is not the problem.

Fundamentally, South Africa is far healthier than Argentina, Turkey or Brazil and government deficits and growth all look better here than in the average emerging market and, as the Big Mac index shows, we are now cheaper than anyone else.

Maybe a free-floating currency is not so good if you are a very small country in the world context. (The OECD has admitted this in a book called **Don't Fix, Don't Float**.) As a percentage to GDP, the rand is one of the most liquid currencies on the planet and the 11th most traded, yet SA is only the 35th largest economy in the world. Leave out the Euro countries and we're about 25th, but that still means that, for our economy's size, the rand's turnover is ahead of everything else.

As I write, export stocks on the JSE have shown annualised growth of more than 250% over the past month. Maybe investors will see this fact and the rand might show some increase against the dollar.

In fact, the Big Mac index shows that the rand is about 61 per cent undervalued when compared with the dollar, 66 per cent against the Danish krona and 65 per cent against the British pound.

3

South Africa has been blessed with Political Leadership since 1994 that far outstrips the quality of leadership it endured since the Jan Smuts era in 1948. Nelson Mandela rates with the political leaders of the century, but he managed the honeymoon period of the new era. Thabo Mbeki was always going to have the more difficult time. Leadership is a lonely job, and much of the criticism of Mbeki is with respect to his "autocratic style" and perceived stubbornness. These are traits often associated with leaders who achieve results. He has made his mistakes - and he will make more, but most of the reasons for the good news in this book must ultimately rest with him.

Political Leadership
An External Perspective

Part 1
Chris Landsberg
Director, Centre for Policy Studies, Johannesburg

Rarely in the history of world affairs has a young democracy with the relative size and power of South Africa exerted so much influence and leadership as does this liberated republic.

Indeed, South Africa exerts a global leadership incommensurate with its size and capabilities. It typically punches above its weight, and generally commands a respect by the developing and the developed worlds alike - North and South.

The Republic, with a GDP of some $148 billion, is what President Thabo Mbeki called "a country of two nations".

The one nation is the chronically underdeveloped majority population. The other incorporates a small section of the population and is highly developed and largely white. The underdeveloped nation shares living standards similar to those of the people in Congo-Brazzaville, whereas the first world nation maintains standards similar to Spain. Together with Brazil, South Africa remains the world's most unequal society.

Thus, South Africa is, at best, a middle-ranked power with significant socio-economic challenges located in the southern tip of Africa. Yet, despite this profile and challenge, the Republic conducts a diplomacy and international influence that is generally reserved for the great powers of the world.

South Africa exerts a global leadership incommensurate with its size and capabilities. It punches above its weight.

Rarely in the history of world affairs has a young democracy ...
exerted so much influence and leadership as does this liberated republic.

Its heightened international influence is a far cry from the apartheid decades when South Africa was a heavily-ostracised state conducting domestic policies of white-minority domination and racial oppression; politics that were fundamentally out of step with the post-World War II era of decolonisation and the self-determination of people.

In gradual fashion, South Africa became, between 1948 and 1989, one of the world's most isolated states and thousands of conferences, seminars and other events were organised throughout the world to fight apartheid.

Since the achievement of a negotiated settlement of the apartheid problem in 1994, South Africa has emerged as a pivotal state in regional and global affairs. It has articulated a foreign policy that is geared towards bringing about the politics of "redress" between North and South, and between Africa and the former colonial powers, as founded in initiatives like the African Union and its development programme, the New Partnership for Africa's Development (NEPAD). The clear goal is to bring about international redress by playing a bridge role between these divided blocks in world affairs.

South Africa's foreign policy since 1994 has worked to bring about a rules-based global order through a commitment to multilateralism and negotiating global rules, norms and values. The country has promoted greater and more effective "global governance" and positioned itself to become the number one destination in the world chosen by people to host key global conferences and important negotiation attempts.

South Africa is the foremost international bridge-builder in world affairs, extracting commitments from opposing and competing sides by negotiating deals that would bring about change.

Multilateralism and Leadership

South Africa's global leadership was exercised mainly through multilateralism. For example, while the Bush administration in the United States is increasingly unilateralist in its foreign policy, South Africa has adopted a policy of promoting solutions to global and international problems and issues in ways that reinforce, not negate, the role of organisations such as the United Nations, the Southern African Development Community (SADC), and the recently established African Union (AU). It also places a high premium on transforming the international financial architecture so as to prevent the use of these organisations for unilateral agendas and purposes.

Key international meetings include South Africa's hosting of the 1995 UNCTAD Summit, the 1998 Non-Aligned Movement (NAM) Summit, the 13th International Conference on HIV/Aids, the 2001 World Conference Against Racism in partnerships with the United Nations Human Rights Commission, the 2002 Africa Union, and the World Summit on Sustainable Development. In terms of anti-racism, South Africa has emerged as a leading nation in tackling this global challenge.

South Africa assumed the chair of the Non Aligned Movement in 1998 and became the first chair of the AU. Just as the country pursues a policy of transformation and reconstruction at home, so its foreign policy seeks to reform the UN Security Council and the Bretton Woods institutions, notably the World Bank and the IMF.

South Africa has long been concerned that the UN Security Council continues to mirror power relations as they were in 1945, and that reform has been desperately slow. In being committed to a better and safer world, Pretoria believes that, as the premiere agency charged with maintaining international peace and security, the Security Council must become democratic and representative of all the peoples of the world.

South Africa has reinforced the role of the Secretary General as a key player in addressing and finding solutions to peace, security and stability issues confronting the international community and has stressed that the UN itself has major flaws that need correcting.

One way of doing this is to opt for the expansion of the Council in both permanent and non-permanent categories as well as the use of the veto. In accordance with this, SA has actively promoted the African position for two permanent seats to be allocated to this continent.

Pretoria has come out against efforts to manipulate the UN, particularly the Security Council, by the US and other great powers in order to achieve unilateral objectives which do not coincide with the interests of the broader international community.

Africa: Primus Inter Pares

The Republic has elevated Africa to a position of pride of place in its international relations. Africa is South Africa's comparative advantage in the world; it is part and parcel of its national interest. Our foreign policy seeks the achievement of a peaceful and prosperous Africa, and, in the words of the foreign policy commander-in-chief, Thabo Mbeki, "a better world for all". During the United Nations Millennium Summit in September 2000, Mbeki called on world leaders to commit themselves to help the continent extricate itself from economic marginalisation, poverty and conflicts.

Since 1995, government has articulated the vision of an African Renaissance, essentially a call for continental, economic, political and social renewal. This defines our approach to the political, economic and social challenges of Africa and is a foreign policy doctrine that seeks to mobilise the world around the idea that this is the "African Renaissance Century".

In line with this clarion call, South Africa continues to emphasise the need for both a credible peace in Angola and post-conflict reconstruction in that country.

The Government was also in the vanguard to bring about a New Partnership for Africa's Development (NEPAD), an initiative to spur development after decades of failures as a result of the legacies of colonialism and the Cold War, bad governance, conflicts and unsound economic policies.

The NEPAD plan of action has identified five critical issues as essential to bolstering Africa's development chances:
1   Democracy, governance, peace and security
2. Economic and corporate governance
3. Infrastructure and information technology
4. Human resource development
5. Agriculture and market access.
NEPAD seeks to generate new forms of co-operation between Africa and the developed world based on mutual accountability and responsibility.

Over and above these multilateral African initiatives, South Africa continues to work towards a resolution of the Western Sahara issue by focusing on the UN Settlement Plan. In Lesotho, between 1998 and 2002, South Africa played a key role through the extended SADC (involving Botswana, Zimbabwe, Mozambique and Namibia) to bring about a credible election in that country and to help stabilise it in the post-election period.

In the Horn of Africa, South Africa again supported multilateralism by coming out in favour of the IDAG-led peace process to try and bring an end to the 18-year old Sudan civil war.

Since 1995, government has articulated the vision of an African Renaissance, essentially a call for continental, economic, political and social renewal.

Governance and Capacity-building

In this difficult age of global confusion and power politics, South Africa backs the continued existence of an independent and empowered African Commission on Human and Peoples' Rights under the AU so as to ensure an effective delivery mechanism.

The accent is on the importance of a global order more committed to human rights and the same can be said about SADC where South Africa supported early implementation of protocols, particularly those on free trade, politics, defence and security co-operation.

The view has been that the entry into force of these protocols will allow for the establishment of a free trade area and appropriate SADC interventions to restore stability and security in the region, as well as boosting international investor confidence and attracting foreign direct investment to the regional economy.

The Government has lobbied intensively for the SADC restructuring process and believes that the issue of capacity building is critical to the successful implementation of the NEPAD process. It has focused on the need to develop detailed action plans in each project area, and believes that these should always be followed up by a mobilisation of resources to address identified capacity constraints.

South Africa has a clear policy of promoting adherence to democratic benchmarks and governance indicators set up by Africans and for Africans in order to benefit from the renewed focus on African ownership. Indeed, it is South Africa's policy that the democratisation process currently underway on the continent must be reinforced and sustained. Governance is a key way of securing such sustainability.

The Zimbabwean and Namibian developments have the potential to thwart this approach because they contradict it, and also because the SA Government's reaction has not been consistent.

Many commentators argue that the lack of decisive action in this regard could terminally jeopardise NEPAD, but Mugabe's removal as deputy chairman of SADC is a small step in the right direction.

The link between socio-economic development and adherence to democratic principles and good governance is strongly emphasised in South Africa's diplomacy and the country seeks to align itself with groupings of democratic countries on the continent and globally.

A doctrine of foreign policy is that governments that come to power and/or attempt to retain power through unconstitutional means must be isolated and resisted. Emerging democracies require sustained support and assistance from partners in both the North and South and there is a policy of facilitating political dialogue with donor countries in order to engage with these countries constructively in promoting democracy and good governance.

Democratisation and Conflict Resolution

South Africa is committed to ensuring that the Inter-Congolese Dialogue (ICD), which began at Sun City in February 2002, will bare fruit. South Africa, in support of the MONUC process, contributed to finding a lasting solution to the conflict in the Democratic Republic of Congo (DRC). In Lesotho, South Africa aimed at bringing stability and social and economic development to the mountain kingdom by continuing to engage Lesotho through the SADC Troika. In Burundi, there was a crucial need to strengthen the Arusha Process and SA provided specific training to Burundi to provide an internal protection unit, while soliciting support for the deployment of an international peacekeeping force.

The Zimbabwe question forced itself onto the agenda by 2000, and through the "quiet diplomacy" strategy, the President provided visionary leadership and a voice of reason, by continuing to engage the Zimbabwean President in co-operative partnership.

Pretoria called for free and fair democratic elections in March 2002 and sent election observes under the auspices of the SADC Parliamentary Forum, the multisectoral South

Africa Observer Mission (SAOM), etc. South Africa tried to bring about a political rapprochement between the MDC and Zanu-PF in order to ensure peace and stability, as well as an economic recovery in Zimbabwe. This has not been successful.

In Sudan, South Africa supported and encouraged the IGAD peace process and Egyptian/Libyan Initiative, but stressed that IGAD was key. South Africa was mandated by the OAU in 1998 to address the constitutional crisis in the Comoros and the South African Independent Electoral Commission (IEC) provided assistance in co-operation with the relevant authorities in the Comoros.

The International Bridge-builder

The Republic's foreign policy seeks to build bridges and close the divides between North and South, as well as foster solidarity between South and South.

In terms of South-South co-operation, the Republic sought to increase its relations with countries like Algeria, Nigeria, Egypt, Brazil, India and, (outside this group) China, and touted the idea of a G-8 of the South.

A key goal of the South-South strategy is to develop a co-ordinated approach to globalisation and to ensure that the developing South plays a more active and meaningful role in global institutions. In the long run, South Africa wishes to develop the notion of alliances between countries of the South so as to maximise the interface of the developing world on globalisation.

South Africa has touted the idea of a G-8 of the South to include amongst others China, India, Brazil, Nigeria, Egypt and Algeria.

Humanitarian Issues

Pretoria developed a clear policy of promoting relief for humanitarian crisis situations. Indeed, it applied funding from the African Renaissance Fund to the relief of complex humanitarian emergencies and natural disasters in Africa. It has put on the SADC agenda the idea of establishing regional and sub-regional mechanisms to deal with humanitarian crises, and develop national, sub-regional and regional capacities.

It has stressed the need actively to co-ordinate and co-operate with the relevant international organisations such as the UNHCR, UNICEF, the International Committee of the Red Cross (ICRC) and the World Food Programme, as well as government and non-government relief agencies. This again speaks to the issue of multilateralism.

Pretoria continued to work within the national disaster management framework to address any problems that impact directly on South Africa, such as refugees and victims of famine from Zimbabwe.

Global Governance and Regionalism

Foreign policy is committed to the utilisation of opportunities to achieve solutions to socio-economic, stability and security challenges through regional approaches. Pretoria encourages inter-regional co-operation on issues of mutual concern and where there are similarities in approaches. Co-operation between SADC and the EU, SADC and the Gulf Co-operation Council (GCC), and SADC and Mercosur are strongly encouraged.

Peace-keeping and Peace-enforcement

In an age of Western military disengagement and shirking of responsibilities from Africa, South Africa has underlined the need to develop national, sub-regional and regional capacities effectively to address peacekeeping requirements in Africa. Still, South Africa remains committed to multilateralism, as it is committed to obtaining UN Security Council endorsement for any peacekeeping operation that it embarks upon. But South Africa maintains a strong focus on conflict prevention as a key measure in maintaining security and stability, while, at the same time, continuing to support and participate in specific peacekeeping operations.

As such, South Africa believes in facilitating political dialogue between warring factions and states, so as to promote conflict-prevention, management and resolution in Africa. Pretoria is also actively involved in post-conflict reconstruction and development.

South Africa's effect on world governance in the last 8 years has been nothing short of astounding.

The way forward

South Africa's international relations, and its global leadership over the past eight years, have consolidated its image as a stable democracy founded on racial and cultural diversity that seeks to bring about a more equitable, rules-based global order. As a democracy, the onus will remain on South Africa to continue to show leadership in terms of redressing global imbalances between Africa and the South on the one hand and the developed world on the other.

South Africa will have to remain deeply committed to multilateralism and continue to make contributions towards regional and global democratisation, and peace and security. It will need to harness and bolster its skills to pursue a proactive role in the prevention, management and resolution of conflicts. Given its own achievements in the fields of democracy, good governance, transparency and accountability, it is well placed to continue promoting these norms and values internationally.

A particular challenge remains for South Africa to make contributions towards creating and maintaining an international environment conducive to a culture of human rights in order to enhance domestic, regional and international peace and security. This will continue to resonate as a unique challenge for a country that itself is a shining light for the sort of reform it seeks in world order.

Annotated Bibliography

Department of Foreign Affairs, Department of Foreign Affairs of the Republic of South Africa, Annual Report 2000/2001, Pretoria, 2002.

Department of Foreign Affairs, Heads of Mission Conference, Vaal River Document on Strategic Planning, January 1999, Pretoria, 2000.

Dorina A. Bekoe, Task Force Meeting, Peacemaking in Southern Africa: The Role and Potential of the Southern African Development Community (SADC), International Peace Academy and the Centre for Africa's International Relations, Johannesburg, October 2002.

Dorina A. Bekoe and Chris Landsberg, NEPAD: African Initiative, New Partnership? International Peace Academy (IPA), IPA Workshop Report, New York, 16 July 2002.

The New Partnership for Africa's Development (NEPAD), NEPAD Workshop on Indicators, Benchmarks and Processes for the African Peer Review Mechanism (APRM), Cape Town, 7 to 8 October 2002.

NEPAD Secretariat, NEPAD at Work, Summary of NEPAD Action Plans, Midrand, July 2002.

Political Leadership
An Internal Perspective

Part 2
Professor Tom Lodge
Head of Department of Political Studies - University of the Witwatersrand

In the Background

Thabo Mbeki's status as a likely future leader of the ANC was well established two decades before he became South Africa's president.

There were challengers, of course: Chris Hani, wildly popular in the MK guerilla training camps during the 1980s and Cyril Ramaphosa, favoured by both the ANC's left wing and the internal "struggle movement" that had developed around the UDF and the trade unions.

But, of the younger generation of ANC leaders, Mbeki was the best known outside his organisation, both as Oliver Tambo's personal assistant and as the ANC's "foreign minister". In the latter stages of the ANC's exile, he had been more or less consciously groomed for succession.

To the Foreground

That is not to say Mbeki didn't earn his place at the ANC's helm. In preparing the ground for the party's assumption of power, Mbeki played a key role. That the ANC managed to draw into its fold important activists within the Black Consciousness Movement (despite the antipathy to them in certain senior quarters of the organisation) was, at least partly, attributable to Mbeki's presence in Swaziland in the mid-1970s, at a time when the first wave of political exiles appeared in Mbabane after initial efforts by the Government to clamp down on the South African Students' Organisation - two years before the Soweto uprising.

In the 1980s, it was Mbeki who was chiefly responsible for cultivating a relationship between the ANC and those western governments which had previously treated African liberation movements with disdain. He also managed the

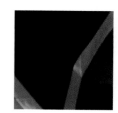

initial contacts between the ANC and Afrikaner intellectuals as well as South African business representatives. And it was mainly Mbeki who created the space within the ANC for the beginnings of a discussion on constitutional proposals.

Mbeki deserves a major proportion of the credit for the ANC's extraordinary transition from a revolutionary insurgency to an organisation willing to work within the confines of liberal democracy. Though he played an inconspicuous role in the constitutional negotiations between 1992 and 1994, out of the public eye he was a major participant in the efforts to bring the white right into the political settlement as well as inducing Inkatha's participation in the elections.

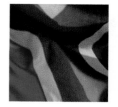

In KwaZulu-Natal, he made a vital contribution to the peacemaking that followed the 1994 poll. Mbeki's skills as a conciliator may not have been suited to the brinkmanship and gambles of constitutional bargaining in which Cyril Ramaphosa excelled, but, without his backroom diplomacy, it is unlikely that the settlement would have been as comprehensive and inclusive as it turned out to be.

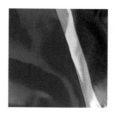

Mbeki deserves a major proportion of the credit for the ANC's extraordinary transition from a revolutionary insurgency to a liberal democratic organisation.

It is notable that at the recent ANC congress, no major policies were changed, but it was resolved to improve communication.

Parallel Reality and Delivery Successes

As an elected politician and a leader of Government, his record provokes a range of differing views. Mbeki's admirers suggest that, as Mandela's virtual prime minister between 1994 and 1999, he merits much of the praise for the achievements of the ANC's first administration, at least with respect to the management of a modest economic revival, the construction of a fairly co-ordinated public administration out of the bizarre degree of fragmentation which represented apartheid's legacy, and the quite evident effort invested in making party, government, and administration, socially as well as politically as representative as possible.

In foreign policy - which is discussed separately in this volume - South Africa's international status was partly, of course, a reflection of Mandela's global celebrity status. South Africa's slowly-improving relationship with the rest of Africa is mainly a consequence of the priority Mbeki placed on continental affairs. It is in the detail that different views are presented.

Economic Reform

Depending which side of the ideological spectrum you inhabit, you either approve of the tough economic conservatism that has been manifest in the Government's handling of public finance, or you view it as regressive.

Certainly Mbeki's authority on economic issues has been very obvious. While the technicalities have remained the domain of his ministers and the Reserve Bank, the consistency with which the Government has defended or pursued deficit reduction, trade liberalisation, domestic deregulation, counter-inflationary measures and reductions

in public sector employment, is an expression of Mbeki's determination and, let it be said, courage.

Of course, the Government's opponents on its right have suggested that GEAR's implementation has been uneven and its targets remain unfulfilled, but no one can accuse Mbeki of courting public popularity at the expense of sound financial policies.

Civil Service Reform

When Mbeki succeeded Mandela, commentators suggested that a more businesslike approach would prevail with respect to "delivery". In other words, the time for protracted consultative kinds of policy-making was over.

A streamlined and efficient civil service would get down to the business of improving social infrastructure and the Government would be less sensitive to special pleading on behalf of minority groups for the maintenance of privileged treatment.

Such predictions were only partly true. It is true that Mbeki dismissed several of the less effective ministers from Mandela's cabinet. The considerable improvement in pubic education over the past three years is certainly one consequence of more effective direction right from the top of this key arena of social reform. Mbeki's Government presided over a most remarkable - and rapid - re-organisation of local government and it is at least arguable that the essential frontline administration needed for the large-scale delivery of better services to deprived communities is now in place.

The Mbeki Government has been more willing than its predecessor to discipline venal notables and dishonest bureaucrats and to admit that rent-seeking is on the increase. Corruption is now acknowledged as a major challenge for government whereas five years ago it was dismissed as a bad habit from the apartheid past.

Parallel Reality and Delivery Problems

Aside from these achievements, Mbeki's credentials as a "delivery president" look rather less impressive. Points of criticism have been:

- The slow pace of land reform (partly a consequence of a protracted policy review)
- The inertia which for a while appeared to affect housing construction (though this field has experienced a recent revival)
- The degeneration of public health.

Public Health

The real damage to his reputation as the leader of a compassionate government has been in the addressing of the Aids crisis. In fact, compared to all of sub-Saharan Africa, South African preventative health measures against HIV-Aids are substantial and well organised but the President's publicly expressed doubts about the depth of the crisis and his scepticism about the medical explanations of its causes has certainly limited the effectiveness of his government's efforts to counter the epidemic.

As long as hospitals, as is the case in at least two provinces, continue - as a consequence of political interference - to refuse medication to people who desperately need it, then Mbeki and his cabinet colleagues should not escape censure.

One especially depressing aspect of Mbeki's interventions in the field of Aids science has been the general silencing of any dissent from his views within the movement he leads.

Tolerance

Generally, since 1999, the ANC has become more intellectually repressive, more likely to react fiercely to criticism, and more autocratic in its internal management. Partly, of course, this is the consequence of the Government's adoption of policies unpopular with rank and file, but it is also a reflection of a leadership style that discourages even gentle criticism from party loyalists.

Corruption is now acknowledged as a major challenge for government whereas five years ago it was dismissed as a bad habit from the apartheid past.

This tendency has wider implications. In Parliament the ANC caucus is much less likely to hold the executive to account than it was pre-1999 and, at the moment, we are witnessing an especially clumsy attempt to limit the independence of public broadcasting. On the other hand, government has been fairly punctilious in its respect for the integrity and autonomy of the courts.

It is quite likely that the closure of the Reconstruction and Development Programme (RDP) office in 1996, at Mbeki's instigation (and the subsequent abandonment of efforts to encourage a participatory style of development project conception and implementation), may have allowed for more rapid and, in certain respect, more efficient "delivery".

However, the RDP, as a visionary concept that could mobilise people around a nation-building programme, died with its reduction to a set of routinely published welfare statistics. Soon, the 2001 census results will tell us, with a degree of authority, whether the Government has succeeded in significantly reducing poverty in the past five years. At present, sample surveys present conflicting findings.

Pan-African Patriotism

Mbeki's efforts to replace the egalitarian and democratic ideals of the RDP with pan-Africanism have only been partly successful. Certainly, the new politics of African identity has helped to unite behind the ANC a rapidly growing African middle class - though to Mbeki's very considerable credit he has taken pains to define African citizenship in ways that allow all South African citizens subscription to continental patriotism.

One can make a case that Mbeki's approach to pan-African politics - Zimbabwe notwithstanding - has consolidated South African capacity to lead the continent. But most South Africans are not especially animated by Mbeki's revival of African unity. Opinion polls suggest that his leadership has lost popular endorsement since his accession and that, as a visionary, his ideals and goals are too abstract or too remote to gain a response from ordinary people.

The Future

After eight years of ANC rule, many South Africans believe that the Government is managing the country well. There is ample evidence of a range of reforms, initiatives and actions coming together to form a critical mass of what many believe to be good government.

Yes, Aids, Zimbabwe and pardoning have raised many eyebrows and caused a disproportionate amount of ill-feeling, press exposure and sadly, damaged reputation. But, as the chapters in this book reflect, a much greater proportion of what has been achieved, has, even for most ardent critics, exceeded expectations. Mbeki, and the ANC for that matter, have not communicated these successes all that well. It is pleasing therefore to note that, at the recent ANC congress, no major policy changes were taken, but it was resolved to improve communication.

What next? On several occasions, Mbeki has stated publicly his disapproval of presidents who stay beyond their constitutional terms - or use their party's control of parliament to change the rules to allow them to remain in power. So, in 2009, we are set to have a new president.

Given the ANC's own timetable for settling such matters, by 2007 we are likely to know who that will be.

It is a bit odd that, today, the succession field seems so open. In the past, the ANC has approached the replacement of its leadership in a most decorous and stately fashion, with signals and pointers to likely candidates being set many years in advance. Mbeki has discouraged such a process and, because tight discipline within the ANC inhibits any competition between personal factions, no new leaders are unlikely to emerge spontaneously.

Possibly the most important challenge facing Mbeki in the next five years will be to delegate sufficient authority to allow for his replacement to be as seamless a process as his accession.

When Mbeki succeeded Mandela, commentators suggested that a more businesslike approach would prevail with respect to "delivery".

Possibly the most important challenge facing Mbeki in the next five years will be to delegate sufficient authority to allow for his replacement to be as seamless a process as his accession.

48

The overwhelming majority of the vote secured by the ANC in our first two elections has both positive and negative aspects. On the one hand we have a government virtually assured of long tenure. This has allowed the implementation of long term plans sometimes at the expense of short term benefits to its franchise. On the other hand, especially given Africa's record, there is the risk of high-handedness and arrogance - strong and vocal opposition politics combined with a free press and an independent constitutional court are the safeguards.

Government and Opposition

Are the Checks and Balances Intact?

Dr F van Zyl Slabbert

Perhaps in politics, more so than in most disciplines, amnesia plays a disproportionate role. The quality of analysis so often depends on what one forgets, or even chooses to ignore. For example, the constitutional structure between Government and Opposition in South Africa is not yet four years old. It is true that the Constitution was finalised in 1996, but 1999 was the first election held under the current Constitution and the first opening of Parliament only took place after that. So Thabo Mbeki (Government) and Tony Leon (Opposition) have been going at each other, under the current Constitution, for less than four years.

And yet, when one reads the regular weekly columns on Parliamentary politics or watches/listens to TV and radio, it is sometimes not difficult to get the impression that South Africa rivals Westminster in its history and rituals of Parliament. The sense of outrage and shock at Parliamentary convention being flouted or contravened, presupposes a well institutionalised Parliamentary culture as part of our daily political life. This is of course very encouraging as far as consolidating democracy is concerned, for it would be disastrous if no one cared that Parliament was being abused. But, it is also important not to forget how young our Parliament (and Democracy) is, and how remarkably well we have performed considering where we came from.

" THERE IS STILL A
POSSIBILITY OF PEACE, BUT
UNFORTUNATELY
THERE IS STILL A POSSIBILITY
OF WAR "
PEREZ DE CUELLAR

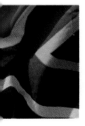

However, it should also not be forgotten that up until then, the concepts of Government and Opposition had a completely different relationship and meaning toward one another. Every conceivable strategy and tactic was used to oppress and oppose. It was a fight to the death between "the system" and "the struggle" and by the time De Klerk made his speech, South Africa was in an antagonistic, brutalised and polarised state of emergency. Anyone who had studied the documents, speeches and policy positions of the major antagonists during that time, i.e. the National Party Government and the African National Congress, could come to no other conclusion then, that a liberal democratic constitution as a "solution" to South Africa's conflict, was the very last thing on their minds. Yet, that is precisely what they negotiated. Such a Constitution introduced a notion of Government and Opposition that was the complete antithesis of what had gone before. A cursory reading of the pain, bitterness and suffering reflected in the reports of the Truth and Reconciliation Commission will show how remarkable such a development is in the South African context.

The country went through three phases of transition from 1990 until the present: The first phase 1990 - 1994 was the negotiation phase proper; the second 1994-1999 was the interim phase and the third 1999 - the present is the final phase. Each phase involved all three levels of Government - National, Provincial and Local. For example, approximately 650 local government municipalities had to convert themselves into negotiating forums and negotiate an interim phase of local government. This was done under the auspices of the Local Government Transition Act. Nationally an Interim Constitution was negotiated which led to a Government of National Unity that was elected in the first non-racial democratic elections in April, 1994. At the same time, a Constituent Assembly was appointed which negotiated the current Constitution that was finalised in 1996. The 1999 general election was the first under the final constitution and led to the current structure between Government and Opposition.

However, not by a long shot was it as plain sailing as it reads above. There were bombings, massacres, assassinations and armed confrontations. In KwaZulu-Natal the ANC and IFP were killing each other's members, "third force" accusations were brought against the State by the ANC, particularly after the Boiphatong massacre. At one stage Mandela accused de Klerk of "killing my people".

Where did we come from?

On the 2nd February, 1990, F W de Klerk, then State President of the old apartheid South Africa, made an extraordinary speech in the old apartheid Parliament that unlocked the future which South Africa is coming to terms with at the moment. It was then a future that had been struggled for, and fought against, since the formation of Union in 1910, and made even more inconceivable by the coming to power of the Nationalist Party Government in 1948. That was 12 years ago. Most of the world, particularly those involved in the struggle against apartheid, is familiar with what happened in those 12 years. Commentators and analysts have still not run out of breathless adjectives of wonderment, and bewilderment, trying to come to grips with the rapidity and depth of change that took place.

Commentators have still not run out of breathless adjectives of wonderment and bewilderment.

(In fact, the relationship between them deteriorated steadily until de Klerk walked out of the Government of National Unity in 1996.) Buthelezi and General Constand Viljoen walked out of negotiations and formed an independent Freedom Front (threatening to boycott the 1994 elections and continuing the struggle by "other means"). General Viljoen was heard to say, often, that he had 30 000 men under arms ready to do battle at a moment's notice.

Q. Which one is the Armed Struggle?

THE RIGHT TO BEAR ARMS

It took sustained and intense behind the scenes talks to persuade both to participate in the 1994 elections. In fact, this was achieved literally three weeks before the elections, so that special arrangements had to be made to get the IFP on the ballot papers. In the meantime, the right wing assassinated Chris Hani, invaded Mbabatho and bombed the CBD of Johannesburg. The country was on a knife edge. The concept of Government and Opposition was fluid and ambiguous and an undercurrent of anarchy and repression was in evidence. If ever there was a time that South Africa had to prove it had the leadership and the character to walk through this period of turbulence and keep the process on track, it was then. Eventually all the major parties that could cause irreparable damage, came to the table and chose peace rather than violence. Their leaders have to be commended without exception: Mandela, De Klerk, Viljoen and Buthelezi. Especially, Mandela played a pivotal conciliatory role.

The April 1994 elections brought into being a Government of National Unity. It was agreed that such a government would be in place until 1999 when the first elections under the final Constitution would take place and the agreement responsible for a Government of National Unity would no longer be in force. It was an extraordinary time. The leader of the NP that dominated politics in South Africa from 1948, became a Deputy President under President Mandela and sat in the same cabinet of a Government of National Unity. The ANC and NP were partners in governing South Africa from 1994. There was no real awareness of Government and Opposition. It was more a time of symbolic transition and reconciliation - a new flag, trying to strive for a new unity of purpose. Even when De Klerk left the Government of National Unity in 1996 to go into opposition, it was not taken very seriously. In fact some within the NP said it was his greatest mistake if he wished the NP to remain a force in national politics. The subsequent fortunes of the NP seemed to prove this to be so.

In the meantime, the DP under the leadership of Tony Leon, seized the opportunity to propagate the idea of opposition politics in a liberal democratic constitution. It was a novel experience for many South Africans. The idea of "genuine opposition" was always associated with somehow subverting the State. Now a liberation movement that had successfully subverted the State was the Government in South Africa. Why oppose it? Even the NP was part of the Government of National Unity! De Klerk's defection from the Government of National Unity was proof to Leon and the DP that too late De Klerk realised that he had been co-opted and could not really lead a "genuine" Parliamentary opposition. For Leon, the time had come to "fight back".

It is to Mandela's lasting credit that he managed the succession to his own leadership with consummate dignity and grace.

Thabo Mbeki became the leader of the ANC. He would become the first democratically elected president under a liberal democratic constitution in South Africa. That happened less than four years ago. The 1999 election also saw Tony Leon of the DP become the first democratically elected Leader of the Opposition under the new Constitution. A new relationship between Government and Opposition was born, one so fundamentally different to what had gone before that it stretched credulity to its utmost to take it seriously. And yet, it is there for all to see.

Government and Opposition Under a Liberal Democratic Constitution in South Africa

It would be a serious distortion of reality to reduce the relationship between Government and Opposition to the competition between the party in power and those in opposition. Multi-party competition for electoral support is only one of many checks and balances against the abuse of power by any party or government. Chapter One of the Constitution spells out the Founding Provisions; Chapter Two the Bill of Rights; Chapter Eight the Courts and Administration; Chapter Nine specifically refers to State Institutions supporting Constitutional Democracy. These are: the Public Protector; the Human Rights Commission; the Commission for the Promotion and Protection of the Rights of Cultural, Religious and Linguistic Communities; the Commission for Gender Equality; the Auditor-General and the Electoral Commission.

What are the implications of all of this?

Firstly, that the Constitution is supreme and justiciable under a Constitutional Court. Since 1996 the Government has been charged in this Court and judgements given against it for behaving unconstitutionally. More important, Government in each instance accepted the judgement of the Court. Secondly, the Constitution creates a massive space for civil society action where a variety of special interest lobbies can petition and mobilise support for special causes. Thus the Treatment Action Campaign (TAC) successfully petitioned the Constitutional Court on the Government's policy on Neviropine. Thirdly, political parties can canvass freely for political support under the guidelines of the Independent Electoral Commission and the Electoral Act to see to it that elections are held as freely and fairly as possible.

So, has South Africa moved from a brutalised, polarised society to a smooth functioning liberal democracy overnight?

Of course not. There have been, and still are, many transitional problems that could threaten the consolidation of a young democracy. A high crime rate is symptomatic of rapid urbanisation, unemployment and poverty. Imported crime, especially drug syndicates, pose a serious threat to the youth. Urbanisation combined with pressure for housing causes dislocated urban communities. These are problems South Africa has in common with many developing countries. In many of them, the temptation to suspend democracy in favour of some authoritarian/dictatorial attempt to cope with, or even ignore these problems, has been too strong to resist.

South Africa has chosen a different path - a democratic one. Even though the State battles with the efficient delivery of services, particularly at the Provincial and Local levels of Government, there has not been any serious attempt to subvert the Constitution or engage in violent and subversive action. In fact, despite all of these problems, South Africa has experienced remarkable political stability. There seems to be a high degree of unspoken consensus amongst all major parties that South Africa should pursue a multiplicity of goals concurrently. There must be democracy and growth, human rights and law and order; fiscal discipline and delivery of services, privatisation and job creation. This is a pretty tall order for any country, but especially for a developing one. No wonder that there are political tensions that reveal themselves between and within parties on how these balls should be kept in the air at the same time. Privatisation is an issue within the ANC alliance, crime and law and order a major issue between Government and opposition parties. But no-one has ever suggested that these tensions should be resolved outside the framework of the Constitution.

An interesting and very important facet of the relationship between Government and Opposition in South Africa is the obvious tension between modernity and traditionalism. Almost 25 per cent of the voters in South Africa live under, and many accept, traditional authority. This is almost the antithesis of authority and leadership in a liberal democracy. This is worth mentioning because traditionalism is a countervailing source of power and therefore potential opposition in an emerging liberal democracy. South Africa has been fortunate in having leaders like Mandela, Buthelezi, and Pateko Holomisa that could traffic between modernity and traditionalism and try to reconcile the obvious conflicts between them. This problem remains unresolved at the moment, but the Constitution, in Chapter Twelve, specifically makes provision for a way to be found to accommodate traditional leaders within a liberal democracy. So far traditionalism has been a source of political stability rather than instability in South Africa. But, most important, there is no attempt to sweep its relevance under the carpet, or ignore it.

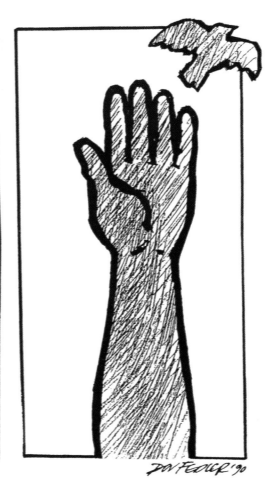

No liberal democracy can be seriously discussed without reference to the Fourth Estate. The media in South Africa, printed, radio and television, have played at times an adversarial and a supportive role to Government and Parliament. Competing sources of information and opinion are freely available and accessible. Clause 16 of the Constitution states unequivocally: "Everyone has the right to freedom of expression, which includes freedom of the press and other media, freedom to receive or impart information of ideas, freedom of artistic creativity, academic freedom and freedom of scientific research."

To repeat: it would be a serious distortion of reality to reduce the relationship between Government and Opposition to a competition between the government in power and parties in opposition. The ANC vs DA, or ANC vs IFP, or ANC vs UDM "show" has to be understood against the checks and balances spelt out above. Whatever the burning issues of the day: Zimbabwe, Aids, sustainable development, racism, poverty alleviation, etc., and however strongly they divide parties, NGOs and special interest lobbies, they are mediated through the checks and balances typical of a liberal democratic constitution. And South Africa has one of the most classical liberal democratic constitutions in the world. (That is why the recent debate on Liberalism in South Africa got trapped in the quagmire of its own assumptions.)

Most important to remember is that where there is strong constitutional government, politicians are inevitably and, for them, inconceivably, groomed for obscurity.

> Considering where we have been
> and what we have gone through,
> the future is rich with promise.

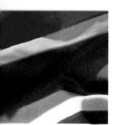  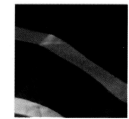

In all socio-political analyses there are the so-called "wild cards", major, even cataclysmic events that force one to go back to the drawing boards. For example, 11th September, 2001, "Globalisation and its Discontents" (as Stiglitz calls it), the USA attacking Iraq and so on. Assumptions about national sovereignty, constitutional government, international relations and allies have to be revisited and their relevance for our own domestic situation rescrutinised. South Africa is as subject to the "ceteris paribus" (all things being equal) clause as any other country.

So, all things being equal, how is South Africa shaping? The Berlin Wall fell in October 1989. This symbolised the collapse of organised Communism and the end of the Cold War. It also precipitated fundamental regime changes in a host of countries in Eastern Europe, USSR, Africa, Latin America and South East Asia. Also in South Africa. Some chose democracy in the liberal democratic sense, others not. If we use the period from then, until now, as a baseline of comparison, how many countries have managed to:

(a) Achieve democratic political stability?

(b) Raise 37 per cent of budget from personal income tax?

(c) Have a duly elected Government successfully challenged more than once in the Constitutional Court?

(d) Have a peaceful and dignified succession of political leadership?

(e) Tolerate a wide variety of special interest mobilisation in civil society?

(f) Still maintain a positive growth rate of between 2 to 3 per cent per annum; reduce its deficit before borrowing substantially; curb inflation and cope with most of the political fallout that tough economic measures generate?

(g) Still have a functioning state despite severe problems of delivery?

Considering where we were little more than 12 years ago, and with a new structured relationship between government and opposition not yet four years old, is this not an impressive balance sheet?

What about the future? The future is potential, not reality. Considering where we have been and what we have gone through, the future is rich with promise. That is, of course, all things being equal.

5

In fast changing times people look to secure and safe havens - in which to live and to invest. If South Africa is to retain its talent and attract the capital necessary for transformation and growth, it has to have a predictable set of financial management policies and effective fiscal practices. Our record over the past 8 years has been exemplary - there is no reason to suspect that anything is about to change.

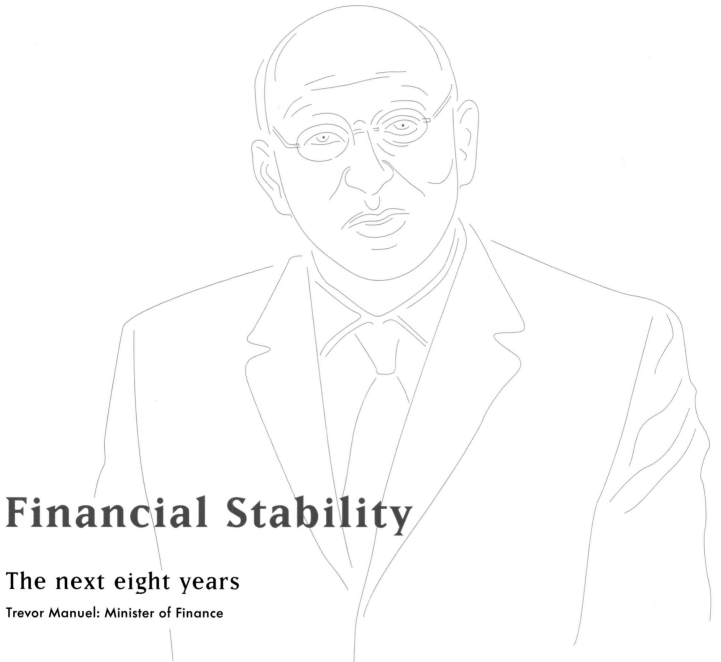

Financial Stability

The next eight years

Trevor Manuel: Minister of Finance

In a complex and unforgiving world, South Africa has taken strides to improve macroeconomic and financial health and stability.

The importance of financial stability in the modern global economy is aptly described in the words of The Financial Stability Institute, a body created in 1999 - by the Bank for International Settlements and the Basle Committee on Banking Supervision - to assist supervisors around the world in improving and strengthening their financial systems.

According to the Institute:

"Financial stability is crucial for sustained economic growth and cannot be achieved without strong financial systems. Weak financial systems can destabilise local economies, making them more vulnerable to external shocks, and may threaten global financial markets.

Effective financial-sector supervision promotes stability by ensuring that financial institutions operate in a safe and sound manner. Financial institutions must have adequate risk-management policies and procedures and operate with sufficient levels of capital. Skilled supervisors are key to effective financial sector supervision. Supervisors must understand the risks inherent in financial activities and establish an adequate framework of supervision and regulation."

Since the East Asian financial crisis, progress has been made in strengthening the international financial architecture in an effort to create greater stability in both domestic markets and the global system. Stability concerns have gained ascendancy (and remain under continuous discussion) in a wide range of groups under the auspices of the G7, G10, G20, IMF, BIS, OECD, etc.

We have gained international acceptance as a stable small emerging-market country with an open economy.

The governments policy is unequivocal - they are committed to a gradual process of exchange control liberalisation.

The interrelationship between macroeconomic stability and financial sector soundness

Macroeconomic stability and financial sector soundness are generally recognised as the most important factors for economic growth. These factors are mutually reinforcing, in that macroeconomic stability is vital for financial sector development and, in turn, a sound and well-functioning financial sector is essential to macroeconomic stability. It is therefore incumbent on a Government to address both these key factors simultaneously. Our Government has done this successfully.

South Africa has attained many economic achievements since the opening of our economy in 1994 including:

- more competitive industries
- more rapid economic growth
- sustainable fiscal balances

As a small, open, emerging-market economy, South Africa has undertaken macroeconomic reforms and fiscal consolidation since 1996 and has pursued a path of gradual external liberalisation.

We can proudly say in that in such a short period we have, through a consistent economic policy, achieved macroeconomic stability and we have our macroeconomic fundamentals in place. This is demonstrated by our resilience to external shocks, which is presently illustrated

by our economy achieving economic growth of 2.2 per cent for 2001. GDP growth for the second quarter of this year (2002) was a healthy 3.2 per cent, with growth for the year expected to be around 2.5 per cent.

This resilience can be attributed to prudent fiscal and monetary policies, along with the benefits of the economic restructuring that has taken place over the past decade. South Africa's foreign financing requirements are limited and the external debt burden moderate.

However, on the financial stability front, there is room in South Africa for improvement, particularly in regard to consolidating and, thereby, further strengthening, the structure of our financial sector regulatory and supervisory framework.

International acceptance

We can confidently say that we have gained international acceptance as a stable small emerging-market country with an open economy. While some commentators may point to the continued existence of exchange controls and may call for a "big bang" approach to exchange control relaxation, most of these commentators have, at the same time, recognised the complexities and pitfalls inherent in rapid capital account liberalisation.

Mindful of this, Government's stated commitment has always been clear and unequivocal - we are committed to a gradual process of exchange control liberalisation that takes into account critical sequencing considerations. A sustainable development path requires that certain conditions be in place before proceeding to full capital account convertibility.

Following almost 10 years of capital outflows, South Africa has experienced capital inflows averaging around 6% of GDP per annum.

Impact of Globalisation

Over the past two decades, there has been a tumultuous change in the size and structure of global financial markets.

The first half of the 1990s saw an expansion of private financial flows from developed to developing countries, which was widely welcomed as a positive contribution to development. However, the second half of the decade revealed that these private flows were reversible - resulting in serious declines in output, investment and employment, as well as increases in poverty. The volatility in portfolio capital flows causes many macroeconomic problems for developing economies, particularly in the short-term, when international investment sentiments may change very quickly and, often, unpredictably.

South Africa's re-entry into the global system came at a time when that system was being altered through increasing globalisation. Through a gradual process, our liberalisation of the financial sector was eased into the global economy.

In this prudent manner, we gained easier access to the surplus saving of the more mature industrial countries of the world. Consequently, the level of foreign investment in South Africa has increased dramatically.

Following almost 10 years of capital outflows, South Africa has experienced capital inflows averaging around six per cent of GDP per annum. The bulk of South Africa's capital inflows, however, are in the form of portfolio investment, especially bond flows. The scale of inward portfolio investment in the late 1990s was considerably higher than in other emerging economies. This is largely a function of the depth and sophistication of the domestic debt and equity markets.

The large inflow of funds over the past few years has enabled the Reserve Bank to increase the country's official reserves from the equivalent of 5.3 weeks worth of imports of goods and services in 1996 to 17.6 weeks at the end of 2001. The increase in capital inflows and the country's official reserves in recent years has been the main enabler of the substantial relaxation of exchange controls and reduction in the net open forward position of the SA Reserve Bank, over the period.

Although South Africa was not immune to the East Asian crisis and its contagion effects, our banking sector passed

a test of strength in showing remarkable resilience during this period. This was due to our robust financial system and sound financial sector, which was reaffirmed in the 2000 Financial System Stability Assessment ("FSSA") of South Africa, a result of the joint IMF/World Bank Financial Sector Assessment Program ("FSAP").

The FSSA evaluation of the South African financial system described it as robust, highly developed, sophisticated and well-regulated, with a strong banking system, a well-developed securities market, a strong presence of institutional investors, and low corporate leverage.

The way forward

A key factor that has helped insulate South Africa from the worst of the current turmoil in South America has remained its sound financial system, with an impressive legal framework in quality and scope for the financial sector and robust legal institutions.

In this regard, it must be mentioned that the IMF Article IV Consultation Report of June 2002 commended South Africa's good progress in following-up on the recommendations of the initial February 2000 Financial System Stability Assessment.

South Africas foreign exchange reserves have increased from 5.3 weeks cover in 1996 to 17.6 weeks cover by the end of 2001.

But this does not mean that there is no room for improvement and circumspection. This year, the effectiveness of our banking supervisors and regulators has been tested. The cases of Regal Treasury Bank, Unifer/Unibank, Saambou Bank and BOE Bank are strong indicators that we need to review continuously the effectiveness of our regulatory system and our approach to supervising our banking system.

Supervisory capacity

An important part of financial stability remains effective financial supervision - a task made difficult by information deficiencies among depositors, financial institutions and borrowers, which may create incentives to take undue risk.

Effective financial supervision can successfully counteract this behaviour by promoting adequate capital standards, effective risk management and transparency. However, it requires skilled supervisors who can quickly understand the inherent risks in financial activities, identify the best ways to anticipate, manage and control these risks; and establish an adequate framework of prudential regulation.

We require strong supervisors who are backed up by institutional and legal support to help them enforce regulations and apply corrective measures firmly, but timeously.

In South Africa, increasing capacity for more robust on-site supervision is an important issue that we need to address. The ability of the supervisor to detect and effectively resolve problems within any given bank before they threaten the financial soundness of a bank is crucial. These are the type of issues relating to risk management, capital adequacy, and corporate governance, which need to be addressed at an international level.

For regulation to be efficient, it is essential that the domain of the supervisor / regulator is the same as the domain of the market that is regulated. To achieve such efficiency, establishing a single supervisory institutional framework for the financial services sector in South Africa is required.

The focus of the new single supervisory agency must be on delivering a professional, high-quality and cost-effective service that advances and administers a regulatory framework, which contributes to public confidence in the financial services industry. However, the success of the new framework will lie in proper co-ordination and communication (exchange of information) and, as such, will require a significant improvement in the exchange of information and co-ordination across financial sectors among regulators, both domestically and globally.

The Basle Capital Accord and proposed Basle II

The 1988 Basle Capital Accord and proposed Basle II are potentially the most important regulatory developments since the East Asian crisis. The proposed modification of the Capital Accord could have profound impact on international bank lending in terms of its level, cost and cycle.

Although the objectives and principles of Basle II are welcomed, we are alive to the concerns that have been raised that these changes may paradoxically increase the risk of crises and discourage international bank lending to developing countries.

With the proposed implementation date for Basle II now set at 2006, South Africa needs to ensure that it has in place the required supervisory capacity to implement what will be a more rigorous capital framework. Within the context of the Basle II proposals, the issue of access to banking issues must also be accommodated in South Africa.

Despite our sophisticated financial markets, too many South Africans still have little or no recourse to financial services. Accordingly, access to banking will remain an issue for the foreseeable future and, therefore, Government's response and the challenge to our supervisors, must be how these issues are best captured in the framework of the Basle II proposals.

Corporate governance

The mammoth failures in corporate governance, represented by Enron and Worldcom, have redefined the US corporate landscape and ushered in an era of global reform and accountability. In South Africa, we have initiated a process of corporate reform beginning with a general acceptance of an independent, private-sector sponsored code of corporate governance (the King Code of Corporate Governance - which is similar to the outcome of the Cadbury Report in the United Kingdom).

This year, we have favourably completed a World Bank Report on the Observance of Standards and Codes on Accounting and Auditing and Corporate Governance this assessed our country's compliance with international standards and codes on corporate governance and auditing and accounting standards. Our Government is furthermore considering draft legislation that gives legal backing to accounting standards and which changes the governance of the accounting and auditing professions.

Combating money laundering and terrorist financing
In the past year, increased attention has been given to the issues of combating money laundering and terrorist financing. The cumulative effect of money laundering activities harms a country's reputation and impacts on its financial stability, as it tends to destabilise the foundations of a nation's financial system. The quick flow of laundered funds takes control of economic policy away from government, making policy difficult to achieve. In addition, money laundering distorts business decisions, increases the risk of bank failures, creates liquidity problems in financial markets, and diminishes tax revenue - thereby indirectly prejudicing honest taxpayers.

South Africa has comprehensive and world-leading legislation to combat money laundering and terrorist funding.

There is a growing global realisation that there is a need to keep ill-begotten funds out of global financial systems. Worldwide, countries are establishing or improving financial intelligence units to prevent money laundering and to combat terrorist financing. South Africa has itself embarked on an ambitious programme to establish its own Financial Intelligence Centre, founded on some of the most comprehensive and leading legislation.

No country can implement anti-money laundering measures in isolation and South Africa has recently joined the East and Southern African Anti-money laundering Group, the Financial Action Task Force ("FATF") regional co-ordinating body. In due course we will seek full membership of the FATF and other bodies responsible for the combating of money laundering and terrorist financing.

"WHAT DO YOU MEAN WE'RE BANKRUPT?"

Conclusion
Over the past few years, Government has taken steps to improve both macroeconomic and financial stability. During this period, Government has had to make policy choices in a complex and often unforgiving world. At the centre of the range of policy choices that our Government faces lies the principle that South Africa is an open economy. In that environment, it is inevitable that, from time to time, there will be turbulence. The events of late last year were clearly one of those times.

It is tempting in the current volatile global times to look for quick fixes or hasty policy responses. But this, invariably, leads to unintended consequences and policy uncertainty. Rather, as our own experience and that of other countries internationally has borne out, the best response in such circumstances is to be confident that the policy choices we have made, and the good performance of the economy that we have achieved over the past five or six years, will support the ongoing growth and sustainable development that the South African economy needs in the years ahead.

In going forward, we must ensure that appropriate macroeconomic fundamentals remain in place, that a sound and well-regulated financial system exists to promote financial stability, including prudential regulation, and that social safety nets are in place to protect the poor against the potential social costs of globalisation.

The South African financial system is described as robust, highly developed, sophisticated and well regulated - Joint IMF/ World Bank assessment 2000.

There's no doubt that the achievement of fiscal and financial discipline has been one of the great achievements of the ANC Government since 1994.

But fiscal discipline is a means to an end, not an end in itself, and government policies have come in for criticism from both the left and the right. The key problem is that virtue has brought little reward in the shape of a higher growth rate: economic growth remains stubbornly around three per cent, only half of what was originally envisaged at this stage of transformation.

While there has indeed been a considerable inflow of foreign funds in recent years, as Trevor Manuel admits, it has mainly been in portfolio investment and not direct investment in new productive capacity - with a few notable exceptions, like minerals beneficiation (which unfortunately provides few permanent jobs) and the motor industry. In any event, even this inflow has slackened considerably, and at times gone into reverse, this year.

A major failure here has been the slow pace of privatisation of state-owned and public enterprises like South African Airways, the Airports Company, Telkom and Eskom. The initial sale of a minority stake in SAA to Swissair had to be reversed; a sell-off of the Airports Company seemed to be imminent two years ago, but mysteriously went no further; and though the offer for a further Telkom tranche is back on track, given what has happened to world telecoms markets in recent years, it will realise considerably less than what was originally hoped.

Manuel repeats Government's "clear and unequivocal" commitment to a gradual phasing-out of exchange control, but in practice this has gone backwards in some respects: the asset-swap mechanism has been scrapped and not replaced, and the real value of individual offshore investment and travel allowances has fallen steeply with the depreciation of the rand. Manuel also warned earlier this year that even when remaining institutional forex curbs will be lifted, they will be replaced by "prudential" investment guidelines which will in effect be the same thing under another name.

While effective supervision of the financial sector is clearly necessary, and everyone will support efforts to make the existing regime more effective, the case for a single supervisory institutional framework for the financial services sector is not as cut and dried as Manuel asserts. A monolithic regulator could well prove too bureaucratic and expensive, as is being found in other jurisdictions.

As eminent an authority as Reserve Bank Governor Tito Mboweni has rejected the idea of a single supervisor, arguing cogently that bank supervision should remain under the aegis of the central bank. No doubt there are elements of turf protection on both sides; but, however much this may be the case, the fact is there are merits on both sides of the debate.

Criticism from the left centres on the fact that market-friendly policies have brought no relief to the chronic unemployment situation; indeed, more jobs have been destroyed than created in the private sector, while corporate profits have on the whole been buoyant. The left would prefer to see less emphasis on reducing the budget deficit and more on government spending to create jobs and improve social services. They see the ANC as having betrayed the revolution and sold out to international capitalism. To them, financial stability and "fiscal consolidation" as practised by this Government are not an achievement, but a disaster.

They may have learnt nothing from the collapse of the Soviet economy; but, while neo-liberals argue that disappointing growth shows that Government has not done enough to throw the economy open to market forces, so radicals argue that the persistence of high unemployment proves that it is not interventionist enough.

Editorial Comment
Manuel has a tight rope to walk, balancing the COSATU strike on privatisation against the corporate demands for a freer market. Given the extent to which these forces oppose each other, his balancing act has been remarkable, and has been widely acknowledged in the international community by those who know.

Manuel's balancing act has been remarkable, and is widely acknowledged in the international community by those who know.

It is often asked, is there more corruption under the ANC than there was under the Nats? Or is the difference that prior to the early 90s you could go to jail for printing the story? Now it really doesn't matter. What does matter is that a free press is one of the greatest guarantees of democratic and just rule - both from a government and a corporate point of view. A free press underpins the very fabric of truth in modern society.

6

Freedom of Speech
and the Media - Robust or Rundown

Peter Bruce, Editor: Business Day

Baptism of Fire

Shortly before South Africa's second democratic general election in June 1999, an idea began to form in my head. I was editor of the **Financial Mail**, the country's biggest weekly news and business magazine. The election was trundling along calmly. There seemed to be few contentious issues and the winner was a foregone conclusion. The African National Congress would take it by a landslide and the new President of the country would be Thabo Mbeki. I decided to oppose the ANC in the poll and to carry a prominent endorsement of a rival party, the (then) newly-formed United Democratic Movement (UDM). South Africa, in my view, needed a strong, black-led, opposition and I thought the UDM might be it.

Three weeks before the election we ran the endorsement on our cover and in an expanded editorial. What happened next was truly amazing.

The phone rang. It was Cyril Ramaphosa, arguably the most popular member of the ANC national executive. He was cross. He was also chairman of the company that publishes the **Financial Mail**. I knew I was in trouble. I had hugely embarrassed the owners of the magazine, who it might reasonably be said were supportive of the ANC. What I didn't know was how little trouble I was in.

Ramaphosa was given some space in the next issue of the magazine to reply to my endorsement, there were radio shows and some cartoons in the press, and it was over.

After the election (the UDM did well, but has subsequently fallen apart somewhat), I went to an ANC victory party and was greeted by one party leader as, "the bravest man in the country", to much cheering and teasing. A week later I was at a dinner where Mbeki was speaking. When he saw me he broke away from his group to greet me warmly, pat me on the back and tell me how much he had enjoyed the whole spectacle of the endorsement. And that was it. Of course, some party hacks and newspaper columnists called for my head, but I was struck by the maturity and good humour in the Government response to my endorsement. This is Africa - shouldn't I be fortunate to escape with my head?

The fact is, the government of the day carried my attack and opposition with good grace and composure. I could not have been more impressed.

Journalism under the Nats was generally a subversive affair.

The Press is Free

And I now get extremely angry with editors, journalists and armchair commentators who somehow believe the media in SA is being squeezed by the Government. It isn't. As editors we are freer now than at probably any time in the history of journalism in this country. What is in doubt is whether we use that freedom or whether we may not be just a little scared of it. Do we censor ourselves?

In the apartheid era, before the first democratic election in 1994, the SA press had had a torrid time. Or parts of it. The media divided into largely ideological or party political lines. Of course, the national broadcaster, the SABC, was tightly controlled by the ruling white National Party. The Afrikaans press strongly supported the National Party (the Nats). The English language press was divided. Some editors were fiercely (and bravely) anti apartheid. Some were uncomfortable with apartheid but equally uncomfortable with majority rule. Others supported it but took exception to the quasi-socialist economics that buttressed Afrikaner nationalism. The law was frequently used against troublesome editors, the braver of whom fought back. The late Donald Woods, former editor of the **Daily Dispatch** in East London, had, by the age of 35, entirely refurnished his home with the proceeds of libel actions against National Party politicians who tried to label him a communist (which it was illegal then to be).

Interestingly the new generation entering journalism do not have an apparent political agenda. They are more serious about journalistic independence.

More So than it Used to Be

But journalism under the Nats was a generally subversive affair. To an extent, the core tasks, telling a story with balance and from a distance became impossible. You could not ignore apartheid or be unmoved by it. Journalism suffered and we became a one-story country. Newsrooms lost, or stopped valuing the expertise of people who were specialists in health policy, or housing. Political writers were king and the road to editorship most ran through the press gallery in Parliament. Worse, perhaps, newspaper managements discovered that advertisers were happy to "sponsor" editorial in supplements and surveys which focussed either on their areas of business or on their companies specifically. This meant that managements were happy to hire young and inexperienced journalists. They were not set very high professional goals.

Thus, the onset of democracy in 1994 caught the press and most of the media off guard. Newsrooms were run down, kept alive in most cases by one or two star performers. Pay was low, motivation even more so and, into this scenario, black journalists began knocking at the door of a largely white-edited and white-managed media. They were aided by an almost immediate debate among the new black policy elite about the need for "transformation" (of colour) in the media.

Most newspapers, TV and radio stations in the country are now edited and managed by blacks or other so-called "previously disadvantaged" citizens.

That debate took many forms. For some, blacks in the media would soften perceived opposition to the new black government while, to others, black journalists would naturally champion the national interests of the new country. The debate took various forms and was carried mostly in the very newspapers the black elite was criticising. The pressure to "transform" the media reached a peak in 1998 when the Human Rights Commission (HRC), claiming it had been pressed by black professionals, announced it would conduct an investigation into racism in the media. The commission became a flashpoint between black and white journalists and, when the HRC issued subpoenas for its hearings, blacks applauded and whites resisted. Eventually, a compromise was reached.

Editors were invited to the hearing on the understanding that they would, in fact, attend. To my mind, the hearings were a disappointment, as were the conclusions reached by the HRC. Was the "racism in the media" a question of content, as some HRC research seemed to imply? Or was it to be found in the demographics of the newsrooms? The hearings never really resolved this. Other editors found the atmosphere in the hearings refreshing and energising, nothing like the inquisition many had feared. But time will best resolve the questions raised at the hearings and the questions asked there will cease to be important and will be replaced in the public mind by others.

Black influence over editorial and over management has grown rapidly. Most newspapers in the country are now edited by blacks or other so-called "previously disadvantaged" citizens. State radio and TV is managed and edited by blacks as is the country's increasingly successful independent TV channel, E-TV.

The Future

What is really exciting about this is that the change has by no means resulted in a meeker media. In fact, I foresee a time when South Africans wonder how they ever survived with the tame media of the 1990s and the early 2000s. An awesome thing is happening in journalism. We are growing up and understanding, black and white, that our professionalism is what matters most, that our independence is our security. I used to be scared for press freedom in South Africa. I no longer am. Not because the Government is benign. It is, relatively. But that can change in any country.

In fact, as I write, the Government is pressing for legislation to be introduced which would allow it to approve or not approve of editorial policies at the SABC. That is clearly wrong but one cannot blame the politicians for trying it on.

The really cool thing that is happening in this dispute, however, is that the SABC management, once thought of as docile and compliant to its government shareholder, is fighting back and publicly opposing the minister responsible for broadcasting. That is the spirit that is beginning to dominate in the media. We are losing our fear of the state and beginning to back ourselves, both journalists and managers alike.

An awesome thing is happening in journalism. We are growing up, black and white, understanding that our independence is our security.

I now see the quality of young, mostly black people entering the industry. They are, say, 19 years old. That means they were 10 when Nelson Mandela was released from prison. They have known little of the horrors of apartheid, and how hopeless the future was for blacks. Instead, they are confident, well-educated, free people who want to make a contribution, survive on merit and compete with the best. Interestingly, the new generation entering journalism do not have an apparent political agenda, and seem to be much more serious about journalistic independence than anything else. They are certainly not open to being manipulated politically.

My fears, if I have them, are economic. As technology changes the media, can traditional elements of it like the press survive? The collapse of the local currency has hugely increased the cost of newsprint and the general state of the world economy has decimated advertising revenues, not just in South Africa, but everywhere. In tough times, it is hard to hire bright new people and I ache when I think of the wonderful talent we have had to overlook. I hope it comes right. I also hope the Government is doing the right things to make it come right.

If not, we will be on their backs, independent, free, boisterous, patriotic and proud. That is the state of the media in South Africa. And that is the way it should be.

7

South Africa needs to transform to a country where poverty and unemployment are things of the past. This is a large and daunting task. And whilst the government needs to deal with the immediacy of the problem, it also needs to create sustainable conditions that systematically reduce both employment and consequently poverty. South Africa is blessed with abundant resources, willing people and access to world class technology. International trade is the key to future prosperity for our nation.

International Trade
A Future Perspective

Alec Erwin: Minister of Trade and Industry

Blue Skies Ahead

The end of apartheid and the holding of our first democratic election in 1994 opened up the world for South Africa.

After decades of increasing isolationism, in a steadily declining siege economy, political freedom created a whole new universe of economic opportunities.

Like most blessings, however, the re-entry of South Africa into the world economy was a mixed one. On the one hand, we had access to fresh markets but, on the other, the new democratic government had almost no time to prepare for the competitiveness of the world economy.

It was a case of sink or swim, with trade treaties to be negotiated, markets to be investigated, and complex trading and tariff systems to be dealt with. In 1994, the South African Rip van Winkle found himself awake in a world economy utterly transformed, with information and communication technologies fundamentally changing the nature of business.

Since then, South Africa's global economic interests have formed around two major issues: market access and economic development. This country has successfully focussed on the multilateral trading system and on selecting key strategic partners as sources of investment and for market access.

Almost all countries now are part of regional trading blocs. Going at it alone is simply not an option and we have had to think carefully about which partnerships are best in our economic interest. This process involves matters of choice and priority, which means core strategic thinking and a good understanding of the world economy and what makes it work.

That we have done this so fast and so effectively since 1994, is one of our greatest achievements in the economic arena.

Re-invention

After 1994, South Africa's Department of Trade and Industry (DTI) had to scramble to reinvent itself to provide leadership in an uncertain world. Most recently, the DTI has designed (in collaboration with the full range of key stakeholders) an Integrated Manufacturing Strategy (IMS) that encapsulates South Africa's economic strategies into the future.

In essence, the IMS has taken on broad global realities such as the shift away from raw materials and cheap, labour-intensive, heavy industry to what is increasingly known as the "knowledge economy" where ideas, information and technology integrate and are much more important than muscle and commodities.

Political freedom has opened up a whole new universe of economic opportunity.

Good Progress

How well have we done? The answer is very well indeed, as shown in Table 1 on the growth of South Africa's exports as a percentage of output since 1994.

Manufacturing Exports - Up!

The rising export orientation of South African manufacturing is consistent with global trends. Manufacturing's share of total exports rose from 35 per cent in 1994 to more than 50 per cent at the end of the 1990s. Similarly, the share of primary products in merchandise trade declined from 64 per cent in 1968-70 to 37 per cent in 1998-2000.

Despite our significant raw material resources, primary products make up a smaller share of our exports than for most other African countries - only Morocco, Madagascar, Mauritius and Tunisia have a lower share of primary products in merchandise trade (WTO, 2002).

The consistency and the magnitude of exports strongly suggests that exporting has become a permanent and critical feature for many manufacturing firms. Far more consistent and deeper engagement with export markets, by many more manufacturing firms, is likely to enhance efficiencies. The learning entailed in competing in demanding markets is likely to have reinforced the evident rise in the productivity of the manufacturing sector.

High Technology Sector - Up!

Looking at the technological composition of output, South African manufacturing has seen the share of the low technology sectors decline; the share of medium technology remains constant, while the high-tech sectors have seen a steady increase. Currently, the latter contribute more than 41 per cent to total manufacturing value added.

Exports as a Share of Manufacturing Output - Up!

There has been a steady increase in the share of exports in manufacturing output. Whereas, in 1994, exports constituted 14 per cent of manufactured output, this had doubled to 28 per cent in 2001. Moreover, rising export orientation has been consistent - even in periods when domestic demand has been strong and universal - and is characteristic of all manufacturing sectors.

In 1994, the new democratic government had almost no time to prepare ... It was a case of sink or swim.

More and more, winning nations in the international arena are those that are able to compete for export markets through adding value, such as design, innovation, services, marketing, distribution and so on. For example, a well-crafted Italian shoe is worlds away from a rawhide sandal. South Africa is able now to make much better use of its raw materials and to export these in value-added forms, from gold jewellery to motor cars.

Whole new areas of business have opened up in crafts and cultural industries, computer software development and services such as call centres.

South Africa's integrated manufacturing depends on a global economic strategy that will promote exports and attract investments and technology to those high-opportunity sectors that will drive industrial development.

They range from the service sectors, like tourism and financial and management services (where South Africa is becoming a leading supplier into the African continent), to value-added manufacturers and entirely new areas of activity, such as biotechnology.

At the same time, trade policy is also vital for enhancing our international competitiveness, and South Africa has successfully embarked on a fundamental upheaval of its tariff policies, including free trade agreements with selected key markets.

How well have we done? The answer is very well indeed.

Exports as a Percentage of Manufactured Output, 1994 and 2001

Sector	1994 (%)	2001 (%)	% of Total Exports in 2001
• General and special purpose	16.8	80.0	12.5
• Other transport equipment	33.9	86.3	2.0
• Radio, television and communication	8.2	59.3	1.8
• Professional equipment	28.3	72.9	0.9
• Furniture	18.0	51.4	2.3
• Motor vehicles, trailers	8.9	28.4	13.3
• Rubber products	7.3	23.4	0.9
• Wood and wood products	14.1	27.8	1.8
• Wearing apparel	6.0	18.7	1.5
• Electrical machinery	7.5	19.2	1.9
• Basic chemicals	36.1	46.5	8.4
• Other chemical products	8.8	18.9	4.0
• Glass and glass products	8.8	18.3	0.4
• Coke and refined petroleum	18.9	27.5	7.5
• Beverages	5.8	14.3	2.5
• Textiles	12.1	20.1	1.6
• Basic precious and non-ferrous metals	44.4	50.8	6.5
• Fabricated metal products	5.6	11.8	2.3
• Paper and paper products	20.5	26.0	4.7
• Other non-metallic minerals	5.8	11.2	0.9
• Plastic products	3.3	8.5	0.8
• Food and food products	8.5	13.6	6.6
• Tanning and dressing of leather	33.2	38.2	0.8
• Basic iron and steel products	48.8	52.4	13.3
• Other manufacturing industries	0.8	4.2	0.5
• Footwear	3.5	5.5	0.1
• Publishing and printing	2.0	3.4	0.3
• Total manufacturing	14.3	27.7	

Table 1: Manufacturing - Ratio of Exports to Output, 1994 and 2001

Source: Department of Trade and Industry, March 2002

Exporting has become a permanent and critical feature for manufacturing firms.

Since 1994, the focus has been on international market access and economic development.

SA's Leading Role in World Trade Organisation Negotiations

The rules of the international trading system are adjudicated by the World Trade Organisation (WTO), where South Africa is currently playing a leading role in the Doha round of negotiations set for 2003. We will be fighting for a better share of key European and US markets which are protected by unfair and uncompetitive tariff barriers, such as in agriculture. Since 1994, we have learned to fight our corner to such an extent that, at no time before, has the underdeveloped South been able to negotiate off a more co-ordinated, strategic and researched footing. This has resulted in a fairer world trading order for our products. We will benefit greatly from this in the decade ahead.

In the meantime, in 2000 we concluded a free trade agreement with our single biggest global trade partner, the European Union, hammering out our share of that lucrative market.

Closer to home, success in the past two years includes the building blocks for regional free trade via the Southern African Development Community (SADC) and the Southern African Customs Union (SACU).

These are further given a hard business sense through the Spatial Development Initiatives (SDIs) launched by South Africa with its neighbours, the Maputo Corridor being only one example of this, producing huge downstream benefits ranging from the Mozal project to the Pande gasfields and transfrontier peace parks. These initiatives are extending further into the subcontinent, particularly with peace in Angola and the first signs of a cessation of conflict in central Africa and the Great Lakes region.

Sorting Out Priorities

The next priorities are our other main trading partners. Within the key North American market, we are reaping the benefits of the Africa Growth and Opportunities Act (AGOA), which lifts key tariff barriers on our exports, such as in textiles.

A bi-national commission with the US has also done its share to open up that market for South Africa, and it is worth noting that when the US recently implemented punitive tariffs on some steel imports, it exempted South Africa from this. Increasingly South Africa is becoming part of a global supply chain network, adding value to raw materials for export to developing nations.

Motor Industry Success

Much of this is epitomised by the spectacular success of the South African motor industry's export drive since 1997. From BMW to Toyota, South African right-hand drive vehicles are sweeping the world, outperforming the best in terms of quality.

Our vehicle exports have risen from 15 764 in 1995 to 130 000 in 2002 ... and climbing. Exports as a percentage of domestic production have risen from 4 per cent of the total to 26.5 per cent, earning R15 billion for South Africa.

The vehicle components industry is booming, from leather seats to catalytic converters. The export of cars and components is forecast to earn R40 billion this year. (See also Chapter 22 on Labour Productivity.)

New Markets

These exports, and others, are also going to new markets, as South Africa seeks to diversify strategically our trading networks and tie them in via new trade agreements.

Thus, some of our key markets for the decade ahead will be India, China (a massive opportunity for us, and one where trade is growing rapidly), Nigeria (South African breakthroughs in cellphone networks there are a good example), Egypt, Russia, Latin America via the Mercosur FTA, and Saudi Arabia.

This does not exclude other opportunities, but rather provides us with strategic starting points to enter other markets in those regions. South Africa's global trading network is much more balanced and less dependent on the business cycles of a few established traditional markets.

Increasingly South Africa is becoming part of a global supply chain network.

Conclusion - Shared Vision, New Era, Exciting Opportunities

All of these achievements are in addition to the emergng opportunities surrounding President Mbeki's New Programme for Africa's Development (NEPAD) initiative.

Although it is early days yet, and the path ahead is fraught with obstacles, NEPAD has been warmly endorsed by the major economies as Africa's best chance to make this the African century.

For the first time, Africans have a shared vision of a prosperous and democratic future based on sound economic principles. We can break the cycle of underdevelopment, poverty and social strife that has for so long held this continent back from achieving its real potential.

We will confound the armchair critics. Those South Africans with the courage, the foresight and the energy to stay the course will find themselves richly rewarded in the longer term.

In the arena of expanding opportunities in the world economy, South Africa stands at the beginning of a whole new era, replete with exciting opportunities. What is more, our presence in the harsh world of the global economy, following a steep learning curve over the past decade, shows we can compete with the best and fight our corner as one of the most competitive trading nations in the world.

Very exciting times lie ahead for South Africans!

We will confound the armchair critics. Those South Africans with the courage to stay the course will be richly rewarded.

Achievements

Minister Alec Erwin makes a compelling case that the short and medium prospects for the South African economy are strongly positive.

Since 1994, the DTI has led the successful reintegration of South Africa into the global economy and, at a general level, the South African economy is adjusting satisfactorily to the challenges.

Our economy has gone through structural changes induced by systematic trade liberalisation. It is an inescapable fact that the pre-1994 economic growth path based on import substitution, high tariffs, subsidies and anti-competitive measures, has been dismantled. This transition, from an inward-focused, protected manufacturing sector to an outward-oriented development strategy, is often fraught with painful trade-offs and adjustments.

A special feature, however, of our transition, has been that difficult decisions about our re-entry into the world economy were taken with stakeholder support. This involved explicitly identifying the economic and social dimensions of trade and industrial policy.

Having dialogue on contentious issues is one thing, negotiating agreements with social partners such as organised labour and business, is another.

Our success in negotiating agreements and achieving consensus on difficult economic policy matters is often taken for granted. Nedlac (the National Economic Development and Labour Council) has been a critical institution in this regard.

At Nedlac, Government comes together with organised business, organised labour and community groups at a national level to discuss and try to reach consensus on issues of social and economic policy.

Government has been particularly successful in negotiating agreements with its social partners in the trade and industry policy chamber of Nedlac. Some examples in recent years include the SA-EU trade agreement, the SADC trade agreement and competition policy.

Leadership Role in Multilateral Institutions

The South African economy is relatively small in a global context. Yet the impact and leadership role our key economic policy makers have had on the global stage, has been remarkable. There is wide appreciation and acknowledgement for the role played in multilateral institutions such as the World Bank, IMF and the WTO.

South Africa has been a rallying force amongst the developing countries in these forums (World Bank, IMF and WTO).

Challenges

Foreign Direct Investment

Attracting foreign direct investment is important as a potential remedy for meeting the domestic capital shortfalls caused by our low savings rate, but out record of success has been disappointing. A critical challenge facing DTI and Government in general is to identify the barriers, real or perceived, to changing perceptions about South Africa as an investment destination.

Most foreign investors do not know of our efficient physical infrastructure of roads, rail and air transport, our well-developed communications network supported by reliable and cost-effective electricity supplies. Many do not know that our stock exchange is the 11th largest in the world in terms of market capitalisation. In this regard, significant scope and opportunity still exist to accelerate the pace of privatisation and the restructuring of state-owned enterprises.

Employment

Our scorecard on job creation is probably the most disappointing. The Government is confronted with the difficult challenge of combining short-term job creation strategies while laying the basis for long-term job creation and sustainable growth.

Unemployment is arguably the most significant constraint on South Africa's future economic development. In many countries, employment growth has come from small and medium enterprises. Government's performance in creating conditions to facilitate the rapid expansion of SMMEs, has been mixed at best. An integrated approach is needed to address the problem of structural unemployment. Failure to confront the job creation challenge will threaten the stability of our democracy. An explicit medium-term employment strategy will go a long way towards placing job creation at the centre of economic policy.

Beneficiation

There is still an inherent bias in South African manufacturing towards upstream resource-based industry. Despite some diversification, primary commodities still dominate South Africa's trade profile. The promotion of beneficiation of South Africa's mineral commodities remains a crucial challenge. In this regard, the recently unveiled Empowerment Charter for the mining industry allows companies to offset the value of the level of beneficiation achieved against ownership commitments on black economic empowerment. This provision of the Charter demonstrates that beneficiation ranks high on the priority list and should lead to new investment and job creation opportunities in the future.

Conclusion

A solid economic foundation has been laid with the remarkable degree of macroeconomic stability we achieved under difficult global economic pressures. The focus now has to shift to policies geared to achieving job creation, skills development, attracting foreign investment and building internationally competitive industries. The new industrial policy framework is primarily focused on improving competitiveness. Achieving this cannot come from trade policy alone. A more effective alignment between competition policy, trade and industrial policy as well as exchange rate policy is required.

However, despite the acknowledged progress, we still need to grapple with the challenge of finding an appropriate and sustainable growth path to propel our economy to new levels.

The focus must now shift to job creation, skills development, attracting foreign investment and building internationally competitive industries.

South Africa's constitution is widely acclaimed as the finest liberal democratic constitution in the world. That it emerged from the chaos of the time was remarkable. That is has stood the test of time is a blessing. It underpins the progress in every facet of out lives. It is the cornerstone of good governance going forward.

The Constitution and the Constitutional Court [1]

Chief Justice Chaskalson

The history of South Africa from the mid-sixteenth century is one of colonialism, white political domination and, ultimately, apartheid.

Apartheid, adopted as policy by the South African government in 1948, was a powerful ideology that left no facet of life untouched. It was institutionalised in the law through statutes and regulations which sought to classify and control the lives of South Africans, advancing the interests of the already dominant white community and marginalising blacks, the great majority of the population. It was enforced through the application of harsh and unjust laws which were rightly condemned by the international community as gross violations of human rights.

Apartheid caused poverty, degradation and suffering, denying to the overwhelming majority of South Africans access to proper education, to work opportunities other than in menial occupations, to the ownership and occupation of most of the land, and to fundamental rights and freedoms essential to self-esteem and self-development. It relegated those who were not white to inferior status in society and required them to live in humiliating conditions. Through migrant labour and pass law policies, it separated families and this had a devastating impact on family life. Ultimately it resulted in enormous social and economic disparities between blacks and whites which still exist in South Africa today.

After a long and protracted struggle during which many people lost their lives and freedom, apartheid was brought to an end in South Africa. This was achieved through negotiations between the political leaders of the country who accepted that the best hope for our country lay neither in oppression nor war, but in a commitment to reconciliation and the reconstruction of our society.

These negotiations led to a political settlement that was recorded as "a solemn pact" in an interim constitution which came into force in April 1994.

Power to the People

"(The future) can now be addressed on the basis that there is a need for understanding but not for vengeance, a need for reparation but not for retaliation, a need for ubuntu but not for victimisation".

- The Interim Constitution

The Interim Constitution

The interim Constitution contained an extensive Bill of Rights and included a resolution on national unity and reconciliation, that begins by saying, "This Constitution provides a historic bridge between the past of a deeply divided society characterised by strife, conflict, untold suffering and injustice and a future founded on the recognition of human rights, democracy and peaceful coexistence and development of opportunities for all South Africans, irrespective of colour, race, class, belief or sex."

It goes on to stress the imperatives of unity and reconciliation and the need to lay a firm foundation for the future in order to transcend the divisions and strife of the past. This, it said, "can now be addressed on the basis that there is a need for understanding but not for vengeance, a need for reparation but not for retaliation, a need for ubuntu but not for victimisation".

The interim Constitution put an end to institutional discrimination and contained far-reaching guarantees of human rights. The new democracy that it promised was ratified and confirmed by a constitution adopted by an elected Constitutional Assembly in 1996 which came into force in February 1997. This is the Constitution that is currently in force.

"And South Africa has one of the most classical liberal democratic constitutions in the world" Frederik van Zyl Slabbert

The 1996 Constitution

In the preamble to the 1996 Constitution the injustice of the past is acknowledged, and a commitment is made to improve the quality of life of all citizens and to free the potential of each person. There is also a commitment to building a non-racial and non-sexist society in which fundamental human rights are respected. The founding values of the legal order thus established are also identified in the Constitution. They are: human dignity, the achievement of equality, the advancement of human rights and freedoms including non-sexism and non-racism, and respect for certain of the fundamental principles of democracy – the rule of law, universal adult suffrage, a national common voters roll, regular elections

and a multi-party system of democratic government to ensure accountability, responsiveness and openness.

The Bill of Rights

The founding values of the Constitution are articulated in a Bill of Rights which is referred to in the Constitution as "A cornerstone of democracy in South Africa [which] enshrines the rights of all people in our country and affirms the democratic values of human dignity, equality and freedom".[2]

As in every constitutional democracy, the rights that everyone has under the bill of rights are not absolute. They may be limited but only in terms of a law of general application, and only to the extent that the limitation is reasonable and justifiable in an open and democratic society based on human dignity, equality and freedom.[3] The limitations enquiry under the Constitution calls for a proportionality analysis, involving the balancing of different interests in the context of the relevant legislative and social setting.

The Bill of Rights entrenches internationally recognised rights and freedoms such as the right to life, equal protection of the law, freedom of expression, freedom of movement, access to courts, fair trials and protection against unreasonable searches. The rights of people who have been arrested, detained or accused are spelt out in detail and freedom of religion, belief and opinion, and of assembly and association are guaranteed.

The influence of our history can be seen in the formulation of the rights and in the inclusion of rights not commonly found in Bills of Rights. Thus, there is not only an equal protection clause but also a right of everyone to have their dignity respected and protected, and detailed provisions prohibiting discrimination. The equal protection clause guarantees that: "everyone is equal before the law and has the right to equal protection and benefit of the law".[4]

The anti-discrimination clause prohibits unfair discrimination on grounds including "race, gender, sex, pregnancy, marital status, ethnic or social origin, colour, sexual orientation, age, disability, religion, conscience, belief, culture, language and birth".[5]

Discrimination on one of these grounds is presumed to be unfair unless the contrary is established. This protection against discrimination is binding not only on the state but also on individuals. Its reach is therefore extremely broad.

"People turned out in their millions to vote. Queues were multiracial for the first time. The atmosphere was electric - and full of joy and peace."

A cornerstone of democracy in South Africa enshrines the rights of all people in our country and affirms the democratic values of human dignity, equality and freedom.

Section 7.1 of the Constitution

In reaction to the draconian security legislation of the past, the right to freedom and security of the person specifically provides for the right not to be deprived of freedom arbitrarily and without just cause, not to be detained without trial, not to be tortured in any way and not to be treated or punished in a cruel, inhuman or degrading way.

So, too, the right to privacy that everyone has includes the right not to have their person, home or property searched, their possessions seized or the privacy of their communications infringed. Similarly, the response to the history of censorship, state control of electronic media, laws restricting the freedom of the press and interference with the autonomy of universities, is shown in the formulation of the right to freedom of expression which in specific terms includes freedom of the press and other media, freedom to receive or impart information or ideas, freedom of artistic creativity, academic freedom and freedom of scientific research.

Freedom of movement and residence includes the right to a passport and to leave the Republic, while freedom of assembly includes the right to demonstrate, to picket and to present petitions. In almost all the civil and political rights entrenched in the Constitution there can be seen a right that was denied under apartheid.

In reaction to the closed and authoritarian society of the past, the Bill of Rights makes provision for fair labour rights, a right to have access to information held by the state, and to information held by any other person if that is necessary for the exercise or protection of any right, a right to just administrative action, and to an environment that is not harmful to their health or well-being.

The Constitution recognises that ours is an unequal society. It sets as one of the founding values, not "equality" but the "achievement of equality", and imposes positive duties on the state to address the legacy of apartheid, by requiring it to take action to achieve the progressive realisation of socio-economic rights to housing, health care, food, water and social security. It also recognises "the nation's commitment to land reform, and to reforms to bring about equitable access to all South Africa's natural resources"[6] and requires the state "to take reasonable legislative and other measures within its available resources to foster conditions which enable citizens to gain access to land on an equitable basis."[7]

"AND THEY SAY SOWETO HAS A POLLUTION PROBLEM?"

Government is based on the will of the people and every citizen is equally protected by the law. (Preamble to the Constitution.)

The Constitutional Court

These rights can only be given effect to if there are impartial, independent courts to administer their application. Key to the establishment of the Constitution was the setting up of the Constitutional Court - a new court that would be the highest in respect of all constitutional matters. Set up in 1994, the Court has 11 judges, including the Chief Justice and the Deputy Chief Justice of South Africa. The Constitution establishes a Judicial Service Commission to play a key role in the appointment of the members of the Court. This is a body consisting primarily of judges, practising lawyers and members of parliament.

The Constitutional Court functions primarily as a court of appeal although there are special circumstances in which matters may be brought directly to it. Its decisions are binding on all courts and all organs of state including parliament and the executive.

The judgments of the Constitutional Court have been cited with approval by superior courts of many other countries and regions, including the European Court of Justice,[8] the Supreme Court of Canada,[9] the Court of Appeal in England,[10] the Court of Appeal in Zealand[11], the Namibian Supreme Court[12] and the Judicial Committee of the Privy Council.[13]

The Separation of Powers

Our Constitution is premised on a separation of powers between the legislature, the executive and the judiciary. Their powers are defined in the Constitution. The judicial power requires courts to interpret and uphold the Constitution, and this inevitably gives rise to a potential tension between the courts and the other arms of government. The tension exists in all cases where the legislature or the executive has made choices that are challenged in the courts. This tension has to be managed by the courts and the Constitutional Court has said that it will be necessary to develop a doctrine of separation of powers that "reflects a delicate balancing, informed both by South Africa's history and its new dispensation, between the need, on the one hand, to control government by separating powers and enforcing checks and balances and, on the other, to avoid diffusing power so completely that the government is unable to take timely measures in the public interest".[14]

Judgments of the Court

Courts have an important role to play in the transformation demanded by the Constitution. In doing this, they need to be sensitive to the role of the legislature and the executive in a democratic system of government and to the difficulties inherent in governing a country with a history such as ours, where resources are limited and demands are multifarious.

Similarly, the legislature and executive must show and have shown a deep rooted respect for the rule of law and constitutionalism. This is evident from the government's response to one of the Court's early judgments in 1995 when the Court held that President Nelson Mandela had acted unconstitutionally with regard to local government elections and declared invalid his actions in this regard.[15] Despite the fact that the matter was politically sensitive and had potentially far-reaching consequences, President Mandela appeared in public to stress that he fully accepted the Court's decision, that the Court was the final constitutional arbiter on the constitutionality of his presidential actions, that the Constitution was supreme and that the Court's judgment had to be followed unconditionally.

As the Court has stressed in a recent judgement, "The government has always respected and executed orders of this Court. There is no reason to believe that it will not do so in the present case."[16]

The fact that the Constitutional Court is sensitive to its role in a democracy and respects boundaries that are inherent in the separation of powers, does not mean that it is a passive court. On the contrary it has not hesitated to give judgments, not always popular, holding that laws or conduct of the state and its officials are inconsistent with the Constitution. It has for instance invalidated capital punishment,[17] corporal punishment,[18] the criminalising of sodomy,[19] presumptions of fact in a number of different criminal law statutes that had the effect of placing the burden of proof in criminal cases on the accused,[20] unduly short periods of prescription in respect of claims against the state,[21] regulations of the education department that discriminate against foreign employees,[22] immigration regulations that discriminate against married couples where one partner is not South African[23] and homosexual couples,[24] the denial of prisoners' rights to vote[25] and the state's housing policy in the Western Cape.[26]

"Since 1996, the Government has been challenged in this court and judgements given against it for behaving unconstitutionally. More important, Government in each instance accepted the judgement of the court." Frederik van Zyl Slabbert

The Court has also held that the government acted unreasonably and unconstitutionally in failing to make an anti-retroviral drug broadly available to pregnant women who were HIV-positive in order to reduce the risk of mother-to-child transmission of HIV. The Court ordered the government to remove the restrictions on the availability of the drug, to make the drug available for this purpose, to train counsellors for its use and to take reasonable steps to progressively extend testing and counselling throughout the country.[33]

Conclusion

South Africa remains a profoundly unequal country with many challenges still to be dealt with. However, there can be little doubt that the supremacy of the Constitution and the respect that is given to it by both the courts and the government will assist the country in dealing with such challenges. In this way, the aims of the Constitution set out in its preamble, can be fulfilled. "Heal the divisions of the past and establish a society based on democratic values, social justice and fundamental human rights; lay the foundations for a democratic and open society in which government is based on the will of the people and every citizen is equally protected by law; improve the quality of life of all citizens and free the potential of each person; and build a united and democratic South Africa able to take its rightful place as a sovereign state in the family of nations."

It has also held that the government acted unlawfully in handing over to the FBI a suspect wanted in the USA for terrorist acts which carry the death sentence, without securing an undertaking from the USA that the death sentence would not be imposed;[27] that prosecutors cannot withhold witness statements from an accused person without compelling reasons for doing so;[28] that a Liquor Bill was unconstitutional because it unjustifiably encroached on provincial powers;[29] that the national airline acted unlawfully in discriminating against a job applicant because he was HIV positive[30] and that same-sex couples in life partnerships are entitled to pension benefits[31] and to jointly adopt children.[32]

1   This chapter is based on published and unpublished speeches given by Chief Justice Chaskalson. It was prepared by the Chief Justice's researchers: Steven Budlender, Sivakalay Pather and Nasreen Rajab.
2   Section 7(1) of the Constitution.
3   Section 36 of the Constitution.
4   Section 9(1) of the Constitution.
5   Section 9(3) of the Constitution.
6   Section 25(4) of the Constitution.
7   Section 25(5) of the Constitution.
8   Saunders v. The United Kingdom [1996] 23 EHRR 313.
9   Arsenault-Cameron v. Prince Edward Island [1999] 3 S.C.R. 851; United States of America v. Burns [2001] 1 S.C.R. 283.
10 R. v. P. [2001] E.W.J. No. 3798 (CA); Pearce v. Mayfield [2001] E.W.J. No. 3675 (CA).
11
12 S v. Shikunga and Another 2000 (1) SA 616 (NmS).
13 La Campagnie Sucière v. Mauritius [1995] J.C.J. No. 53; Matadeen v. Pointu [1998] J.C.J No.10; Reg. v. Reyes [2002] J.C.J. No.11.
14 De Lange v. Smuts NO and Others 1998 (3) SA 785 (CC); 1998 (7) BCLR 779 (CC) at para 60.
15 Executive Council, Western Cape v. Minister of Provincial Affairs and Constitutional Development and Another; Executive Council, KwaZulu-Natal v. President of the Republic of South Africa and Others 2000 (1) SA 661 (CC); 1999 (12) BCLR 1360 (CC).
16 Minister of Health and Others v. Treatment Action Campaign and Others CCT 08/02, currently unreported judgment delivered on 5 July 2002, at para 129.
17 S v. Makwanyane and Another 1995 (3) SA 391 (CC); 1995 (6) BCLR 665 (CC).
18 S v. Williams and Others 1995 (3) SA 632 (CC); 1995 (7) BCLR 861 (CC).
19 National Coalition for Gay and Lesbian Equality and Another v. Minister of

    Justice and Others 1999 (1) SA 6 (CC); 1998 (12) BCLR 1517 (CC).
20 For example S v. Bhulwana; S v Gwadiso 1996 (1) SA 388 (CC); 1995 (12) BCLR 1579 (CC).
21 Moise v. Transitional Local Council of Greater Germiston and Others 2001 (4) SA 491 (CC); 2001 (8) BCLR 765 (CC).
22 Larbi-Odam and Others v. Member of the Executive Council for Education (North-West Province) and Another 1998 (1) SA 745 (CC); 1997 (12) BCLR 1655 (CC).
23 Dawood and Another v. Minister of Home Affairs and Others; Shalabi and Another v. Minister of Home Affairs and Others; Thomas and Another v. Minister of Home Affairs and Others 2000 (3) SA 936 (CC); 2000 (8) BCLR 837 (CC).
24 National Coalition for Gay and Lesbian Equality and Others v. Minister of Home Affairs and Others 2000 (2) SA 1 (CC); 2000 (1) BCLR 39 (CC).
25 August and Another v. Electoral Commission and Others 1999 (3) SA 1 (CC); 1999 (4) BCLR 363 (CC).
26 Government of the Republic of South Africa and Others v. Grootboom and Others 2001 (1) SA 46 (CC); 2000 (11) BCLR 1169 (CC).
27 Mohamed and Another v. President of the RSA and Others 2001 (3) SA 893 (CC); 2001 (7) BCLR 685 (CC).
28 Shabalala and Others v. Attorney-General of the Transvaal and Another 1996 (1) SA 725 (CC); 1995 (12) BCLR 1593 (CC).
29 Ex parte President of the Republic of South Africa In re: Constitutionality of the Liquor Bill 2000 (1) SA 732) (CC); 2000 (1) BCLR 1 (CC).
30 Hoffmann v. SA Airways 2001 (1) SA 1(CC); 2000 (11) BCLR 1211 (CC).
31 Satchwell v. President of the Republic of South Africa and Another CCT 45/01, currently reported judgment delivered on 25 July 2002.
32 Du Toit and Another v. Minister for Welfare and Population Development and Another CCT 40/01, currently unreported judgment delivered on 10 September 2002.
33 Minister of Health and Others v. Treatment Action Campaign and Others CCT 08/02, currently unreported judgment delivered on 5 July 2002.

If South Africa ever needs another patriotic holiday, perhaps 5 July could be celebrated as Constitution Day.

The date doesn't commemorate the founding or the signing of the document that serves as a blueprint for the new South Africa; it is the date of this year's landmark decision by the Consitutional Court ordering the Government to make nevirapine, the antiretroviral drug that reduces the risk of mother-to-child transmission of HIV during birth, broadly available.

The majority decision, rejecting a Government appeal against a Pretoria High Court ruling last year that nevirapine should be made available in public hospitals and clinics, found that the Government policy restricting the use of the drug was both unreasonable and unconstitutional. The decision was celebrated not only for its potential to save the lives of thousands of infants but also for its affirmation of the Constitution's core values: that the protection of human rights overrides even government policy in our new democracy.

Living proof that the court's decision is saving babies from the agony of Aids, can be found at the weekly nevirapine clinic held at the Coronation Hospital for Women and Children west of Johannesburg.

In mid-October, about 50 mothers attended with their babies. The clinic is an island of hope in a sea of pain and despair. Staff said the numbers attending this clinic (and others around the country) were increasing weekly.

Healthy babies born to HIV-positive mothers are checked for infection five times in their first year and, if they test HIV-negative at 12 months, they are considered safe from the infection.

Dr Ashraf Coovadia, who supervises the clinic, said early indications were that the use of nevirapine had reduced the transmission rate to 10 percent of births, compared with 30 per cent of births without nevirapine treatment.

Geoffrey Mlauli, a counsellor at the hospital, said that because many of the mothers who passed through the clinic were illiterate, they had only a sketchy understanding of the emotional public debate over the the use of nevirapine. "However, every pregnant mother who was aware of being HIV-positive, wants nevirapine," said Mlauli.

"The shock of a pregnant woman who is informed that she is HIV-positive is a terrible thing to see. Her first reaction is to try to save her baby. Expectant mothers seem to forget their own state and their only thoughts are for the child. Only later does the fear become about themselves.

"But there is nothing to describe the relief and happiness the mothers feel when they are told that their babies are free of the disease."

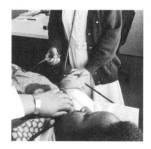

Only one of the mothers, many of whom fear stigmatisation in their home communities for carrying the disease, was prepared to speak. She was one of many women who were given nevirapine before the Constitutional Court decision. And her two-year-old is healthy: "I don't understand why the Government did not want the people to have nevirapine, but all I can say is that I am happy that the judges made a choice to help all the people."

Mlauli said that, while the court's decision would save many lives, public health professionals remained deeply concerned that there was no provision to supply antiretroviral cocktails to HIV-positive mothers, and so delay the onset of Aids.

"We do all this work to save the children, but there is nothing we can do for the mothers, except advise them how to lead healthy lives and inform them about herbal and alternative remedies," he said.

"A great deal of work and education is still needed for these people to fully understand their rights."

Enshrined is our constitution is the right of all South African to adequate housing. Although the process is far from complete, the progress made by government and the private sector is quite simply staggering. The provision of housing, electricity, water and sanitation is the first step towards the building of a resilient and stable community. The next step in the provision of community centres, clinics, schools, parks, law and order and of course commercial opportunity.

9

⬟ Housing Infrastructure
From Shanties to Suburbia

Sankie Mthembi-Mahanyele: Minister of Housing

"Give every family a house with electricity, fresh water and sanitation and you build a nation's foundation."

Housing Delivery Since 1994

Housing stands out as one of the Government's great achievements.

Each working day since the democratic government began in 1994, some 500 new houses have been built for the poor people of South Africa. In less than eight years, the Government has developed new housing policies and delivered 1.4 million homes benefiting 6 million people. As part of enhancing security of tenure to the historically disadvantaged, the Government has also transferred 398 000 old municipal houses to two million people who have been renting them.

In short, the housing programme has benefited one million people per year for the past eight years. This contribution by the Government has created an asset base of R50 billion for the historically marginalised people. About 22 000 emerging contractors and developers have been assisted to carry out the projects, thus helping to integrate the disadvantaged into the mainstream economy.

The housing delivery programme takes a number of approaches aimed at addressing the diverse needs of the home seekers. These include the People's Housing Process, Rental Programme, Hostels Redevelopment Programme, Savings Programme and Rapid Land Release Programme.

Starting at the Beginning

The Constitution of this country states that all South Africans have a right to adequate housing. It also states that it is the duty of the Government to take reasonable legislative and other measures, within available resources, to achieve the realisation of this right on a progressive basis. The housing policy is guided by, among others, the following principles:

- People-centred development and partnerships
- Skills transfer and economic empowerment
- Fairness and equity, and choice
- Quality, affordability and innovation and
- Sustainability and fiscal affordability.

The policy is being undertaken in terms of the following seven key strategies:

- Stabilising the housing environment
- Mobilising housing credit
- Providing subsidy assistance
- Supporting the people's housing process
- Rationalising institutional capacity
- Facilitating speedy release and servicing of land and
- Co-ordinating government investment in development.

Housing has become the catalyst for creating sustainable human settlements. The challenge is that other sustainability issues be addressed simultaneously through housing delivery and management. In effect, the housing challenge ceases to be a question of the number of housing units delivered each year. Instead, housing delivery and habitation are translated into a vehicle to achieve multiple goals and outcomes over the basic requirement for shelter.

The Four Pillars of Sustainability

Sustainability in housing and human settlement can be understood in terms of four pillars that support sustainable development. Projects should:

- Address environmental challenges
- Generate economic empowerment
- Enhance social capital and
- Build institutional capacity.

Each of these pillars interacts with the others in the development process. For example, economic and social sustainability are interrelated and meet at the points of poverty alleviation. Whereas waste management clearly falls under the environmental pillar, it also dynamically interacts with the economic and social pillars to generate opportunities for job creation, entrepreneurship and empowerment through waste recycling and disposal services.

Addressing Environmental Challenges

This pillar covers responses to conventional environmental challenges of resource depletion - the resource limits - either due to over-exploitation or pollution from by-products of economic production and consumption. Housing needs to be viewed as an opportunity for addressing the resource limits of our environment through efficient consumption of non-renewable resources and minimising pollution impacts on our environment: The key issues and sub-components of this pillar are:

- Land conservation, urban integration and greening;
- Energy efficiency and renewable energy
- Water conservation
- Alternative sanitation and resource recovery
- Waste management and resource recovery and
- Materials efficiency.

Adding energy-efficient measures to housing units can be costly in the short term. Energy efficiency allows a household to enjoy the same or higher energy service at lower levels of energy consumption, thus contributing to cost-saving on combustible fuels or electricity. This also applies to water conservation interventions, waste management and material efficiency.

Never in the history of the world has a country the size of South Africa housed 20 per cent of its most disadvantaged people in 8 years.

Generating Economic Empowerment

Poverty alleviation is undoubtedly the key development challenge of the developing world. This becomes even more daunting in view of the job losses and growing unemployment due to retrenchment in private and public sector organisations. Due to the apartheid legacy, poverty in South Africa bears a racial dimension, which undermines political stability. Consequently, economic empowerment of previously disadvantaged groups is a unique South African sustainability challenge.

The main sustainability responses for housing under this category include:

- Access to land and security of tenure - including informal settlement upgrade and rural land reform
- Job creation, entrepreneurship and emerging contractor support
- Affordability and alternative finance
- Cost saving through appropriate location, energy, efficiency and water conservation
- Provision for transformation and home-based enterprises
- Empowerment for women and previously disadvantaged groups
- Overcoming racial segregation
- Diversified accommodation with regard to tenure and the unique needs of each household and
- Integration of social-cultural amenities and services.

Enhancing Social Capital

Sustainable housing should address poverty alleviation by responding to the socio-cultural needs and practices of beneficiary households and communities. This needs to be addressed at household level to accommodate extended families, the aged and Aids orphans. At community level, social amenities like schools, libraries, police stations, recreation centres and clinics are integrated into settlements. Sustainable housing requires that this be implemented. In addition, sustainable housing must ensure that disabled people, the aged and those dealing with the impact of HIV/Aids are adequately accommodated. Sustainable human settlements can only emerge from integrated housing with three dimensions:

- Overcoming racial segregation
- Diversified accommodation with regard to tenure and the unique needs of each household and
- Integration of socio-cultural amenities and services.

Integrated and sustainable housing requires easy access to social-cultural amenities and services like schools, police stations, clinics, libraries, recreation and shops.

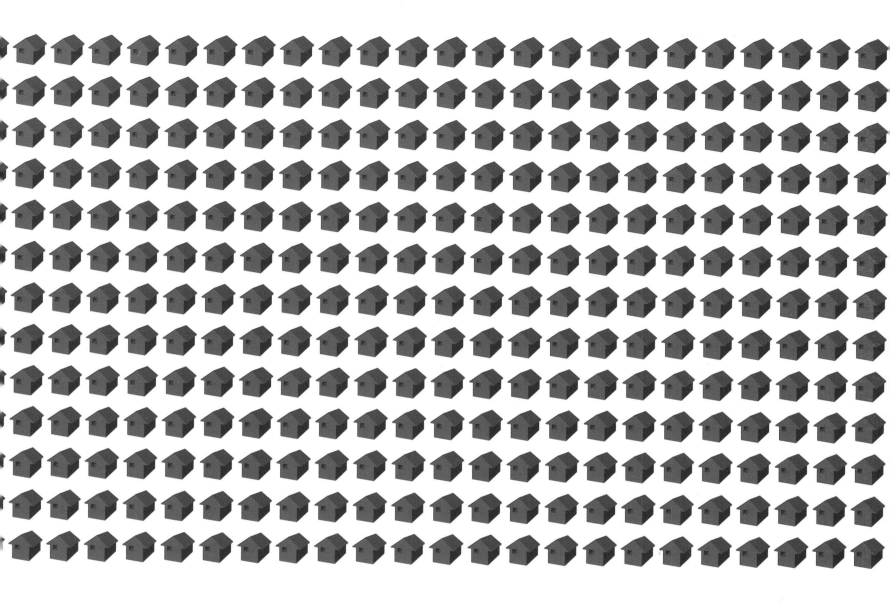

Housing for the Disadvantaged

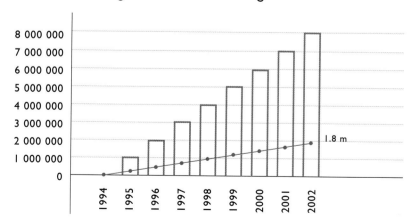

8 000 000	
7 000 000	
6 000 000	
5 000 000	
4 000 000	
3 000 000	
2 000 000	1.8 m
1 000 000	
0	

1994 1995 1996 1997 1998 1999 2000 2001 2002

- People Benefiting
- Houses Made Available

The housing programme has created an asset base of R50 billion for the historically marginalised people, 22 000 emerging contractors have been established.

Building Institutional Capacity

Istitutional sustainability relates to the need for stable, inclusive, transparent, accountable and efficient decision-making, and implementation systems which can optimise limited resources. This is critical for achieving sustainable housing and human settlements.

It is concerned with housing environments long after that last brick is laid - with ongoing management and maintenance. The key institutions that comprise stakeholders of housing development are:

- Public sector - all government and semi-public structures involved in housing delivery, including multi and bi-lateral donor communities
- Private sector - all private organisations/entities involved in housing delivery
- Civil society - non-governmental organisations and community-based organisations involved in networking among the first two sectors and the beneficiaries
- Beneficiaries - households and communities who are direct recipients of housing.

Public-private partnerships are critical for leveraging private sector finance and other inputs. Partnering with NGOs and CBOs in projects is crucial for the contribution of professionals who have close relationships with beneficiaries.

The People's Housing Process

The South African housing programme, promoting self-building by beneficiaries through state assistance, has gained much acceptance from the homeless people in recent years. The current mood of the communities towards the People's Housing Process or PHP in South Africa shows that this programme has been overwhelmingly embraced by the housing beneficiaries and other role-players.

Today, the PHP has already yielded more than 18 000 houses. Recent statistics released by the Department show that all the provinces are starting to put more emphasis on the people's housing process. The number of the total PHP-related subsidies that have been approved this year alone has more than doubled since the programme's inception. Expert opinion has marveled at the creative manner in which poor communities have energised and mobilised the funding of this programme.

The general feeling is that the housing savings schemes are the engine rooms of the PHP as they offer people an opportunity to invest whatever little they can afford. On the other hand, more traditional saving schemes have also played a role. Minister Mthembi-Mahanyele describes "as very productive" the features of the multitudes of housing savings schemes, in which the members, the poor and homeless, build collective savings, which they can then use to loan to each other to fulfil their housing and other social needs or collectively buy material for their houses. Furthermore, the management of these savings lies entirely in the hands of the community, a responsibility which becomes an important training tool.

This innovative approach adds a spark in the sustainable development that the housing policy seeks to promote. The pilot urban agricultural model that some communities have adopted to integrate farming with residential development and the greening of surroundings in their places of residence, are some of the features recently adopted by many housing beneficiaries as a contribution to sustainable human settlements.

Mthembi-Mahanyele says she supports this initiative as it promotes healthy air and clear lungs for a community's well-being. The Minister maintains that vegetables and fruit trees always add value to a community's nutritional requirements.

Whereas many people within and outside the housing sector are still trying to understand the zeal and strength of the homeless people, the SA Homeless People's Federation has taken the issue of self-development even further. In trying to build communities through housing, the Federation has adopted an approach that will enhance socio-economic development in poor communities, as can be observed from a number of social and economic initiatives that the Federation has undertaken in various areas.

This is perhaps the reason why both the Government and the Federation describe their partnership as a tried and tested one. The partnership has indeed transformed the culture of housing delivery in many areas to that of self-reliance.

The people's housing process has, to date, managed to produce professionals from both the classroom and outside - architects, bricklayers, carpenters and good administrators. Who could have thought that, at this stage, South Africa would have encouraged and motivated its citizens to establish small and medium enterprises such as brick manufacturing and welding plants?

Has anyone ever thought of the skills women of this country possess in the field of construction?

Well, judging by the pace at which communities are embracing the PHP programme, it is projected that the delivery of housing through the People's Housing Process will pass the 10 per cent quota that the Government has set as a target of the houses delivered through the PHP this year.

Because most PHP projects are dominated by women - both as entrepreneurs and beneficiaries - the housing sector is also heading for a balance in men and women working within the construction industry.

The People's Housing Process is an ancient practice closely associated with African culture. This is the reason why the Government has decided to adopt it as part of its development programme.

NURCHA

The National Urban Reconstruction and Housing Agency (NURCHA), which helps unlock housing finance, has made great strides towards assisting emerging contractors, especially women. The Agency has since mobilised projects worth R77 million for women contactors through its guarantees. One of the female contractors assisted by NURCHA is Irene Mahlangu from Mpumalanga Province who, without formal education, has already handled projects worth R40 million through the assistance from NURCHA.

Both the Departments of Housing and Public Works are working closely with emerging contractors. Despite giving technical assistance to this group through its agencies and provincial departments, the Government is also mobilising the private sector to assist them and a number are beginning to heed this call. Nu-Way Housing Developments has recently allocated building contracts totalling R11 million to the emerging sector.

Rural Housing

The Rural Home Loan Fund (RHLF), which disburses housing finance to rural households, also has, as its main target, rural dwellers who are mostly unable to access housing finance. RHLF has already disbursed R199 million to rural households. More importantly, the Fund has ensured that, among the intermediaries used to disburse this money on the Fund's behalf, there are also emerging entrepreneurs

as micro-lenders. Recently, five women-owned micro-finance businesses have received credit of more than R50 million and grant support of more than R1 million from RHLF.

Energy Efficient Housing

Working together with communities to find out their needs can yield better results in the application of new technology - as was the case with the eMbalenhle Air Quality project carried out in 40 houses near Secunda. Various technological solutions in different combinations were introduced to the 40 households. These included new low-smoke stoves, low-smoke coal, proper chimneys, gas appliances and thermal insulation.

The outcome was marvellous. Insulating the house thermally was found to be an effective measure in reducing indoor pollution levels by up to 30 per cent. Even more significantly, users reported huge reduction of up to 50 per cent in coal consumption. This not only reduced internal pollution, but also the outside pollution as well and that of the settlement as a whole. People also liked insulation because it helps to keep dust outside.

Affordable Rental Housing

The Government has also embarked on a rental programme. The projects vary from pure rental to "rent to own" in which people pay rent for a particular period and then buy the units.

More than 35 000 units of these homes have been built throughout the country and a number of housing associations have been established to help bring the historically disadvantaged communities into the property market. Apart from the new projects, the Government is also encouraging housing associations to revive old buildings that are underutilised and convert them into affordable rental accommodation.

Conclusion

The housing environment inherited by the democratic government in 1994 had severe abnormalities as a result of the policies and political turbulence of the pre-democratic era. The national housing policy formulated and implemented since then has gone a long way towards addressing these problems.

Energy Efficient Housing

South Africans can be justly proud of what they have achieved in the provision of low-income housing:

- The quantity of delivery has been impressive
- New and important legislation has been passed
- Special-purpose housing finance vehicles have been formed
- Consumer protection measures enjoy a much higher priority than in the past
- Rental housing provision has become an important focus and
- Microlenders are providing billions of rands in loans to support incremental building projects.

We remain with complex challenges in the years ahead, but sound policies have been put in place and the appropriate emphases exist to enable South Africa to rack up further housing successes in the future.

The housing subsidy offered by Government to all households with incomes below R3500 per month forms the bedrock of the delivery process. To complement the subsidy, and in order to deliver quality housing, savings and personal equity need to be added into the mix.

Government must therefore be commended for re-emphasising the importance of personal savings and for devising mechanisms (together with the National Urban Reconstruction and Housing in particular) for tapping these savings. Equally, the energy being given to accelerating self-help housing delivery, via the so-called Peoples' Housing Process, is laudable. The real challenge for Government in this regard is to work appropriately to support community driven self-help processes in a manner that does not constrain and overly administer them.

On funding issues generally, the fact that no conventional loans provided by the commercial banks are on offer for homes costing less than approximately R70 000, is a harsh reality which we have to accept.

Government - and the Minister of Housing in particular - has castigated the banking sector for years about their commitment to housing the poor.

The truth of the matter is that:
- The home loan product offered by banks is not suited to the low-income market
- Banks are cautious about lending to communities of limited means and
- Real concerns about enforcing the rule of law to recover bad debts still exist.

However, the position is not all doom and gloom. Today, the microlending industry, warts and all (and, yes, there are unsavoury elements to it) is worth some R14 billion. Importantly, from a housing perspective, a significant portion of this financing (estimated R3 billion) is being used directly for housing additions, improvements, etc. The Rural Housing Loan Fund is but one example of many finance companies making much needed credit available to the poor.

Great strides in the area of consumer protection also need to be highlighted. The passing of the Housing Consumer Protection Measures Act, the establishment of the National Home Builders Registration Council (NHBRC), and the very recent extension of protection measures to include houses built with government-provided subsidy (value R21 300) is to be welcomed.

The housing sector has had to clean up its act and this is only right and proper if all South Africans are to have reasonable standards of housing.

The growth in social housing (i.e. lower income rental provision) is another feature of note. Approximately 20 000 such rental units, mostly provided by not-for-profit housing associations, now provide South Africans of limited means with rental housing alternatives, outside of the typical "township" context. Such schemes are usually well-located in relation to employment, city centres, and other amenities. They also contribute in significant ways to urban regeneration and reinvestment back into the declining parts of our cities. The growth in the provision of "transitional housing" in urban locations is another trend of note. This housing, which is basic in nature, offers new urban residents, secure, affordable short-stay rental options.

An area of massive challenge is to induce the providers of commercial finance to offer loans for social housing. It is unfortunate that the National Housing Finance Corporation (NHFC) has a virtual monopoly in providing loans to this sector. Moreover, their lack of capacity to respond timeously to loan applications by a service-oriented staff will almost certainly change in an environment of enhanced competition from other financial players.

In this regard, the recent loan made available by ABSA to the Johannesburg Housing Company deserves special mention. Hopefully, this is the start of a flood to come.

One area of significant concern is the responsibility placed by the Housing Act (and by recent changes to the procurement regime) on local authorities to drive housing delivery for low-income communities. Not only is the willingness to do this absent in certain such authorities, but many lack the capacity, skills and experience to play such a role and, above all, most authorities, both large and small, are desperately trying to limit their financial commitments when adequate cost recovery in poor communities remains a problem.

This is an area that needs vigorous and creative management if local authorities are to be the new engines of housing delivery for the poor.

Perhaps, however, the most pressing challenge derives directly from the acres and acres of new low-income, low-density suburbs built since 1994, the additional 1.4 million new homes which are seen by many as a "badge" of success.

Yes, this could be said to lay a platform for the development of new communities. In truth, we will all be saddled with millstones in the future unless South Africa can:

· Enrich these suburbs with other facilities and amenities
· Promote the generation of employment and income-creating opportunities which are meaningful and sustainable and
· Increase occupational levels to those which can sustain the cost of the transport and infrastructure networks.

These millstones will be financial in nature, but perhaps most crucially, the social implications of large urban neighbourhoods of spatially-disadvantaged and poorly-employed people could be a legacy for decades to come.

A suggestion going forward is that the corporate sector become involved in "adopting a township" as Barloworld has done with its involvement in the Habitat for Humanity project in KwaZulu-Natal, and as the Durban Business Community has done in Cato Manor, similar to the Business against Crime initiative of adopting a police station.

"Adoption" would mean collaboration with the local community on social-infrastructure. The Government can't do this alone, it needs the creativity and energy of the SA Business Community, already regarded for establishing new global standards for government/private sector collaboration.

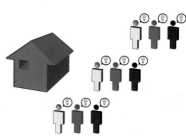

begin and a committee elected by the tenants ensured active community participation right from the start. The restoration process took two years and the building was refurbished until the JHC could offer 65 single and double rooms. In the year 2000, the rent for a single room was R305 per month, with communal toilets and washing facilities, excluding electricity.

Today, it is mainly single parent families with young children who occupy Douglas Rooms. The children attend a crèche in a converted house nearby which was also purchased by the JHC and is run by the Methodist Church.

In this way the housing environment is sensitive to the needs of its tenants. The childcare centre accommodates 45 children and provides training for unemployed mothers in JHC buildings. At the crèche, the children of Douglas Rooms are given first preference, with the remaining places going to children from the area. This provides a point of contact for tenants with members of their community.

The Douglas Rooms project captures the challenges presented by occupied slum buildings: excising tenants, co-ordinating the physical refurbishment with tenants still in residence, and getting tenants who have lived in a culture of non-payment for almost two years to accept the discipline of regular instalments for rent and service.

An old, dilapidated building, called Douglas Rooms, was taken over by the Johannesburg Housing Company or JHC - a non-profit housing entity. The demand for accommodation in this well-located neighbourhood had filled the building with tenants who sublet their small rooms to pay rent - causing severe overcrowding.

Then the council cut off the electricity. The landlord did no maintenance, and water leaked through rusted pipes. A fire, sparked by a candle in one of the rooms, destroyed the roof of an entire wing. The building became increasingly squalid and, after running up considerable debts, the owner absconded along with the deposits paid by the tenants.

The building, by then, was a haven for drug lords and housed seven noisy shebeens. The JHC was asked to buy the building by a delegation of tenants, the bondholder and the council. A long period of negotiations began with the tenants, who were in sympathy with the JHC's social housing aims.

Shebeens and brothels were closed and those not wanting to sign the lease with JHC left the building. Now, the slow process of transforming a slum into a community could

The building was a haven for drug lords. Shebeens and brothels were closed. A culture of non-payment has been turned to regular payment for rent and services by mainly single parent families.

They became masters of their own destiny -pushing back the frontiers of poverty.

A recent PHP project occurred at Midrand in Johannesburg at a small community called Ivory Park. Eight years ago, Ivory Park was a place of crime and violence, an overcrowded informal settlement with inferior housing.

But, four years ago, the women took it upon themselves to transform and develop the area into a respected settlement with decent housing. Armed with serviced sites and oozing confidence, but with a deficiency of administration and construction skills, the women organised themselves. With limited income, they each managed to invest about R3 a day towards their project. They also offered their own sweat, rolling up their sleeves and producing structures of good quality that have since changed the complexion of the settlement.

With the support of other communities and Government, they became masters of their own destiny and lent a hand to push back the frontiers of poverty.

The 50 homes already built by this group have proved that, although people may be unskilled, they can learn a variety of skills and build their own homes. This is the strategy that the Government has been using to help the historically disadvantaged, including women and the youth. Many people have received training courses in bricklaying, plastering, plumbing, administration and other construction and management trades.

Further assistance, especially from the private sector, helps promote the development of construction-related enterprises such as brick-making and welding, as was the case with this group. With a brick-making machine donated by the SABC and by selling some of the bricks they made, they accumulated enough money to buy a welding machine which has since helped them establish a window and doorframes plant.

One of the Government's priorities has always been helping women to gain economic independence, take control of their lives and fully participate in the society in which they live, thus improving their status and the security and well-being of their children.

The PHP is one of the strategies the Government and its agencies have put in place aimed at promoting and empowering women.

10

There is a direct and strong correlation between the level of education of the citizens of a developing nation, and its propensity to grow and increase employment for its population. The rebuilding of what amounted to a deliberately inequitable educational system had to be a national priority. Given the scale of the job to be done, Government has made great strides towards this objective. Working with the private sector will deliver optimal results from both a qualitative and quantitative point of view.

Education: Preparing the Nation

Professor Kader Asmal: Minister of Education

Historical Perspective

Education has made a contribution towards preparing the nation for our new democracy, although there is still much to be done.

Freedom was achieved in 1994, and in 1996, the first non-discriminatory education legislation was introduced. The South African Schools Act created a single national education system, and repealed the Bantu Education Act of 1953, which was designed to ensure that black people were forever consigned to a destiny of manual labour and were mentally oppressed through a stripping of their dignity and self-worth.

One of the central instruments in the reconstruction of education has been the establishment of a National Qualifications Framework. All programmes are carried on the framework, and this provides for the portability of all qualifications in support of a model of flexible, lifelong learning.

Within the unified education system, we have been able to track and analyse the changes taking place in our society. We have one census, one voters' roll, and one education system in which we all participate. We have established baselines against which we can measure our progress and are able to record the historic process of reconstructing a nation.

Using these, we are able to table to the President (and the public at large) "quarterly reports on the state of education". These have been consolidated into a publication entitled, **Achievements Since 1994**, which was published by the Ministry of Education to allow ordinary people to appreciate what has been done, with their help, in such a short time. This has helped also to entrench a culture of democratic accountability, which is necessary for our continued development and growth.

In 1999, on assuming office, President Mbeki posed the question. Is our system ready for the challenges of the 21st century? These challenges include the pressures of globalisation, the use of new technologies in the workplace and a radical transformation of the way in which we, as people, relate to each other.

A brief answer to the President is that we are not yet ready, although we are responding to all the above challenges. We have isolated two fronts on which we must do battle: access and success. We want more children and students to be studying, and we also want to be sure that teaching programmes are of a high quality and that students succeed.

Challenge One

Access

In regard to issues of access, our first test for any laws or policies of the Ministry is to ask how they will affect the ability of the poorest to benefit from the limited state resources available. As a result, we have some extraordinary provisions: for example, the poorest 20 per cent of schools are funded at seven times the level of the richest 20 per cent - a massive redistribution of resources. Anyone who earns less than 10 times the school fees is automatically exempted from payment of the fees.

In these and other ways we have attempted to protect the rights of the poor to access state services, without diminishing the quality of provision in wealthier schools.

The education system is divided into three layers:

- General education and training (the first 10 years, including a reception year)
- Further education and training (the next three years, with an orientation towards vocational and technical streams)
- Higher education, including universities and technicons.

In 1999, on assuming office, President Mbeki posed the question: Is our educational system ready for the challenges of the 21st century? The brief answer is: "No, we are not yet ready, although we are responding to all the above challenges."

General Education and Training

Our responses in regard to schools have been directed at two levels.

Firstly, we have sought to improve the quantitative aspects of the system in terms of infrastructure, facilities and access to education. This has been an urgent imperative since 1994, following the appalling legacy of apartheid which deliberately contributed to the under-development of the majority of our people.

Dilapidated schools, without water, sanitation or other necessities, and staffed by poorly trained teachers, ensured that the outputs of the system did not contribute to the economic or social empowerment of black people.

The School Register of Needs is one of the key markers of our development, and reports on the physical state of our schools. We have directed significant resources towards the improvement of the physical infrastructure, building and refurbishing schools, providing libraries and laboratories, and ensuring that water, sanitation and communication needs are met.

The average number of learners per classroom has decreased from 43 in 1996, to 35 in 2000. In 1996, 40 per cent of all schools had no water; in 2000 this was reduced to 34 per cent. There is a 68 per cent improvement in the provision of sanitation, although some 16 per cent of schools still have no toilet facilities. The number of schools without phones, a crucial management tool, has dropped from 59 to 34 per cent.

We have made progress although there is still much to be done. Increasingly, we must look towards integrative government services, where the provision of libraries, community centres and sports facilities become a joint initiative of the education departments and local government structures. Because the resources for these huge tasks are not sufficient, we have sought and found the support of the international and local business community to assist in these tasks.

The most obvious have been those new schools which former President Mandela has persuaded local businesses to build in some of the most deprived rural areas in the country, but these should not overshadow the systematic work done by the provincial departments in trying to improve the facilities at schools.

Schooling - Improving Access

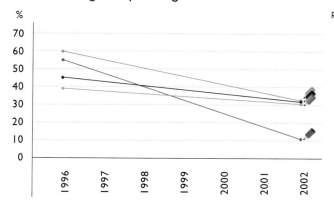

%
70
60
50
40
30
20
10
0

1996 1997 1998 1999 2000 2001 2002

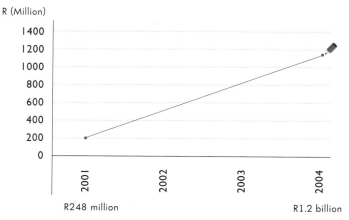 Learners per classroom

 Schools without sanitation

 Schools with no water

 Schools without phones

Spend on Adult Basic Education and Training

R (Million)
1400
1200
1000
800
600
400
200
0

2001 2002 2003 2004

R248 million   R1.2 billion

In 2001, we spent R248 million on adult education; in 2004, we will spend R1.2 billion.

As a result of these developments, we have managed to achieve the universal provision of general education, with places in schools available to all within the compulsory age cohort (7 to 15 years). Because of under- and over-age enrolments, and poor flow-through, we have gross enrolment ratios over 100 per cent in some areas.

Because state resources are limited, we have taken the principled decision to target these resources to the poorest of the poor. Using the nodal areas identified under the presidential poverty-alleviation programmes, we have been able to maximise our influence in those areas most disadvantaged by the years of apartheid.

To compensate for this targeted approach to funding, schools in wealthier areas have been encouraged to raise fees from parents to supplement the grant from the state. In some cases the revenue from fees far exceeds the state subsidy, confirming the willingness of those who can pay for a quality education to do so.

In return, we have also established a highly democratised system of school governance, with parents, teachers and even students taking part in all policy and funding decisions of the school. This has entailed a huge mobilisation exercise, and over 80 000 school governors are elected every three years to assist on a voluntary basis with the governance of schools.

Not content with the current levels of access, we are intent on further expanding the provision of state education. One of the priority areas is to provide a basic education, including literacy training, to the millions of South African who were denied an education under apartheid. Adult basic education and training is being expanded through the establishment of training centres, and at present there are 400 000 adults pursuing formal qualifications (equivalent to a Grade 9 school certificate), and another 400 000 in various literacy programmes, which may serve as a platform for further study.

In 2001, we spent R248 million on adult education; in 2004, this will increase to R1.2 billion - a four-fold increase in as many years.

In regard to the school system, we are expanding access through two initiatives. A major component is the provision of a pre-school reception year (Grade R) to all learners turning five, which is being implemented as from 2003. By 2008, we plan to have all 800 000 children of this age group in an early childhood development programme.

The benefits of this provision on learner achievement have been demonstrated in many different contexts, but will likely have most impact on children from poorer households. For this reason, the programme will initially be rolled out in the poverty stricken rural and urban districts identified as "nodal areas" for urgent attention.

Since 1996, we have benchmarked our national examination papers with the Scottish qualification authorities, and pass rates for school learners increased from below 50 per cent to over 60 per cent.

The other expansion of the school sector is through the inclusion of children with special education needs, and who experience barriers to learning. This includes children with physical, emotional or intellectual difficulties, and it is our intention to ensure that all schools become "full-service schools", able to cater for all children, whatever their special needs. It is estimated that up to 280 000 children could be out of school because of the barriers they experience, and we must remedy this. Their inclusion will be a crucial step towards truly universal access for all.

In regard to schools, we can conclude that from a position of 17 racially and spatially defined departments in 1994, we have created a single national system of education, providing opportunities to all our children. There are not yet equal opportunities, but, no longer by design, and an enabling framework is in place for parents to take the lead in school development. In addition, the system is non-discriminatory and democratic, and promotes the building of a proud nation.

Further Education and Training

The technical and vocational system of education inherited in 1994 was largely defunct, and offered irrelevant and poor quality programmes to a small number of students. The institutions were located in places that were not accessible to learners, and those who did attend the technical colleges were often seen as failures or drop-outs.

We have taken steps to establish an entirely new system of technical and vocational education, in line with modern employment needs and practices. This restructuring is being implemented in support of the Human Resource Development Strategy of the country, entitled "A Nation at Work for a Better Life for All". Under the new framework, which builds a bridge between school and work, this sector will remain vibrant and responsive to the changing needs of society - both in the workplace and in the broader social sense.

We are turning our colleges into high-status institutions, and ensuring that the programmes are relevant and of high quality. Students who graduate must have the trust of employers, and thus, the stigma of vocational education will be removed by demonstrating its value in the labour market.

The business sector has been both supportive and influential in this restructuring of the sector, and fully understands the centrality of these institutions to social and economic development. The Department of Education works closely with the Department of Labour to ensure that we remain responsive to the changing economic environment.

Higher Education

The landscape of higher education has been under review for a number of years, and significant changes are being introduced into the sector. The system is expensive, taking up a large share of the total education budget, and it is poorly organised in many respects, with the result that we have not seen quality graduates emerging from many of these institutions. We have been able to reach a national consensus on the need for a re-organisation of the institutional landscape in a bid to refocus and strengthen the system.

The National Plan for Higher Education has been published recently for comment, after which the Minister will make a decision. The new system is expected to comprise 21 institutions: 11 universities, 6 technicons and 4 comprehensive tertiary institutions. In some cases new institutions will be created through the merging of one or more universities or technikons and these are expected to deliver higher education on a more rational and equitable basis.

Institutions that are not involved in a restructuring process will also be required to consider their own institutional cultures, and align these with the national values of our country. Linked to this is the new Academic Policy for Higher Education, which will link the provision of programme subsidies to emerging national priorities.

Participation rates are set to increase from 15 to 20 per cent over the next four years, and students will be supported by the national Students' Financial Aid Scheme, which is allocated over R800 million per year by the Department of Education.

Lydia Gates

Challenge Two
Success

The second major thrust is around the success of learners. One measure of success is the quality of the school exit examinations. Following the integration of the racial departments in 1996, the national pass rate was below 50 per cent, largely reflecting the poor state of black education. Since then, we have introduced national examination papers in the five most popular subjects, and these have been benchmarked with the Scottish qualification authorities.

Despite this rigorous standard, we have managed to improve to a level of 60 per cent last year, and hope to improve even further in years to come. One of the less obvious examination statistics is a dramatic reduction in the number of non-functioning schools, which yielded results below 40 per cent. Many of these schools serve the poor, and a reduction in their number is a key contribution to better service for these people.

Part of the reason for these improvements is the increased levels of accountability that have been built into the system. Senior managers are held to performance contracts and school managers and teachers are increasingly subject to performance standards.

We have instituted a policy of Whole School Evaluation, which complements an internal process of self-appraisal for development purposes. Another instrument provides a measure of systemic performance, all of which enable us to measure what is happening in schools, and to intervene where necessary.

The other contributor to quality is the school curriculum. We have adopted an outcomes-based system of education, which is appropriate to our time and context. This approach has been well accepted by teachers and parents. More recently, we have introduced revisions to the curriculum statement, making the design more rigorous and user-friendly.

Included in the revisions are a much stronger and more explicit set of values. Human rights, democracy and inclusivity are the underpinning principles of the curriculum, and the Values in Education initiative adds explicitly to this thrust.

We also manage the South African History Project, to ensure that the extraordinary history of our country is remembered, and known by our children, so that we are never forced to relive it. All of these are designed to foster greater integration and understanding in society. The complementary role of arts, culture and school sport must also be recognised.

Our human resources are recognised as the greatest asset of this country. The Human Resource Development Strategy recognised the role of education in three different regards:

- The development of the foundations for social participation, through general education
- The development of specific knowledge, skills and values, appropriate to career or vocational aspirations, provided by technical and vocational further education and training institutions
- The contribution to research and development, through the knowledge production role of higher education institutions.

Underlying all of these must be an acknowledgement of our place in Africa, as part of a globalising world, at the turn of the 21st century.

We must explore the boundaries, and promote creativity and innovation. But this innovation must be grounded in the real needs of our people, and it should draw on their rich heritage of indigenous knowledge systems.

Education is not new to Africa, and it is our historical task as a Ministry of Education to reflect and influence the making of a prosperous, modern South Africa.

National Minister of Education, Kader Asmal, says: "Education has made a contribution towards preparing the nation for our new democracy, although there is still much to be done."

This is a fair reflection on what has been achieved since 1994 and he and the many other people involved in transforming education can be proud of the progress that has been made.

Policies inherited from the apartheid years were inappropriate for a democratic South Africa and a new vision for integrated, holistic and logical systems of education and training had to be articulated, given legal formulation and translated into policy.

Implementation began under former national Minister of Education, Sibusiso Bengu, and has been pursued, energetically, under Asmal. Meticulous attention to process has been a characteristic in developing these new systems. Various groups worked on policy initiatives before 1994 and the concept of a National Qualifications Framework emerged as the way in which the Government would widen opportunities for learning.

Many academics were involved in its planning, some of whom were brought into Government when the ANC came to power. Certain universities established Education Policy Units to analyse developments and to critique policy. However, being in power brings imperatives for decision and action, and this policy of wide consultation became more difficult to follow.

Surely, no one can fault the idealism that is reflected in the policies that Asmal and the various departments of education are implementing. Where questions may be asked is around the feasibility of timelines and the allocation of resources.

For example, the principled decision to target resources to the poorest of the poor can be applauded. It is splendid that the poorest 20 per cent of schools are funded at seven times the level of the richest 20 per cent. In practice,

however, teachers' salaries and benefits take so large a proportion of available funding (and the higher paid teachers tend to be in more affluent schools) that the redistributions achieved through allocations are small in real terms.

Surely no one can fault the idealism that is reflected in the policies of the Education Department.

Inclusion

Another example of the difficulty of matching policy with reality can be seen in the decision to ensure that all schools become "full-service schools", able to provide for all children, whatever their special needs. The decision was taken after wide consultation and participation, again reflecting Government's belief in democratic process.

Many people believe that policies of inclusion have worked in other countries and that it is appropriate for South Africa to go this route. Moreover, research indicates ways in which inclusion should be implemented. The White Paper 6 on Learners With Special Education Needs was generally well received, with the idealism that underlies so much of education policy being expressed by Asmal when he said, "Integration will enable us, as a country, to finally lay claim to the status of cherishing all our children equally."

Those responsible for the White Paper envisaged that implementation would be gradual and carried out in as cost-effective and efficient a manner as possible. Despite this common sense approach, however, there is concern about the extent to which specialised support services are available in schools. Some argue that the reality is that children with special needs are in some cases being, "mainstreamed by default", with little or no support. They end with marked emotional problems and move through grades with little educational attainment. Many of these children are referred to child psychiatry or to child mental health resources because there is no other support available, and this places huge strains on these institutions.

The Government has made considerable progress in making the system ready for the challenges of the 21st century. They deserve much credit.

105

2002

Higher Education

In 1997, Government committed itself to a comprehensive higher education transformation agenda.

The higher education system is seen as a key engine in driving and contributing to the reconstruction and development of South African society. Because apartheid created massive social-structural inequities, far-reaching changes in higher education are essential if there is to be equity of access and opportunity for social advancement. In March 2001, Minister Asmal presented the National Plan for Higher Education and put forward an ambitious timetable of implementation and he insisted that, "The Plan is not up for further consultation and certainly not for negotiation."

It has not proved that simple.

Creating single institutions out of two or more entities is no easy task and there are considerable political risks in doing so. It was only in May 2002 that the plans for the restructuring of higher education were approved by the cabinet. Nevertheless, there is strong support for them and they are logical.

There are a number of major challenges facing universities and technicons. Obtaining sustainable funding is an obvious one, and it has concerned South Africans for many years. Another is increasing the access to higher education. In Africa, South Africa ranks second only to Egypt in the number of higher education students per 100 000 of the population, but this is still well below the ratios in developed countries.

The quality of courses offered and the competency of graduates are other key factors. Relevance is also significant. There is strong pressure for rationalisation and for concentration on courses that have obvious relevance for the world of work. These quite easily become financially viable. Little research has been done, however, on the impact of such rationalisation. It might be that the financial savings are not as great as envisaged and that other advantages are lost.

Decisions taken elsewhere can also impact on higher education. For example, there has always been a steady stream of aspirant teachers taking degrees in geography and history. It appears that the introduction of outcomes-based education, in a way that combines traditional subjects into learning areas, might have led to a dwindling number of students in these courses, perhaps for the good or perhaps to the detriment of institutions. There is no research available to help one assess the consequences of there being fewer teachers in these subjects.

The New Academic Policy will provide generic standards against which judgments will be made for the registration of qualifications on the National Qualifications Framework. Accreditation of programmes by the Council on Higher Education's Quality Committee will be a condition for the state subsidisation of programmes offered in public institutions.

Time will tell whether a single, integrated and co-ordinated education and training system is appropriate for higher education. Some also question whether an outcomes and credit-based modular and programmes-based system is the best for this level.

The higher education system
is seen as a key engine driving the reconstruction of South African society.

A final comment on this sector.

Higher education institutions will not change without pressure being exerted. Given the importance of the sector both for the economic development of the country and for the advancement of individuals, Asmal is right to be aggressive in his demands for change.

Nevertheless, eyebrows will be raised in institutions with a corporate memory of Christian National Education at the statement that, "institutions that are not involved in a restructuring process will also be required to consider their own institutional cultures, and align these with the national values of our country".

Conclusion

Asmal and the National Department of Education have been diligent and aggressive in improving the quantitative aspects of the system and have made considerable progress in making the system ready for the challenges of the 21st century. They deserve much credit.

If I have one concern it is that the drive for control and results might lead to too much intervention - by those with political power - into areas of detail.

If the big decisions are right, the small ones will take care of themselves. Even if mistakes are sometimes made, educators who are given power and encouraged to be creative will be positive and full of energy.

Quantity, Quality and Quandary

Dr Jane Hofmeyr: National Executive Director - Independent Schools Association of Southern Africa

The advent of democratic government in 1994 inaugurated the restructuring of the 19 former apartheid education departments into one national and nine provincial departments, and brought about far-reaching policy changes in every sphere of education.

The country had the benefit of international expertise in developing its new policy frameworks, which have attracted international acclaim. Of particular significance has been the decision to move to outcomes-based education and training, linked through a national qualifications framework.

Quantitative Issues: Great Strides

The change must be understood against a background of huge inequalities in education as a result of apartheid, and the fact that South Africa spends 21 per cent of its national budget and six per cent of its Gross Domestic Product on education. This makes it one of the highest spenders on education in upper middle-income, developing countries.

The new education policy frameworks have attracted international acclaim.

South Africa has made great quantitative strides, with near universal education for children aged 7 to 16 years.

107

South Africa has made huge quantitative strides and achieved near universal education for children aged 7 to 16 years. As a developing country, this is an exceptional achievement, particularly as 50 per cent of the learners are female. The school sector consists of some 12 million pupils, 28 000 schools and 350 000 educators.

The Schools Act (1995) re-organised the many different types of apartheid schools into only two categories: public (state) and independent (private) schools. The independent school sector is small with some 2 000 schools and around 500 000 pupils, but it is growing rapidly and has become very diverse, serving every socio-economic level and type of community.

Recent research by the Human Sciences Research Council shows that, far from being a predominantly white and elitist sector, the highest percentage of independent schools in any province now charge fees below R6000 per annum and 66 per cent of the learners are black. Where the country has fallen down on access is in the area of technical and vocational education, where only one per cent of senior secondary learners are in further education training colleges, compared with 50 per cent on average in the OECD countries.

In addition, as Minister Asmal has noted, despite the considerable efforts made to improve the physical infrastructure of schools, there are still huge gaps in the provision of basic services such as water, toilets and telephones. Here, one of the greatest concerns is the unspent capital budgets for education in most of the provinces - pointing to a lack of departmental capacity rather than a lack of funds.

Qualitative Issues: Great Concerns

Despite the high level of state expenditure and considerable private contributions, the country has not yet been able to eliminate the inherited inequalities from decades of apartheid, and improve the quality of education. For most of the past decade, less than 50 per cent of candidates have passed the final school-leaving examination.

In the 1994/5 and 1999 Third International Maths and Science Survey, South Africa came last. In both the public and independent sectors, schools range from the very best to the very worst. While the independent sector has world-class schools that increasingly attract international pupils, it is also plagued by unregistered "fly-by-night" schools that provide very poor education, exploit parents and pupils, and appear and disappear at will.

Within the public sector there are also excellent ex-white suburban schools, that are now racially integrated and achieve 100 per cent pass rates, but there are also dysfunctional township schools, which only achieve 0 to 20 per cent pass rates and where the culture of teaching and learning has broken down as a result of years of resistance to apartheid.

Although the 2000 and 2001 examination pass rates of 60 per cent indicate that, for the first time, the overall quality of schooling is improving as a result of considerable efforts by Government and the private sector, the key challenge of raising the general level of quality remains.

Great Challenges

Education in South Africa faces other significant challenges:

- A looming teacher shortage
- A very small pool of science and mathematics competencies
- The impact of HIV/Aids on the teaching force and pupils
- High youth unemployment.

Meeting all of these challenges is made more difficult by the lack of sufficient management capacity in the education system to implement the ambitious new policies - another sad legacy of apartheid. A massive collaborative effort by all sectors of the country and public-private partnerships is essential to address these issues.

The 2001 pass rate of over 60% indicates that the quality of schooling is improving.

At the western end of Attridgeville, near Pretoria, where the houses turn to a sprawl of shacks and shanties spreading like corrugated iron ivy creeping ever higher and further along the stony ridge, Banareng Primary School is an oasis of plenty.

On a hot, clear October day, the school's gardens - with orderly beds of cabbages, spinach, onions, herbs and a mosaic of flowers springing from every crevice and corner - were the launchpad for the national roll-out of the Department of Education's Awareness Campaign on the School Nutrition Programme.

It coincided with Imbizo Week, when government politicians and officials held community meetings all over the country to interact directly with the people who elected, giving them a chance to raise concerns with the person at the top. The marquee was packed to bursting with the parents of Banareng's 670 pupils and the mothers' hats, of all shapes, atop their best outfits, showed that they were here to celebrate and not to complain (apart from concerns about overcrowding).

At a podium bedecked with produce like a church altar on harvest day, speaker after speaker celebrated Banareng as an example and an inspiration to the nation. And, there is much to celebrate at Banareng. The vegetable gardens, started with help from a BMW community outreach programme, provide a hot meal for every pupil every day and affordable food for the neighbourhood. Paulina Sethole, Banareng's principal for the past four years and a teacher there since 1973, brims with pride as she recalls how, in 1999, the parents rallied around to turn the school grounds from a wilderness into a garden. "The children were suffering in class, they were often sick and we knew that many were hungry because they came from shacks where there was no money," she said. "A hungry child cannot be taught, but since we have begun the feeding, absenteeism is low and the academic results are much better," says Paulina and she adds that the teachers have woven the gardens into their curriculum, starting with counting for the grade ones through to practical biology in higher classes.

"Those same children brought the bricks one at a time to build the beds; on Mondays they bring scraps to make compost and now they are learning what recycling really means."

Paulus Sebea, chief gardener, smiles and says: "I think my school is number one. It makes me so happy to see the children happy and growing and I am pleased to show teachers from other schools how to do what we have done here. I feed the children and I feed the nation."

As he turns away to join the throng, the slogan written on the wall behind says it all: "It takes a village to raise a child."

"I feed the children, and I feed the nation."
Paulus Sebea, chief gardener

Agriculture in the "old" South Africa was both unsustainable and inequitable. Its transformation has been hailed worldwide. It is largely deregulated and unsubsidised and is thriving. The gross value of agricultural income has doubled since 1994, and the value of agricultural exports has risen by 80% over the same period. Farming is not yet equitable, but the land reform process is in place and is yielding sustainable results. More importantly, the land redistribution process is substantially supported by both black and white farming communities.

11

Agriculture and Transformation
Broadening Participation and Improving Performance

Derek Hanekom: Member of Parliament, Department of Agriculture

In 1994, when the new government was elected into office, an agricultural sector was inherited that was neither competitive nor sustainable. Furthermore, the ownership of agricultural land and resources was highly concentrated and racially skewed as a result of dispossession and discriminatory laws. The Government was confronted with a number of policy challenges:

The sector needed to be restructured to make it:

- More competitive
- More sustainable and
- More equitable.

The Marketing Environment and State Control
Probably the single most important factor contributing to the inefficiencies in the sector was the system of state control of the marketing of agricultural products. The measures of control varied greatly between commodities. Maize, for example, was subjected to both price-fixing and a prescribed single marketing channel. Farmers were compelled to sell their maize to the local co-operative at a price that was announced annually by the Minister of Agriculture. Deciduous fruit and citrus farmers could only export their fruit through an agency appointed by the state.

These interventions were in place in terms of the Marketing Act, which had been on the statute books for 60 years. The policy environment was not competitive and not conducive to growth. Other policies, such as subsidised credit and a tax regime favourable to capital investment, had jointly resulted in unsustainably high levels of farm debt and a systematic displacement of labour.

In short, the farming sector was not making its potential contribution to export earnings, to employment or to economic growth, and the interventions were not compatible with a market economy.

In 1994, the agricultural sector was neither competitive nor sustainable.

Drought subsidies, combined with price guarantees, resulted in the cultivation of marginal land and the complete absence of sensible risk management among farmers.

Deregulation

In 1996, the Marketing of Agricultural Products Act was approved by Parliament and the old Marketing Act was finally repealed. This ushered in a period of dramatic reforms because the new act allowed for certain interventions and statutory measures, but not of a market-distorting nature.

It was designed to put an end to all the unnecessary controls to promote trade and encourage competition, and to open up opportunity for new entrants. Statutory measures were effectively limited to the approval of levy applications by participants (described as "affected groups") in an industry, and certain criteria had to be met for these requests to be approved. The levies were essentially to fund research, for trade promotion and market information.

The National Agricultural Marketing Council and Deregulation

A body called the National Agricultural Marketing Council was established to oversee the termination of marketing schemes and the closure of the all-powerful control boards that had dominated agriculture in South Africa for so many years. What followed in the year to come (1997) was probably the most rapid far-reaching deregulation the world had seen. The process was remarkably smooth, a high degree of "buy-in" was achieved through exhaustive consultations and negotiations, and the final results were good.

A number of other policy changes accompanied the marketing reforms and various subsidies to farmers that were inequitable, unsustainable or encouraged bad farming practices were discontinued during the same period.

One example of this was the end of drought subsidies, mainly to maize farmers, that had placed an enormous fiscal burden on the state in earlier years. This, combined with price guarantees, had encouraged cultivation of marginal lands, and had resulted in the complete absence of sensible risk management among maize farmers.

Although all farmers are aware that South Africa is a drought-prone country, it was not something that they had to worry about unduly - if the drought came the state would pay!

Agriculture and Sustainable Practice

Farmers in South Africa can no longer be accused of being a burden to the state or the taxpayer. They are operating in a deregulated and competitive environment and performing well without receiving any form of subsidy from the state. Export earnings have increased and, in general, farming practices have become more sustainable. Among the agricultural exporting countries of the world, South Africa is probably the least subsidised.

It is difficult to assess with certainty what real impact deregulation has had on farming. The falling exchange rate has given export earnings a boost, but has raised input costs, especially fuel. The recent interest rate hikes will also affect farm profits.

But the latest economic review from the Department of Agriculture paints an interesting picture. Gross farm income was estimated at R57.9 billion - an 18.6 per cent improvement over the previous year! This occurred over a period when overall growth in the economy was somewhat sluggish. For the same period the value of agricultural exports grew by 28.2 per cent to R22.3 billion.

Global Challenges

The sector is clearly performing well and there is little doubt that it could perform even better in a more favourable global environment, with less protectionism in the major markets of the West, and without the massive subsidies that have the effect of limiting market opportunity and depressing commodity prices.

Last year, in a deregulated economy and with no state subsidy, farm income was up 18.6 per cent and exports were up 28.2 per cent to R22.3 billion.

These are the new issues and challenges that our Government has to take up, not only on behalf of South African farmers, but as a global challenge affecting all developing countries. President Mbeki has raised the issue at various forums, including the recent World Summit on Sustainable Development held in Johannesburg.

The effects of farm subsidies in the richer countries of the world should not be underestimated. Research done by the University of Stellenbosch shows that $360 billion is spent annually in the United States and the European Union. The shift away from direct price subsidies is an improvement, but does not change things all that much - farmers continue producing large surpluses, not because they have any competitive advantage, or because they are better farmers, but because they receive money from their governments. World targets on poverty reduction will never be met if this issue is not addressed.

Domestic Challenges

While there is nothing wrong with proclaiming the success of deregulation in the agricultural sector, we must be mindful of the policy challenges outside the arena of trade and marketing that have not yet been addressed and are now surfacing strongly in policy debates. Alongside the growth in farm incomes and the increases in exports, millions of South Africans are malnourished, and poverty levels have not been reduced. Inequality remains high.

The issue of who derives the benefits of South Africa's wealth-yielding assets cannot be ignored. It is unlikely that sustained growth can be achieved without reducing inequality, and the immediacy of devastating poverty and hunger cannot wait until we have achieved our desired growth levels.

The good news is that the reduction in our country's fiscal deficit, the increase in revenue collection and the economic successes of the past few years have put the Government in a much stronger position to tackle these problems with intensified vigour. Social grants have increased, but, in many cases, large families are entirely dependent on the grants one person may receive and there are many people who find themselves without jobs or family members to support them and who do not qualify for grants. Consideration will have to be given to extending the social security system, or to increase job opportunities through public works programmes and to supporting small and informal enterprises and agricultural land reform.

Farming subsidies, particularly in the US and the EU, provide a barrier to free trade and to the development of the world's poorer communities.

Gross Value of Agricultural Income Between 1994 and 2002

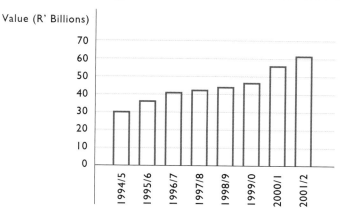

Source: Dirk Blignaut, Senior Economist
(Directorate Agricultural Statistics) Department of Agriculture

Gross Value of Agricultural Exports Between 1994 and 2002

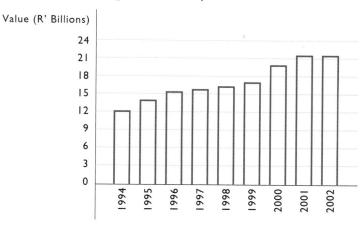

Source: Hans Scheepers, Senior Economist
(Directorate Agricultural Statistics) Department of Agriculture

Land Reform

Land reform, although it will necessarily constitute part of an overall attempt to reduce inequality and eradicate poverty, has to be approached extremely carefully. It differs from other measures in a land. Especially good agricultural land is finite. Clearly land reform on its own does nothing to alleviate poverty; what is important is how the opportunity is used and by whom. There is enough evidence to show that ill-considered land reform programmes can exacerbate poverty and do serious harm to an economy. The international experience of several unsuccessful land

reform attempts has given rise to some scepticism. The truth is that many efforts have been embarked on for political reasons or out of desperation, after years of ignoring the grievances of the landless without having given the less dramatic approach - state-assisted, but market-based land reform - a chance to work.

In this regard, although a lot more will have to be done, and the pattern of land ownership remains racially skewed, South Africa is basically on the right track. Not all projects have been success stories, but many have been. Much has been learned and there is no reason why the pace should not pick up, without doing harm to the economy. The results of the economic review clearly indicate that the sector is flourishing, and there is no reason why this should not continue.

Land reform will help reduce inequality and poverty. Our farmers are positive and proactive on this issue.

When land reform started after the first democratic elections in 1994, there was anxiety and some resistance to the very notion. The Minister at the time gave assurances that land would not be confiscated, and that it would be a fair process. The message was sent out repeatedly that it was not land reform that was threatening, but rather it would be the absence of land reform that would cause instability and tension. Today, there is general acceptance among farmers of the need for land reform, and investment in agriculture has not declined. There is healthy co-operation between the main organisations representing black and white farmers and the Department of Agriculture.

There is every reason to be optimistic, but at the same time to be wary of complacency. There is understandable restlessness and impatience amongst those who were dispossessed of their land, who feel the process is too slow. The challenge of achieving greater equality in the sector, and bringing justice to those who were dispossessed, needs to be tackled with a sense of urgency, but, at the same time, with care and intelligence.

Government's Role

The role of the State has changed from what it was in 1996 and earlier. In the area of trade, the national department assists farmers in opening up opportunities through negotiations and agreements with trading partners. Quality compliance and standards in fruit and citrus exports are monitored and maintained by a body called the Perishable Products Export Control Board.

From a single company doing all the exports with state-granted monopoly power, there are now no fewer than 250 registered exporters of fruit and citrus. In the process, new markets have been found and total exports have increased.

In domestic marketing the interventionist role of the State has come to an end, the 23 control boards have been shut down and the role of Government is now limited to market information and approval of levy applications by industry to fund essential services.

The normal agricultural services such as research, training, extension and finance (through the Land Bank) continue to be provided by the national and provincial departments of agriculture and the Agricultural Research Centre.

Conclusion

Far-reaching and necessary changes have occurred in agriculture in the past few years. The sector has become increasingly competitive and efficient. As shown, the results have been impressive, and agriculture is making a significant contribution to growth, to export earnings and employment.

There are still a number of challenges, in particular land reform, food insecurity and poverty. Although a lot more needs to be done, these issues are being addressed by the Government. In land reform, due process is followed and it is done in a just and fair manner. This is contributing to a long-term, stable atmosphere, which is conducive to further growth and investment in agriculture.

Agriculture is making a significant contribution to growth, to export earnings and to employment.

Rick Dillon and Pannie Human know all about the deep primal need for land reform in South Africa. Every day landless black people pass through their office in Harrismith in the Free State taking the first steps on a journey of hope.

Dillon, an agricultural consultant, and Human, an attorney, have combined their talents to offer a one-stop service to help aspirant farmers access government grants to buy land on the open market. In the past year they have assisted 123 applicants in 32 projects in the province to buy a total of 7600 hectares at a total cost of R12.7 million of which R8.6 million was grant aid. The Land Redistribution for Agricultural Development Programme, aimed at promoting a class of full-time black commercial farmers, introduced in October 2001 at the instigation of Thoko Didiza, the Minister of Agriculture and Land Affairs, offers landless individuals grants of up to R100 000 each.

Until 1999, the Government provided R16 000 grants to buy land for people who earned less than R1500 a month. Communities were organised into communal property associations, but it proved difficult to use the scheme to establish new viable commercial farms.

Now the Government has set a target of establishing 70 000 black commercial farmers under its land reform programme by 2017.

The key to both the success of the new grant programme and the success of the applicants is that the amount of the grant is tied to the amount of the contribution made by the applicant. Every applicant is considered to bring sweat equity worth R5000 which qualifies for a grant of R20 000.

But that won't buy much of a farm, and that is where Dillon's expertise comes in. "This programme is the key to land reform in South Africa, it is well-conceived and it enables people who are committed to farming to own their land," says Dillon, as an assistant helps a man clad in the blue overalls of a farm labourer understand the applications process.

As he leaves, Samuel Mokoena arrives and Dillon does a run though the numbers for him. "I have been trying to get a farm for five years now," says Mokoena who has been leasing land to graze his small herd of cattle. "The land has worked well for me, but it is not mine."

Mokoena is delighted when Dillon tells him to start looking for a property in the R170 000 range, the amount he can muster when his assets (10 cattle and two old tractors), a loan and the government grant are added together. To make it, Mokoena will have to sell his BMW sedan and replace it with a bakkie. The value can then be considered as part of his own contribution.

"I was born from the farm and all I have wanted in my life is to produce food for South Africa," Mokoena says. "We are very happy that we can work together with white people and be equal with everything."

"People are amazed at how we can make the system work for them by simply manipulating the balance between the land and the contribution of the individual," says Dillon. "The policy is excellent, it rewards a man for the efforts he has made."

Next in the office is Daniel Moloi who has arrived to sign transfer documents for a 228 hectare farm. He has built up a taxi business after working 10 years as a gardener and 10 years as a machinery operator. His latest venture was harvesting 35 tonnes of wheat from 22 hectares of rented land near Bethlehem. "With taxis you can make a lot of money, but I want to produce food," he says with the fulfilment of his lifelong dream just a penstroke away.

"Now the hard work starts. We cannot just sit on the land, we must be careful to work so the Government can help the next man."

As an industry, tourism can create more jobs than any other. It is also a hard currency earner. The attainment of both of these consequences is of critical national importance. The evidence in 2002 is that since 9/11 and the December 2001 decline in the exchange rate, tourism has grown rapidly. South Africa is suddenly considered both safe and very affordable. The World Summit, the Cricket World Cup and hopefully the Soccer World Cup in 2010 provide a showcase of our hospitality. The challenge is to develop and sustain an African uniqueness that has global appeal.

12

Tourism in South Africa

New Vision, New Direction, Greater Participation

Cheryl Carolus, CEO: South African Tourism

Our Vision

SA Tourism is excited and challenged by the new path it has mapped out to ensure that our vision for growth in tourism is realised.

We have fundamentally changed the way we go about marketing and developing this country as a destination, but are confident that we have the market intelligence and ability to realise our targets. At the heart of our new strategy is our ambition to become:

- Focused in a way that ensures our scarce resources obtain the highest possible yield against the objectives of growth in volume, spend, length of stay, distribution and lower seasonality as the key tourism drivers of economic growth, job creation and transformation;
- Customer-driven to ensure that we understand what our customers need (within the constraints of our own principles and values) and deliver the experience;

- Strategic in our approach so as to ensure that we deal with the major issues and challenges for growth, and don't get side-tracked into a myriad of smaller issues that detract from our core mandate; and
- Leaders in the industry to ensure that our strategy is implemented, and that the benefits accrue to our customers and the widest possible sectors of South African society.

Going forward, SA Tourism has already started to align itself organisationally in the direction of this new strategy. We will be actively engaging with role-players throughout government, the local trade and our international partners to create the conditions in which we become a single team in promoting South Africa.

Desirable, world class, sophisticated and truly African - these are the attributes of our land.

We have fundamentally
changed the way we
market the country as a
destination.

New Direction - World-class and Different

Desirable, world-class, sophisticated and truly African - these are the attributes our land and our people have to offer as we forge ahead to make this country a globally preferred destination. Historically, we have not utilised these attributes to the extent that we could have done. In the past two years, a renewed effort to position South Africa as an exciting place to visit has enjoyed high priority on the national agenda.

As South Africa moved into the era of democracy, the nation was captured by the promise and potential for tourism and the benefits it would bring to the people of our country as an economic driver for sustainable jobs and foreign exchange. Now, after years of isolation, the country has emerged as an attractive destination and is striving to position itself within this high-growth industry as a world-class contender.

Tourism is already one of the fastest growing industries in South Africa, contributing nearly 4.9 per cent of GDP.

Tourism Feedback

SA Tourism regularly interviews departing tourists at international airports to get a measure of the success of our marketing efforts and to track their experience in our country.

Our Welcome

Some of the answers are predictable. Many visitors come for the wildlife but are taken by the diverse natural beauty of South Africa, and are really moved by our people. The warmth of the welcome, the courteous hospitality, and the friendly exuberance make it the experience of a lifetime.

Our welcome is especially African and gives us an edge over many of our competitor destinations. More and more, experienced adventure travellers seek the cultural facet that other destinations can't offer.

Our wildlife, people and natural beauty make South Africa unique for the international traveller. Currently we have six million tourists visiting every year, 4.5 million from Africa and 1.5 million from the rest of the world (mostly Europe). Our potential as a destination of first choice is considerable!

Tourism Growth Post 1994

South Africa has seen degrowth in foreign arrivals. For the period 1994 to 2000, the compound annual growth rate (CAGR) of arrivals was eight per cent. The strong growth we saw in overseas visitors in 1996/7 convinced many that South Africa was on an upward swing that required relatively little effort to sustain. The optimism of the period was perhaps most strongly reflected in government policy documents that suggested targets for tourism arrivals as high as 15 per cent growth per year until 2010.

Foreign arrivals to South Africa have been flat at just under six million arrivals per annum since 1998, but strong growth from our key source markets, such as the UK, started positively with 14.6 per cent (month on month) growth in January 2002. South Africa has benefited from the 9/11 tragedy in the sense that many tourists diverted their travel plans away from the Middle East, USA and Europe and came here. Our reputation as a "safe" destination has improved considerably.

In response to this rise in demand after 1994, many existing and new tourism businesses have expanded capacity, developed new products, and are attempting to become increasingly competitive.

However, the period after 1998 has been more sobering when the arrivals growth rate dropped back to a mere 0.4 per cent, partly attributed to a decline in arrivals from some of our neighbours. This slowdown is raising many questions about the constraints to further expansion. The critical issue is that the honeymoon of the "democracy dividend" is over. Currently, the growth rates in overall arrivals are far below those experienced in many other regions of the world, including the rest of Africa. To manage this proactively, SA Tourism has embarked on a growth strategy to create a more focused, customer-driven approach.

Tourism is one of the fastest growing industries in South Africa. It already contributes 4.9 per cent to GDP.

Overall Visitor Arrivals to SA

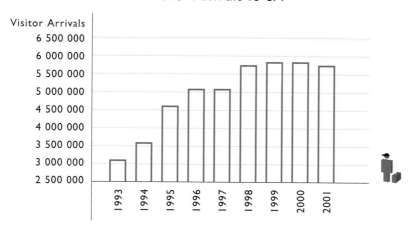

Visitor Arrivals

6 500 000	
6 000 000	
5 500 000	
5 000 000	
4 500 000	
4 000 000	
3 500 000	
3 000 000	
2 500 000	

1993 1994 1995 1996 1997 1998 1999 2000 2001

They come for the wildlife,
and are really moved by our people.

Arrivals Growth to SA Compared

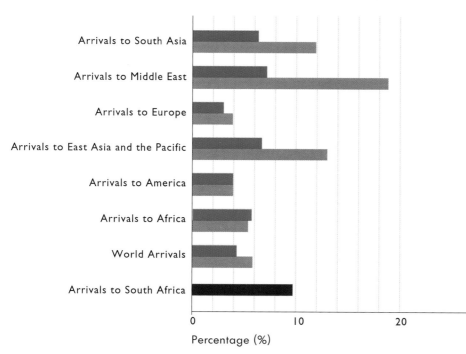

Arrivals to South Asia
Arrivals to Middle East
Arrivals to Europe
Arrivals to East Asia and the Pacific
Arrivals to America
Arrivals to Africa
World Arrivals
Arrivals to South Africa

0   10   20

Percentage (%)

In the period 1998 to 2000, SA tourism
growth slowed. But 9/11 and the
devaluation of the rand in 2001 has
caused the growth levels to revert to
double digits in 2002.

Compound Annual Growth Rate of Arrivals
● WTO Forecast (95-20)
● Actual Arrivals (98-00)
● Arrivals to SA (93-00)

Source: Tourism Market Trends, WTO 2001 Edition: Tourism Highlights 2001, WTO. Copyright© 2002 SA Tourism and the Monitor Group.

Tourism is a real partnership between government, the tourism industry and the public.

Tourism Growth Strategy

The Tourism Growth Strategy or TGS marks a new beginning. Over the past nine months, we have done intensive research to understand the international market and make critical choices about where we should spend our marketing time and money.

We believe we have the people, product, climate, and the experience that most international leisure travellers are looking for. Our strategy has clear targets and we regularly monitor our performance. In addition we have built strong relationships with our provincial partners and the industry to grow a broad-based tourism sector for all South Africans. The TGS represents a significant step in SA Tourism's transformation from being an administrative organisation of the past to one that is able to grow the market effectively. The process lays a key strategic foundation for the new SA Tourism to take up the lead in deploying its resources to secure an increase in those markets which hold the greatest potential to deliver.

In doing this, SA Tourism recognises that the process of arriving at a strategy involves choices about which markets to focus on, which segments within these markets to target, with what message and through which medium. And all these choices must be informed by deep insight and understanding about markets and customers. We have thus moved away from deriving strategy from opinion and anecdote, and towards answering two key questions with data and deep analysis:

- Behind which customers do we organise ourselves to win?
- How do we target these customers?

In answering these questions, SA Tourism has undertaken to become a customer-focused organisation. Thus, the strategy on sustainable growth from international tourism markets will be based on demand, rather than solely on what we have to offer, or what we as South Africans believe foreign tourists may want.

Marketing is, however, only one piece of the puzzle which makes up a competitive destination. The development of product and the effective organisation of the channel, combined with the marketing message, make up the proposition. Product and channel strategy are, for the most part, outside of SA Tourism's mandate, but we recognise that marketing strategy must integrate them. At the same time, our deep research into customers and markets will deliver insights that are as useful to the product owners and channels as they are to us. For this reason, SA Tourism has created a process that engages with partners and stakeholders and enables SA Tourism to share its learnings. At the same time, we will be working closely with government at all levels, feeding insights and data to inform tourism policy, development and investment programmes, as well as to enable government to focus its efforts on key strategic areas as it works to unblock regulatory and other barriers to tourism growth.

All of these processes must be located within a broader framework for tourism development and considerable effort is being made to ensure that our strategy speaks to the key thrust of our national objectives - not least because it is domestic tourism which delivers the demand off which many of our programmes are based. For all of these reasons, the strategy has been founded on a set of five key objectives.

Key Objectives for Growth

Increase Volume	➡	Increase tourism volume at high and sustainable rates.
Increase Spend	➡	Increase total spend by tourists in South Africa.
Optimise Length of Stay	➡	Optimise length of stay to maximise revenue yield to SA.
Improve Distribution	➡	Improve volume and spend distribution around the country, and throughout the year.
Promote Transformation	➡	Improve activity and spend patterns to enable transformation and promote black economic empowerment.

In developing the strategy to deliver on these objectives, SA Tourism has had to ensure that it makes the best choices about where to deploy its limited resources. To do this, the entire process was managed through five operating principles:

- Focus - The process of developing the strategy had to focus on the major issues for growth, and on the core areas in the international market where growth could be obtained in the short-term, but with a focused approach to understanding the medium and long-term opportunities.
- Data-driven - All decisions had to be based on fact and sound analysis.
- Consultative - The process employed was consultative, incorporating input from as many stakeholders as possible.
- Transparent - The logic for all decisions was transparent to those involved in the process.
- Capacity building - SA Tourism has established a Strategic Research Unit to provide ongoing market intelligence and strategic advice to the organisation.

Greater Participation

Guided by a policy framework for tourism development (White Paper on Tourism), the collaborative tourism action (cluster) process was launched with the aim to achieve collective action among the key stakeholders to enhance marketing, investment, skills and infrastructure development. The Tourism Forum was established in December 1998, comprising leadership drawn from government, business,

public institutions and labour, with the common purpose of ensuring growth and development of the tourism sector. The Forum agreed to support the following key strategic areas:

- Sustainable funding mechanisms
- Information systems
- Human resource development programmes
- International marketing
- the Welcome Campaign.

Subsequently, a number of programmes were launched in line with the guidelines as set out in the White Paper:

1. Poverty-relief funding

Since 1999, the Department of Environmental Affairs and Tourism (DEAT) has funded more than 200 community tourism projects throughout the country. About R300 million has been spent which has resulted in creating more than 600 000 temporary jobs and 1100 permanent jobs. Most projects have been of a tourism infrastructure or product development nature. These projects are categorised into product development; infrastructure development; capacity-building and training; establishment of small, medium and micro-enterprises (SMMEs); and business development projects.

2. Marketing strategy

In 2000/01, for the first time in the history of the promotion of South African tourism, the marketing budget more than doubled. Central government contributed R150 million, the Business Trust R50 million and the Tourism Business Council R25 million. South Africa's marketing strategy includes the following initiatives:

2.1 International Marketing Scheme (ITMAS)

The objective of ITMAS is to partially compensate small to medium-sized business for certain costs incurred in terms of activities designed to promote South African tourism internationally. Of the R4 million fund, more than R1.5 million was spent in 2000 to benefit approximately 682 entrepreneurs. For 2001, part of the fund subsidised 139 black emerging entrepreneurs to attend Indaba 2001 in Durban, Africa's premier annual tourist exhibition. Indaba 2001 was also used as a platform to launch the Emerging Tourism Entrepreneur of the Year Award, an incentive to increase South African entrepreneurs' participation in the tourism industry and create "can do" role models.

2.2 Welcome Campaign

Launched in December 1999 by the Minister of Environmental Affairs and Tourism, the Welcome Campaign encourages all South Africans to embrace tourism and share South Africa's rich natural and cultural heritage. Underpinning the Campaign is the message that tourism is the fastest growing contributor to South Africa's future economic prosperity, and is playing a key role in job creation and socio-economic upliftment. In February 2001, SA Tourism augmented the Welcome Campaign with an inspiring television and cinema commercial that relayed the message "For every eight tourists one job is created", but sometimes a single tourist can spark an industry. In 2002, Welcome was linked to the Jo'burg Summit on Sustainable Development. The South African welcome pledge was launched with the opening line "Smile and say hola to tourists".

Another facet of the campaign is Tourism Month. This annual promotion, held in September, is designed to promote a culture of tourism amongst all South Africans. It boosts South Africans' interest in both exploring and preserving the country's vast number of diverse tourist sights and provincial icons.

2.3 International and local marketing

Following the launch of SA Tourism's new corporate identity in October 2000, a R150 million international marketing initiative was launched in November at the World Travel Market in London. Tactics included the London cabby campaign; extensive billboard advertising in Germany and the Netherlands; high-profile print campaigns in the United States, United Kingdom, France, Germany and the Netherlands; live broadcasts from South Africa by 15 US radio stations; media tours of South Africa for foreign journalists; and meetings with hundreds of foreign and local stakeholders in the travel industry. To complement this awareness-building campaign, South African Tourism launched the Circle of Sunshine (endorsed by Archbishop Desmond Tutu) in London in November 2000. The Circle of Sunshine is an expanding network of "ambassadors" (expatriates, business leaders and celebrities) who have links with South Africa and who want to motivate others to make this country a priority holiday destination. It has also been launched in Germany and promoted in South Africa and will be launched in other key markets.

Celebrate South Africa was another vehicle used to promote the country. This six-week festival showcased South Africa's performing talent, arts, crafts, fashion and cuisine from April to May 2001 in London.

2.4 Transformation

In November 2001, Cabinet endorsed the Tourism Transformation Strategy produced by Department of Environmental Affairs and Tourism (DEAT). The Strategy includes a three-year action plan aimed at transforming the industry. The first part has been completed and has resulted in the formation of a forum of organisations that provide assistance to tourism enterprises. DEAT has compiled an information booklet with details and procedures for assistance and a database of black-owned tourism businesses within the broad travel, tourism and hospitality sector.

2.5 Tourism Enterprise Programme (TEP)

DEAT, the Business Trust and Ebony Consulting International launched the R129 million TEP to promote growth in the tourism industry, and it is expected to create about 10 000 jobs in the next few years. The primary objective of the programme is the development of skills capacity and the participation of 75 per cent of historically disadvantaged enterprises within the tourism economy.

2.6 Human resource development

Education and training is considered one of the pillars of the development of a new, responsible tourism culture in South Africa. DEAT has supported the full introduction of Travel and Tourism and Hospitality Studies as a subject in schools by finalising a curriculum.

Two exciting projects which are in their second year, run by SA Tourism, are the Amathuba tour guide training project and the Emerging Tourism Entrepreneur of the Year Award (ETEYA). Amathuba is run in conjunction with the German Government and Carl Duisberg Gesellschaft. In total, 60 students will enjoy a 12-month all-expenses-paid training course in Germany. ETEYA has attracted nearly 180 entries over the past two years. These awards are designed to encourage and sustain the development of SMMEs in the tourism and hospitality sector, within the broader objectives of job creation and economic empowerment. Each finalist is granted the opportunity to showcase products at the World Travel Market and the overall winner receives a cash injection into the business.

World Summit on Sustainable Development (WSSD)

The successful hosting of the WSSD had many spin-off benefits for South Africa as a world-class destination. More than 40 000 international guests were treated to the hospitality and efficiency of Johannesburg and South Africa

more than proved its ability to host such a gathering of diverse cultures and interests.

The Minister of Environmental Affairs and Tourism has released figures from a study on the economic impact of the WSSD which indicate that about R8.3 billion was injected into the economy by government and the private sector and will certainly leave a lasting legacy for South Africans. About R2.6 billion was from direct expenditure contributing around one per cent to GDP.

According to departure polls, many delegates plan on coming back to South Africa on holiday together with family and friends. The possible economic spin-offs from tourism growth will benefit our larger goals of economic empowerment and job creation.

During the Summit, SA Tourism hosted media tours around the country so that journalists could see sustainable development in action. They visited several community projects around tourism and environmental management, each one involving a high degree of community participation with resultant job creation and economic and social benefits. The media were highly impressed with the tenacity and creativity shown by South Africans in dealing with daily challenges.

Cricket World Cup
During the Cricket World Cup in 2003 , South Africa will once more be thrown into the spotlight. For tourism, there are exciting possibilities to showcase our product to a receptive audience.

Cricket has a huge following in our key growth markets such as the United Kingdom, India, Australia and Kenya. SA Tourism, together with the provinces, will be investing great effort to position South Africa as a viable leisure destination. This will be done through media tours and massive coverage during the World Cup. Our strategic focus will be to highlight national icons through broadcasts during the game.

Growth and Development Summit
A major conference for government and business to discuss issues of confidence and investment is planned. This represents a significant opportunity to develop a South African growth and development strategy with an important stakeholder group.

The Way Forward
We have all realised that the winning formula for tourism growth is the quality of the tourism. What makes people speak glowingly about us and makes them return, is the lasting impression left by our service, our hospitality and our warmth. Tourism has the potential to contribute to nation building and pride in South Africa. Hence the cry: "Tourism is everyone's business - play your part." In making the country aware and seeing first hand the economic and social benefits of tourism, we are creating ambassadors out of ordinary people.

As we move forward to develop a selling proposition for tourism internationally, we are building on the strengths, which are: our natural beauty, wildlife, sun and the warmth of our people. An added advantage is that we are rooted in Africa and we are able to build on this. Tourism is a real partnership - between government at all levels, the tourism industry and the public. This partnership has to move along with a common understanding of our ultimate objectives and develop the means to get there. A narrow, one-dimensional approach will not work. We hope that the tourism growth strategy, which is all encompassing, will be embraced by everyone so that we can truly focus on making South Africa a desirable, world-class destination.

Tourism in and to South Africa

Gail McCann, CEO: Southern Africa Tourism Services Association

Southern African Tourism Services Association (SATSA) with its members being "Your credible tourism partners in South and Southern Africa" plays an important role in tourism in and to South Africa. SATSA and its members, ranging from the largest tour operator to the smallest guest house constantly strive for professionalism and integrity in inbound tourism. This is to ensure the growth and recognition of the South African Tourism industry as a sustainable contributor to the South African economy.

> **The World Summit on sustainable development firmly placed South Africa in a position to be competitive with the best. The Cricket World Cup in 2003 will elevate South Africa to heights never dreamt of.**

South Africa needs to be a proactive player in the global dynamics of an ever changing tourism environment. The Tourism Growth Strategy by South African Tourism is to be commended and gives renewed impetus to confidence in the economy by encouraging:
- New developments
- Foreign investment
- Job creation.

Tourism was only recently identified by government as a major contributor to the economy. The tourism economy now contributes 7.1 per cent of South Africa's GDP and we expect the figures to rise to 8.1 per cent next year. SA Tourism's shift towards targeted and intense tactical marketing is determined to make South Africa the number one long haul destination in the world. The effort and success of the World Summit on Sustainable Development firmly placed South Africa in a position to be competitive

with the best and the rest. The Cricket World cup in 2003 will elevate South Africa to heights never dreamt off.

Our unique and diverse tourism attractions will become the most sought after in the world. Tourism in South Africa remains the catalyst for the future economic and social development of South Africa and we will continue to embrace this shining light through all adversity, to create prosperity for all South Africans.

However, there are a number of important issues that South African Tourism needs to address:
- Ensure continuous collaboration with industry and industry associations. (Statistics are a way to determine trends, but alone, will not give the full picture)
- Remove blockages that stunt growth in this sector
- Build ongoing partnership, co-operation and focus with the private sector and government
- Co-ordinate efforts in mobilising South Africans to travel within their borders
- Encourage education in schools on the benefits of tourism
- Promote social responsibility programmes in boardrooms focussing on tourism.

South African Tourism understands that we all want to achieve a common goal.

> **Being proudly South African as an industry will only happen if co-operation and collaboration exists at every level.**

No Sushi in Soweto

"Tourism in Soweto", she says "is a growing business. It's going to create jobs for people."

Minah Makhoro has been a nurse all her working life, a profession she chose because of her love for people. Eventually, though, nursing the very ill took an emotional toll and she started looking for another occupation. This required a review of her skills, her responsibilities as a married mother and, most importantly, the future of business in South Africa. As an option, she says, tourism was the most natural choice.

"As a black person, hospitality is important to me and I entertain a lot. My family comes from different parts of the country, and they've always put up at our house. I ended up getting entertainment in my bloodstream by hosting people all the time. I realised I was doing it well and people appreciated it. I got presents and I thought, 'Why don't I generate income from it?' And that's how the idea of starting a bed and breakfast came about." Minah and her husband, Morris, owned a house in Protea North on the western edge of the conglomeration of townships known as Soweto.

"We used to rent out the house, but we did not get much income from it. That's when it occurred to us that this was an opportunity to create something in our own community that could generate income and promote Soweto." They began renovations in 2001, but it was not all smooth sailing. "The start was very difficult. We had to take a second bond but, halfway through renovations, the money finished so we had to stop the work and get another bond." Eventually the house was completed; it contains three double bedrooms with en-suite showers and bathrooms, a bar, a dining area and a large kitchen.

Today, 2422 Mosala Street, Protea North, is the Basiea Bed and Breakfast (Basiea is a clan name) and, with its distinctive peach and yellow colouring, the building stands out from its yellow-brick neighbours. Staff were employed, but two obstacles remained - raising capital and attracting guests.

Finding funding for her business from the private or public sector proved difficult and the bureaucracy and contradictions nearly made her give up. Her luck changed when she met Queen Mokgopo, a tour operator, during preparations for the World Summit on Sustainable Development. Queen had a background in tourism, but had decided in 2000 to try her hand at her own business.

Queen recalls: "We met, and discovered that we had common ideas and common reasoning and we became friends. Now, I give you the tour, and Minah will give you the accommodation." With almost no marketing, Minah opened her doors on 22 August, 2002. "The next day I got one Japanese guy who was in town for the Summit. He went back and told his colleagues about our food. On the 24th I got four Japanese guys, and so it went until the end of the Summit. The Japanese visitors wanted a Sowetan experience and African cuisine (we don't serve sushi) and that is what they got. Eventually they were taking mini-buses all around Soweto by themselves. On a typical day, tourists would come and experience our food, experience the feeling of being in Soweto, the feel of being with people in their own environment, the freedom of moving around the streets and meeting the locals." Minah says that tourism in Soweto is a growing business.

"It's going to create jobs for people, as long as we market it well. But we are going to have to come up with something that's going to sell this part of Soweto, because everybody goes up to Orlando West to see Nelson Mandela's old home." Makhoro refuses to let the difficulties she faces get her down. "We can see the future in the tourism industry and the good news is that we have started. We have the guts because we have started. We don't fear failure because I'm looking forward to a bright future where Queen will own her own bus, and I will own a lodge, not in the Magaliesberg, but here, in Soweto."

13

20 Years ago, Greenpeace were considered environmental extremists. The ozone problem was just exaggerated hype from a group of bunny-hugging radicals. Now we know that they were right, and the world was wrong - on almost every issue. The new South Africa gave us a chance to start afresh - environmentally that is. We had much to be proud of. A better start than most. But the timing of our new dispensation could not have been better for the Sustainable Environment debate. The World Summit in Johannesburg linked poverty relief to unfair trading practice and both to the sound, sustainable use of our resources. South Africa has pioneered much of the debate on sustainability, permaculture and ecotourism.

South Africa is experiencing a tidal wave of public concern and support for the protection of our environment.

Environmental Management

Sustainability Initiatives

Dr Chrispian Olver: Director General, Department of Environmental Affairs and Tourism

When the United Nations Conference on Environment and Development convened the Rio Earth Summit in 1992, the world came of age. The decision to adopt and promote sustainable development was a defining moment in the history of social progress, peace and development in the world.

Two years later, in 1994, our country was to elect a democratic government that would be expected to set in motion solid implementation mechanisms on the agreements reached at that summit.

This Summit could not have come at a better time for the billions of people on the planet. For the people of South Africa, with a new government based on their will, it meant the challenge of integrating social development with economic prosperity and environmental protection. Both Rio and 27 April (the day South Africans went to the polls in 1994) represented an idea whose time had come and moved the world's people closer to the possibility of living in harmony with our environment and our volk. Today, eight years since the new democratic government was installed and 10 years since the Rio Summit, we are able to reflect on the good news and the progress we have made.

South Africa hosts the World Summit on Sustainable Development.

In 2002, we hosted the World Summit on Sustainable Development. It was another defining moment when we, as Africans, hosted and led a process that took the principles of Rio into action. Through the New Partnership for African Development or NEPAD, we have set a motion in process to rethink the prosperity and revival of our continent as a beacon of good governance, democracy, human rights and with an improved quality of life for our generation and those to come.

The past 10 years have taught us that, unless we incorporate environmental considerations into our development planning and implementation, we will discover that the future of our species, bio-diversity and the natural balance of our planet as we know it today, cannot be assured.

In addition, we are overwhelmed with concern for the overall environmental crisis facing our worlds - both the rich and the poor. Added to that is a view that the advanced nations are attempting to manipulate, in their own self-interest, the global and, in particular, the African environment and natural resources.

The past 10 years have taught us that, unless we use our resources sustainably, the natural balance of our planet cannot be assured.

South Africa's New Environmental Policy Framework

We, as a matter of priority, set ourselves a range of objectives for development, driven by a cognisance of the emergency at hand. Our focus was on:

- good governance
- effective resource management
- conservation and
- co-operation with other developing countries.

Central to South Africa's new Environmental Policy framework is a broad vision founded on respect for all the relevant principles and themes of environmentalism and sustainable development, recognising that environmental degradation is not only a function of failing markets and poverty, but also of institutional failure at both the micro-household level and the macro-government level.

What progress have we made?

Looking back at developments in the Department of Environmental Affairs and Tourism over the past years, we have made considerable progress in both growing tourism and managing our environment. Guided by political directives from our Minister, Mr Valli Moosa, our strategy and vision was to deliver, across the length and breadth of our land, a better life for all South Africans. Safeguarding the environment and promoting the growth of tourism in the context of the principle of sustainable development is our major challenge.

The Department of Environmental Affairs and Tourism's strategic "positioning statement" is now well established as "building unity in action for change" and " lending a hand, to push back the frontiers of poverty". Both are central to our building of a new society.

In the past two years, we have, at a domestic level:

- Raised awareness about the achievements of our country via improved media coverage and reporting
- Highlighted what we have done in the area of job creation via improved reporting and
- Encouraged the promotion of responsible tourism through an award system.

On an international level, we have:

- Signed a number of agreements with (among others) Norway, Finland, the UK, Iran, Algeria and Japan

All our science and technologies, and all our social institutions become dysfunctional if the natural life systems cease to function.

- Entered into dealings with the Global Environment Facility, United Nations Environment Programme and World Bank on grants and partnerships around technology transfer and capacity building
- Acceded to international Conventions like CITES and Rotterdam, Stockholm and Kyoto on the importance of global responsibility towards the environment.

At government level, we have initiated joint initiatives with, for example:

- The Department of Minerals and Energy on the asbestos problems, the Pebble Bed Modular Reactor Programme and the Coega Project to ensure responsible management of the environment
- Our regional neighbours in terms of tourism marketing and transfrontier national parks and
- Namibia and Angola on our shared fishing resources.

On a broader front, we have concentrated on:

- Poverty alleviation through the Poverty Relief Fund, releasing more than R32 million to tourism projects all over the country.
- The transformation of the tourism industry, which has included the development of solid partnership in the areas of learnerships, tour guide training, a tourism safety campaign and a revolutionised hospitality grading scheme.
- Marine and coastal matters where we are working on a sustainable system of fishing quotas that ensures community benefit and sees that the South African fishing industry is managed responsibly.
- A National Conservation Strategy and a National Conservation Act, ushering into a new system of bio-diversity management and conservation that has, as its tenets, the increase in the number of national protected areas, in consultation with the provinces.

We will approach the coming years even more determined to grow tourism and to manage the environment and strengthen Government's objective of ensuring "a better life for all".

Future prospects. What needs to be done?

South Africa is experiencing a tidal wave of public concern and support for the protection of our environment. It is appropriate, given our history, that our constitution calls for conservation and environmental protection within the context of sustainable development.

Environmental degradation is a function both of failure at the micro-household level and the macro-government level.

In this regard, it compels us to protect the environment and also promote social and economic development.

Everyone agrees that these challenges require a partnership between governments of the North and the South, and between governments, civil society and the private sector.

Aid from the rich to the poor is important and must be increased. Of equal, if not greater, importance is the need to remove obstacles to economic activity in developing countries.

While some of these matters must be negotiated in the World Trade Organisation, the World Summit on Sustainable Development could not have been silent on the obstacles to poverty eradication, and there is hope emerging from the agreements we reached in Johannesburg.

The World Summit was an opportunity for the formation of a global partnership to roll back poverty. We remain confident that the world leaders who gathered here will take back an action plan of hope to the poor and destitute and thereby open a new chapter in human solidarity.

It has been an enormous privilege for South Africa to host the biggest global gathering yet. It has provided us with a unique opportunity for the promotion of our country as a tourism destination and as a place to do business. It constituted a net economic gain rather than simply a financial burden on the taxpayer and a logistical inconvenience on the residents of Johannesburg and was, in fact, a good example of sustainable development!

Biodiversity and Conservation for the Future

South Africa is the third most biodiverse country in the world, rich in natural resources which, if used in a sustainable manner, can yield social and economic benefits for ourselves and for future generations.

In this context we will continue to consolidate the protection of our biodiversity and the wonders of nature by employing a range of tools.

These include:

- National, provincial and municipal parks
- Transfrontier conservation areas
- Biosphere reserves which allow for mixed land use within a conservation area
- Contractual parks where the land is the property of a community
- Private nature reserves and marine protected areas;
- The listing of world heritage sites
- The implementation of international rules for the trade in endangered species
- The world-renowned Working for Water and Working for Wetlands programmes
- The collection and research work of the National Botanical Institute
- The research work of the marine and coastal management branch of the Department and the research work and breeding projects of South African national parks and the provincial conservation authorities
- Further discussions with the Eastern Cape with a view to establishing the Pondoland National Park as part of the economic growth of the Wild Coast
- Further discussions with Mpumalanga Province on the protection of the Sabie River catchment area, which is contiguous with the Blyde River Nature Reserve
- Establishing a representative sample of biodiversity in a system of protected areas in the Protected Areas Bill which will be tabled in Parliament soon
- An acknowledgement that conservation and economic development must go hand in hand. Our conservation areas, rather than being a burden on taxpayers, must contribute to job creation and socio-economic upliftment and
- The promotion of our natural heritage sites must continue to serve as a foundation of the tourism industry, as well as symbols of national pride. For example, the Cradle of Humankind and the proposed Mapungubwe Heritage Area are two of our country's sites that confirm South Africa as the birthplace of mankind.

Tourism Prospects and Small, Micro and Medium Enterprise (SMME) Development

The Department has published a booklet that, for the first time, provides a consolidated set of information on all government and government-related support programmes. A database of black-owned tourism enterprises has been compiled in order to assist government departments to meet affirmative procurement targets.

A public-private tourism transformation forum to promote black economic empowerment has been established, with representation from the Department of Environmental Affairs and Tourism, the Tourism Business Council, the Development Bank of SA, the Industrial Development Corporation and the Departments of Trade and Industry and Labour.

A New Era in Fisheries Management

The allocation of long-term fishing rights is now complete. The process undertaken constitutes both a modernisation and a deep transformation of the fishing industry. The introduction of predictability, transparency and fairness into the rights allocation process has resulted in stability in the industry and, for the first time, fishing enterprises are able to take rational investment decisions.

This transformation of the industry is far-reaching and, in the hake trawl sector, which is the biggest quota, 73 per cent of all rights holders are majority black-owned concerns. During the apartheid era, the total allowable catch was divided among only six white-owned companies. This year 51 companies have been allocated hake trawl quotas. South Africa has among the best managed fish stocks in the world and, this year, we have been able to determine a record total allowable catch of 257 978 tonnes, an increase of 75 978 from 2001, and further determined the total allowable catch for anchovies for 2002 to be 259 726 tonnes. This makes the catch 158 per cent higher than the 1994 figures, largely due to sound fisheries management.

These successful models come at a time when half the European fishing fleet is at a standstill because they have had to reduce the total allowable catch, partly because of years of reckless over-fishing. With this in mind, Europe has asked for access to South African waters as part of the EU-SA trade agreement. We have refused and we have no intention of changing this position.

Through Operation Neptune, a combined project with the South African Police Service, we are combating the poaching of abalone as part of our efforts to protect this precious resource from extinction. The operation has been highly successful and has led to large amounts of poached abalone being seized and numerous arrests have been made.

However, despite the best efforts of Operation Neptune, the abalone resource remains under pressure. Criminals continue to poach, denying many coastal communities the opportunity of making a living from proper and sustainable exploitation. Unless urgent steps are taken, abalone could soon become commercially extinct.

Mobilising our people

We will continue to find ways of communicating with the public. This year we participated actively in the Imbizo Week. We have also placed a special emphasis on community radio stations and we provide information on our website.

With the Summit behind us, our people wait eagerly for us to call on them to lend a hand in the implementation of the decisions taken in Johannesburg and, through a rigorous campaign of outreach, we will make that call. In June 2002, we announced the Government's intention to set up the Cleanest Town Competition aimed at encouraging the nation to take pride in its surroundings and work together with Government in cleaning up their towns.

It was greeted with much enthusiasm and, in the process, achieved its objective - to raise awareness on the importance and the benefits of a clean environment and urge people to change their attitude and behaviour towards their surroundings. We will continue to develop new ways of ensuring that all sectors are engaged through programmes of mass participation and, through that, ensure that the earth is protected for those from whom we have borrowed it: the future generations.

Conclusion

Thomas Berry in his book 'The Great Work - Our Way Into the Future' says "The future can exist only when we understand the universe as composed of subjects to be communed with not as objects to be exploited. 'Use' as our primary relationship with the planet must be abandoned. While there are critical issues of providing food, shelter and livelihood to vast numbers of peoples, these issues themselves ultimately depend on our capacity to sustain the natural world so that the natural world can sustain us. All our sciences and technologies and all our social institutions become dysfunctional if the natural life systems cease to function. Intimacy with the planet, with its wonder and beauty and the full depth of its meaning, is what enables an integral human relationship with the planet to function. It is only possible for humans to attain their true flourishing while honouring the other modes of earthly beings. The fulfilment of the earth community is to get caught up in the grandeur of existence itself and in admiration of those mysterious powers whence all this has emerged.

"Nourishment of both the outer body and the inner spirit will be achieved in intimate association with each other or not at all. That we can now understand and work towards this fulfilment is the challenging future that opens up before us in these early years of the 21st century."

"History is governed by those overarching movements that give shape and meaning to life by relating the human venture to the larger destinies of the universe. Creating such a movement might be called the great work of a people. There have been great works in the past in Greece ... in Rome ... in India ... in China ... in America. All of these efforts have made significant contributions to the human venture but they were all limited in their fulfilment and bear the marks of our deeply human flaws and imperfections.

"The great work now as we move into a new millennium, is to carry out the transition from a period of human devastation of the earth to a period when humans would be present to the planet in a mutually beneficial manner. Such a transition has no historical parallel since the geo-biological transition that took place 67 million years ago when the period of the dinosaurs was terminated and the new biological age began. So now we awaken to a period of intensive disarray in the biological structure and the functioning of the planet."

These are the challenges that face the Department of Environmental Affairs and Tourism.

Nourishment of both the outer body and the inner spirit will be achieved in intimate association with each other - or not at all.

In 1972, my first exposure to the SA Government was in reversing their attempt to expropriate land under wildlife to perpetuate the now failed homeland policy. During the two decades that followed, it became apparent that the Government, both intellectually and through its institutional structures, had little understanding of sustainable environmental management. The importance of the environment and the global tourism opportunities were lost as the apartheid ideology prevailed. After the 1994 elections, the importance of international tourism and sustainable environmental management was recognised.

Many of the perspectives articulated in this chapter by Dr Chrispian Olver, are valid. South Africans should be proud of their achievements in this field over the past eight years, evidenced by the opportunity to showcase the country by hosting the World Summit on Sustainable Development 2002 in Johannesburg.

At its inception, the new SA Government understood the importance of sound environmental management, the promotion of tourism and how these two forces interact to alleviate poverty. In particular, the manner in which Government has overhauled its institutional structures is to be commended.

The Department of Environmental Affairs and Tourism and the Department of Water Affairs and Forestry are excellent examples of the creation of world-class institutional frameworks, equipped to deal with the challenges and complexities. Perhaps the greatest achievement of the past eight years has been the interdepartmental co-operation established to ensure an integrated strategy.

The creation of both an internal and external perception that South Africa is becoming a desirable world destination for discerning travellers has contributed to a vibrant tourism industry which has, in turn, created job and small business opportunities, vital to poverty alleviation. The private sector has responded and progress is being made in the creation of new wildlife reserves.

The most dramatic development has been the creation of the transfrontier parks, which will, in my opinion, be the greatest development on the African continent for the next 100 years. We, as a country, serve as an example to the rest of the world, as these magnificent parks unfold owing to the combined efforts of inter-government co-operation, NGO support, private sector funding and community involvement.

Furthermore, Government has enabled the private sector to develop tourism in these parks. It would not be unreasonable to suggest that South Africa is leading the world in re-instating biodiversity on a macro scale, not to mention that our ecotourism model is recognised as a world leader.

I would concur that the marine coastal fisheries legislation by Government, whilst not perfect, has understood the pressing needs and dangers of overfishing and the importance of the maintenance of biodiversity both on land and in the sea. It is interesting to note the growth of marine ecotourism, especially whale and shark watching. As a passionate South African who has been involved in the conservation industry for more than 30 years, I salute the progress that is being made in promoting tourism and in the creation of new parks and conservancies. It is heartening to witness the advances being made in environmental management, particularly the care of river catchments. This will go a long way to alleviating regional poverty through the creation of business opportunities and the provision of natural resources (water) on a sustainable basis.

An issue that will, however, require more urgent attention is the continued degradation in many parts of South Africa due to inappropriate land use. SA is a low rainfall country. The legacy of the homeland system, combined with abusive farming practice, remains with us today.

In Africa, land is an emotive issue. However, in the final analysis, it is not who owns the land that matters, but that it is used in a sustainable manner. Government will need to ensure that legislation takes into account the inescapable

134

At its inception, the new SA Government understood the importance of sound environmental management and the promotion of tourism and how the two could work together to alleviate poverty

perspective

fact that land must be used in accordance with prevailing ecological conditions (rainfall, soil, etc.) if the long-term environmental strategy is to be sustainable. I am reminded of Alan Paton's passage in **Cry the Beloved Country**:

"The grass is rich and matted, you cannot see the soil. It holds the rain and mist. And they seep into the ground, feeding the streams in every kloof. It is well tended and not too many cattle feed on it, not too many fires burn it, laying bare the soil. Stand unshod upon it, for the ground is holy, being even as it came from the Creator. Keep it, guard it, care for it - for it keeps men, guards men, cares for men. Destroy it, and man is destroyed."

On the matter of ecotourism, I would caution in two areas. There is no doubt that the South African ecotourism models are economically and ecologically sustainable. However, at this time they are not politically sustainable. Transformation and equity participation in the industry must reflect South African society as a prerequisite for long-term sustainability. Both Government and the private sector will need to address this issue.

Equally, the previously disadvantaged rural communities of SA will need to move away from past entitlement attitudes towards a more progressive approach with new hope, new horizons and new initiatives.

Secondly, I would caution that we all recognise tourism as a double-edged sword. There are numerous examples across the world, where overuse of the natural resource has led to its destruction.

Africa, and in particular South Africa, still has a precious commodity - landscapes devoid of human intervention and development. Such wild, open spaces will become increasingly valuable and, therefore, any development on indigenous wild land should be undertaken with caution and we should, wherever possible, seek to advance the green frontiers and reduce development in those areas. Vigilance on the Environmental Impact Assessment process will need to be rigorous.

All South Africans should look back with pride over the achievements of the past eight years and give credit to our leadership. More importantly, we should look forward with hope and anticipation towards greater prosperity, providing we understand that there are limits to growth in tourism and the demands that can be realistically placed on the environment.

Dr Chrispian Olver's paper would suggest that his Minister and Government recognise both these facts and the many competing forces that are being imposed on the environment. The Department of Environmental Affairs and Tourism is doing an adequate job in addressing the issues coherently and in a balanced manner.

It is never a perfect world and there is always room for improvement. Particularly in the micromanagement of the multitude of projects currently underway in SA, more work is needed to clear the blockages and increase the co-operation. However, at a macro level we should acknowledge and celebrate **SOUTH AFRICA, The Good News** in environment and tourism, and look forward toward a common future where we are all proudly South African, with aligned interests.

"Ask not what your country can do for you, but what you can do for your country." John F Kennedy

You can wait for development to trickle down to you, or you can claim a spot in the queue for creative solutions.

How can you buy or sell the sky, the warmth of the land?

The idea is strange to us. If we do not own the freshness of the air and the sparkle of the water, how can you buy them? Every part of this earth is sacred to my people. The earth is our mother, we are part of the earth and it is part of us. The perfumed flowers are our sisters; the deer, the horse, the great eagle, these are our brothers. The rocky crests, the juices in the meadows, the body heat of the pony, and man ... all belong to the same family.

This shining water that moves in the streams and rivers, it is sacred. The rivers are our brothers, they quench our thirst and feed our children. Give the rivers the kindness you would give any brother.

We know that modern man does not understand our ways. He kidnaps the earth from his children. He treats his mother the earth, and his brother the sky, as things to be bought, plundered, sold like sheep or bright beads. His appetite will devour the earth and leave behind only a desert.

Our ways are different. The sight of cities pains the eyes. There is no quiet place. No place to hear the unfurling of leaves in spring or the rustle of the insect's wings. The clatter only seems to insult the ears. What is there to life if a man cannot hear the lonely cry of the whippoorwill or the arguments of the frogs around the pond at night?

The air is precious to us, for all things share the same breath, the beast, the tree, the man, they all share the same breath.

The wind that gave our grandfather his first breath also receives his last sigh. You must keep this place sacred as a place where man can go to taste the wind that is sweetened by the meadow's flowers.

Man must treat the beasts of this land as his brothers. For what is man without the beasts? If all the beasts were gone, man would die from a great loneliness of the spirit. For whatever happens to the beasts, soon happens to man. All things are connected.

You must teach your children so that they will respect the land. Teach your children that the earth is our mother. Whatever befalls the earth befalls the sons of earth. If men spit upon the ground, they spit upon themselves. The earth does not belong to man; man belongs to the earth. All things are connected like the blood which unites one family. All things are connected.

We may be brothers after all. Our God is the same God. His compassion is equal for all men. The earth is precious to Him, and to harm the earth is to heap contempt on its creator.

Our destiny is a mystery to us, for we do not understand when the buffalo are all slaughtered, the wild horses are tamed and the secret corners of the forest destroyed.

Where is the thicket? Gone.
Where is the eagle? Gone.
The end of living and the beginning of survival.

Even households with no income are scraping together a R400 fee for a yard water connection after Ronnie Kasrils, the Minister of Water Affairs and Forestry, kept a promise made in October 200,1 to bring piped water to the 40 000 people of the Oskraal district in North West Province.

By the beginning of this year, Kasrils' department had allocated R15 million to the project, enough to provide safe water to street standpipes in the villages of Oskraal, Rabokala, Madidi, Rankotia, Rampa and Ramogaodi, in the former Boputhatswana homeland, about 70 kilometres north-west of Pretoria.

This was set to be a life-changing transformation in a parched area where a few borehole owners have made a handsome living over the years by selling water to their neighbours. For the poorest of the poor – large families sustained by old age pensions – finding R10 a day to buy water (or walking several kilometres to collect water of dubious quality) made every day a struggle to survive.

But more good news was in store for the 5000 families in the six villages. The Madibeng Local Municipality (formerly the ultra-conservative Brits council) devised innovative financial gearing, including using high-quality PVC pipes donated to South Africa by the Peoples Republic of China, to reduce the standard R2200 yard-water connection fee to a more affordable R400.

Household connections, using a variable-flow valve invented by Brits Engineer, Malcolm Morris, ensured that every family could access the free monthly minimum supply of 6000 litres promised by the government in the Water For All campaign launched this year.

Councillor Jan Engelbrecht, the Madibeng executive member responsible for water and electricity, said he had been overwhelmed by the community's support and willingness to pay for the scheme in an area where the average income was around R1000 a month.

A key element of water supply projects is that they are designed to be labour intensive. Willie de Waal, the resident engineer for the Oskraal project contractor, Bigen Africa, said using manual labour for the laying of pipes and backfilling added about 20 per cent to the overall cost, but this was offset by the benefits of employing 300 people from the local community on the six-month project.

The Department of Water Affairs and Forestry's R4 billion rollout of clean drinking water to more than 7.4 million people since 1994 – more than half the estimated 14 million rural people who did not have access to safe water at the time of the first democratic election – is one of the country's biggest success stories.

"At our present rate of progress, the remaining 7 million people will all have received clean water by 2008, far surpassing the millennium target agreed by heads of state in 2000," Kasrils said on the eve of the World Summit for Sustainable Development. In KwaZulu-Natal "1.2 million people have been given accelerated access to piped water, protecting those communities from outbreaks of cholera that have affected rural communities in the province since dormant bacteria were activated by the floods in 2000".

In the parallel but more expensive and technically demanding area of Sanitation, Kasrils says the aim is to ensure that all people in the country enjoy basic sanitation by 2010. Basic sanitation is defined as a ventilated pit-latrine or equivalent, which does not pollute valuable ground-water reserves.

14

Businessmen and homekeepers know the formula well. One can only spend what one earns. And when the need for transformation is as large as it was for South Africa in 1994, it must have come as a great dissapointment to the ANC that the coffers were bare. The South African Revenue Service has dramatically changed this by increasing tax revenues while the Government simultaneously lowered tax rates. The ability of the Government to deliver over the last 8 years is in no small measure due to their success.

Tax Collection
Spreading the Net

Pravin Gordhan: Commissioner - South African Revenue Service

Editorial Comment

Enhanced tax collection is one of the major reasons that South Africa has been able to reduce its deficit from 7.6 per cent of GDP in 1993 to 1.6 per cent in 2002.

This has been acclaimed by the World Bank.

As Rudolf Gouws says (in Chapter 2): "A positive fiscal development is the fact that raising the tax-to-GDP ratio has not been as a result of higher taxes (these have in fact been reduced), but of greatly improved revenue collection. The benefits of this fiscal consolidation have been seen in, at first, the halting of a strong upward trend in the Government debt-to-GDP ratio and, since 1996, the decline in the ratio from 49.5 per cent to 42.9 per cent (with a projected fall to 37.4 per cent by 2004/5)."

It was critical to reduce the tax rate in order to position South Africa as an attractive nation for skilled people and new investments.

However, our transformation needed funding. It is to the credit of the ANC and the ability of SARS that prudent economic policy has prevailed. This has put the ANC into a position where it can responsibly improve the rate of welfare and support for social transformation while, at the same time, stimulating the economy through tax reduction. This is a significant achievement. As the IMF noted: "Recent changes in economic thinking in South Africa have been no less impressive than the country's political transformation."

In this chapter, Pravin Gordhan outlines the SARS strategy in continuing this good work.

Enhanced tax collection is one of the major enablers of
the Government's achievement in reducing our deficit from
7.6 per cent of GDP in 1993 to 1.6 per cent in 2002.

The number of active taxpayers has more than doubled since 1994 - a major reason for increased tax revenues.

Introduction

SARS, in terms of the South African Revenue Service Act, 1997 (Act 34 of 1997) is an organ of state within the public administration, but an institution outside of the public service.

SARS aims to provide improved, transparent and client-orientated service to ensure optimum and equitable collection of revenues.

Its main functions are to:
- Collect:
  - All national taxes, duties and levies
  - Revenue that may be accumulated under any other legislation, as is agreed upon between SARS and an organ of state or institution entitled to the revenue
- Protect the borders against illegal importation and exportation of goods
- Advise the minister on all revenue-related matters.

The Legacy Inherited After 1994

The former Inland Revenue and Customs and Excise Departments, inherited by SARS after 1994, were, in their time, an incubator and instrument of apartheid. SARS's transformation programme, Siyakha (We are Building), has, over the past four years, been radical enough to re-engineer the organisation into an efficient tax and customs administration. The legacy included:

Systems and Technology
- The organisation had limited automation and old, non-integrated systems coupled with outdated and/or unreliable hardware and software.

Processes
- SARS was a function-driven organisation and the processes were not integrated.

Human Resources
- The organisation had very limited skills in the fields of information technology, management and accounting. Instead, there was a steep organisational structure, which resulted in low staff morale and internal fraud.
- In terms of race and gender, there was a major imbalance.

Financial
- Although SARS is required to comply with GAAP in terms of the SARS Act, there were no definitive norms and standards for compiling annual financial statements. Poor systems and skill levels resulted in weak financial controls.

Communication and Service
- Communication, both internal and external, and taxpayer service, were extremely poor. There was a lack of control over key resources, such as border posts.

Tax Systems
- Following the demise of the homelands, SARS inherited 11 tax administrations, all with different rate structures. High corporate tax rates, fiscal drag, excessive exemptions, low compliance levels and high fraud had narrowed the tax base.

Customs
- A lack of proper systems and manual processes resulted in unreliable and inadequate data, prohibiting effective and efficient customs administration.

SARS's Key Achievements

To address the inefficiencies of the past, and in order to raise the status of the SARS as a leading revenue-collection and customs-control organisation, the Siyakha transformation initiative was implemented in 1999.

The foundations of Siyakha embrace our contribution to developmental governance and citizenship: "A culture in which both government and citizens have a mutual responsibility to sustain democracy and foster development".

The key challenges during the past four years included initiating innovative ways of reforming and modernising the tax system; introducing the capital gains tax; investing in human resource reorganisation and development; and building both regional and local partnerships with various stakeholders and taxpayer groups.

In 2002, SARS exceeded the printed revenue target of R234 billion by R15.2 billion.

Tax revenues are up over 150 per cent since 1994 but tax rates are down.

This surplus is mainly due to:

- Improved revenue collection: increases in a gross operating surplus of companies, higher commodity prices, faster processing of returns. Improved collection resulted in considerable growth in revenues.
- Compliance: a 62 per cent increase in audit results due to a more focused, targeted enforcement; the introduction of collections outbound call centres and improved anti-smuggling measures and border control have resulted in greater compliance.
- Special customer enforcement actions: round tripping in the fishing industry and improved drug seizures have increased customs enforcement.
- Operational policy changes: the introduction of computerised risk profiling and the introduction of integrated compliance across all tax types; the signing of memoranda of understanding with our neighbours has led to improved operational policy changes.
- Legislation: the introduction of capital gains tax and the changes to the Revenue Laws Amendment Act have improved collection.
- Strategy and planning: implementing a performance management system and formalising the business planning process have made a significant difference.

Actual Collections Per Year
Total Budget Revenue (as per budget review 2002)

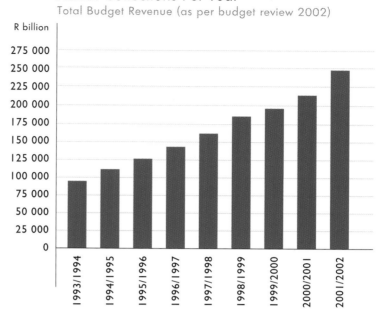

Number of Taxpayers Registered

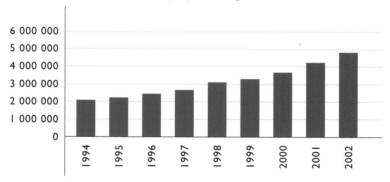

- Technology: improving the technology of collection in the area of capital gains tax, unemployment insurance, pay as you earn and systems-process security have improved efficiencies.
- Finance: an unqualified opinion on our own accounts for the past two successive years; the finalisation of Generally Recognised Accounting Practice (GRAP) and the progressive implementation of Generally Accepted Accounting Practice (GAAP) in respect of administrative revenue have made a significant difference.
- People: improved staff development; the deployment of management teams, the implementation of an Employee Assistance Programme, and the implementation of the Accredited Certified Chartered Accounts (ACCA) Qualification Programme have improved the competence of our staff enormously.

SARS interventions will reflect the optimal balance between encouraging and enforcing compliance.

- Service improvement: the establishment of a dedicated service presence in all our offices and the implementation of service performance measures; the monitoring of complaints and improved service at customs ports of entry have significantly improved our service delivery.

SARS's Future Prospects

Since 1994, SARS has steadily increased its effectiveness as an entity concerned with the collection of taxes, duties and levies. In the near future, there will be further enhancement of the organisational capability on an enterprise-wide basis, underpinned by technology enablement and cultural transformation.

SARS has made significant strides in the years following administrative autonomy, specifically in terms of enhancing processing efficiency and implementing a more focused compliance approach. More recently, the implementation of Siyakha in KZN heralded much-needed infrastructure and processing changes.

Building on this platform, technology enablement and a strategic enterprise-wide approach will be employed to enhance SARS change capability. The scope of transformation is clearly substantial and critical in order to enhance the economic and social well-being of the South African nation.

The following factors are imposing greater pressure for SARS to anticipate and lead change in South Africa in the near future:
- The speed of information transfer and the increasing pace of economic transactions

- The quality revolution and the need for greater accountability and value-add regarding the use of government resources
- The time compression of business cycles
- The influence of interactivity, proliferation of the Internet and increased volume of business transactions in the market place resulting from a networked, globalised world
- The changing landscape of business following the recent accounting scandals and misrepresentation in financial reporting
- A renewed and changing focus on national security in the wake of the September 11 terrorist attacks on the US
- Regional integration: SADC, financial and trade liberalisation and the impact of NEPAD
- The power and effectiveness of human and business networks, locally and internationally
- Adoption of mass service customisation and market segmentation philosophies
- A community approach to the way business, government and its citizens collaborate for a better and more effective and productive society.

The SARS response to these dynamic drivers will depend largely on its ability to conceptualise the future and turn that vision into a reality through strategic leadership and management. In addition, the organisational culture and learning environment will provide us with the required flexibility to respond timeously and appropriately to the changing internal and external environment.

A key component is the leveraging of scarce resources and core competence resulting from feasible integration of customs and tax administrations. As such, it will enable an integrated and unified view across taxpayers/traders affairs while still acknowledging the inherent peculiarities of each.

This approach dovetails with the next wave of SARS transformation that will see the strengthening of operational and strategic vehicles in an aligned way, supported by technology to herald in a new enterprise-wide performance and governance culture. Pivotal to the success of this phase will be the creation of adaptive legal, business and technology architectures, and strategic leadership to support and drive the planned changes.

SARS's new "electronic" administration - creates real-time transactions, reduced bureaucracy and less paperwork.

SARS will continue modernising and customising its services to serve the South African taxpaying population and trade community better. In seeking to optimise the compliance landscape in South Africa, SARS interventions will reflect the optimal balance between encouraging compliance and enforcing compliance.

In this regard, the legal, business and technology environment will facilitate the process of adequately and comprehensively addressing stakeholder needs and aspirations with due cognisance of the underlying compliance behaviour.

Strategic intent, and total business solutions that provide SARS with a comparative advantage to deliver its mandate, will provide the frame of reference. Value-added technology investments will deliver a key resource that will successfully position SARS as an "electronic" administration. This will entail offering multi-channel interactions and migrating to a real-time transacting environment that significantly reduces the need for bureaucratic paper processes: a policy that actively supports the South African e-government gateway.

The creation of significant organisational capability and flexibility in a learning environment will suitably position SARS to leverage on technology and shape the South African compliance landscape in a positive way that will yield innumerable benefits in the future. This is in addition to merely providing and sustaining the revenue on an annual basis to fund government spending.

Conclusion

It is often said that the only certainties in life are "death and taxes". We have been faced with considerable challenges in improving the tax net, tax administration, service and collection. We acknowledge that there is room for further improvement and we will continually strive to create the right balance between tax rates on the one hand and the extent of collection on the other.

The only certainties in life are "death and taxes" -
We are certain SARS would like to wish all South Africans a
longer and more prosperous life!

144
A Fresh Thought: Lower Taxes, More Revenue
Steven Levitt: Formerly Executive Director of Macsteel Holdings and Director of Companies

perspec*tive*

In 1999, I was asked by Pravin Gordhan, then Acting Commissioner for South African Revenue Services, to assist in building a new organisation. I agreed to commit limited time to the project but, after a few months, I found that there was so much to do, working amidst individuals spurred on by passion, that my involvement spanned nearly a year.

Under different circumstances, SARS would have been defined as a superb business model. More than 100 branches throughout the country, not to mention the collection points at every border; and its cost to income ratio was a meagre one per cent of revenues generated. Yet the organisation was suffering from the effects of its new-found freedom, released from the shackles of public service, while operating as a public administrator under state control. Elementary tools such as cost budgets, with which to pace the expenditure patterns of the organisation seemed to have fallen by the wayside, or were not redesigned to cope with the new independence.

Coupled with this was an even tougher minded National Treasury, determined to curtail overspend by government departments while, simultaneously, insisting that all operate within allocated expenditure constraints. My experience and interests were soon put to work to assist with rebuilding the basics.

There are two overlying thoughts that capture my recollections during my early involvement in this project. The first is that, as is so often the case in the business world, the choice of the CEO may appear controversial from the outside and, in this instance, the new commissioner's qualifications were more in keeping with, perhaps, the academic world.

A fresh approach is what transpired, with the kind of intellect and latitude that many organisations aspire to when confronted with change. Civil servants, many of whom had grown up in a system that fostered compliance within tight constraints, were finding themselves led by a new breed of manager.

Pravin Gordhan actively encouraged free thought. Executive meetings seldom adhered to the formal agenda. New ideas were brainstormed and innovative approaches evolved. Then, a combination of a formal secretariat and the need for fast action, ensured that the matter was attended to at the very next opportunity.

Employees who were too fixed in the old mould blended into the tapestry of the existing 14 000 employees (whose profile is only too well understood by the taxpayer!). On the other hand, young and energetic members of the workforce were swiftly identified and given new mandates and responsibilities.

Seldom was the refrain heard that members of the formerly disadvantaged communities did not possess the skills necessary to do the job. The profile at the top was systematically altered, almost on a monthly basis, and those who coped with the rigours of executive responsibility thrived. Very soon, those with qualities found their comfort levels, in many cases very different from their past work experience.

Business people will generally concur that most organisations benefit from fresh thought and an attitude that turns things inside out. And, the further removed an entrepreneur is from daily functions, the more chance there is of excessive spend to continue with the status quo.

Budgeted annual resource allocation was then already in excess of R2 billion and tender processes and commitments tended to concentrate heavily on due process, and less on evaluation of effective alternatives. There were significant savings on basic costs as we rethought the rationale for expenditure structures and renegotiated with suppliers.

If government departments equipped themselves to deal with the private sector on an equal footing, the savings in spend would be matched by a compensating reduction in the exceptional margins that many private sector businesses covet from their sales to the public sector, for the benefit of all.

To my mind this is exactly what SARS has done and it is not by coincidence that the state revenue collection has been so meaningfully improved.

Young, energetic employees were swiftly identified and given new mandates. It is no coincidence that revenue collection has improved.

Of the entire fabric of South African life, sport has along with Nelson Mandela played the greatest role in bringing our nation together. When the anthem is played and the flags are flying there is hardly a spectator who does not feel a special pride. Over the last 8 years our children have begun to witness that it is talent and determination, not colour, race or creed that distinguishes sports people. Sport is the leading edge example of what empowerment, active cooperation and respect can yield.

Sport

Isolation, Transformation, Emulation

Dr Joe Phaahla: CEO of the South African Sports Commission

Isolation – Running an Uneven Race

During the years of isolation, sport was characterised by clandestine agreements between the previous Government and the corporate sector for the benefit of both sides. Boycotts were countered by pumping finance into rebel tours and receiving tax rebates in return. Although it may be argued that, initially, isolation did have spin-offs for these beneficiaries (at the expense of the majority of the oppressed people), eventually the "No normal sport in an abnormal society" slogan began to take its toll.

During this time, it was broadly the white South African sports people who enjoyed international participation as they were affiliated to organisations that resisted the isolation strategy of the global anti-apartheid movement.

"Madiba Magic" virtually assured success in the early days. Playing for your country took on a whole new meaning.

saw this as an opportunity to develop strategies for catching up with the rest of the world. To some extent this is still the case.

Bringing together a divided people after so many years remains a major task for most sporting codes, although there are some wonderful examples of success.

Participation – The Playing Fields Even

During the early 1990s, more South Africans were able to represent their country on the world stage. Not surprisingly, the support they received was overwhelming. "Madiba Magic" became the catchword as Mandela's support at various events became part of his statesmanship.

Our athletes were given a resounding welcome at the Olympic Games in Barcelona in 1992 (before our first election), as an integrated team under a neutral flag with the IOC anthem. This was followed by the 1994 Commonwealth Games in Victoria, Canada. Winning the World Cup Rugby (1995), and the Africa Cup of Nations (1996) and being overall winners in the 1995 All Africa Games in Zimbabwe were resounding achievements. This was followed by an increase in the medal count during the subsequent Olympic Games in Atlanta in 1996, securing the bronze medal in the World Cup Netball in 1995 and finishing a credible fifth position in the Commonwealth Games in Kuala Lumpur (1998) and in Manchester (2002). We continued to do well in a number of other sporting events and were again overall winner at the All Africa Games in 1999 (Johannesburg). In the Cricket World Cup in 1999 we lost the semi-final to Australia. Josiah Tugwane won the gold medal in the marathon at the Atlanta Olympics in 1996; and we have qualified twice for the Soccer World Cup.

We also managed to host several global events in South Africa and were lauded for the professional manner in which this was done.

These events ranged from minor individual sports to macro events such as:
- World Beach Volleyball Tournament in 1994 and 1995
- World Corporate Games in Johannesburg (1994)
- African Junior Table Tennis competition in 1996

While these tactics were being employed to counteract isolation, sporting losses were suffered by all South Africans, both black and white:

- Declining technical skills at international level
- Non-participation at international level
- Non-recognition of performances of athletes and officials
- Stigma of being associated with racism and
- Lack of appropriate development consistent with global best practice.

These losses were largely overlooked as white South Africans continued to interact informally with the West and the Americas while sham events like the Black XI vs White XI soccer matches divided people even further.

During the late 1980s and early 90s, more and more South Africans became disaffected with the artificial divisions in sport. Concurrently there were black athletes and officials who felt that they were not prepared to waste their talent during the period of isolation and were doing everything in their power to engage with the outside world while also condemning apartheid. Some of these athletes and officials ultimately took up citizenship in other countries and turned away from pursuing their efforts to end apartheid. When the boycott ended in the early 90s, we were faced with new challenges to integrate and unite sports federations and manage the re-entry of South Africa into the international arena.

The levels of interest from the various sectors differed - white sport federations were hungry for world competition, black sport federations were ill-prepared and largely ill-equipped. Most of our representative teams were mainly white and not representative of the majority, but were ready for competition; whereas most of our "black" teams

Paralympic Games - South Africa: Medals (1992-2000)

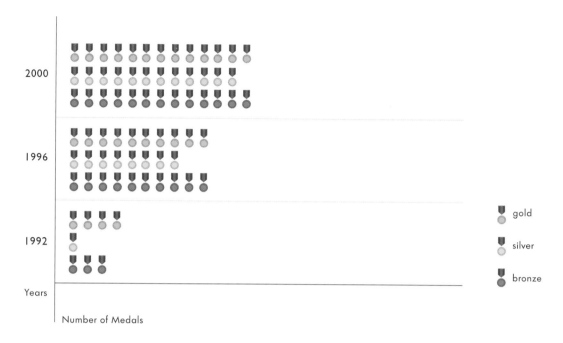

- African Cup of Nations in 1996
- World Cup Rugby in 1995
- All Africa Games in 1999 and
- The Lennox Lewis/Hassim Rahman boxing bonanza.

Following the internationally acknowledged success of the World Summit on Sustainable Development in Johannesburg, we are confident of being awarded the Football World Cup in 2010.

Having some of our local boys signing up with some of the top European teams (Sibusiso Zuma - Denmark; Lucas Radebe - Leeds; Quinton Fortune - Manchester United and Benni McCarthy - Ajax Amsterdam) is cause for celebration. Individual athletes have also continued to make us proud: Ernie Els and Retief Goosen in golf, Baby Jake Matlala in boxing and our various track and field athletes and swimmers.

It should however not be forgotten that some of our biggest ambassadors have been the Amakrokokroko in the Paralympic Games. The team finished a remarkable 13th out of 122 countries with 38 medals (13 gold, 12 silver and 13 bronze) in 2000.

Bringing together a divided people after so many years remains a major task. But there are wonderful examples.

Olympic Games – South Africa: Medals (1992-2000)

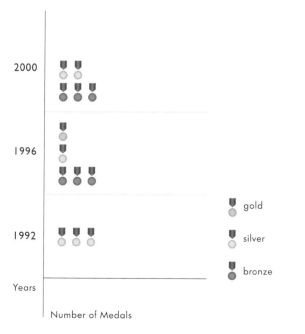

Years

Number of Medals

Commonwealth Games – South Africa: Medals (1994-2002)

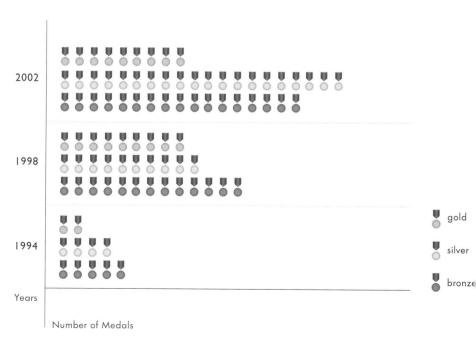

Years

Number of Medals

The South African Sports Commission was established in 1998 to co-ordinate, promote, develop, administer and resource sport and recreation. This included co-ordinating the various sporting bodies and federations across the country.

The Sports Commission vision is to lead South Africa to world-class sporting excellence, and specifically to:
- Improve opportunities for all South Africans to participate in sport and recreation;
- Work in partnership with stakeholders by striving to meet their human resource and infrastructure needs; and
- Ensure the management, promotion and co-ordination of sport and recreation is administered with excellence.

The extent to which these objectives have been achieved is exemplified by the recent scrapping of quotas in cricket at the highest level and the growing number of black rugby stars playing first-class rugby and in the Springbok team, just to mention two. There is now a truly positive atmosphere on our sporting fields and in our stadiums. Participation across the board demonstrates a great belief in the country and its abilities. This was marked by the unified support in the bid for hosting the Olympic Games 2004 in Cape Town as well as the rekindled bid for the 2010 Soccer World Cup event after the first attempt (for 2006) eluded us.

Emulation – an International Benchmark

The management of sport (both technically and in its role as a source of national pride) in South Africa has become the role model for the rest of the continent as illustrated by the assistance rendered to the hosting of the African Cup of Nations in Burkina Faso (2000) and in Mali (2002).

More recently, a delegation from Northern Ireland, interested in how we have managed to integrate our sport, remarked that our achievements are generally regarded as the international benchmark, especially the sense of unity created for the average South African. Their primary interest was how to change the political climate - using sport as the imperative.

Sport showed South Africans of all colours that they were stronger together.

Conclusion

Sport has made a major contribution to changes in our political climate. Just visit any sports stadium at any event: the spectators are unified behind the flag, behind our teams and behind each other. Our sportsmen and women are held in high regard no matter what their discipline, and our reputation as an international sporting venue improves every year.

The recent staging of the inaugural South African Youth Games in Tshwane is yet another milestone in delivering a truly diverse and unified society. The spirit that was displayed by the participants, while supporting each other in the quest for medals, was clearly heartwarming as it transposed our history. The games displayed not only multiracialism, but multiculturalism.

Sport is probably one of the best examples of empowerment in South Africa and has been responsible for creating:

- Opportunities for the underprivileged with talent;
- Heroes in new parts of the country;
- Acceptance that quotas can be positive initially, and can be quickly removed once they've done their job;
- A growing sense of community and national spirit; and
- A world-first in the compilation of a national anthem (combining the old with the new) that every South African is proud of!

Remarkably, the South African miracle continues as more and more sportsmen and women from all walks of South African life become outstanding ambassadors for our country.

We have transformed our sport from divisional to integrational over the last eight years.

Basil D'Oliveira is a name that has a special meaning for South African cricket. In 1968, the South African Government banned D'Oliveira from participating in a tour of this country by the English national cricket team on the basis that he was a "coloured" person from Cape Town.

D'Oliveira, a right hander with a test average of more than 40, had emigrated to the United Kingdom because of racial discrimination in South African sport and, on the basis of his skin colour, he was declared unwelcome in the country by then prime minister, BJ Vorster.

The incident precipitated South Africa's 20-year ban from the international game, but today, cricket is at the forefront of transformation and deracialisation of South African sport.

Since unbanning, cricket has worked hard at changing its image, and the introduction of programmes aimed at including the black majority has led to the inclusion of black players of such quality that they can no longer be referred to as "affirmative action" choices.

Today, Herschelle Gibbs, another Cape Town "coloured", is first choice as South Africa's opening batsman. Makhaya Ntini is a top black fast bowler from the Eastern Cape and other black players such as Justin Ontong, Roger Telemachus, Mfuneko Ngam and Ashwell Prince make regular appearances in the South African side.

A young man from Soweto, however, probably best illustrates how much the game has actually changed since the days of Vorster and D'Oliveira. Enoch Nkwe is 19 years old, and played his maiden game for the Gauteng provincial team in the early summer of the 2002/2003 season. Nkwe not only scored a century in his first-class debut, but also became the youngest ever centurion for his province. The tonne did not come easily.

The team was on the brink of disaster on 117 for 5 when Nkwe walked to the crease. He occupied it for the best part of six hours, in an innings reminiscent of Michael Atherton at his tenacious best. This meant having to contend with the frustrations of fast bowler, Andre Nel, who had already made a name for himself by hitting South Africa's

best-loved fast bowler, Alan Donald, on the head in a provincial game.

Nkwe was in the nervous 90s when he gently drove a ball straight back to Nel, who retaliated by throwing it at the batsman, hitting him on the ankle, and leaving him writhing in pain for several minutes. Nkwe got up, made his hundred, and was eventually out for 106.

Even non-cricketers paid attention to this event. Not only was it a maiden debut, but Nkwe's stoic defence, vicious square cutting and above all, his ability to keep calm under the most trying circumstances, made him an instant hero.

At the age of 11, Nkwe first encountered the sport while waiting for a schoolfriend. He watched a game in progress, and was asked whether he would like to take part. "I wasn't doing anything and I thought I'd join in. Their coach asked me if I wanted to play the game. At that time I didn't really give a damn about cricket and never really knew what it was about."

Even non-cricketers paid attention to Nkwe's 106. It was a symbol of the untapped human potential in our country.

After playing in the junior leagues, he was offered a bursary to one of Johannesburg's top cricketing schools, St Stithians College, where his game was developed under close mentorship. In making his first first-class century, Nkwe may have done more than most people for South African cricket, sport and race relations.

His remarks afterwards bear testimony to this: "I felt honoured (making the century). I will tell my township folks to persevere with playing the game, to believe in themselves and have faith in their ability."

16

Crime is one of the single biggest reasons that many of our most productive people have left our shores. And although crime levels worldwide are rapidly increasing, the lack of substantial progress in law and order in South Africa is simply unacceptable to the majority of the population. With public/private sector partnerships that are amongst the most innovative in the world, not only are we beginning to turn the tide, but we are establishing new approaches and new technologies that are becoming international benchmarks.

Crime is still a problem in SA, but remarkable success has been achived in stabilising it and bringing it under control.

The War Against Crime

Is the tide starting to turn?
Bold initiatives taken years ago are starting to pay off.

James Fitzgerald: Chairman of Business against Crime

Crime is still a problem in South Africa, but remarkable success has been achieved in stabilising it and bringing it under control, thanks to efforts from government, the police and the private sector.

For example:

- Courts have been streamlined to handle cases faster and more efficiently.
- Corruption is being eliminated from vehicle registration offices.
- The disappearance of dockets - once a favourite method for offenders to escape punishment - has been eliminated at many courts.
- The illegal re-registration of vehicles - a preferred method of putting stolen or hijacked cars back on the road - has been eliminated at six major licensing offices in Gauteng, SA's largest province.
- Video surveillance in city centres has dramatically cut street crime, prompting businesses and shoppers to consider returning, or, at least, not leaving.
- Sexual offences are being handled with greater efficiency and sensitivity, while victims are getting much-needed support.
- The fight against commercial and organised crime has already led to landmark convictions.
- The partnership between the private sector initiative, Business Against Crime (BAC), and the Government, is being hailed as one of the best in the world.
- The country is attracting more foreign investment, tourism, and international conferences like the recent World Summit on Sustainable Development, signifying a growing sense of security among foreigners.

Even though these and other projects may not have been rolled out to the whole country, they represent a significant start.

Bold Initiatives Mark the Start of a Fight

The first step in 1996 was the preparation of a National Crime Prevention Strategy (NCPS) by the Government, in conjunction with the private sector. This was followed by the appointment of Meyer Kahn, head of one of SA's largest corporations, as Chief Executive Officer of the SA Police Service, for a two-year period. With funding from the private sector, additional full-time business executives were appointed to assist in the implementation of the NCPS. And then, late in 1996, following an appeal to the business community by Nelson Mandela, Business Against Crime (BAC), was formed. This business coalition pooled its expertise, time and money to partner government in the fight against crime by bringing a corporate approach to strategy, transferring appropriate skills and driving deliverable solutions to specific projects. So much so that Deputy President, Jacob Zuma, recently hailed the partnership as unique and recommitted government to on-going support.

Senior business executives now sit on the newly-formed board of directors of the Department of Justice and Constitutional Development (DoJ & CD), which operates in an advisory and good governance capacity, complete with an audit, remuneration and budget committee to ensure a new, commercialised framework.

The business coalition has pooled its expertise, time and money to partner government in the fight against crime.

A Performance Enhancement Programme (PEP) by the DoJ & CD and a Service Delivery Improvement Programme (SDIP) by the South African Police Service (SAPS) is now achieving sustainable results. In recognition of the work done by all, Mr Hassen Ebrahim, a Deputy Director-General in the DoJ & CD has recently been nominated as one of the finalists for the African Achievers Award in the category of Public Sector Service Delivery. While crime figures in certain categories remain high, the most violent crimes such as armed robbery, murder and rape have stabilised, albeit at unacceptably high levels.

Rape Rate: January to September 1994-2001

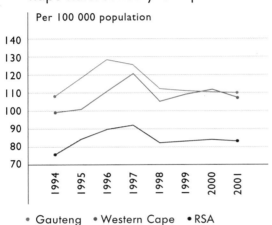

Per 100 000 population

• Gauteng • Western Cape • RSA

Murder Rate: January to September 1994-2001

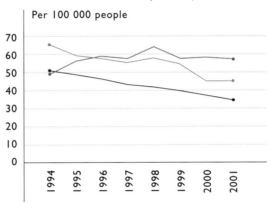

Per 100 000 people

• Gauteng • Western Cape • SA

Upgrading the Criminal Justice System

The Integrated Justice Programme, at a cost of R2 billion is upgrading the country's once creaking criminal justice system, with a suite of projects and initiatives to be delivered over five years.

This programme is ratified and supported by international organisations and local agencies such as the European Union, the Royal Netherlands, USAID, the South African Business Trust, Business Against Crime and Irish Aid. It aims to ensure that offenders are effectively managed throughout the process of investigation, prosecution and incarceration, and that justice is effected swiftly.

Pilot project results have been spectacular:
- The time it takes to bring a case to court at the revamped Port Elizabeth court centre has dropped by 178 days and saved the taxpayer more than R8 million.
- The percentage of cases finalised within the 60-day target set for magistrates' courts increased by 17 cases per court from 365 to 382, again representing sizeable savings for the taxpayer.

- Improved work procedures saw the average case preparation time fall by 11 days from 173 days to 162 days, ensuring a speedier trial for suspects.
- Police dockets that once disappeared at the rate of up to 27 a month are now available without fail on the day the accused is brought to trial.

Case Processing Time (Average)

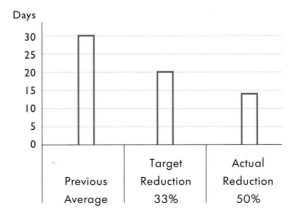

Days

| | Previous Average | Target Reduction 33% | Actual Reduction 50% |

And, in an exciting new development, the United States Agency for International Development (USAID) has financed a $25 million Criminal Justice Strengthening Programme (CJSP) in conjunction with the Department of Justice and Constitutional Development and BAC over three years to make significant improvements through projects that address court services, sexual offences, prosecution, legal education and finance.

Unquestionably the programme will have far-reaching effects on the administration of justice in South Africa by:

- Improving capacity and reducing the backlog at courts
- Reducing the number of prisoners awaiting trial through swifter trials, and reducing pressure on overcrowded jails
- Treating victims of sex-related crime with greater sensitivity
- Improving case-management control to stop cases falling through the cracks .

The four business units within the Department that will directly lead the programme include: Court Services, the Sexual Offences and Community Affairs Unit of the National Prosecuting Authority, the Justice College and the Office of the Chief Financial Officer.

Cutting Crime in Schools

The Thiisa Thuto schools crime prevention programme has been a huge success - and has been adopted by the United Nations, which describes it as the best of its kind in the world.

The pilot programme run at 44 Soweto schools saw crime across the board plummet by 78 per cent from August 2000 to July 2001 while attendance increased by 70 per cent over the same period.

And, thanks to the introduction of non-violent means of conflict resolution, pass rates at schools where the project is running increased by 87 per cent during the same period. Parents have reported that even discipline at home has improved.

Because of its success, this programme, spearheaded by Business Against Crime, is being implemented in many other parts of the country by government agencies.

These are the Thiisa Thuto schools crime prevention programme results

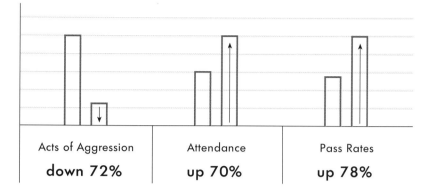

Acts of Aggression	Attendance	Pass Rates
down 72%	**up 70%**	**up 78%**

"Thiisa Thuto," the schools crime prevention programme, has been adopted by the United Nations as the best of its kind in the world.

Increase in Number of Convictions (Pretoria Initiative)

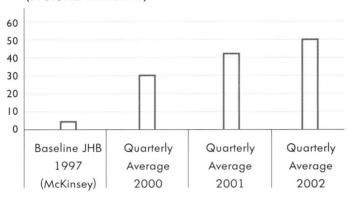

1200% Increase!

Conviction Rate (%) Planned vs Actual

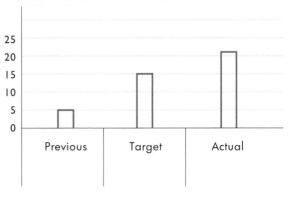

400% Increase!

Cracking Down on Commercial Crime

- The Commercial Crime Project has resulted in the perpetrators of commercial crime being increasingly brought to book. For example, three people who masterminded a R35 milllion share fraud scheme were recently convicted; and a landmark legal precedent was established with the first-ever plea-bargain judgement.
- The first successful racketeering case was brought against a foreign resident who used a fake Reserve Bank website to commit fraud against victims worldwide.
- An offender (in a telling demonstration of the co-operation between government and the private sector), changed his plea to guilty on over 100 charges of fraud after being faced with senior counsel from the private sector acting for the prosecution.

The entire fight against commercial crime is a collective effort between Business Against Crime, the police, the National Prosecuting Authority, the Department of Justice and Constitutional Development and various business associations. A trust fund has been established that allows the state to engage the best senior counsel in the private sector to manage the prosecution in complex commercial cases.

Commercial crime detectives have gone on specially designed training courses, and legislation has been enacted to give the commercial crime units greater rights in handling the proceeds of crime and seizing the assets of suspected criminals.

New computer systems have been installed to enable a co-ordinated and integrated approach to syndicate crime activity, structural changes have been made in the police's commercial crime units, and closer ties have been forged between these units and the Office for Serious Economic Offences.

Partnering Against Organised Crime

The fight against organised crime is another example of effective partnership between the public sector and the private sector, covering syndicated crimes in:

- Drugs
- Corruption
- Illegal firearms
- Vehicle theft (with 120 000 cars stolen or hi-jacked every year, there is special emphasis on this).

The vehicle crime programme is geared towards removing the commercial benefit derived from stolen vehicles and vehicle parts, and to increase syndicate crime prosecution. Its most notable achievements are:

- The fraudulent registration of vehicles - one of the most favoured methods of re-registering hijacked and stolen vehicles - has been reduced to almost nothing at the six licensing offices where the programme is running, while more than 200 cases of fraud are pending against previously corrupt employees.
- Vehicle parts, vehicle accessories and copper cable were incorporated into the Second-hand Goods Act with effect from January 2000.

> The new system should bring vehicle crime under control within the next few years.
> Guus Wesselink - Netherlands

- Electronic information interfaces were built between the police and the Department of Transport to facilitate mutual access to vital information.
- The private and public sectors have agreed to a national vehicle identification programme aimed at verifying all vehicles in the national car park. The objective of this plan, which is currently being worked on, is to remove all illegally registered vehicles from the roads.
- Illegal vehicle parts businesses (chop shops) are being identified and closed down through joint operations by the police, army, air force and the Department of Justice and Constitutional Development. Business Against Crime contributes to the strategic and tactical planning of the operations, and provides operational project management skills. (In a recent operation, more than 20 suspected illegal chop shops were raided, resulting in over 100 criminal cases being opened after the discovery of more than 80 stolen vehicles and 23 000 distinct car parts ranging from doors to engines.)

At a conference on vehicle crime held in Pretoria in July 2002, Guus Wesselink, Director of the Foundation for Tackling Vehicle Crime in the Netherlands, said: "New systems being implemented by all relevant government departments and members of the private sector, assisted by Business Against Crime, should bring it under control within the next few years."

Ray Carroll, Executive Director of the National Motor Vehicle Theft Reduction Council of Australia, said: "There are only three effective partnerships between the public sector and the private sector in vehicle crime prevention in the world.

The Business Against Crime model is so good that it could be transplanted virtually intact to almost any country where vehicle crime is a problem."

Video Surveillance Reduces Street Crime

Operated in conjunction with law enforcement agencies, local government and municipalities, the Video Surveillance Programme has reduced street crime by up to 80 per cent wherever it is in operation. Conviction rates have gone up, average response time to incidents has come down to under one minute, and the number of police required to patrol the areas has been reduced by 90 per cent.

The programme, started in Cape Town, has now been introduced to Johannesburg where dozens of video cameras keep a watchful eye over the Central Business District. The most conservative estimate is that it has reduced street crime there by 60 per cent.

And Elsewhere on the Crime Front

In order to improve the quality of justice in the old "homeland" states established by the previous government, magistrates and prosecutors will receive on-the-job training from retired magistrates and prosecutors.

Corruption and theft of trust monies (fines, alimony, bail, etc.) within the justice system is under scrutiny, and outsourcing the handling of cash to commercial banks is being evaluated.

Divorced women in rural areas who currently have to travel long distances to collect their alimony grants will see a new, more user-friendly and secure system that will enable them to draw their money at local pay points.

Our challenge is to roll out our successful pilot projects, and roll back the criminals.

Courts are being made more accessible and efficient through the appointment of professional managers to relieve magistrates and prosecutors of their day-to-day administrative duties. Currently, some 20 administrative managers and 52 financial managers are being appointed to manage a national standardisation of service delivery at court level.

Within the police force, a business partnership network with local police service centres has been established in 107 locations of the targeted 340 places that account for 85 per cent of the crime in South Africa. In addition, 119 victim support schemes provide free and confidential counselling to nearly 5000 victims of crime every month - most of whom previously could not afford this service. It has been described as "world class" by none other than Dame Helen Reeves, Chief Executive of Victim Support in the United Kingdom.

Conclusion

There is no question that we have turned the corner in the "war against crime" and it is encouraging to review the extent of co-operation between government, the private sector and the general public in what is increasingly being viewed as world-class practice.

Over the past 6 years, the piloting of the projects described in this chapter have set our course. Our challenge now is to roll them out and to roll back the criminals.

Most commentators will agree, crime is on the increase worldwide. As **Time Magazine** said in their 2001 annual review of the future: "One of the major challenges we face is who is in charge - the good guys or the bad guys?"

It is heartwarming to note just how many of the crime fighting initiatives undertaken in South Africa have attracted praise from overseas countries - perhaps the surest sign yet that we are on the right track.

Of course, we've still got a long way to go; but we have turned the tide.

Tell the story of how two female European tourists were seen window-shopping, late one Saturday night on the mean streets of downtown Johannesburg, and watch the shocked expressions as the listeners prepare themselves for another tale of horror.

But, this story has a happy ending. Blissfully unaware that protective eyes were watching them, the carefree duo spent a couple of hours wandering the pavements, "on the wrong side of the tracks", before taking a taxi back to their suburban hotel.

Two years ago, chances were that the pair would have been robbed or worse - another bloody statistic in what used to be the murder capital of the world. "Used to be, but not any more," says Russell Williams as he demonstrates how the matrix of high-powered cameras that make up the City of Johannesburg's electronic surveillance system was able to watch every step the women took, while street-wise camera operators warned nearby police patrols to keep a discreet eye on them. "In Johannesburg, Big Brother is not watching you," says Russell. "He's is watching over you and he is winning the war against crime." In the 30 square-kilometre monitored area, the surveillance system has:

- Helped reduce crime by more than 60 per cent
- Cut police emergency response times to 60 seconds
- underpinned the restoration of growing public confidence in the CBD.

Street crime - muggings, hi-jackings, armed robberies, rapes and murders - rose to alarming levels in the city in the late 1990s. Visitors were warned to stay off the streets and people from the suburbs were afraid to venture into Africa's biggest commercial hub. Fear of crime topped the list of reasons businesses gave as they fled the city in droves, leaving office buildings empty and accelerating the cycle of decay and despair. Falling crime figures are only part of the story. The success of the public-private sector drive to revitalise the CBD (which has a capital base of R35 billion) can also be measured in declining A-grade office vacancies, and rising interest in inner-city properties and development opportunities. Business Against Crime Surveillance Technology, a company set up to establish and operate the facility's management system, started work in April 2000 in partnership with the Johannesburg Development Agency, the South African Police Service and the Johannesburg Metropolitan Police Department. The network is also being used by traffic officials for event management, and by facilities managers for maintenance inspections.

Crime figures are only part of the story. A Grade office vancancies are also in decline.

The inner city's surveillance network was increased to 200 cameras ahead of the World Summit on Sustainable Development held in August 2002 and another 120 cameras will be installed by the end of the year. The whole system was designed and developed in South Africa and uses high-powered, US-made, Sensormatic cameras, but 78 per cent of the equipment for the network was sourced and manufactured locally.

A key element is that each camera can be watched by the others around it and the performance of the network is ensured by adherence to international ISO9000 quality-assurance standards. The intuition and experience of the more than 120 operators who monitor the screens around the clock help them read body language and recognise danger signs, enabling them to despatch police to approach and deter a suspect, or render assistance, before someone has called for help. "Most people don't know where the cameras are or who is watching but they know they are being taken care of," says Williams.

Crime in the 30 square kilometre area has declined by 60 per cent. Police emergency response time has been cut to 60 seconds.

We have understood for some time the Black Economic Empowerment principles that will underpin the Government's new BEE strategy to be issued towards the end of 2002. If one regards them solely from the moral point of view, they surely are easy to defend. But in this chapter, for the first time, the real power of the capacity effects of true empowerment become both crystal clear and compelling. After all, what would our national cricket team be without Ntini and Gibbs?

Black Economic Empowerment
Changing the South African Business Landscape

Cyril Ramaphosa

The BEE process is intended as a collaborative one.

Where were we?

In 1993, Sanlam sold 10 per cent of its stake in Metropolitan to a black consortium called Methold in what became known as the first empowerment transaction. Since then, the SA business landscape has been fundamentally transformed by black economic empowerment or BEE.

These transactional activities are only one component of BEE though many of the early deals were wiped out by the 1998 market crash. Other areas of BEE activity in companies include increasing support for small business development through targeted procurement, employment equity reporting and the design of skills development plans.

From Government's perspective, various programmes and strategies have been implemented. These are aimed at economically empowering previously disadvantaged people, and include:
· Infrastructure development programmes
· Land reform
· Human resource development.

To some, BEE seems to have travelled full circle. Looking back they ask whether we have made much progress?

Schisms in the Landscape

South African society does remain characterised by vast inequalities in income and access to productive assets. Women still remain subordinated in terms of income, job opportunities and power relations.

Ownership and the control by black people of key industries and of productive land, remains minimal. In the skilled professions and in the ownership and management of small and medium-sized enterprise, there remains limited participation by black people. The economic structure still excludes the vast majority from ownership of fixed assets and the possession of advanced skills that would facilitate the accumulation of wealth.

However, despite this performance, BEE has transformed and will continue to transform the business landscape.

What is meant by BEE?

Our understanding of BEE and the complexities in implementation has vastly improved. Much of this is as a result of the experiences of black business people and the, often hard, lessons they have learnt.

The Black Economic Empowerment Commission (BEECom), which falls under the auspices of the Black Business Council (BBC), also added tremendous insight into BEE, through its analysis of these experiences and its consideration of the meaning and rationale of BEE.

Since the term BEE was first used in the early 1990s, there have been two interpretations of the concept. First, there was a narrow definition that was promoted by the media, the corporate sector and financial institutions. According to this definition, BEE is equated with the development of a black capitalist class. The narrow definition focuses on the entry and transaction activities of black people in business.

The 1994 economy had neither the income levels nor advanced entrepreneurial and skills levels to sustain growth.

The second is a broad definition that has since been adopted by the Black Economic Empowerment Commission. It argues that BEE is:

- An integrated and coherent socio-economic process
- Located in the context of the country's national transformation programme, the RDP
- Aimed at redressing the imbalances of the past by seeking to substantially and equitably transfer and confer the ownership, management and control of South Africa's financial and economic resources to the majority of its citizens
- Ensuring broader and meaningful participation in the economy by black people to achieve sustainable development and prosperity.

This definition, as put forward by the BEECom and contained in a report it submitted to Government in March 2001, has, in principle, been accepted by the Government. The BEECom argued that there is both a moral and an economic case for the implementation of an integrated national BEE strategy and that it is not possible to achieve sustained, higher levels of economic growth without targeted programmes to increase substantially black participation in the economy. Following the submission of the BEECom report, Government began drafting a strategy on BEE to outline its understanding of the core interventions.

The BEE Commission argued that there is both a moral and an economic case for true empowerment.

The Cabinet Legkotla, in January 2002, considered a draft of the Government's strategy on BEE. The President's State of the Nation address in February referred to it in some detail. Giving approval in principle, the July Legkotla asked for a final document to be submitted to Cabinet.

The adoption of a BEE strategy is imminent and can be expected before the close of the year (2002). Many of the initiatives, which have been raised in relation to the strategy, are being implemented.

Government's commitment to promote certainty through clear policy, guidelines and regulation as well as more

effective use of its instruments to channel support to BEE, is extremely positive and signifies a move towards a more sustainable BEE through the participation of all businesses and stakeholders.

BEE - Are there benefits?
Beyond definitional issues, the economy and business have already benefited from increasing participation by black people. Despite the barriers, there are new entrants in most sectors of the economy and there is increasing awareness of corporations towards the need to broaden the shareholder base and to take heed of the interests of consumers or communities. New business opportunities have been created through government procurement, licensing activities, and the private sector implementing targeted procurement policies.

In most industries, there are black people with an increasingly influential stake over the direction of business and there are black companies who we can say are key industry players.

Those companies that have embraced the elements of BEE have been able to expand their market share through access to new business and thereby grow their companies.

Black people participating at a professional or executive level in the management teams and boards of corporations have added new experience and views in the traditionally closed boardroom environs.

Government's financial institutions have developed innovative ways of providing finance to support BEE entrants in competitive sectors of the economy and learnt valuable lessons about providing packaged support to suit the different needs of entrepreneurs.

Stakeholders in the liquid fuels and mining sectors have agreed on BEE charters that outline targets and instruments for their industries and, in the financial sector, there is activity to prepare a charter.

Companies are reporting on employment equity, and are implementing skills-development plans; and all stakeholders are beginning to understand the central role of Sector Educations and Training Authorities (SETAs).

Higher growth rates and more equitable income distribution are not possible until the majority are productively integrated into the economy.

There are attempts to broaden the ownership base through innovative community empowerment schemes, employee and retail schemes, as well as to support to collective forms of ownership.

A Landscape with Fewer Schisms

While we are still far from where we want to be, South Africa has a very different business environment from the one we had eight years ago. BEE has transformed the business landscape and will continue to do so. It is good for the economy, principally because it is about unleashing the potential of South Africans and promoting human dignity through enabling participation by black people in meaningful economic activities.

We have learnt valuable lessons about BEE, business development and growth. It has long been recognised that a growth path that does not address inequalities is unsustainable, both socially and politically.

There is a vast literature which argues that an economy is more likely to become competitive if it can increase the participation of people in production (Japan and Germany), through inter-firm networks or clusters (Italy and New Zealand) and through social pacts between government, labour and business (Ireland and Sweden).

These processes increase productivity on the shop floor, increase the collective efficiency of industrial districts and local economies and create high levels of certainty and predictability for both domestic and foreign investors at a national level.

Increasing the participation of women in the economy has massive knock-on effects in nutrition levels, child mortality, literacy and health of people, thereby increasing the overall productivity of the nation.

In most competitive economies, small and medium-sized business is the lifeblood of the economy, creating low-cost, labour-intensive employment, innovation, increased competition and efficiency (USA, Italy, Taiwan).

A growth path that does not address inequalities is unsustainable socially, politically and ecomonically.

The inequalities in SA do result in an economy that inherently performs below its potential because the income earned and generated by the majority is too low. The economy has neither the income levels nor advanced entrepreneurial and skill levels to sustain economic growth and development.

Consequently, a higher rate of growth, increased employment and more equitable income distribution will not be achieved if the majority of our population are not fully and productively integrated.

BEE Strategy

A BEE strategy is thus, in the first instance, a new and creative growth path (for companies, industries and the economy) that combines the processes of increased competitiveness of the national economy with robust programmes targeted at unleashing creative resources and potential of South Africa's people.

Today, as stakeholders anxiously await the announcement from Government on its strategies, aimed at increasing meaningful black participation in economic activities, BEE continues to change the business landscape.

The question on the minds of many is: What next?

For the private sector, the challenge is to renew commitment, seize the initiative, design BEE programmes, monitor and report on progress in implementation and actively participate in industry forums with other stakeholders to set industry standards and to outline industry-specific BEE initiatives.

Government's Strategy

First, it provides for a policy and definition of BEE and the indicators against which BEE would be implemented. It also proposes national outcomes targets and proposes stakeholders to agree on more specific targets against which BEE would be measured.

Secondly, the strategy provides for various instruments to enable the participation of black people in the economy. These include:

- The design of an enabling, stable and predictable regulatory framework that allows for the issuing of codes of practice that set out empowerment measurement indicators, definitions and guidelines.

- New programme innovations, in the areas of procurement, access to finance, state asset restructuring and licensing, to enable the Government to accelerate BEE.

- The promotion of partnerships with particular emphasis on their role as instruments that would assist in achieving BEE, through industry and corporate BEE programmes industry charters and company reporting.

- The establishment of the Black Economic Empowerment Advisory Council, which is aimed at providing considered advice to the Government and at achieving institutional and societal consensus on the implementation of BEE.

To elaborate on one area: an integral part of the BEE strategy will be the design of corporate and industry BEE programmes, where possible, in partnership with industry stakeholders.

The Government has stated that it will be pursuing the establishment of partnerships with the private sector, built around the specific circumstances and empowerment determinants of different industries. The approach is underlined by the belief that Government, on its own, cannot address all the opportunities and constraints that determine the scope for empowerment in the economy. Furthermore, BEE implementation, and issues such as targets, should take account of variations across industries and should be informed by the experiences of the corporates themselves.

The process is intended as a collaborative one that assists corporates and industries to design and implement empowerment solutions through empowerment charters and other programmes.

These BEE programmes and charters should contribute towards meeting national BEE objectives and the acceleration of economic growth in a mutually reinforcing way.[1] In some instances charters will be the outcome, in others, some common understanding of standards or targets. In all instances it is expected that companies, (especially listed ones) and those of a larger size would design and implement their own BEE initiatives, whether or not an industry develops a programme.

It is expected that, once the charters or industry standards are complete and agreed to, they could be submitted to the BEE Advisory Council for endorsement and the standards derived from them may be issued as codes of practice in terms of the proposed legislation.

The charters will not all be driven entirely from Government and they will not all run in the same manner. This is precisely why individual corporates should begin the process of designing BEE strategies and thereby develop industry experience. It can be expected that corporates and industries should address the following indicators in implementing BEE:[2]

- Ownership and control (BEE ownership and partnerships, investment in BEE, support for broad-based and collective forms of ownership)
- Human resource and skills development (employees and consumer financial education)
- Employment equity and diversity training
- Enterprise facilitation including procurement (market share)
- Income (remuneration spend and contribution to job creation eg learnerships)
- Corporate social investment has been considered a relevant BEE indicator in some industries.

In the financial sector, indicators could include access to financial services and capital (lending patterns) as well as investment in targeted sectors.

It is envisaged that strategies, programmes and targets could be designed for each indicator, for sectors and sub-sectors.

Conclusion

In conclusion, the degree to which BEE is achieved will be measured by the extent to which different stakeholders are addressed by these strategies. BEE must impact as widely as possible in order for it to have the desired result of economic growth.

BEE is positive for business and for the economy because of the promise of what it can deliver.

It must therefore be implemented. It's the very acceptance that is good for our economy. It already has, and will continue, to change the business landscape.

---

1   Similar initiatives have been undertaken in mineral and in liquid fuels, in tourism and in agriculture.
2   These have been highlighted in the Government's strategy on BEE and utilised in liquid fuels and mining charters.

BEE is good for the economy, principally because it unleashes potential - economic, intellectual and moral.

After putting himself through school with money raised playing dice, Herman Mashaba managed to get out of the ghetto and enrol for a degree in administration.

But, in the early 1980s, South Africa's universities were a hotbed of political activity, and his studies ground to a halt when his institution was shut down by the authorities after unrest on campus.

Back in his home township of Hammanskraal near Pretoria, Herman had two options:

- Return to the life of a gambler, a dangerous occupation since he was the "knocksman", the man who holds the money, or
- Start working for someone else.

"When I came back to the township, one of the things I did, for the first two years, was focus on trying to leave the country, but I had no contacts.

Mashaba funded his school fees playing dice - he was a "knocksman" - now he represents SA at the G8 in support of NEPAD.

"I became a door-to-door salesman. I sold insurance, worked for one company for seven months and another one for 23 months and, in the process, I bought myself a car. Then I decided to throw that up and I went back to gambling."

In 1985, Herman managed to raise a R30 000 loan, and decided to get into the black haircare business. He and a friend mixed chemicals in a backyard. After some trial and error, Black Like Me was a household name in South Africa by 1992.

The company was highly entrepreneurial, selling directly to salons until the brand was well-known enough to be sold through retail outlets. Unfortunately a fire destroyed his entire factory in 1993, an event he wryly describes as putting "a strain on my cash flow".

Within months, Herman was back in business and four years later sold the Black Like Me brand to Colgate. This sale, says Herman, was the only time he ever lost money. Frustrated by the lack of growth in his product, Herman bought the business back in 1999, and began focusing on Africa and Europe.

"One of the reasons I sold the business to Colgate was to tap into their infrastructure so that I could make the product international. Unfortunately that did not happen."

"The wheels of big companies like that move very very slowly, and this business needs speed. If you don't have speed, you're dead. I've proved that speed counts, because when I bought the business back, I had no money left. I put it into buying the company and ran it hand-to-mouth."

In 2001, Black Like Me turned over R51 million, and produced six-and-a-half million units of product, a 46 per cent improvement on the previous year.

Herman's company now controls 10 per cent of the South African haircare market which is estimated to be worth between R600 and R800 million a year.

The brand launched in London early in 2002, in partnership with colour manufacturer Renbow International. (The black haircare market in the UK is said to be worth £65 million.)

In the rest of Africa, a R600 to R800 million market, Black Like Me operates in Ethiopia, Cameroon, Zambia and Kenya, and Herman has appointed a specialist dedicated to developing the market.

Today, Black Like Me is commonly used as an example of successful black entrepreneurship in South Africa, to the extent that Herman represented Africa at a G8 Conference in support of Nepad (New Partnership for Africa's Development), held in Germany in April 2002.

One of the students who exemplify these values is Sello Kgosimore. Sello is 23 years old and grew up with his grandparents on a farm near Wesselsbron in the Free State. He attended a farm school until Standard Five after which he went to high school in Welkom.

Although Sello passed matric with an exemption and excelled in other areas such as leadership and boxing, his options post-matric were limited. Before hearing about CIDA, he applied to the airforce and to a Johannesburg business college that offered a one-year diploma. Neither of these was particularly appealing to Sello, whose goal was to educate himself to reach his highest potential. Technicons and universities were beyond his financial means and were intimidating to someone with a schooling background that was perceived to be somewhat lacking in academic and life-skill training.

Sello began his university career somewhat astounded but unequivocally eager.

When CIDA sent out their first invitations for applications, Sello's school principal and guidance teacher encouraged him to apply. To an ambitious young man from a small Free State town, the opportunity to pursue an undergraduate degree in business on a campus in the middle of bustling Johannesburg was thrilling. His consistent academic performance and contribution to his school community ensured him one of the first few spots at CIDA.

Three years later, Sello is within close range of graduating with a BBA, which he has enriched with professional Microsoft qualifications and certificates in stock-taking, trade and tourism and personal money management. These skills are all part of what he teaches to teenagers in Qwa Qwa over the school holidays. He has held down a part-time job at Edgars and been on student teams responsible for cleaning, conducting tours of the campus and co-ordinating accommodation and celebrations (a big part of CIDA student life!). Sello is also the President of the CIDA Student Governing Body and, as such, leads

a large campus and regularly addresses top local and international business people. He has taken courses in public speaking and advanced meditation at CIDA.

Sello plans to be a chartered accountant and to do his honours degree in accounting at RAU, which has underwritten the CIDA accounting curriculum and extends valuable support to aspirant CIDA accountants. He will use this background and experience to develop and run his own businesses, the aim of which, he says, is to employ as many people as possible.

Already Sello is using experience gained in the entrepreneurship programme to begin buying and renting property. This is to generate income for postgraduate study and to support his mother, a domestic worker whose highest qualification is Standard Two.

The need and value of CIDA is even more apparent from talking with this excited young man than from surveying the university's statistics and successes (see chapter 25). He talks articulately and intelligently about his belief in hard work, in taking full responsibility for one's choices and about the positive future of Africa.

He credits CIDA for the opportunity to develop these attitudes and for providing him with "a family and much more than just an education of theories". It is inspiring to know that Sello's story is currently one of thousands and potentially one of millions. While CIDA still has to innovate solutions to many challenges (the most crucial of which is providing students with safe, inner-city accommodation) its model of education is already proving to be unique in its creativity, cost-effectiveness and potential replicability.

Sello plans to be a chartered accountant.

CIDA still has to innovate solutions to many challenges, the most crucial of which is providing students with safe inner city accommodation.

18

The concepts Black and White, which for so long coloured our political landscape, are as deficient when it comes to things cultural as they were for the rest of society. Quite simply, the rest of the colours of the rainbow do make a difference to one's options. It is not surprising then that the liberalisation of the arts has had a massive influence on the quantity, the quality and the creativity of our cultural output as a nation.

Chameleons Colour and Culture

Christopher Till:
Director - Apartheid Museum

1985 had at least 1000 "chameleons"

Political staff
PARLIAMENT - More than 1000 people officially changed colour last year.

They were reclassified from one race group to another by the stroke of a government pen.

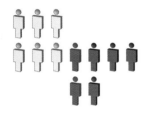

Details of what is dubbed "the chameleon dance" were given in reply to Opposition questions in Parliament.
The Minister of Home Affairs, Mr Stoffel Botha, disclosed that during 1985:
· 702 coloured people turned white
· 19 whites became coloured
· 1 Indian became white
· 3 Chinese became white
· 50 Indians became coloured
· 43 coloureds became Indians
· 21 Indians became Malay
· 30 Malays went Indian
· 249 blacks became coloured
· 20 coloureds became black
· 2 blacks became "other Asians"
· 1 black was classified Griqua
· 11 coloureds became Chinese
· 3 coloureds went Malay
· 1 Chinese became coloured
· 8 Malays became coloured
· No blacks became white and no whites became black.

The Star, 21 March 1986

The preoccupation of the apartheid era with colour and the tragic absurdity of the previous government's approach is reflected in the bizarre article which appeared in **The Star** newspaper in 1986.

The ability of South Africans to change colour at the stroke of a pen and the thump of an official stamp would be funny if it were not so painful.

Archbishop Desmond Tutu described South Africa as the rainbow nation, which presupposes a pot of gold. The chameleon nation is that pot of gold.

The chameleon, with its slow, jerky, forward movement, continually adapting its colour to its environment, is the metaphor for the new South African cultural landscape.

Colour is certainly a descriptive ingredient for the arts, whether it be sound colour, a colour palette, colourful language or fashion colours. These different elements of each area of our arts and culture have a particular hue that speaks of rich diversity.

The (cultural) landscape has changed forever and those that stride across it are as identifiable as the colours and form of the new South Africa flag.

Cindarella

The arts are often described as the Cinderella of the ball, fighting a rear guard action to catch the attention of funders. Some would say that this also extends to attracting an audience. This has been no less true for South Africa. Culture, for some, existed prior to 1994 only with a capital "K" with the emphasis being on, "rugby, braaivleis, sunny skies and Chevrolet."

Support for the arts was largely confined to official monolithic edifices constructed at great expense, icons of grandiose vision, white supremacy and Wagnerian grandeur. The State Theatre in Pretoria, the Nico Malan Theatre in Cape Town, the Sand du Plessis Teatre in Bloemfontein and the Playhouse in Durban were the bastions of state sponsorship and absorbed the annual budget to further the high arts of ballet, opera and theatre companies along with symphony orchestras. Don Giovanni, Rigalletto, Swan Lake and Beethoven's Fifth were lavishly staged, complete with invited stars and guest conductors. In contrast, the Market Theatre, a vanguard of local productions, received no funding from state coffers, nor did any other art forms except those included under the performing arts councils.

The Foundation for the Creative Arts is Established

In the late 1980s, cultural practitioners gathered in Cape Town, at the invitation of the then Government, and established a structure by which state funds could be channelled into the arts (other than performing arts). This took the form of the Foundation for Creative Arts, which began life with the grand total of R2 million to dispense annually. With the unbanning of the ANC, PAC and other resistance movements in the early 1990s, a new era in the cultural arena began.

Efforts to engage with the returning politicos and exiles and with locally-based activists began with the ANC primarily being the arbiter of what would and would not be sanctioned in this pre-election period.

Sanctions are Lifted

As part of this dialogue, a move began to transform cultural institutions through engagement. Those who resisted were isolated by the new breed of cultural activists. A march to the State Theatre, protesting the incalcitrance of its director and board, who refused to see the reality of

a society and country on the move, was broken up by police, using teargas.

Consultative and joint working groups sprang up with representatives from both sides of the cultural and political spectrum. And so began the chameleon dance towards creating new, representative and acceptable structures. And with this came the selective removal of cultural sanctions.

The first major company to visit South Africa for many years was Arthur Mitchell's Harlem Dance Company (a group of world-renowned black dancers) and they performed at the opening of the newly-renovated and extended Civic Theatre. This gave an insight into the exciting world to come.

The long-standing Standard Bank National Festival of the Arts initiated transformation, looking to encourage the local community and showcasing black artists. Dollar Brand returned as Abdullah Ibrahim at the Grahamstown Festival of the Arts. At the time, the city was bedecked with posters for a show called, "In Search of Stoffel Botha's Brain". As you may recall, Stoffel Botha was the Minister who listed the various colour transmutations quoted at the beginning of this story.

Culture for some existed prior to 1994 only with a capital "K."

171

The New Era

Given the division between one community denied the right to resources and another expectant of resources, the issue of who would get what became paramount. Our transition brought about a new energy in response to the uncertainty of the time.

The Arts Alive Festival, set in the metropolitan cultural heartland of the Newtown Cultural Precinct - home to the Market Theatre, Kippies Jazz Club, the Federated Union of Black Artists (FUBA), and a host of cultural players - set itself up as an international festival with its artistic roots focused in Africa.

A succession of West African musicians, Manu Dubangu, Salif Kaiter, Ismael Lo, Baba Maal and Angelique Kidjo, shared the billing with local artists when they rocked audiences at Mega Music and Zoo Lake. West African sounds mingled with those from Soweto and Alexandra.

The Dutch group, Dog Troup, performed their street theatre in the streets of Newtown and the urban/rural sounds of Malaga reverberated off the walls of the Electric Workshop, a recycled remnant of the area's industrial past.

The Dance Factory underlined the power of movement and the synthesis of traditional and classical dance styles. Artists and curators from across the world arrived for the preparation of the biggest art event to be held in Africa. The first Johannesburg Biennale subsequently brought about the participation of 62 countries. South Africa was part of the world again.

The colours of the new flag, universally adopted with pride, became a symbol of the Chameleon Nation.

The National Arts Coalition, a civil society body, established a forum for debate, tasking itself with developing guidelines for a new government to use in preparing an arts policy. It held an international conference, " Bringing Cinderella to the Ball: Arts and Culture to the new SA".

Dr Ben Ngubane was sworn in as the Minister of Arts, Culture, Science and Technology with Winnie Madikizela-Mandela as the Deputy Minister. The expectation of the arts community was, on the one hand, one of excitement and entitlement and on the other (among the established arts organisations) one of uncertainty.

While progress at times may seem slow and jerky, it has been inexorable and persistant.

The Arts and Culture Trust, a private sector funding initiative, was launched with President Nelson Mandela as its patron, and the Arts and Culture Task Group (ACTAG), a body of artists, educators and arts administrators, was appointed to look into the policy and principles for a White Paper on the arts.

The transformation of the political landscape was now poised to reach every aspect of society.

Restructuring the organisations and processes consuming the majority of the funds allocated for arts and culture was at the top of the agenda. Democratising the arts required funding. The uneven distribution of resources was to form the basis of Government's strategic thrust.

This began in 1995 with the announcement by the Department of Arts Culture, Science and Technology of a 15 per cent cut in the budgets of the performing arts councils, with these funds to be distributed to the nine provinces. The principle of gradually reducing funding to the performing arts councils, and redistributing these resources, had begun.

In September 1996, the Cabinet adopted, as official government policy, the White Paper on Arts and Culture and Heritage. This met with mixed reaction as many of the principles developed by the National Arts Coalition and ACTAG were not included, but it set a framework for the arts to develop.

The policy set out the underlying values of arts, culture and heritage as being a basic human right and not a luxury and with freedom of expression, as guaranteed under the Constitution. It also promised that the resources for developing arts and culture would be justly and fairly dispensed.

Adaptation and Regeneration

The establishment of the National Arts Council, which took over the resources and function of the Foundation for the Creative Arts, put in place the new mechanism for distributing state funds.

An independent organisation, Business in Support of the Arts (BASA), established itself in 1997 to encourage the business sector to invest in arts and culture.

Adaptation and regeneration is part of the process of assimilating the ideological, philosophical and practical realities which define arts and culture in post-apartheid South Africa.

The cultural landscape entered a new era of transforming itself. In many cases it mirrored the title of a show by local comedian, Pieter Dirk Uys: "Adapt or Dye" (sic).

The heyday of the Performing Arts Councils and their various companies and orchestras was also to undergo a chameleon change. Some died, others adapted or changed form, name, repertoire and colour.

- The National Symphony Orchestra closed and reopened as a Section 21 Company, finally disbanded and was reformed as the Johannesburg Philharmonic Orchestra.
- The State Theatre was mothballed after its final performance of the ballet, "The Merry Widow."
- The Nico Malan presented Puccini's "La Boheime: Noir" with an all black cast.
- The Durban Playhouse announced retrenchments and reduced its activities to resolve a budget deficit created by funding cutbacks.
- The State Theatre Ballet Company and the Organisation of African Unity celebrated Africa Day at the State Theatre ... with both turning 35.
- Cabab Ballet closed and relaunched itself as the Cape Town City Ballet joining forces with the State Theatre Ballet for the first time in a production at the Nico Malan Theatre in Cape Town.
- Cabab Opera changed its name to Cape Town Opera, established as a Section 21 Company, and signed an agreement with the Western Cape Department of Labour to train black opera singers.
- Two orchestras, the Cape Town Symphony and Cape Town Philarmonic, combined to form one orchestra.

- The Transvaal Philarmonic Orchestra changed its name to the new Philamonic Orchestra Pretoria.
- Capab changed its name to Artscape and the Nico Malan to the Kamma Theatre.
- The South African Ballet Theatre, made up largely of former State Theatre ballet dancers, was launched with a self-funded production of "Giselle".
- The J C Strijdom Square collapsed on the anniversary of the old Republic Day (May 31) resulting in the closure of the State Theatre amid safety fears.
- The State Theatre was relaunched as a venue available for companies to rent.
- The Fantastic Flying Fish Company, made up mainly of former Durban Playhouse members, was launched.
- The City of Johannesburg cut funding to the Civic Theatre by 40 per cent or R12 million.

The new approach to funding and the trials and tribulations of the performing arts councils and the formal sector was a process that initiated self-reliance and adaption.

Chameleon metamorphosis has seen a considerable downsizing of the performing arts sector.

Downside and Upside

There were immediate casualties in the infrastructure that employed professional artists.

The gains have been the redefinition of arts and culture in South Africa and the cross-fertilisation and hybrid forms that have been (and are being) produced. Narrow definition and predictable productions have given way to experimentation and a cross-over effect. Self-reliance and innovation has been born of necessity.

The National Arts Council, tasked with dispensing funds to the wider community of artists, began to fulfil its mandate to bring equity to the arts and cultural dispensation by distributing funds to artists, cultural institutions and NGOs.

The idea is to reflect fully cultural diversity through promotion and creation of a wide list of disciplines from literature and drama, music, opera and photography, to visual arts and crafts.

The cultural landscape transformed, signalled by the Pieter Dirk Uys production "Adapt or Dye" (sic).

The Stage is Set

The principles and policies for government support for the arts are largely in place, having followed a process of defining and refining since 1994. The Department of Arts and Culture, in its current strategic plan, has identified the challenge as shifting the funding needs away from serving the minority, to explore the previously neglected arts and exploiting their economic potential. This is measured against the country's move in the cultural area from exclusivity to inclusivity and the stated policy framework of the White Paper on Arts and Culture. One criticism is that the redirection of resources to ad hoc projects away from professional, well-resourced companies, is spreading the jam too thinly, mitigating against critical mass and sustainability.

The discussion around funding is an obvious topic as the avenues for obtaining the means to produce are limited. However, the vibrancy of the arts is such that, despite this, the diversity and quality of arts and culture in South Africa is unquestioned. The arts and cultural sector is as it should be - independent and challenging. If anything, the cultural activism of the early nineties is returning to challenge the track record of the formal arts sector and policies of Government with regard to the delivery of promised support.

The arts are, to a degree, always an instrument of challenge and change, and the perspective which the arts bring to society is part of the questioning, made possible by the freedom of expression this country allows. Any attempts at diminishing this would and should elicit a vigorous response from the sector.

In a recent article in **Time Magazine** on the arts in Argentina (which is experiencing a boom and revival, against the backdrop of four years of economic chaos), the very nature of arts and culture is underlined. Titled, "The Art of Recession", the high value Argentines place on culture is demonstrated by the fact that the Government still spends five per cent of its budget ($42 million) on the arts. "While people are calling for cuts in military or political spending, nobody wants cuts in culture," the cultural secretary for Buenos Aires is quoted as saying. "The crisis has helped us value what we have."

South Africa experienced this phenomenon during the years of apartheid where institutions like the Market Theatre (and other cultural icons and individual artists) responded to the situation with powerful commentary and product. The difference is that no state funding was received and the only support came from international agencies. This has largely dried up since the 1994 elections.

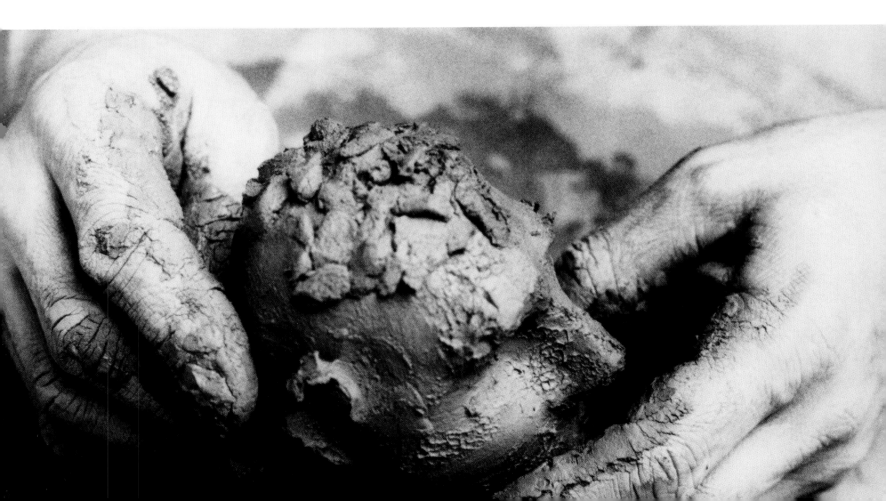

Will the Curtain Go Up?

The challenge facing the arts, culture and heritage sector is to find, develop and grow the kind of audience that created the example in Argentina where arts and culture form an essential part of the national psyche.

The discussion and examples about change in the focus and funding mechanisms of the state described in this story, are one part of the equation. The other is the ability of arts practitioners to renegotiate their place in the changed landscape and to find the leverage to open doors.

The post-apartheid era has provided a new set of challenges and adjustments. The opening up of society and access in every sphere of life, the euphoria and liberalisation, have created new opportunities. A new language and vocabulary has had to be found; there are new causes and issues.

In the performing arts, this is principally found in contemporary dance and opera. The visual arts, by their iconoclastic nature, have long followed their own path and the music of South Africa has translated itself into a genre whose roots are unmistakeable.

The South African Star is Born

Protest and resistance have moved to introspection and reflection. South Africa is part of the world again and we have had to make sense of local and universal influences and issues.

This is both a stimulus and inhibitor. The stimulus has given rise to an arts and cultural mélange that is producing a South African cultural identity which has found a place on stages, museums, catwalks, shops and the airwaves of the world. Festivals and exhibitions, concerts and compact discs display the tag, "Made in South Africa", and their imagery and sound have a powerful identity. Writers, actors, artists, musicians and crafts people have made the local and world arena theirs and are widely recognised and respected.

The landscape has changed forever and those who stride it are as identifiable as the colours and form of the new South African flag.

Funding questions and the structuring of the arts will continue to occupy the cultural agenda and the need to address these important building blocks should not be underestimated. The interaction between national policy, provincial responsibility and local delivery will have to face the needs of individuals and institutional arts, culture and heritage practitioners, taking cognisance of successes and failures to date.

It is the legacy of the arts, not only to have survived the neglect and division of the past and the attrition that followed, but to redefine and renew themselves by changing colour, form and shape to adapt to the environment in which they operate.

From Mamelodi to Moscow, Amsterdam to Amersfort and Davos to Daveyton, South African arts and culture have spread across the cultural radar. From local halls in the townships to the bright lights of Broadway, the West End and towns and cities on all six continents, South Africans and their cultural and artistic presence can be found. The dance of the chameleon described in the 1985 article has transformed itself. A random sample of this reclassification celebrates the energy and diversity of South Africa's identity and achievement.

1994-2002 had at least 1 000 "Chameleons"
- 1 Exhibition, "Art against Apartheid", conceived in Paris in 1983, opens on the walls of Parliament replacing apartheid-era images
- 400 South African artists, representing Africa, take part in the end of the millennium festival in Nantes, France
- 1 Commonwealth Writer's Prize is awarded to Ronnie Govender for his **Cato Manor Stories**
- 2 Booker Prizes won by J M Coetzee
- 3 Nominations for David Kramer's "Kat & Kings" at the Laurence Olivier Awards, London
- 4 Ballet Theatre Afrikan dancers, the first black dancers selected to compete in the Prix de Lausanne
- 2 Awards won by Theatre for Africa at the Edinburgh Festival
- 1 Daimler Chrysler sculpture award for Jane Alexander
- 1 Grammy nomination for Miriam Makeba for her album "Homeland"

The chameleon, in addition to its ability to change colour, has a grasping tail, a long tongue and eyes which swivel independently.

- 2 Honours for artist William Kentridge: a retrospective exhibition show in Washington, New York, and Chicago (and he won the Carnegie medal)
- 2 International awards for Yizo Yizo, in the Best International Television Series category in Geneva and the prestigious Japan Prize for Educational Television.
- 1 Solo exhibition at the Guggenheim Museum, New York, for photographer David Goldblatt.
- 2 Films by Anand Singh, "Cry the Beloved Country" and Paljas receive critical acclaim and a distinguished producer award for him from the Californian Film Festival.
- 1 World Music Award for Lucky Dube for the best African recording artist.
- 2 Hiroshuma Awards, one to John Kani and the other to Antjie Krog for their contribution to peace through their work.
- 4 Grammy nominations for Ladysmith Black Mambazo.
- 1 of 16 choreographic works chosen from 32 countries by Vincent Mantsoe, performed at the Recontes Choreographiques Internationals in Paris and Europe.
- 160 artists from around the world participate in the 2nd Johannesburg Biennale.
- 1 Royal Command Performance for Richard Loring's "African Footprint".

... and so on.

The chameleon, in addition to its ability to change colour, has a grasping tail, a long tongue and eyes that are able to swivel independently. These attributes serve the chameleon nation well.

To hang on and persevere when the going gets tough, to move with lightening speed to snatch the smallest opportunity and make something of it, a gaze which looks forward and back at the same time never forgetting where the journey began, and to be inspired by the progress made - while this progress at times may seem slow and jerky, it has been inexorable and constant.

The ability to change colour is to adapt to new circumstances and situations and to show how all the colours of the rainbow are able to be reproduced in a dazzling display of virtuosity, adaptability and beauty. This makes the chameleon nation one to be reckoned with and proud of.

Gone are the days of colour being a measure of discrimination and ability. The chameleon dance is alive and well but to another tune -
Nkosi Sikelel' iAfrica, "God Bless Africa".

These attributes serve the chameleon nation well.

There are few museums in the world where guides burst into tears when they reach a certain point on a tour.

But at the Apartheid Museum in Johannesburg's southern suburbs, Virginia Thobela regularly breaks down when she reaches the exhibition on the migrant labour system that kept South Africa's mines going during the dark days of legislated discrimination.

"I cry when I take a tour group there. I just can't help it. The thing is, the visitors themselves are crying. You can't hold it," she says.

When she was three years old, Thobela's father left the family home in Thul'Mahashi, Mpumalanga, to seek employment on the mines around Johannesburg.

That was in 1974, and Thobela, now 31, has never seen or heard from Joseph Thobela again.
"Everyone then was coming from different places to Johannesburg searching for gold. That's what my father was doing and he got a job on the mines.

I don't even know which mine. We were just told he was working on the mines. After getting the job, these (migrant labourers) were not paid enough money to even support their families.

The museum is an evocative place. You know you're in for something different when tickets are issued according to the colour of your skin, and there are separate entrances for blacks and whites."

It confuses people, says Thobela, but it works. Children, particularly, demand an explanation from their parents, which, she says, means the system is working brilliantly.

The realities of apartheid can be grim and unnerving. 121 hangman's nooses descend from a ceiling to represent the executions of anti-apartheid activists. Multimedia displays of township violence come alive with the sounds of conflict, a disturbingly long list of apartheid legislation occupies an entire wall. It is an assault on the senses. But it is also an intensely spiritual experience and Thobela believes in the healing power of the museum.

"This is an educational institution. This museum is playing an important role in healing the wounds of the past because people don't really know what apartheid was, and they can learn here."

Apartheid, she says, was an important part of how South African culture has evolved, and for Thobela, future generations need to know what to avoid.

"I enjoy my job though. The tourists are very good. They want to know and they are asking me everything. But everybody is learning every day. We learn from the questions they are asking. If I don't know the answer, I have to go and find out and get back to them, she says. The museum, she adds, is a "history of the bad times", but it is also the foundation of hope.

Some people say we are promoting apartheid. This museum doesn't promote it. It's for everyone to learn so we can build a better country.

This museum says: Yes, we can forgive, but we won't forget. We can't make the same mistake again! Most people say it's a way for the coming generations to build a better country," she says.

19

In 1994 most white South Africans were anxious that standards in our educational and medical services may fall. Most black South Africans were looking forward to the improvements they had fought for. In fact the provision of world class Private Medical Care has exploded onto the scene. The poorer people in our community have not had immediate access to this service. The challenge for private enterprise is to devise programmes that meet the needs of the bulk of our population. Until poverty and unemployment have been successfully addressed, the challenge for the Government will be to improve health delivery to the poor and to urgently work with private enterprise and NGO's to devise on effective framework to relieve the social and economic effects of HIV/Aids.

Medical Facilities
- Terminal, Curable or on the Mend?

Adrian Gore, Discovery CEO

A national asset of world-class quality

It looked like a copy of Playboy with the cover photograph of a pneumatic pair of breasts in a leotard bikini top; but on closer examination, it turned out to be the September 20 edition of Financial Mail, a serious South African business weekly. The cover story: SILICONE SAFARIS - SA profits from medical tourism.

That is only the most recent - and eye-catching - illustration of the fact that South Africa has one of the most advanced private medical sectors in the world, on a par with what Europe and America have to offer. "Increasing numbers of foreign tourists - mainly from the US and UK - are taking advantage of the low rand and SA's medical excellence to jet in for such pressing medical emergencies as excessive flab, wrinkles and the known ailments of age," the cover story said, adding that "more critical surgical work" such as hip and knee replacements, and even cardiac operations, are also on offer.

The quality of private sector medical care in South Africa is world-class, with the same treatments, drugs and sophisticated surgery routinely on offer as in major Western countries. Access is good, and there are no waiting lists for surgery, whether routine or critical.

South Africa has one of the most advanced and cost-effective private medical sectors in the world.

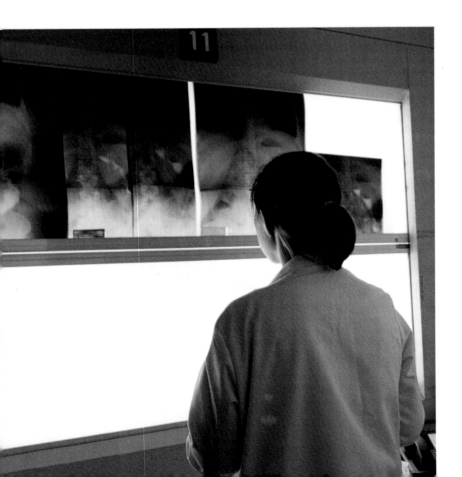

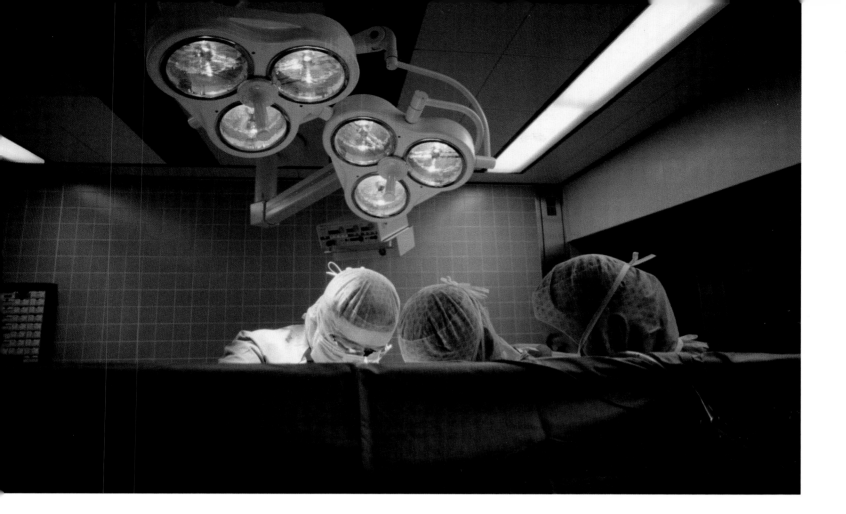

Moreover, the system offers value for money when compared to the West - mainly because prices are dependent on the cost of local labour, which is lower than it is overseas. For example, studies show that the cost in South Africa of common operations such as appendectomies, tonsillectomies, Caesarean-section births and heart by-pass operations are, in dollar terms, between 50 and 75 per cent lower than in the United States.

Perhaps the most remarkable achievement over the past 10 years is that South Africa has become the world's most advanced market in "consumer-driven health-care", which describes the steady global trend towards a health-care market where consumers are genuinely empowered to finance and choose the kind of medical treatment that suits their particular needs.

South Africa has become a laboratory for the rest of the world in this regard, and directors of local health-care companies regularly speak at international conferences and write papers for foreign policy units and think tanks.

The country boasts an invaluable body of consumer-related statistical data about patterns of patient behaviour, medical expenditure, drug consumption and financial management- all of which serve as a useful global benchmark for other countries trying to improve their own health-care systems.

The main impetus for this development came about in 1994 when the authorities deregulated the country's private health insurance market.

For-profit insurers were allowed to enter the field of health-care funding. Given the freedom to innovate and experiment, they soon began offering a wide range of health plans: traditional indemnity plans, preferred-provider plans, managed care plans and the critically important medical savings account plans - a kind of personal bank account which allows users to choose how much to spend on day-to-day medical expenses and, most importantly, to keep whatever money they don't spend.

Hospital Costs · RSA vs · USA ($)

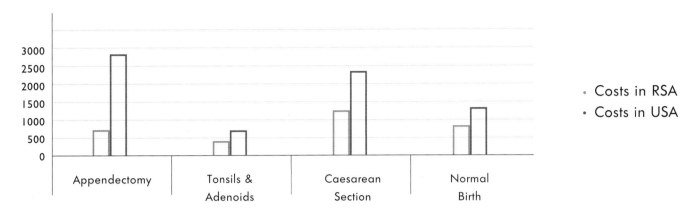

- Costs in RSA
- Costs in USA

The tax authorities allowed employer contributions to medical savings accounts to be tax deductible. Employees were free to use funds in a medical savings account to pay expenses not covered by third-party insurance. Thus, medical savings accounts have been competing with other forms of insurance on a level playing field for several years.

The results have been remarkable: From a zero base in 1994, medical savings accounts in South Africa have captured nearly half of the private health insurance market and have been instrumental in helping to keep health insurance premiums down, reducing non-essential medical expenditure and increasing the solvency of insurers.

As the Harvard Business Review reported earlier this year on the growing trend towards consumer-driven health-care: "When consumers apply pressure on an industry, whether it's retailing or banking, cars or computers, it invariably produces a surge of innovation that increases productivity, reduces prices, improves quality, and expands choices. The essential problem with the health-care industry is that it has been shielded from consumer control - by employers, insurers and the government. As a result, costs have exploded as choices have narrowed."

In fact, South Africa is now the largest and most advanced consumer-driven health-care market in the world, with certain companies way ahead of their overseas counterparts.

For example, Discovery Health, South Africa's largest such company, has over 4-million member-years of experience [one member insured for a full year represents one member-year]. The company takes 30 000 calls a day in its call-centre, processes 1.6 million claims every month, and has pioneered an incentive-based wellness programme which rewards users financially for adopting a healthy lifestyle and undergoing regular preventative medical tests.

As this "inherited memory" of experience in running a consumer-driven health-care system continues to grow, South Africa could, within the next five to 10 years, become a major global processing and administration centre for many of the world's health-care companies. A parallel can be seen in the IT industry, where countries such as India and Ireland have capitalised on their cost-effective, English-speaking computing skills by becoming back-office centres to the international IT industry.

However, because of the legacy of apartheid and the resulting wealth disparities that it created, South Africa's world-class, private health-care system cannot be seen in isolation; in fact, barely 7 million people, or 20 per cent of the population, can afford to use it. Yet these 7 million people fund about 54 per cent of total South African health-care expenditure; they have access to 85 per cent of the country's pharmacists and 75 per cent of all medical specialists.

And for those who can"t afford it?

The rest of the population - by far, the majority - are forced to use the state-funded public health-care-system. As with other state-funded health-care systems (e.g., in Britain and Canada), treatment is essentially free at the point of service, which means that demand is theoretically infinite - with all the problems that this implies in terms of insufficient funding, unsatisfactory service, lack of facilities and medicine, poor working conditions for doctors and nurses, and the flight of skills to the private sector, or, worse, overseas. This has been aggravated by the urgent need for the government to provide, at the very least, basic primary health-care for all citizens.

One could lament the existence of a world-class, private health-care sector enjoyed by barely 20 per cent of the population when the vast majority of South Africans don't have anything near that level of service, and conclude that its importance should somehow be limited or curtailed in the interests of social equity. But one could also take the opposite view - namely that we should be thankful for the existence of this world-class private health-care system because it provides an existing infrastructure (in terms of skills, technology and funding expertise) to build a more broadly based system for the entire population.

It is a national asset. Without it, the problems facing the public sector would be far worse - not least of all because of the disproportionate effect of HIV/Aids on large sections of the population, and the constant access to drugs and medical treatment that that implies.

Therefore, the critical issue facing the key players in the health-care equation - providers (doctors, pharmacists, hospitals, etc), funders (insurance companies, health-care financiers) and the regulatory authorities - is to strengthen the private health-care system and leverage its capacities for the benefit of those not yet able to afford it. For example, private health insurers are now offering ranges of low-cost funding plans aimed specifically at lower-income earners; this shows that with the right approach, those outside of the private health-care system can be drawn in on terms that are affordable to them.

The biggest challenge facing the private health-care sector is to maintain the ability of its users to pay the insurance premiums that keep it going ... and growing.

Anything that contributed to medical inflation in the broadest sense of the word would result in members of medical schemes having to reduce their benefit levels or drop out of the system altogether. Those remaining would have to pay more, in turn causing more people to drop out - resulting in the ultimate vicious cycle.

After a sustained drop in the past decade, medical inflation started to edge up again in the late nineties mainly as a result of rising inflation in general, made worse by the weaker currency, which increases the import component of medical transactions.

Nevertheless, the key players - funders and providers - remain confident that the benefits of South Africa's world-class private health-care system can gradually be extended to the broader population over time through a pragmatic approach that strengthens rather than weakens the existing structure.

" MAYBE WE SHOULD RETHINK THIS NATIONALISATION THING?"

Costs of operations in private clinics are between 50 and 75% lower than in the USA - and the standard is world class.

The Future

A new spirit of consultation and cooperation between the major players and the regulatory authorities has meant that problems once regarded as insurmountable [e.g. the financial effects of having to provide medical cover to all applicants irrespective of their age or risk profile] are being tackled through innovative solutions such as wellness programmes, late-joiner penalties and appropriate waiting periods for treatment. The legitimate social requirements of the recently promulgated Medical Schemes Act are being balanced with the actuarial rigor and financial discipline upon which any successful health-care system must of necessity rest. As we get this balance right the private health-care system will be able to draw more and more previously excluded citizens into its orbit. This, in turn, will relieve the stresses and strains of the over-burdened public health-care system, freeing it up to deliver the first level of primary health-care to those citizens who need it most.

South Africa will then be able to consolidate its worldwide lead in consumer-driven health-care, and continue to export its know-how and experience to the rest of the world. Indeed, this is already happening in the United States, where Discovery Health's US subsidiary, Destiny Health was described by the Harvard Business Review as one of the "trailblazers" in the US market by giving Americans more choice, more control and more information.

Clearly, our private health-care system is doing something right and this bodes well for the future.

Editorial Comment

As Dr. Olive Shisana points out (see Epilogue), "We have 377 public hospitals, 3387 clinics, and 285 private health-care facilities throughout the country, with a doctor-to-patient ratio of 2.9 doctors per 10 000 patients and a nurse to population ratio of 32 nurses per 10 000 patients.

"Despite this health facility and human resource infrastructure, we still are unable to ensure access to health-care for those who need it most, the poor."

Increasingly, countries are adopting the view that health-care is an individual responsibility, rather like feeding yourself is. In a country such as ours, where poor health, poverty and unemployment problems are endemic, the State does have the responsibility of:
- Basic health-care to the poor
- Inoculation and regulation
- Support for chronic epidemics such as AIDS and TB

Increasingly this will best be handled via public/private partnerships of the very nature that Adrian Gore has referred to. It is unfortunate that the right to dispense antiretrovirals had to end up in the Constitutional Court before the Government was galvanised into action (see Perspective on Health, Poverty and Unemployment), but it is fortunate that there is so much initiative in the private sector and amongst ordinary citizens to make a contribution to this problem in our society. We do have some public infrastructure that is available, but in many areas these facilities are not being maintained at appropriate levels. It is our hope that, as with other public amenities such as housing and water the Government will, with the private sector, and in time, initiate improvements that are just as spectacular.

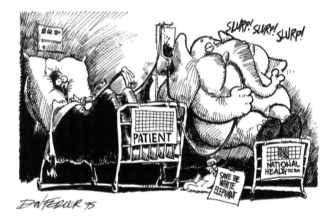

The challenge to the private sector is to build a more broadly based system to meet the needs of the entire population.

Health, Poverty and Unemployment
Steuart Pennington

"In the midst of a hunger crisis and a despondency spawned by increasing joblessness, there is reason to feel buoyant about the constructive work of rebuilding this country, which involves all sectors of our society ... it is about a new South Africanism that cuts across racial and cultural lines ... it is this spirit of oneness, of concern for the less privileged, of accepting the need to have less so others may have more."
- Sunday Times (13 October 2002).

Despite much of the good news presented in the book, it is clear that the top three issues that will make or break South Africa's road to becoming a winning nation are:
- Health
- Poverty
- Unemployment

It is true that approximately four million South Africans still don't have access to fresh water. It is true that large sections of the population are malnourished. It is true that two million of South Africa's 6.5 million children younger than seven suffer from hunger. It is true that HIV/Aids and TB have affected around 20 per cent of the population; and it is true that our unemployment figures range between 25 and 30 per cent of the economically active.

It is argued that when unemployment becomes double digit, the dangers of a social revolution against those in power rise exponentially as that number increases. Without question, indicators such as crime, begging, homelessness and vagrancy are directly connected. It may be asked: With these key social indicators of health, poverty and unemployment at the levels that they are - is there any good news?

There are a number of approaches put forward on how best to deal with health, poverty and unemployment. Some say that it is a government problem and that, via subsidies or income grants, Government should initiate improvements in the form of direct support. Others think it is a macro-economic issue and that provided prerequisites for long-term growth are properly implemented, the trickle-down effect of improved employment will positively impact health and poverty in the long term.

How we deal with the connected issues of Health, Poverty and Unemployment will make or break South Africa.

It is heartening to see the government responding so quickly to what amounts to a crisis affecting poor people.

185

Still others think it is too big a problem for Government on its own, and should be a public/private sector initiative, appropriately institutionalised.

It may be argued that, to some extent, the solution is a combination of all three. In reality any one of the above (or a combination) takes an inordinate amount of time to effect.

Clearly, the Government rates highly the issue of alleviating the plight of the poor and it is possibly even the priority.

As has been said elsewhere in this book, in the years immediately after 1994, there was no money to do this. Now, after eight years of sound financial policy, improved tax collection, better balance of payments etc., there is greater resolve and capacity at government level to make improvements.

The determination by Government to eradicate these three significant imbalances in our society was reported in **The Sunday Times** of 13 October, where the following initiatives were lauded:

- An investigation into the zero-rating of food stuffs
- An agreement with the mostly white mining industry on raising R100 billion to fund black entry into the sector
- A process of widening access to antiretrovirals in public institutions.

"These three developments - each of which represents a mammoth step - indicate a serious effort by the Government to address pressing social, economic and health issues ... it is heartening to see the Government responding so swiftly to what amounts to a crisis affecting poor people."

"Coupled with this is the increase in social grants by between R10 and R20; these are small amounts but they are indicative of the Government's desire to do something." A further example of government initiative is the National Development Agency, set up to deal with poverty eradication and social development, which recently unveiled a new approach to funding that seeks to identify pockets of poverty and then fund community projects proactively, rather than waiting to receive, and then act on, unsolicited applications.

This approach to poverty reduction has been designed to encourage collaboration between government and public entities, civil society organisations, grant makers and the private sector.

There are literally hundreds of diverse South African non-profit organisations that derive some of their funding from the National Development Agency or NDA. Between May 2000 and June 2002, the NDA dispensed nearly R316 million of government and European Union funding to non-profit organisations.

CEO of NDA, Delani Mtagmbu, understands the magnitude of his task. "The biggest risk we now have to democracy is managing the aspirations of the people. Until the two core players in the economy - Government and the private sector - realise that they are not taking a key economic sector into account, both Government and the private sector will be adversely impacted by under-development ... we need to look at creative ways of budgeting, targeting poverty and mobilising additional resources."

He concludes: "Creating jobs is not the only answer. People must be encouraged to develop self-sufficiency. Alongside the village-based development at the micro-level, you need flagship projects at the macro-level to encourage bigger economies of scale, to attract investors and penetrate markets. This is at the core of my approach to development."

But what really astounded us in our research was the growing number of South Africans, from various stakeholder groups, who view these issues as "opportunities for positive action" rather than "problems to escape from".
Some examples:

- The Premier Foods and Metro Cash and Carry initiative to subsidise a 12.5 kg bag of mealie meal (which normally sells for anything between R46 and R54) and so to create a price of R25.99 at their outlets.

- The Ethalaneni Development Trust in KwaZulu-Natal is involved in community food production. Their products are sold to local markets, with surplus food supplied to the community.

- The Caring Network, based in the Western Cape, cares for the sick, the destitute and the dying. According to this organisation's figures, 12 caregivers made 1042 visits to 52 clients in July 2002.

- Feedback - a food distribution scheme - was initially set up to distribute left-over food from film shoots to impoverished organisations in the townships. By March this year, the quantity of food distributed was close to 50 000 kilogrammes a month.

- The Street People Project, an initiative by the City of Cape Town, is another example of an organisation devoted to improving the lives of the estimated 10 000 children who make a living on the street. Primarily, their aim is to get involved before it is too late and rebuild healthy families that can provide for the children themselves.

These are just five out of hundreds of examples of extraordinary projects that have been initiated by ordinary South Africans in their quest to reduce the problems in health, poverty, and unemployment.

These NGOs (some of which are highlighted in our Chapter 25: Private Sector Miracles that are Changing the Nation) are passionately focused on making a positive, sometimes miraculous, contribution in this regard.

Clearly the Government takes seriously the plight of the poor.

perspec*tive*

There is evidence that the job creation tide may have turned. From September 2001 to February 2002, the number of people with jobs increased by a massive 800 000.

187

Conclusion

In a forthright interview, President Mbeki admits that the Government alone cannot resolve these problems, and, in particular, the problem of job creation.

He challenges trade unions, that are at the forefront of the call for more jobs, to use the investment muscle they possess through their provident funds, to channel this money towards the infrastructural development that creates jobs.

This will require the fund managers and their trade union trustees to buy into a different mind-set, one that accepts less return for a more socially conscious investment.

On the upside, however, there is growing evidence that the positive impact of the devaluation in the rand and the knock-on effect (now a permanent feature of our economy) on the tourism industry and the primary and secondary manufacturing sector will start improving employment levels.

Business Day (26 September 2002) reported: "SA workforce grows 0.5 percent in second quarter after construction, manufacturing and mining companies added staff (Statistics SA).

"The total number of people with jobs, including non-registered workers such as hawkers and domestic servants, rose to 11.4 million in February from 10.6 million last September while the economically active population expanded to 16.1 million from 15.4 million. The jobless rate declined to 29.4 per cent from 29.5 per cent."

In just six months, 800 000 jobs were added: now that is a trend going in the right direction!

Parallel reality is a question of how you see it: half-full or half-empty; or how you feel about it: positive or negative.

Those of us who are looking for positive angles, in even the most pervasive social problems, will hopefully conclude that the growing energy devoted to these areas will result in a society that is healthier, better off and increasingly employed. This energy needs support from Government. The chapters in this book indicate that this is increasingly the case.

Many South Africans, from all walks of life, already devote considerable energy, and are making a significant contribution, to reducing these evils in our society. We have a sense that, more and more, South Africans are beginning to care and are beginning to realise that they can, in their own way, make a difference.

(Large parts of this perspective were sourced from the magazine **The Big Issue**, October 2002, issue 63 volume 6. **The Big Issue** is sold by socially-excluded people who buy the magazine at R4.55 and then sell it to the public for R8.95. Projects have been developed to train, teach, empower and equip vendors to find permanent employment and accommodation.)

In a forthright interview, President Mbeki admits that Government alone cannot resolve job creation.

Hlanyane Samuel Hlongoane knew his life was on the right track when he started working on Transnet's eye train as a student volunteer. "The moment I stepped onto Phelophepa, I knew I was in a different world, a world that was about helping and healing," says Hlongoane. That was in 1997 when Hlongoane was a third year optometry student at the University of Natal.

Now qualified, Hlongoane, aged 29, is the resident optometrist on Phelophepa (which means "clean living" in Setswana) and he plans to ride the rails for many years to come. "This is my gift to the community to say thank you for helping me through my life," he says. "If you just sit back and look at other people's problems you are never going to do anything good."

Phelophepa, the R16 million eye clinic on rails, built from old rolling stock in 1993, visits 36 points in South Africa's rural areas between January and September. Since 1994, it has treated almost 350 000 patients, often restoring full sight to patients suffering from cataracts that have reduced their vision to a blurry memory. The train has also brought 450 000 people, half of them children, health education and counselling at a nominal fee. The train's R10 000 a week running costs are subsidised by Transnet and a range of donor companies.

Hlongoane grew up in Hammanskraal north of Pretoria intending to work in eye-health because his mother suffered from myopia caused by glaucoma. He says his first stint on the train opened his own eyes to both the plight of the rural folk, who have dubbed Phelophepa "the miracle train", and to their deep appreciation for the relief it brought them: "Everywhere we stopped, the people flocked to it - it is their only hope. I just got touched by what I saw when I realised how much people needed its services."

After graduating, Hlongoane joined a private optometry practice in Swaziland, but he quickly became disenchanted. "When you work in private practice you must focus all the time on the income and making the business grow," he says. "In private practice everything you do is for money.

But when you work on the train, the emphasis is only on the patients, every patient is treated the same and you must make sure that they are all treated well. We treat people with respect and they respect us."

Hlongoane says other key medical workers on the train, its resident doctor and psychologist, also have a long-term commitment to Phelophepa and its work: "I have also managed to lure a colleague from university to come and work as a pharmacist."

"We all find there is more sense of purpose and fewer problems than in a normal working environment. It is like a family."

After nine months on the move, the train returns to Johannesburg for two months of refurbishment and restocking with equipment. Hlongoane says his team spends the time preparing thousands of packs of instruments and dressings for the next nine-month outing. Life on the train is hard but it is made easier by warm hospitality offered to the eye train staff by the communities in which they work: "The love of the people makes it all worth it. You feel like you are in your own area - highly welcomed and protected."

Since 1994, the train has treated 350 000 people - often restoring full sight.

20

Above all, Aids is a social and humanitarian disaster. It is an epidemic that will touch every South African over and over again during the next 20 years. Critically the attitudes of government, business and of individuals have changed in the last year. There is a recognition that we have a war to fight, that we have to be together on this, that we have choices. To name, blame and shame won't help, we have to have compassion for those affected. Given the recent history of our land we are in no doubt as to which course our country will take.

Aid

Changing the Course of the Epidemic

Stephen Kramer: Head of Aids Research Metropolitan Group

HIV, like many epidemics, is a reflection, to some degree, of a social circumstance that is stressful or in turmoil. Historically, most epidemics have happened in societies which were under stress or were unequal or lacking in cohesion. It was precisely the events that took place in South Africa during the decade after 1990, following the period of apartheid, that enabled the rapid spread. These included migrant labour practices (themselves a reflection of inequality), the low status of women, high levels of violence, rape and sexually transmitted diseases. Add to this the distractions of political change and you have the conditions for a disaster.

Many might say that the only "good news" about HIV/Aids in South Africa is that it can only get better. Not so! It could get worse. It is my belief, however, that there is evidence of a turn for the better.

Essentially HIV has two stages - first comes HIV infection and following that (with a delay of a 5 to 8 years) is the epidemic of Aids sickness.

South Africa has been through the first phase of rapid infection, and is starting to enter a period of disease progression. There are a few markers relating to infection that indicate interventions are beginning to take effect:

𝑋 Recent antenatal clinic figures for HIV show a slower infection rate than might have been expected;

𝑋 The figures for younger women show declining levels. While more evidence is needed to verify what this implies, there are other reasons to believe that a turning point has been reached, but the effects of behavior changes will be felt gradually over time.

The second phase of the epidemic is characterized by Aids-related sickness and death.

S

Clinical Measures

Clinical measures of actual infection levels are of great significance and there are two main types.

In recent antenatal surveys, the rate of infection among pregnant women seems to have slowed, especially in young women. While this needs to be interpreted with caution, as there could be other forces at play, the statistics give reason for optimism.

Then there's the indirect measure - the per cent of pregnant women infected with syphilis. This relates to HIV in two ways. Women with syphilis are more at risk of being infected with HIV, all other things being equal; and high levels of syphilis are also a sign of unsafe sex.

A big decrease in syphilis among this group (the infection rate in 2001 was only 38 per cent of the level two years earlier) shows a change towards safer sex and better treatment.

The proportion of change brought about by safer activity versus treatment is hard to tell but both play a role.

Other sexually transmitted diseases increase the risk of HIV infection by between 10 and 50 times. Therefore, reduced levels of Sexually Transmitted Diseases (STDs) can themselves alter the epidemic.

What does all this mean for the millions of South Africans who are already infected? There is probably cause for optimism in that far too few of these people have access to anti-retroviral drugs which can, for most people, extend life by many years and come close to turning HIV into a chronic but manageable disease.

The cost of these drugs and the surrounding diagnostic tests has been reduced in the past two years, but it is still beyond the means of many South Africans. The only hope for wider access is through private medical aid, company-managed treatment programmes, and via state medical services. Thirdly, there is the issue of Aids orphans. The projections are that the number is likely to peak at two million in the next five to seven years. Massive social intervention will be required to stop the advent of another "lost generation" as these children run the risk of being ignored, becoming uneducated, and ending up on the nation's conscience.

Cause Indicators

In assessing the risk HIV poses to a society, there are a number of things we can look at. None of them is absolute and one can never reduce the risk of an epidemic to a few variables, but the correlations are worth examining.

Social Risk

Epidemics are most severe in societies that are divided - the "other" in such a society is always where risk is perceived to lie, and personalising risk is thus rendered more difficult. Epidemics impact more heavily on societies that are unequal, putting both the rich and the poor in danger, and they tend to be at their worst during times of social change or stress. There are exceptions to these notions, but they are largely valid.

On all three accounts, South Africa was in a situation of extreme risk in the mid-90s when changes were happening in the country.

So, what of the future? While it is hard to measure, there is little doubt that, although still divided, South Africa is less so than it was 10 years ago and that social change is still under way if not accelerating. Indicators show that South Africa's economic inequality has decreased in the past decade, and government policy and measures in place to advance equity will accelerate that process. It might be possible to say that the most stressful period of adjustment is over - making it easier for people to take control of their lives and build a future.

A movement is clearly underway which will mobilise our society in the fight against Aids, in much the same way as it was mobilised to defeat apartheid.

HIV, like many epidemics, is a reflection,
to some degree, of a social circumstance
that is stressful or in turmoil.

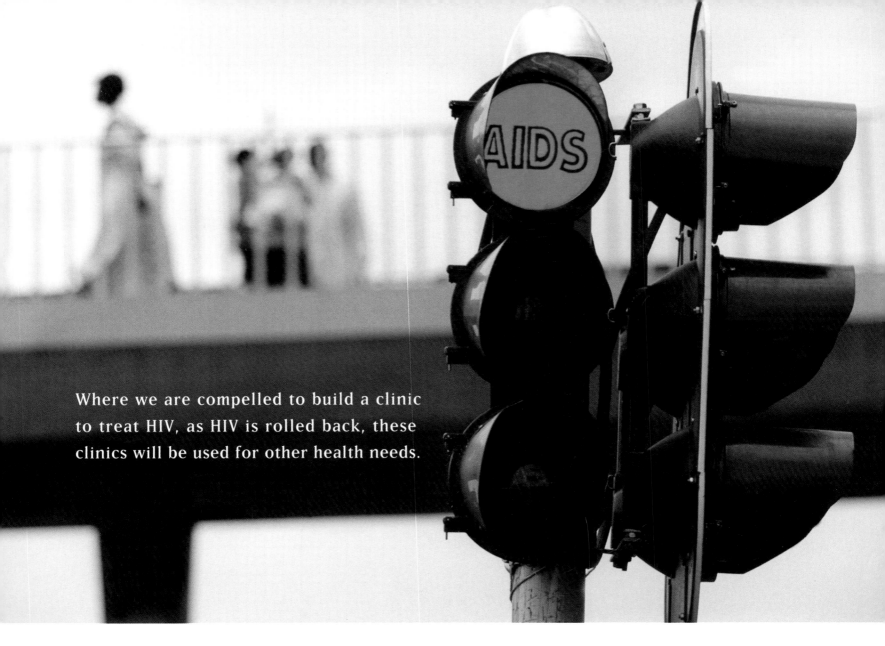

Where we are compelled to build a clinic to treat HIV, as HIV is rolled back, these clinics will be used for other health needs.

Treatment Indicators

Corporate Intervention

There have, in recent months, been announcements by companies of their intention to provide anti-retroviral drugs to staff. These include mining houses, retailers, financial conglomerates and oil companies and the evidence shows that providing treatment not only saves lives, but also saves money.

Many companies that have led the way have done so after analysing the financial implications and they see it as a business decision. Add to this the fact that between four and five million South African's have life assurance and paying death benefits is often more costly than keeping people alive. It is only a matter of time before HIV treatment becomes a standard employee benefit.

Wider access to treatment, beyond the ranks of the employed, is perhaps the greater challenge. The notion that poor people cannot take drugs has been dispelled - in many cases compliance with complex dosage in resource-poor settings has been higher than in developed countries. It is true that these individuals have been selected, and may not reflect the likely outcome of a wider programme - but it is also clear that, with good preparation, most people can take the therapies.

Evidence shows that providing treatment not only saves lives but also saves money.

Individual Intervention

The most compelling lesson learned in modeling and studying this epidemic is that, at any point, concerted action by committed individuals can change its course.

It is never a lost cause. It is never too late to have an impact. This is a particularly nasty disease, in that it robs society of economically productive people, while leaving their dependants, the young and the old, largely unaffected.

Countries in which young adults die in larger numbers than the elderly are usually countries at war and HIV/Aids is set to change the shape of our society. The virus may also compel our people to unite and face a common enemy because it will only be beaten by a concerted effort by South Africans of every background.

Civil Intervention

We see strong signs of a healthy and robust civil response to HIV/Aids. The Treatment Action Campaign has fought a number of court battles favouring treatment ... and won. The South African Medical Association has committed itself to wider treatment access. South African businesses are, in increasing numbers, providing treatment to their staff and a civil movement is clearly underway which will mobilise our society in the fight against Aids, in much the same way as it was mobilised to defeat apartheid.

The danger that HIV further divides South Africa, and that it ultimately increases inequality, is a very real one. It is recognised that social interventions are critical to continue moving SA down the path towards social integration and greater equity - if for no other reason than to fight HIV and other epidemics.

Winning the Battle and the War

Perhaps the key to understanding this disease is that one of two outcomes is possible. It either destroys ... or it is defeated. By fighting HIV, many elements are put in place that will ultimately result in defeating the disease as well as building capacity to deal with other important social issues that are so much part of the health of a developing nation.

Where we are compelled to build a clinic to treat HIV, as HIV is rolled back, these clinics will be used for other health needs.

South African society, under threat, has realised the importance of gender equality, has seen the dangers of breaking up families using the migrant labour system, and has understood the importance of primary health care and of sexual health.

At a broader level, policy makers can clearly show that inequality and disempowerment endanger not only the poor and the weak, but put all people, including the rich and powerful, at risk. South Africa is taking steps to deal with these issues and to protect itself from HIV and, in the process, will protect itself from so much more and consequently become a healthier and happier society. It will require a great deal of effort to reach this goal - an effort that South Africans, who have overcome apartheid, will not and cannot fail to make.

The small Glimmer of Hope

So where is the good news as we wage this battle with Aids? Firstly it would appear that we are beginning to turn the tide of infection and secondly the growing level of co-operation and collaboration between Government, the private sector and the many NGOs may leave us a stronger, more unified society - having fought the battle together, and won.

It is my belief, however, that there is evidence of a turn for the better... The statistics give reason for optimism.

Increasingly the world is a global village. Trade liberation and the internet have rendered information a short term advantage. Any company or country not connected will simply not be involved. Given our virtual isolation in 1995, we have made significant progress so far with connectivity. What we are about to experience with more competition in the fixed line and cellular marketplaces will make our progress seem pedestrian. Interestingly the digital revolution may well be the most effective way to close the gap between the North and the South. The low cost of labour and our high level IT innovation give us competitive advantage in the arena of IT based service provision.

Global Connectedness
SA IT Successes Worldwide

Part 1
Jeremy Ord: Chairman and CEO of Dimension Data

"Talent, passion and hard work can create a myriad of opportunities in life and business. I feel Dimension Data's own success is proof of that, as is the huge international demand for IT-skilled South Africans".

South African information and communication technology (ICT) companies have not only had considerable successes at home, but have earned themselves a strong reputation internationally. The reasons are remarkable, many and varied and will be described further. I believe these successes are due, in no small part, to the attributes that have come to define the new South Africa, its rainbow people and its own political and social successes.

> **South African ICT companies have earned themselves strong reputations internationally.**

I believe our information technology (IT) successes are linked to the characteristics that define living in Africa - a challenging, pioneering continent. In a country that inspires people to excel, instilling a willingness to find workable solutions to past problems, we are continually learning to overcome our differences. These lessons have significantly impacted on our professional lives.

Success in the IT industry has occurred at many levels: from companies becoming world players in their respective fields with pioneering and unique projects, through to a highly competent, motivated and sought after workforce.

Successful Companies
The most prominent include Dimension Data, networking company Datatec, Internet firm Thawte Consulting, accounting software makers Softline, secure electronic payment company Prism and development and implementations company Mosaic, and there are many others.

In the telecoms arena, Telkom has been actively involved in increasing connectivity in Africa through the undersea cable that connects us to Europe and Asia, while Multichoice Africa broadcasts to most parts of Africa and has a significant investment in China.

The South African cellular market has exploded beyond expectation, making us leaders in GSM technology. The two main cellular network providers, Vodacom and MTN, have expanded into Africa and provide many countries with the kind of telephone access that we take for granted.

Indeed, South Africa has long been thought of as the economic superpower of southern Africa, much as Nigeria's robust economy is the key player in West Africa.

Global Reach

Our reach, however, has extended far beyond our neighbours. We also supply world-class services to the North American, European and Asian markets. Our success stories range from companies carrying out international business; to individuals "going international"; to projects that have been initiated and completed from South Africa.

Global People

Our success is a practical demonstration of my feeling about South Africans. We are a great people. South African software engineers, working with network engineers and a host of other participants, were for example able to build a global IT system for the trans-Atlantic company, Premier Farnell.

As many examples show, we're a nation of people with talent, skill, experience and the ability to be globally competitive. Undoubtedly, South Africa has very good information technology skills. Dimension Data is an excellent example of this. Founded in 1983, we now operate in more than 30 countries and our 2001 revenue was $2.5 billion.

South African Skills

South African rugby players are among the finest in the world and can be found playing for clubs overseas, and even other countries. The same is true of our IT professionals.

In the last 10 years we have emerged stronger and more determined. The years of isolation have stimulated our innovative capacity and our will to succeed.

According to a global IT IQ report by US online-testing company, Brainbench, South Africa has the highest concentration of certified professionals in Africa in most critical IT skill areas, and ranks among the top 25 IT IQ countries in the world. This is supported by the fact that South Africa has just less than an estimated five per cent of the $300 billion global software market.

South African IT skills are very much in demand:

- We have people who have broad-based skills in comparison to the narrow, specialised skills found in Europe and North America
- We have greater exposure to a wider variety of technologies, and have accumulated the skills to work with them
- We have broad knowledge and flexibility, enabling us to deal with the convergence issues that will provide much of the IT value-add in the near future
- We have a reputation for working hard.

ICT Education

South Africa's global IT success is, in no small part, due to the kind of people we are. Over the past 10 years, we have emerged stronger and more determined. The isolation could have cowed us, but it seems to have stimulated our innovative capacity and our determination to succeed.

- We are actively educating our people in crucial fields such as IT to ensure we can continue to offer world-class service internationally.

- We have a well-developed technology education system, both through traditional technicons and universities, and innovative education forums.

For example, CIDA, the Community and Individual Development Association, described extensively in this

- Prism is involved in developing a cashless fleet and card management payment solution for the retail petroleum industry, which is being piloted in Saudi Arabia.

SA Innovation

South Africa's own use of technology is also very advanced. In banking we have one of the most sophisticated infrastructures worldwide. We were one of the first countries to develop online banking, with Nedbank and First National Bank launching in 1996 and they were soon followed by the other major players.

In many other areas we have been an early adopter of technology, especially in mobile phones. We have some of the most sophisticated GSM networks in the world in terms of features. The models for pre-paid use, which were developed here, have been so successful that they are used extensively around the world. We also have a very high ratio of cellular to fixed lines.

Similarly, South Africa is one of the few developing countries to have advanced technology in other fields:
- Our nuclear research and research institutes
- Our electricity utility, Eskom, is involved in advanced work on a smaller, more useful pebble-bed nuclear reactor and is also a powerhouse in electricity-generation in Africa, including alternative sources like hydro-electrics
- Sasol is a world leader in petrochemical technology
- Research in satellite technology, principally through the SunSat project at the University of Stellenbosch, has produced a remarkable satellite that was recently launched into orbit. SunSat's primary goal was to do high-resolution photography off low-cost technology. This, in itself, was a huge success and we have gained recognition in the space industry
- Digital image processing development is used in the mining industry to locate mineral deposits through aerial photography. Our mining houses are world-renowned in their own right and have operations throughout Africa, Australia, Europe and North America.

book (Chapter 25), has a very specific technology component, with a syllabus that Dimension Data helped to draft. Lectures are given by members of our staff, and we plan to deepen our involvement in this ground-breaking project.

South African Success Stories
- Many South African ICT businesses now have a global presence. Softline developed home-grown accounting software for the middle-market. They have sizable operations in the US and Australia, and now have a global customer base of about 50 000 customers.

- Mark Shuttleworth's Thawte Consulting, an Internet verification company, was bought by Verisign and this catapulted the Capetonian into a position of becoming the first African in space.

- Prism Holdings recently signed a deal with TM Touch, the GSM network operator subsidiary of Malaysia's giant telecommunications corporation, Telekom Malaysia. They use Prism's aSIMetrix SIM cards, which are the world's first subscriber identification module to incorporate a full suite of crypto, payment and secure multi-application capability. They have also signed a deal with technology services company, SchlumbergerSema, using these cards.

Our banks have one of the most sophisticated infrastructures globally.

There has also been significant interest expressed in South Africa through President Thabo Mbeki's ICT Advisory Council, which has attracted the interest of a number of global players to invest in our technology.

The Department of Trade and Industry has an initiative to market South Africa as a source of low-cost capability in technology, including call centres and in several other areas. It is an exciting project that combines the high level of skill required with the relatively low cost of South African labour, in much the same way that India has captured a sizeable slice of the hardware market (Sahara has a significant global presence).

While Gauteng Province is home to 70 per cent of South Africa's technology companies, Cape Town has launched the Cape Information Technology Initiative (CITI), to attract ICT firms.

To ensure that South Africa remains at the forefront, the Department of Arts, Culture, Science and Technology is focusing on specific areas such as IT, biotech and remote sensing. They have also realigned most of our tertiary education institutions in these directions. In addition, some businesses have been spun out of the security industry. An example is Nanoteq, which writes cryptographic software.

All of these examples show that we are on a strong footing to produce even more success stories and that our enterprising and world-class companies can continue to have an impact internationally.

Government Initiatives

Apart from these technology successes, an unusual and differentiating feature of the South African technology landscape is the number of active small and medium enterprises (SMEs).

In this regard, our Government's project to encourage these SMEs, as well as some well-developed venture capital offerings, is significant. Dimension Data, for example, has initiated a unit called Protocol that is used to invest in successful start-ups. This has, in the past, provided innovations such as online procurement services, automation of procurement in the automotive industry, and online claims processing in the health care industry.

We have also funded some pure technology plays, including a company that has developed systems for bulk SMS distribution and a speech-recognition technology company.

The initiatives of the state-funded Council for Scientific and Industrial Research (CSIR) have given rise to notable achievements in channelling research funds. In fact, the funding for the SunSat project came from the then Foundation for Research and Development, another state-funded body.

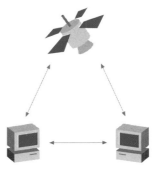

The Future

While we have our eyes on future projects, it is also rewarding to see that there are initiatives on the go to make sure the next generation of South Africans is empowered to participate actively in the global IT industry.

There are a number of NGOs active in the technology sector, such as SchoolNet, which aims to provide connectivity to school children throughout southern Africa. They have been operating successfully for several years and Dimension Data is proud to provide all of the Internet connectivity for them. There is also Gauteng Online, a government-sponsored initiative to ensure all the schools, pupils and teachers in the province have access to the Internet. We are providing the connectivity for the first 35 schools in the programme.

This active use of technology is the best way to address the so-called "digital divide", and a good way to narrow the gap between the haves and the have-nots. Technology closes the gap between the advantaged and disadvantaged communities; innovation and hard work become the distinguishing factor, not history or a strong balance sheet.

Perhaps, most importantly, this is a good way to increase the number of economically active participants in the South African economy. We can expect our ICT reputation to continue to grow globally.

The active use of technology is the best way to address the so-called "digital divide" - to narrow the gap between the haves and the have-nots.

Is South Africa on-line?

Part 2
Clairwyn van der Merwe: Journalist

Even in the latest 4X4, the road to Gaseleka near the Botswana border is bone-jarringly bumpy, not to mention muddy if the rainy season has started.

Not exactly a bustling metropolis, this is the last place you'd expect to find anyone holding a board meeting or preparing financial statements for audit. But, at the local telecentre, this is how things are done.

The centre was started five years ago and has grown into a profitable - and sustainable - community business. The seed funding came from the Universal Service Agency (USA), whose mandate is to boost telecoms access in underserviced areas like Gaseleka.

Originally it only offered basic payphone services to the people of the six surrounding villages, but, now, it has

branched out into accredited computer training and also does postal collection (a convenient touch considering that hardly anyone living here has a street address). Lately, it has been arranging weekly visits by Home Affairs officials so that villagers can apply for identity documents or register births, deaths and marriages.

Community-owned and run, Gaseleka's telecentre is now making enough money to pay eight full-time employees. What's more, it ploughs profits back into the area, either by setting up new community projects or expanding its own range of services. A formally constituted board of directors, representing community members, keeps an eagle eye on the telecentre's running and funding, and sees that the books are audited regularly and professionally.

At another telecentre, near the Kruger National Park in Limpopo Province, the women entrepreneurs running it have added new services like hairdressing and dressmaking. Not long ago, they started offering Internet access to tourists visiting the game reserve.

Kick-starting Rural Growth Through Communications

Small though such successes might seem, they are striking examples of how communications technology can kick-start economic and entrepreneurial activity, even in the poorest of poor rural communities.

"People in rural areas are sometimes more creative than those of us who read their problems through the eyes of Johannesburg," says Dipuo Mvelase, chief executive of the USA. "Often, there is a strong sense of mutual dependence, a fierce determination to make things work in adverse circumstances."

Admittedly, not all of the USA's 103 telecentres (95 of which are in deep rural parts of South Africa) have been as successful as those in Gaseleka and Limpopo.

But, more often than not, says Dipuo, the ones that are thriving tend to be those run and owned by communities who share in the profits and benefit from access to job opportunities and training, not to mention access to emergency services and connectivity with the outside world.

The experience of Vodacom, one of South Africa's three cellular network operators, bears out the entrepreneurial

pulling power of communications. Vodacom's 3171 Phoneshop franchises, housed in renovated shipping containers, have created opportunities for more than 1600 community-based entrepreneurs who run the services on a cash-per-call basis and earn revenues by selling airtime.

With between 52 and 60 million calls being made from these community phones every month, Phoneshop owners are increasingly starting to employ other people to assist them, and some are generating enough revenue to expand or start new ventures.

Now, determined to bridge the rural connectivity gap and, at the same time, stimulate economic growth in rural backwaters, the South African Government is pressing ahead with plans to licence small operators in 29 districts across the country. These rural districts have been targeted specifically because they have fewer than five fixed telephone lines for every 100 people, some of whom still have to walk up to 10 kilometres to reach a phone.

South Africa's telecommunications industry has been busy connecting much of the continent.

As a starting point, licences are being issued in 10 of these districts, one licence for each, with the 10 new operators expected to be up and running by the middle of 2003.

Turning Grand Plans Into Reality

Understandably, the issuing of the licences is generating huge excitement among the communities who, up to now, have been last in the queue for connectivity.

At the same time, ICT policy-makers are keenly aware of perceptions that rural connectivity is a hopeless case, hamstrung by the sheer numbers of people still lacking basic access, the huge cost of installing infrastructure and the poverty problem.

Intent on making this grand plan succeed, players across the South African ICT sector are pulling together to give potential operators all the help they can get.

From the side of the policy-makers and the regulator, ICASA, the entry barriers are being kept as low as possible,

There is light at the end of the communications tunnel for South Africa's rural residents.

skewed in favour of small businesses and local communities. Preference is being given to applicants from historically disadvantaged groups, with an emphasis on companies controlled, managed and owned by women.

Bidders will have to pay only R15 000 to apply for the licences - steep enough to show they're serious but low enough to be within the reach of a cash-constrained small business. Once licensed, the new players will also be getting a free hand in their choice of technology, including voice-over Internet protocol, and, possibly, favourable terms for interconnection with the major operators.

Access to funding will be a key issue for the new operators, who analysts say can realistically expect to spend between R15 million and R100 million each to build their networks. Among those exploring financing possibilities are the Universal Service Agency and the Canadian-funded International Development Research Centre, along with a range of other private and public funding agencies, including the Development Bank of SA and the Industrial Development Corporation.

Others who have thrown their weight behind the under-serviced-area licensing plan include technology empowerment company Forge Ahead BMI-T, which has joined the USA on roadshows to all 10 districts to raise awareness and encourage communities to form broad-based bidding consortia.

"This is an incredible opportunity for local communities and entrepreneurs," says Forge Ahead joint managing director Simon White. "The broader the level of involvement, the greater the chances of turning the Government's good intentions into practical, sustainable reality."

More Competition, More Choice
While it seems there's light at the end of the tunnel for South Africa's rural residents, the overall communications landscape is also being reshaped.

The country is believed to have the fourth fastest-growing cellular market in the world. Three companies compete in the sector, the latest arrival being Cell C, whose services went live in December 2001. Within six months, the new kid on the block had attracted more than 500 000 subscribers, despite the seven-year head start of MTN and Vodacom, who already had well over eight million subscribers between them.

While refusing to embroil themselves in price wars, the accelerated level of cellular competition has sparked off a host of budget-friendly developments like per second billing and discounted pre-paid and contract rates.

Meanwhile, although Cell C's focus right now is on building a base on its home ground, both MTN and Vodacom have turned their gaze northwards. And both appear to have taken in their stride the uniquely African obstacles that operators face in rolling out networks across the continent.

In Nigeria, where MTN claims a 53 per cent share of the mobile market, network rollout costs are about two-and-a-half times higher than in South Africa, thanks to rickety or non-existent infrastructure. Power supply is so erratic that MTN has to use its own diesel generators at almost all base stations. (Keeping these generators fed is no easy matter, either, since the country is plagued with fuel shortages and tanks have to be guarded around the clock.)

Other pitfalls are the wonky state of Nigerian roads, prohibitive customs duties on all imports - and just about all GSM equipment has to be imported - and the absence of any but the most aged maps for network planning.

Despite these snags, MTN's Nigerian network was up and running by the government-set deadline of August 2001. Less than a year after going live, its subscriber base had soared from zero to half a million, nearly three times higher than initial projections.

What's more, the company, which also operates mobile networks in Cameroon, Rwanda, Swaziland and Uganda, is credited with creating 10 000 jobs in Nigeria where, in pre-cellular days, 85 per cent of citizens had reportedly never used a telephone.

Vodacom, too, has been hard at work in Africa, starting with its early investments in Lesotho and then Tanzania, where it took just three months to overtake its three rivals and become the biggest digital cellular network. More recently, the South African-based operator has won GSM licences in Mozambique and the Democratic Republic of Congo and projects that, by 2004, its international arm will be generating around 30 per cent of its operating profits.

Liberalisation Loosens up Fixed-line Market

After years of monopoly, South Africa's fixed-line market is finally loosening up, poised for the entry of a new national player to compete head-on with the incumbent, Telkom.

In May 2002, Telkom emerged from a five-year period of "exclusivity" aimed at preparing itself for competition while meeting government-mandated targets to roll out 2.8 million new lines, improve service quality, and modernise its network.

While consumers and business may have been chaffing at the bit over their lack of choice in fixed-line communications providers, the five-year wait has been well worth it, according to Telkom, which also owns 50 per cent of cellular operator Vodacom.

Since its partial privatisation in early 1997 - a sale that brought $1.26 billion into the country in exchange for 30 per cent of the Government's 100 per cent shareholding - Telkom points to an impressive list of achievements.

Apart from bringing first-time connectivity to almost 2700 villages, the company has connected more than 20 000 schools, clinics, police stations and libraries, and radically cut waiting times for installing and repairing services. Over the same period, it also replaced more than one million non-digital phone lines, enabling it to boast a telephone network that is 99.8 per cent digital, and introduced centralised network management via its world-class national network operations centre near Pretoria.

Global connectivity, long a bone of contention among bandwidth-hungry businesses, has taken a turn for the better. Telkom has been a key player in the development of Africa's most advanced undersea cable system yet, Afrilinque.

Initially dismissed by some as an African pipedream, this $630 million cable system was officially inaugurated in Dakar, Senegal, in May 2002, six years after it was first conceived.

Exciting times lie ahead as the liberalisation process in fixed-line technology unfolds.

Fact Sheet

- 6.6 million mobile phone subscribers
- 4.9 million fixed-line subscribers
- 74 per cent digital network in 1997
- 99.8 per cent digital network in 2002
- 3000 exchange units 1997, 4083 exchange units 2002
- 150 000 ISDN channels 1997, 467 518 ISDN channels 2002
- 127 272 payphone units 1997, 195 399 payphone units 2002
- SA direct service to 54 countries
- PSTN services to 271 destinations.

Bringing together operators from almost 40 nations in Africa, Europe, Australia, Asia and the Americas, the system represents a more cosmopolitan mix of investors than virtually any global cable project that has come before it.

One of the key features of Afrilinque is that it is based on the "owner-operator" business model, meaning that each participant owns a part of the cable and gets to keep the revenue earned through it.

That kind of ownership and control has huge economic significance for Africa. Up to now, many countries have had to rely on foreign operators to route their international traffic - including traffic to and from neighbouring countries. Europe has been the main transit centre for calls within Africa and between Africa and the rest of the world.

The cost of this reliance has been enormous. Every year, up to 80 per cent of Africa's inter-country telecoms revenue has left the continent, translating into an annual exodus

of around $300 million. This figure was forecast to rise dramatically over the next few years, in line with the explosive growth in traffic to and from Africa.

So the new cable system holds the prospect of achieving substantial savings and economic benefits that will grow as other African countries link up with it. The Cape Town/Europe segment has 10 landings in nine African countries, while the segment connecting with Malaysia has a landing that brings India into the system. Land-locked and neighbouring states in Africa will also be able to link into the cable system via satellite and terrestrial connections, spreading the benefits to the continent as a whole.

But it is not just African countries that have jumped at being part of the new cable system. Global telecom operators have contributed approximately half of the total investment of $630 million, lured by the prospect of many more lucrative traffic destinations, as well as a secure, high-speed alternative route for their global traffic.

The link with Europe has a total capacity of 120 gigabits, equalling 5.8 million simultaneous telephone calls, 1.45 million 64 kilobit data channels or more than 2300 television channels. The link between South Africa and Malaysia is even more powerful with a potential total capacity of 130 gigabits, equal to 6.2 million simultaneous telephone calls, 1.5 million 64-kilobit data channels or almost 2500 television channels.

Gearing Up for Growth

Exciting times lie ahead for South Africa's communications sector. As the liberalisation process unfolds, a new national network operator prepares to enter the market, and Government gears up to list a portion of its majority shareholding in Telkom.

Although much of the action will revolve around the big telecoms players on the technology landscape, they certainly won't be stealing all the thunder. Indeed, it's probably the small fry who'll be really worth watching, especially in the country's rural backwaters.

For while South Africa cannot be a serious player in global markets unless it has the connectivity to compete, neither can the country consider itself connected while some of its citizens still slog 10 kilometres or more to make a call.

"Ngifuna amahhashi amane kabangane abane bami kusasa," I said in my best Zulu to the Xhosa herdsman as I climbed off my horse.

I had been fishing for four days with friends along the Mtentu estuary, just north of the Mkambathi reserve on South Africa's Wild Coast.

Early that morning, I had decided to walk five-or-so kilometres up the beach to do some fishing at a point that was highly regarded for cob, garrick and kingfish.

I was on my own and couldn't help feeling a sense of wonderment at having this whole beach to myself. After four hours of fishing, with only one cob to show for it, I was excited at the prospect of returning by the same lovely trail.

After I had walked about a kilometre, a Xhosa herdsman with two horses came up behind me. After a fairly incoherent conversation, me with my Zulu (a combination of Fanakalo learnt on the mines and Zulu learnt at school in Natal), and he with his Xhosa, we agreed that I would ride his other horse along the beach while he took care of my fishing equipment and the two-kilo cob.

It was mid-afternoon, the tide was out, and, although I hadn't ridden for 15 years, I found myself galloping along the beach, mostly in fairly shallow water, ecstatic at the thrill of it. Like some modern version of Lawrence of Arabia, I sped across the wet sand until both the horse and I were exhausted.

It was one of the most thrilling moments of my life.

After a while, the herdsman caught up with me. It was then that I asked him whether, the next day, he could organise four horses for me and my friends (the words, in Zulu, at the beginning of this story).

After a few awkward moments in the conversation, and quite a lot of drawing in the sand, we agreed that the

four horses would arrive at eight the next morning, and that the price for the day's ride would be R40 a head.

Having concluded the deal, I gathered up my fishing equipment and my cob and proceeded to head back to my friends at the camp, assuming he would follow.

"Wait!" said the herdsman. Then and there, on this desolate beach, with no electricity for miles, no evidence of tapped water or habitation other than a few Xhosa huts, my new friend took a cellphone out of his pocket, rapped through the keys and made arrangements for the next day. "No problem, amahashi azobekhona," he beamed.

At 8:00 sharp, he arrived with horses and a broad African smile of hospitality.

I still don't know where he charges it.

At 8am sharp, he arrived with the horses and a broad African smile.

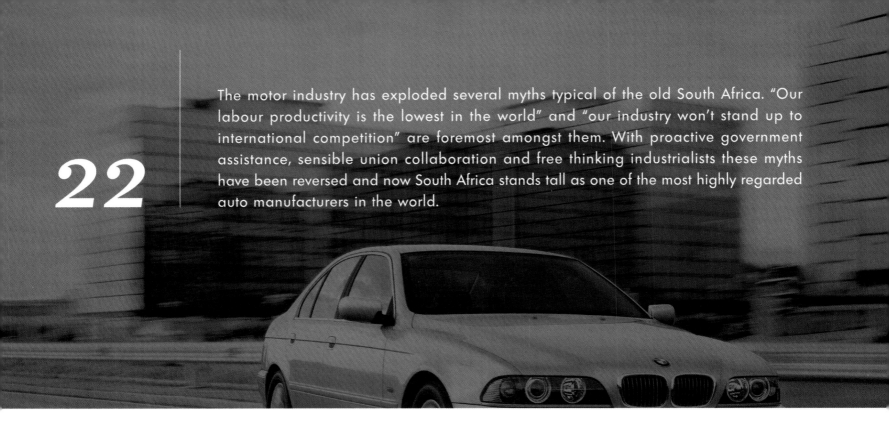

The motor industry has exploded several myths typical of the old South Africa. "Our labour productivity is the lowest in the world" and "our industry won't stand up to international competition" are foremost amongst them. With proactive government assistance, sensible union collaboration and free thinking industrialists these myths have been reversed and now South Africa stands tall as one of the most highly regarded auto manufacturers in the world.

22

Exports and Labour Productivity

- Retooling the Myth

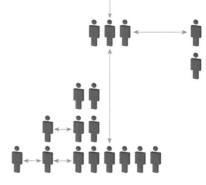

Ian Robertson
Managing Director of BMW South Africa and President of NAAMSA

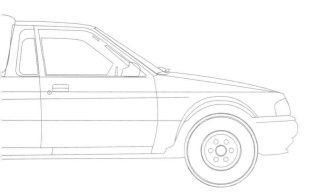

South African manufacturers who had the foresight to re-engineer their businesses for export markets have found that the world is their oyster - none more so than local automotive manufacturers. Ian Robertson, President of the National Association of Automobile Manufacturers of South Africa (NAAMSA) and Managing Director of BMW South Africa, surveys the auto industry's successes to date and challenges for the future.

208

South African vehicle manufacturers and the downstream components sector that has developed in support of our plants prove beyond doubt that locally made products can match and even better world standards. South Africa can become a prime export platform for global markets.

In the automotive manufacturing industry the numbers speak for themselves. In the mid-nineties, South African car makers exported a mere 11 500 vehicles valued at around R750 million. By the end of this year (2002), the respective figures will rise to around 130 000 vehicles valued at R15 billion. And it doesn't end there. Annual vehicle exports could reach as much as 250 000 units if latecomers to the local vehicle export stakes decide to take up the challenge by increasing their manufacturing output for export. The knock-on effect of this export drive among local car makers is most evident in the downstream manufacturing of vehicle components. Component manufacturers have become major exporters in their own right, raising their combined export value from R4 billion in 1996 to an anticipated R20 billion this year.

Massive Benefits for South Africa

The impact on the wider South African economy is dramatic. In 2001, automotive exports from South Africa represented 12 per cent of total exports (up from 1.5 per cent in 1996 and 9 per cent in 2000) and accounted for over 25 per cent of manufacturing GDP. The sector is now the third largest export earner after mining and agriculture, traditionally South Africa's mainstay export earners. Car makers have become vital contributors to the wellbeing of South Africa's economy.

The automotive industry is also a significant and stable employer with an estimated 33 000 jobs in vehicle manufacturing, 47 000 in component and tyre production, and a further 170 000 in the retail motor trade. Downstream employment ricochets out at a ratio of ten to one, meaning the industry as a whole directly and indirectly feeds and supports more than a million people in South Africa.

This is a most encouraging picture, particularly when one considers that just a few years back there were zero export earnings from the automotive industry. The industry was a typical child of the apartheid siege economy - inbred and moribund. Few South African industries were more vulnerable to globalisation than South African car manufacturers. There were not many arguments in favour of establishing a motor manufacturing industry in a developing country. An obvious requirement is close proximity to markets and in this respect South Africa is clearly disadvantaged by its geographical location. Yet the industry managed to read the signs of the times and reengineer itself so that today it is the frontrunner in the country's rapidly growing export economy.

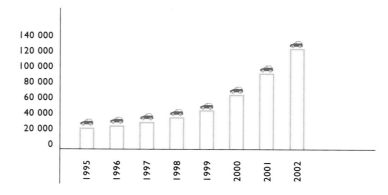

SA Vehicle Exports 1995-2002

SA Vehicle Exports ●
SA Vehicle Component Exports ●

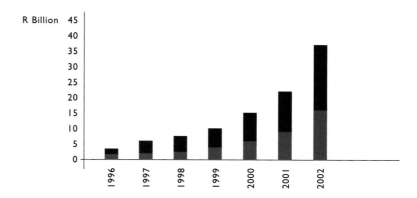

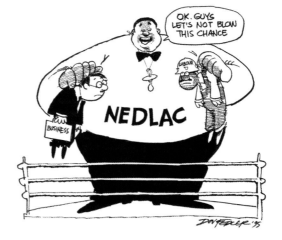

and vehicle component manufacturers and the locomotive effect these gains are having on companies in other sectors provide an object lesson in how companies in developing economies can succeed in global markets. Many South African companies in other sectors are taking a lead from car makers as they too gear up for global competition.

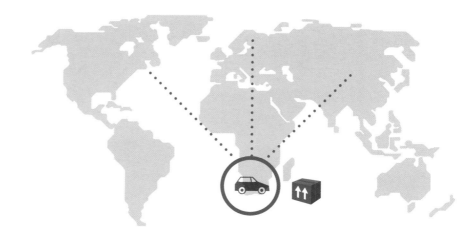

Partnership between Government and the Auto Industry - Export or Die!

Government has played a critical and very positive role in the automotive sector's response to the challenges of globalisation. Without a supportive regulatory framework that encourages and rewards export manufacture, it would not have been possible for the local automotive industry to respond so positively to the new realities of global competition.

Government has been at the very heart of the industry's export gains. Ten years ago there was 150 per cent duty on all imported vehicles and the South African market was completely closed. The heavy hand of government tariffs was everywhere. Prospects for the car making industry's growth were extremely limited as the local market for new vehicles was fast reaching saturation. In consultation with the local industry, government made a commitment to open up the local market to global competition. In essence this meant the vehicle manufacturing industry had to learn how to sustain itself or it would simply disappear. It truly was a case of adapt or die.

The upshot of the consultations was government's decision to introduce the Motor Industry Development Programme, the MIDP. This programme, which provides a legislative framework to the year 2007, provides a system of export incentives for local car and component makers, while gradually reducing import tariffs. In short, manufacturers were given the option of export participation with government backing or export isolation with no support whatsoever. The window of opportunity was closing fast. It had become a question of export or die!

The MIDP's carrot-and-stick approach encourages export growth as it allows importers of vehicles and components to offset the duty payable on imports against the value of their exports. The net effect of the programme has been to transform the industry both qualitatively and quantitatively and to integrate South African-based car and component makers into a global manufacturing network. Today, largely due to the MIDP, South Africa is part of an exclusive global club of quality car makers with real opportunity to make deeper inroads into international markets in the future.

The MIDP has also encouraged local manufacturers to rationalise models so that instead of building a broad range of cars, the focus now is on specific models in order to maximise production capabilities thereby benefiting from economies of scale. At BMW, for example, the full model line-up from the 3, 5 and 7 Series and even a few 8 Series was produced. Today only the 4-door 3 Series model, left and right hand drive, in every engine and specification derivative for local and export markets, is manufactured.

The MIDP has been an extremely sound process thus far and while it will only take the industry up to 2007, NAAMSA is in discussion with government to plan new MIDP horizons for the post-2007 period. Clearly there is great incentive for government to work with the industry to maintain the export momentum and to use export success as a model for other manufacturing sectors to emulate. Equally, vehicle manufacturers will continue to work closely with government to help meet government's broader social goals. It is a symbiotic relationship built on mutual interest and cemented by success. Clearly, it is the type of relationship that points to a winning future.

Business and Labour are Getting it Together

Destiny beckons for local automotive manufacturers. It lies in exploiting South Africa's obvious, though understated, benefits as an export-manufacturing platform. Negative reports in local and foreign media about South African potential is misplaced when there are so many obvious benefits to operating a business here. The country is blessed with abundant raw materials. It has extremely cheap electricity and low fuel costs. Land and rentals are about one fifth of their cost in developed countries and the cost of capital infrastructure in the form of buildings is amongst the cheapest anywhere. The climate is a big plus and labour costs are still competitive, although it must be said that local workers are not yet on a par educationally or productively with, for example, their East European counterparts. But considerable progress has been made and as organised labour reaps the rewards of partnership in the productive process, the only path for South Africa is forwards. Stereotypical South African management thinking about worker ignorance, indolence or apathy rapidly evaporates when our peoples' work ethic and level of knowledge is observed first hand. The commitment of our workforce and their obsession with quality dispels many myths regarding the potential, or otherwise, of South African labour. Indeed, I and my fellow executives are greatly encouraged by the way in which organised labour in South Africa is responding to new global realities. There is growing awareness that we are all challenged by globalisation, that we can only be successful as partners and that South Africa's economic future rests in a working partnership between capital, management and labour.

The proof of the pudding is in the eating. Labour productivity has improved from 7.5 vehicles per employee in 1996 to 12.6 vehicles per employee in 2001. This emerging realisation of the benefit of mutual interests is cause for optimism for the future of South African manufacturing and of the country as a whole. The thirst for knowledge and transfer of skills is evident. BMW, for example, engaged their workforce in over 150 000 hours of training last year.

I believe many of the problems that arise between management and labour are the result of miscommunication. It's like a marriage; we're going to have some arguments and fall-outs, but we're part of the same family and we all want the family to thrive and survive. In a country such as South Africa where unemployment and poverty are endemic, this becomes more than a business imperative, it is a sacred trust. In this regard, the perception that industry in South Africa is in a state of permanent conflict with organised labour is fundamentally wrong, as Anna Starcke points out in her **Starcke Realities** (May 2002). "Labour productivity has exploded, with only China, Sri Lanka, Taiwan and Korea still rated as more productive by the International Labour Organisation. The change has been most dramatic vis-a-vis the erstwhile Asian Tiger economies: according to a 29-country study by the US Bureau of Labour Statistics, SA's manufacturing labour costs, which 20 years ago were 260 per cent that of the average Asian emerging economy, are now down to half the costs in these countries. Likewise, as Tradek Economist Mike Schussler has reported, "SA hourly labour costs in dollars have seen the biggest fall of any country in the 29-country survey, having declined by around 40 per cent since 1995. 'This', says Schüssler, 'gives clearer evidence of an extremely flexible labour market.'

Our experience is different. If employment policies and management approaches are professionally handled and if open lines of responsible communication are in place, there is no problem operating in the South African industrial environment. Because of the country's historical experience, however, there are some understandable legacy problems and NAAMSA has set up a special working group made up of a number of industry role-players to address them. The group has been established specifically to further our understanding of systemic problems and to further improve communication and relationships within the industry. So far the attitudes of all parties represented in this forum have been encouraging. There is no doubt that the general attitude is positive and I believe we are moving in the right direction to secure the industry's long-term future. There is no doubt that all participants in the export initiative including management, labour and government, have a sound understanding of what needs to be done to become and remain internationally competitive. Sustainability requires world-class standards, a full order book and on-time delivery. Failure to deliver in either time or quality dimensions would be terminal.

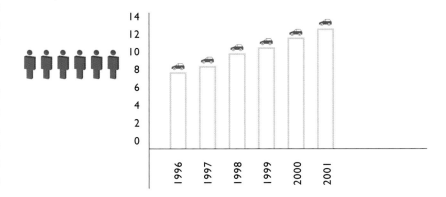

Vehicles per Employee per Day

A Broadening Base as Other Manufacturers Follow

Other companies' subsidiaries in South Africa have joined BMW's thrust into global markets. Volkswagen South Africa started exporting in 1992 when it sold Jettas to China, but its major break came in 1998 when Volkswagen AG gave its South African subsidiary a contract to build the Golf 4. Last year, VWSA exported 29 000 cars.

Ford, after making a considerable investment in its South African plant, now builds 1000 engines a day for export to Ford manufacturing plants worldwide. In 2003, Ford aims to produce 240 000 engines.

DaimlerChrysler entered the export market much later, in September 2000, yet last year (2001) it exported around 31 000 right-hand drive Mercedes-Benz C-Class vehicles from its East London plant, accounting for 77 per cent of total production.

Toyota Motor Corporation of Japan is now considering using its South African subsidiary for export production of its new "globally strategic models". This export output is destined for a number of developed countries, including European destinations in 2005.

Success In the Future

Clearly, there is a ceiling for local vehicle production after which the industry as a whole would require major restructuring. There is still upside potential as South African car makers are not there yet. When it comes to automotive component exports, however, there is no ceiling and this sector will, in my opinion, be the engine for phenomenal export growth in the future. For this to happen, the component industry will have to become less reliant on local automobile manufacturers and will need to mature into a self-sufficient sector identifying, securing and developing its own export markets abroad and ensuring that it achieves truly international competitive benchmarks.

The prospects for the industry and for South Africa are excellent. Before major foreign companies make the kind of investments global motor manufacturers are making in this country, they meticulously survey all potential hazards over the life cycle of their investments. German vehicle manufacturers, which are perhaps the most cautious when it comes to foreign investment, are now heavily engaged in export manufacturing from South Africa and others are following their lead. This kind of investment is only made on the basis of confidence in the future and provided the combination of government incentive and labour productivity provides South Africa with ongoing competitive edge.

"As the Managing Director of BMW South Africa, I am supremely confident in the future of the country and compliment the other local manufacturers. They have grasped the nettle of international competition and shown through their successes what this country and its people are capable of producing. I passionately believe that the automotive manufacturing sector is a South African success story, a real business example of a winning nation and a winning people."

"In a country where unemployment and poverty are endemic, this (cooperation)
becomes more than a business imperative - it's a sacred trust".

At BMW, numerous requests from companies outside the automotive industry are received to share insights on our success as an export manufacturer. Executives are invited to spend some time as observers on the production line at the Rosslyn plant, outside Pretoria, where 3 Series cars for the local and global market are built. This year 55 000 vehicles, 80 per cent of them for export to the most consumer demanding markets such as the USA, Japan, Singapore, Hong Kong, Taiwan, Australia and New Zealand will be built.

A number of senior executives have taken up this challenge and visited the BMW Rosslyn plant where they observed at first-hand how a modern, efficient vehicle manufacturing line operates. Perhaps more importantly, they are exposed to the working men and women who build BMW 3 Series cars for world markets.

BMW's Rosslyn plant is measured against the world's automotive plants in an annual quality study conducted by J.D. Power and Associates in the United States. This survey is considered the global industry benchmark for new-vehicle quality. South African car manufacturers are measured against all their European and American counterparts.

BMW's Rosslyn plant won the Gold Plant Quality Award ranking it first among European and American plants for quality.

As Ian Robertson says: "As an exporter, BMW SA has come a long way. In the early nineties we revitalised the local leather industry when we managed to secure a large slice of the export market for leather upholstery, initially for BMW AG, but later for other European automotive manufacturers. This year, the leather business will be worth over R2 billion."

In 1998, BMW AG approved the subsidiary's transformation from an assembly plant for the local market to a manufacturing plant fully integrated into its global manufacturing and logistics network, exporting mainly to the US, Japan and the Asia Pacific countries. To gear up for this first phase, an initial investment of over a billion rand was made into improved infrastructure, plant and equipment at the Rosslyn plant. This investment was followed by further capital injections in excess of R500 million over the following three years.

By 2000, BMW SA produced 27 500 right and left-hand drive 3-Series for export, and last year, out of a total production volume of 49 000 units, 36 000 were exported, representing around 75 per cent of our total local production - a performance that won BMW the President's Award for Export Achievement.

This year (2002), 43 000 from a total production of 55 000 vehicles will be exported. "At BMW we are proud of this achievement, just as I have no doubt other local car makers share that sense of pride in their own export gains", says Robertson.

"Despite what I believe is often unwarranted negative comment on the state of affairs in South Africa, those in the know understand the country's potential as an export platform. In December 2001, BMW AG agreed to a further R2 billion investment in BMW SA. This announcement can be seen as a major vote of confidence in the country. It means that for at least the next 10 years - which represents the next manufacturing lifecycle of a future BMW model - South Africa is considered to be a safe and profitable place to maintain a significant manufacturing facility.

It is not only inflows of investment from overseas that is sustaining the industry and creating growth. Here in South Africa, positive investment decisions are also being made within our dealer network, which I believe is one of the most advanced, certainly in any developing country, and perhaps in the world.

"The confidence of BMW SA and its dealers is evidenced by the investment of almost R300 million into showrooms, training and new ways of doing business, including e-business. Profitability and confidence within the network is high", Robertson concludes.

South Africa is considered to be a safe and profitable place to maintain a significant manufacturing facility.

One of the great legacies of apartheid was a highly sophisticated transportation system that was almost entirely inwardly focused. One of the greatest changes the world is experiencing is that of globalisation - both of trade and of tourism. It is clear therefore that a radical overhaul of the transportation sector was both necessary and urgent. This is doubly important if one recognises how critical international trade and tourism are to the most pressing social problems our country faces, unemployment and poverty.

23

Transport Infrastructure

Moving forward or going backwards

Mafika Mkwanazi: GCEO - Transnet

Prior to 1994, our transport infrastructure was the envy of Africa and much of the developing world.

However, the system was inwardly focused, mostly a result of our isolation, and very bureaucratic, mostly because of the problems of apartheid.

Since 1994, South Africa has become a fast-changing society faced with a host of challenges as an emerging democracy in an increasingly interconnected world. In order to meet the national goal of sustainable development, the country has developed strategies to improve both its competitiveness in trade and investment, and basic access and mobility for its people.

Transnet is currently investing heavily on infrastructure and this will bring about major advances in the next few years. A critical element of the programmes is the manner in which they are integrated and co-ordinated, not only between themselves and within our borders, but also in how they link to other initiatives. The Maputo Corridor (transport) is a case in point.

Transport is a means to an end and is therefore regarded as a key factor in creating sustainable economic growth. South Africa's transport system plays an important role in

the national economy and in the economics of several other African states that use the South African network and harbours to move their imports and exports.

The Transport System in 1994

The transport system in 1994 did not meet the needs of a globally and locally integrated country and its customers. This was the legacy of the previous regime's strategy.

Urban transport: the urban transport system was set up primarily to carry large numbers of black workers long distances from the townships to employment centres in the service of "separate development".

Freight transport: the freight system was designed to support inward industrialisation, import substitution and relatively cheap transport to key constituencies such as white commercial farmers.

The new South Africa brought with it an opening up of previously sanctioned markets and this caused a surge in traffic through the ports. This is evident in the massive growth in container handling and in the breakbulk sector since 1994.

Our transport
infrastructure is the
envy of the developing
world ...
and indeed some of
the developed world.

Strategic Issues

The strategic issues can be categorised into three groups:

- Cross cutting
- Public and national goals
- Customer-specific issues

The cross cutting issues include:

- Capacity building
- Industry structure
- Institutional delivery
- Financing
- Regional and international economic integration
- Technology
- Infrastructure and flexible capacity
- Global provider trends
- Links to spatial planning

Public and national goals include:

- Safety, health and security
- Environmental protection
- Role of transport in economic development
- Empowerment

Customer-specific issues include:

- Affordable basic access for passengers
- Service/cost trade-off for passengers
- Tourist travel
- Global competitiveness of freight transport
- Logistic services
- System efficiency

It became clear that a new national policy framework was necessary to guide the shaping of transport infrastructure and port development.

National Policy Frameworks

In August 1996, a White Paper on National Transport Policy was released. This was followed in September 1998 by the release of Moving South Africa, a 20-year strategy to implement and achieve the goals of the White Paper. A key focus of the policy framework is to improve South Africa's competitiveness and that of its transport infrastructure and operations through greater efficiency.

The White Paper encouraged intermodal co-ordination, co-operation and sharing of information, in both infrastructure and operations.

The goals here were to:

- Optimise customer service
- Avoid duplication
- Reduce destructive competition
- Minimise total costs
- Maximise social and economic return on investment
- Optimise capacity utilisation
- Achieve a level of integration between transport modes

The White Paper noted that Government needs to focus on policy and strategy formulation (which is its prime role) and substantive regulation (its responsibility) with a reduced direct involvement in operations and in the provision of infrastructure and services (to allow for a more competitive environment).

The White Paper and Commercial Ports Policy (March 2002) states that the port authority would assume responsibility for the maintenance and development of port infrastructure. The principle of competition within a port is also supported.

Government therefore encourages integration, inter-modalism and partnerships between the modes, provided this does not result in monopolies.

The White Paper encouraged civil aviation to promote the national interests of the country in general and to facilitate and enhance the expansion of trade and tourism. In particular, civil aviation policies aim to promote the development of an efficient and productive aviation industry that is capable of competing both domestically and internationally.

218 Other key national policy frameworks include the National rail policy and plan. The National Department of Transport is in the process of developing a national rail transport policy. In order to deliver practically on Government's policy objectives for rail transport, a Strategic Rail Transport Plan will also be developed.

The Gas Act (2001) provides for the promotion of the orderly development of the piped gas industry and establishes a national regulating framework and a national gas regulator. The Act regulates gas pipelines from a construction, commercial and technical perspective.

The national policy frameworks set out the rules of the game for transport and port infrastructure development. The policy frameworks emphasised that economic decisions are subject to general competitive principles applicable to all industries, with a view to maximising consumer choice and satisfaction.

Current Status of Transport and Port Infrastructure in South Africa

Infrastructure plays a vital role in the maintenance and growth of an economy. South Africa has been accepted as the role model in Africa when measured in terms of the quality and size of its infrastructure and its plans for the future. To cope with the demand of an envisaged minimum growth rate of three to four per cent, the Department of Transport shares a huge responsibility not only to maintain what is currently available in terms of transport infrastructure, but also to ensure that the economy receives the necessary infrastructural support to facilitate the anticipated economic growth when and where it is needed. This challenge obviously does not only pertain to the RSA, but also to the region as a whole.

 A new national framework was necessary if transport was not to become the limiting factor to the globalisation of trade and tourism.

The key transport and port infrastructure systems are:
- Commercial ports
- Railways
- Roads
- Telecommunication
- Pipelines
- Airlines

Commercial Port Infrastructure

The National Port Authority of South Africa (NPA), a division of Transnet Limited, is the largest port authority in Southern Africa, controlling seven of the 16 largest ports in the region. These are Richards Bay, Durban, East London, Port Elizabeth, Mossel Bay, Cape Town and Saldanha.

South Africa's seven commercial ports have a significant role to play in ensuring and facilitating sustainable economic growth in the region.

The ports are by far the largest, best-equipped and most efficient network in Africa and not only serve the region but also act as hubs for traffic to and from the coast of East and West Africa. They are also vital to the rest of the southern hemisphere

Rail Infrastructure

The rail network falls under the control of Spoornet (A Division of Transnet) and the South African Rail Commuter Corporation (SARCC). Spoornet provides rail transport for goods and containers and for passengers on the long-haul routes between major cities. The SARCC is, in turn, responsible for providing commuter services in the six major urban centres.

Spoornet is also one of the founding members of the Southern African Railway Association, which focuses on operational efficiency between railroads of the region. The Association represents Benguela Railways in Angola, Botswana Railways, Malawi Railways, Mozambique Railways, TransNamib, Swaziland Railway, Tazara (Tanzania-Zambia Railway Authority), Zambia Railways Limited and National Railways of Zimbabwe and, as such, is key to the growth of trade in Southern Africa.

 **Global supply chains need
an effective and efficient transport
and port infrastructure.**

South Africa's Blue Train was voted "the world's leading luxury train" at the World Trade Awards in 1998 and 1999.

Current Status
Rail Infrastructure in RSA
Key Statistics 2001/02

•	Freight Wagons (active)	88 000
•	Locomotives (active)	2 410
•	Track km	30 400
•	Route km	20 041
•	Freight Tonnages	181.0 million tons
•	Net ton km	105.7 billion ton km
•	Passenger Coaches	2 110
•	Shossholoza Meyl Passengers	3.5 million/year
•	Blue Train Passengers	8 653/year
•	Turnover	R10.6 billion
•	Employees	34 344

Air Infrastructure

The Airport Company operates nine state airports, namely in Bloemfontein, Cape Town, Durban, East London, Johannesburg, Kimberley, Port Elizabeth, George and Upington. Johannesburg, Durban and Cape Town are classified as international airports.

South African Airways (SAA), Comair, Sun Air, SA Express and SA Airlink operate scheduled international air services within Africa and to Europe, Latin America, the Middle and Far East and Australia.

Thirteen independent operators provide internal flights that link up with the internal networks.

SAA is the largest airline in Africa and carries more than five million passengers a year to 503 destinations, either on its own or in partnership with other airlines. In addition to passenger flights, SAA operates four dedicated freighters both within South Africa and abroad and provides technical support for other international airlines.

Road Infrastructure

The national road system includes 1440 kilometres of dual-carriage freeway, 292 kilometres of single carriage freeway and 4401 kilometres of single-carriage main road. The country's primary network is managed by the National Roads Agency. The road transport industry has shown an impressive growth since the mid-1980s. In 1988 there were 400 road operators, today there are 4000.

Pipeline Infrastructure

Since its inception in 1965, Petronet manages, operates and maintains South Africa's strategic network of 3000 kilometres of high-pressure petroleum and gas pipelines.

Products transported are crude oil, leaded and unleaded petrol, diesel, aviation turbine fuel, alcohol and gas. Petroleum products are transported from the coastal and inland refineries to South Africa's main business centres. Gas is transported from Secunda (Mpumalanga) to KwaZulu-Natal.

The Future

Strategic Positioning of Transport and Port Infrastructure

The efficiency of transport and port infrastructure is a key factor in making sure that the costs of doing business in South Africa decrease and that there is an increase in the accessibility and quality of product and service.

Infrastructure developments are at a strategic level: integrated with similar actions in SADC and consistent with the overall ambitions of NEPAD.

Investment - Rail

A national rail plan is in the process of being finalised. Nearly R10 billion is earmarked to improve electrical infrastructure, rolling stock, locomotives, signals, railway stations and network development over the next five years. Spoornet will also expand the refurbishment, repair and maintenance capability of the large number of locomotives and rolling stock leased to a number of African countries.

Coallink (a business unit of Spoornet), transports South Africa's export coal from the mines in Mpumalanga to the Richards Bay coal terminal and has been independently assessed as redefining world-best practice.

Orex (a business unit of Spoornet), an acknowledged world-class operation, hauls iron ore over the world's second-longest (861 km) track. It is the only line of its kind in the country, moving iron ore from mines in the far Northern Cape to steel industries in the Western Cape for export through the port of Saldanha Bay. Orex also transports 900 000 tonnes of bulk cargo for Spoornet's commercial division.

Orex has embarked on a project to increase its annual capacity to 30 million tonnes and has become an international player, providing a diverse range of heavy-haul solutions for growing local and international markets.

Investment - Ports

Over the next few years, a large portion of the National Port Authority's proposed budget of R7.3 billion will go towards the Coega port development. In addition, the deepening of the harbour at East London will continue, along with further development at Richards Bay.

The Port of Durban will create further container capacity by re-modelling Pier One to handle containers and by re-modelling the point berth D - G to accommodate the relocated breakbulk cargoes from Pier One. A car terminal has been created, primarily to serve the BMW export market.

Future NPA projects include:
- Deepening and expansion of the container terminal at Cape Town
- Widening and deepening of Durban entrance channel and remodelling of Maydon Wharf
- Additional berths at Richards Bay to increase the break bulk and bulk liquid to handling capacity

Future South African port operations projects include:
- The expansion and refurbishment of the Saldanha iron ore terminal infrastructure
- The building of the world class car terminal in East London in working partnership with Daimler Chrysler
- Straddle carriers upgrade and purchases.

Investment - SAA

SAA's acquisition of the new Airbus long-haul fleet was heavily influenced by the better economies associated with medium-haul travel into Africa itself, and improved returns from better fuel consumption, freight friendly cargo carriers and reduced pilot training costs.

The acquisition will amount to 53 per cent of the total Transnet infrastructure allocation in 2003.

(Transnet is also making a considerable investment in Telecommunications. This is discussed in chapter 21.)

Investment - Black Economic Empowerment

Transnet's involvement in infrastructure development also supports Black Economic Empowerment (BEE).

Transnet's BEE and procurement policies are designed to promote easy access for contractors and suppliers from the historically disadvantaged communities to enter the mainstream economy.
This policy is continuously being updated to address problems and to cater for new developments in the BEE arena.

Transnet's business partners and/or other established suppliers are persuaded, by means of Transnet's buying power, to assist also in BEE ventures/endeavours (e.g. joint venture agreements, subcontracting, skills transfer agreements as well as their own procurement procedures/ practices).

All Transnet entities (including subsidiaries) are committed to individual BEE targets, cognisant of their positions in the market place, i.e. the availability of BEEs in the markets in which they operate.

Conclusion

Multinational manufacturers, wholesalers and retailers are moving towards increased integration of national, regional and global supply chains. These extended supply chains need effective and efficient transport and port infrastructure to give them a competitive edge in the global market.

Transport and port infrastructure are therefore an important driving force, which shapes economic development and the integration of infrastructure development with industrial and service development along transport corridors.

South Africa is resolute in its strategy of providing the appropriate infrastructure to service the needs of the sub-region. In addition, it is determined to ensure world-class practice and sustained profitability. The investments outlined above will ensure this.

If tourism and manufacturing are to be the employment powerhouse of the future, then our transport infrastructure will be the enabler.

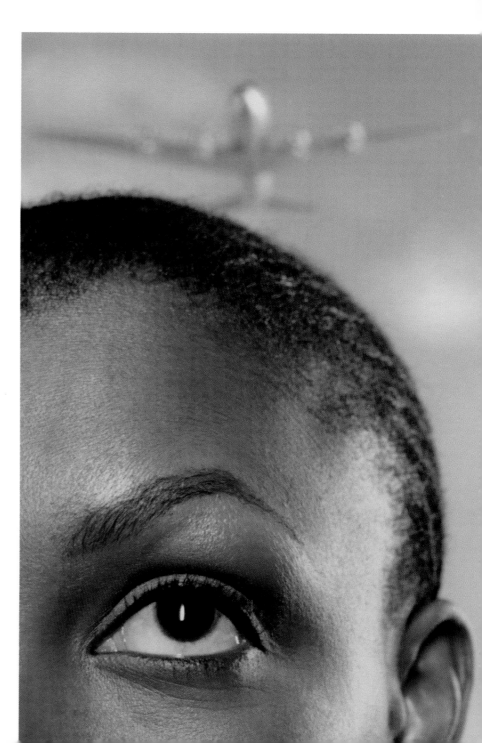

24

Corporate governance is to governments and corporates what quality control is to fast moving consumer goods companies. Brand loyalty happens because consumers build trust in the unwavering quality of the product. And so they buy it again. No self respecting investor, multinational or pensioner wants to put their money into a country or a share that cannot be trusted to deliver consistency, honesty and sound governance. Our corporate governance proposals are considered to be an international benchmark. Enforcing them will bring international respect.

Corporate Governance in SA

An international benchmark

Richard S Wilkinson: Executive Director - Institute of Directors in Southern Africa

Preamble
Corporate governance is a hot topic in corporate corridors around the world.

The rash of corporate failures in some of the world's most sophisticated economies has:
- Raised eyebrows in the business community
- Angered governments
- Disillusioned shareholders and
- Questioned the very foundation of capitalism.

Like many parts of the western world, South Africa has not escaped this contagion, but we have been quick to respond. Both King 1 and King II reports on corporate governance have been hailed as "best of breed" in many sectors of the developed world.

While issues like the triple bottom line are of a fairly technical nature, it is important to recognise that South Africa is considered to have the most advanced proposals in the world when it comes to good corporate governance.

This issue affects all South Africans! If you keep your money in a bank, you need to know how well that bank is managed. Or if you subscribe to a pension fund, you need to know that your money is invested in firms that play by the rules.

Banks, pension funds, public companies and manufacturers who do not employ best practice are more likely to go bust and, when they do, ordinary citizens get hurt.

The good news is that, as a country, we are "on it", ensuring that, as far as possible, the broad interests of all stakeholders are protected.

If management is about running the business, governance is about seeing that it's run properly.

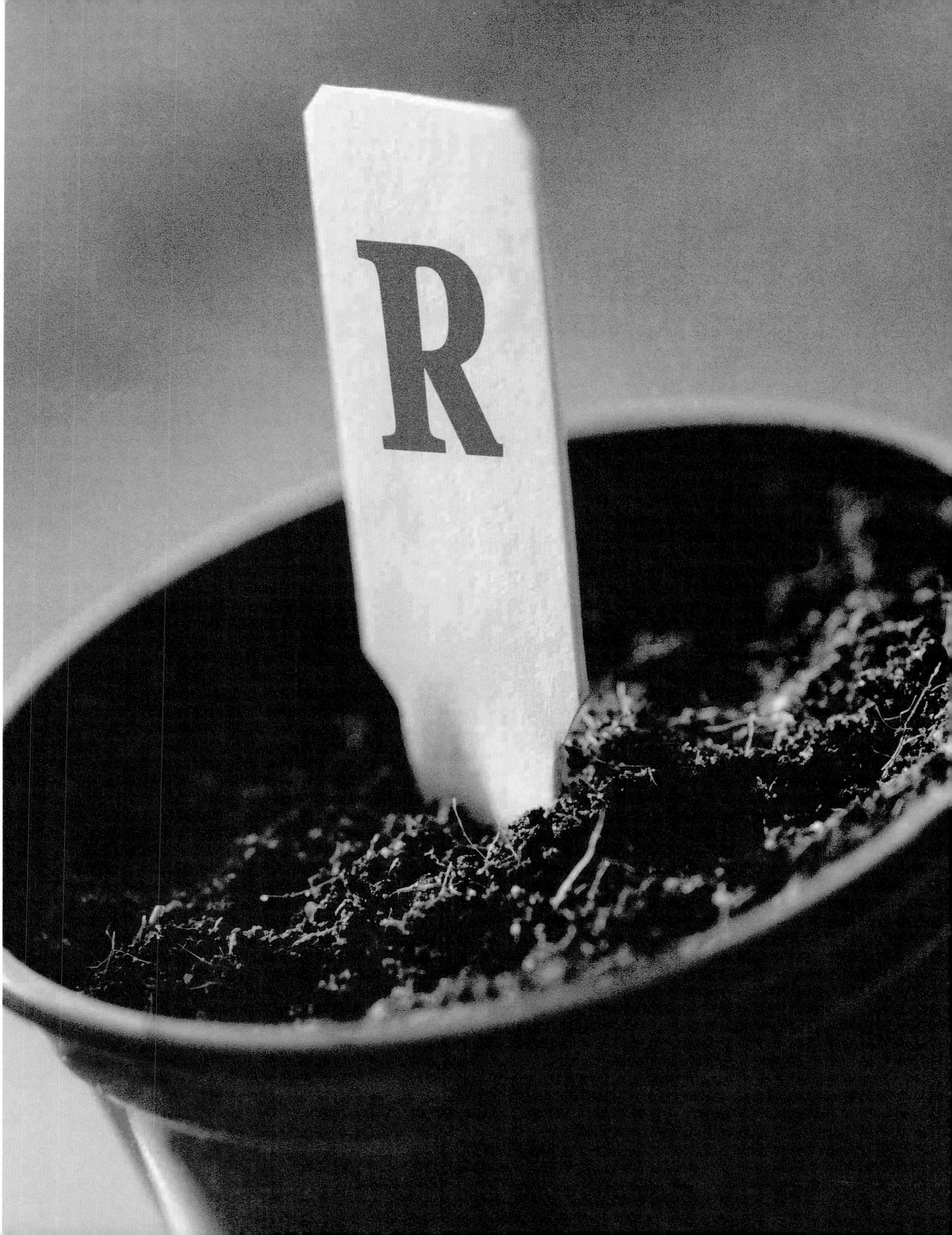
R

A Historical Perspective

Traditionally, corporate governance arrangements were covered in company law and legislation, although Bob Tricker, in his book, **Corporate Governance** (1984) emphasised that, "If management is about running the business, governance is about seeing that it is run properly".

Tricker was the first to coin the phrase corporate governance and also said that the two key elements of governance are:
- Supervising or monitoring management performance and
- Ensuring accountability of management to shareowners.

He also stressed the importance of governing an organisation at the top.

It was, however, the Cadbury Committee Report on the Financial Aspects of Corporate Governance issued in the United Kingdom in December 1992, that gave impetus to improved standards of corporate governance not only in Britain, but worldwide.

The Cadbury Report defined corporate governance as: "The system by which companies are directed and controlled." This was the catalyst for the Institute of Directors in Southern Africa to instigate the initiative to examine the issue. It led to the formation of the King Committee on Corporate Governance in July 1993 and the publication of the King Report on 29 November 1994 (King I - 1994).

While the Cadbury Report looked only at the financial aspects of governance, King I took an inclusive approach - highlighting the importance of economic, social and environmental issues for the stakeholder.

When first issued, the Report received ready acceptance in South Africa although its timing was swamped on the scale of national priorities by the election of the transitional government. This was a time when the national consciousness was directed more at the constitution of the country than on issues of corporate governance

Compliance with the Code of Corporate Practices and Conduct as contained in King I became a listings requirement of the Johannesburg Stock Exchange from 1 July 1995.

Directors were required, in their annual reports, to state that, "the Code of Corporate Practices and Conduct had been adhered to, or if not, in what respects there had not been adherence".

Although this indicated that affected companies had a high level of compliance, there was little enforcement by the regulating authorities and several instances of non-compliance became evident. The next major development was the publication of Principles for Corporate Governance in the Commonwealth as adopted by the Commonwealth Heads of Government Meeting in Durban in November 1999. Once again, although the Principles were adopted unanimously, enforcement has been lax - other than in a few Commonwealth countries, including South Africa.

In May 2000, the Institute of Directors recommended to the King Committee that the 1994 report be reviewed. The main reasons were:
- Local and international developments
- The need to recognise the increasing importance placed on non-financial issues and
- To make recommendations for enforcing compliance.

The Committee accepted the challenge and was reconstituted. Several task teams were then established to undertake a detailed review of specific areas including:
- Boards and Directors
- Accounting and Auditing
- Internal Audit and Control
- Risk Management
- Integrated Sustainability Reporting and
- Compliance and Enforcement.

The task teams consulted extensively and, when the draft report was made available for public comment, interest exceeded expectations both in South Africa and abroad.

The report (KingII) now
sets the international
benchmarks.

The Good News

The King Report on Corporate Governance for South Africa - 2002 (King II Report), released on 23 March 2002, has been hailed as the most comprehensive on the subject anywhere in the world.

A number of authoritative commentators believe that it encapsulates the best of international standards blended with local conditions since it includes the African world view and culture in the context of the governance of companies. This report now sets the international benchmark.

The King II Report and, in particular, the Code of Corporate Practices and Conduct, is a set of principles, not laws or regulations, and contains some unique features regarding the importance of the inclusive approach. For example, stakeholders are encouraged to monitor the application of the Code in the companies in which they are interested and, throughout, qualitative rather than quantitative conformance is encouraged. The Code is outcomes-based and compliance by affected companies took effect for financial years starting on or after 1 March 2002.

Compliance with the principles of good governance by government and the corporate world alike will result in greater foreign and local investment.

Good Corporate Governance Summarised

The section on Boards and Directors emphasises the fact that the focal point of corporate governance is the board, which should have a unitary structure where executive and non-executive directors interact.

The board must monitor and evaluate management and maintain full and effective control over the company. It must reserve specific powers to itself with delegated authority in writing to committees of the board and to management.

The Report recommends that all directors should have unrestricted access to information and be able to seek independent professional advice if in doubt about any aspects of their duties. The board should record the assumptions used in making the going concern statement. In order to be effective, the board should have a balance of executive and non-executive directors, with sufficient of the latter to protect the interests of shareowners (and minorities in particular).

The board needs to consider the demographics of its composition and is urged to encourage shareowner attendance at general meetings. Appointments should be both formal and transparent and the CVs of directors put forward for election (or eligible for re-election) should be included in the notice of meetings.

The Report strongly recommends a clear division of responsibilities at the head of the company to ensure that there is a balance of power and authority and that no one individual has unfettered powers of decision making.

The chairperson is responsible for chairing and controlling board meetings while the CEO has a strategic operational role to manage the business.

It is therefore recommended that the chairperson should preferably be an independent, non-executive director. In the event of the role of chair and CEO being combined, the board should:

- Appoint an independent non-executive director as deputy chair
- Have a strong element of non-executive directors on the board and
- Justify the decision of the combined role each year in the annual report.

The Report also recommends that boards meet regularly, at least once a quarter, although movement towards each alternate month is becoming the norm. The attendance of each director at board and committee meetings must be covered in the annual report.

The King II Report emphasises the importance of board committees with:

- A formal procedure for delegation
- Agreed terms of reference
- Total transparency and
- Full disclosure from board committees to the board.

As a minimum, each affected company should have a committee for audit and remuneration. Others, left to the discretion of the company, are:

- Executive
- Management
- Nomination
- Governance
- Ethics
- Risk management
- Treasury
- Compliance
- Safety, health and environment and
- Human capital.

The company secretary, through the board, plays a pivotal role in corporate governance and should, like newly appointed and re-elected directors, be subject to a, "fit and proper test", to satisfy the board that he or she is not disqualified from holding office.

A further innovation is the introduction of a board charter providing terms of reference, setting out responsibilities of both the board and the individual directors. This charter must identify what is important to an effective unitary board as a working group, but cannot go beyond laws and regulations or the Memorandum and Articles of Association (although it can define the spirit of workings of the board or the "rules of the game").

The King II report defines the responsibility for risk management as resting with the board which is responsible for deciding the appetite or tolerance for risk in pursuit of the goals and objectives of the company.

The board requires reasonable assurance that:

- The risk management and internal control systems provide adequate assurance on the effectiveness and efficiency of operations
- Assets are safe-guarded
- Laws and regulations are complied with
- The sustainability of the business is supported and
- Members of the board can rely on the information being reported to it and that which is passed on to stakeholders.

The assessment should cover risks such as:

- Exposure to physical and operational issues
- Human resources

- Technology
- Business continuity and disaster recovery
- Credit
- The market and
- Compliance.

The Internal Audit (IA) section requires an effective function to be in place that has the respect and co-operation of the board and senior management. IA should report at an appropriate level in the company to accomplish its responsibilities while the head of IA should report administratively to the CEO.

In addition, IA must report at all audit committee meetings and the head of IA must have access to the chair of the audit committee and the board.

A new recommendation is that the appointment or dismissal of the head of IA should require concurrence of the audit committee.

The Integrated Sustainability Reporting section of the report covers what were previously described as "non-financial matters". The board is expected to report at least annually to stakeholders on the nature and extent of its social, transformation, ethical, safety, health and environmental management policies and practices. Each board should determine what it considers relevant for disclosure and should adopt an integrated approach to stakeholder reporting.

The report should disclose non-financial information governed by the principles of reliability, relevance, clarity, comparability, timeliness and verifiability - in terms of the Global Reporting Initiative Sustainability Reporting Guidelines which are presented as an appendix to the King II Report and which were released at the World Summit on Sustainable Development in 2002.

Matters requiring specific consideration in the South African context include practices for reducing workplace accidents against stated objectives and a strategy to address and manage the potential impact of HIV/Aids on the company's activities.

Reporting on environmental issues must reflect current South African law by the application of the Best Practicable Environmental Option Standard.

The report should also highlight policies defining social investment prioritisation, spending and initiatives to support black economic empowerment (with particular regard to procurement practices and investment strategies).

Human capital development, such as number of staff, focus on progress against equity targets, employment training and development initiatives and financial investment should all be disclosed.

Finally, this section calls for each company to engage its stakeholders in determining its standards of ethical behaviour and to demonstrate its commitment to organisational integrity by formalising its standards in a code of ethics.

The Accounting and Auditing section charges the audit committee with investigating and recommending the appointment of external auditors for consideration by the board and these must then be approved by shareowners in general meeting.

Because of the importance of the audit committee, its members are appointed by the board and the majority of candidates should be financially literate and independent non-executive directors. Preferably the chair of the board and the CEO should not be members of the audit committee but may attend by invitation when appropriate.

In the Relations with Shareowners section, dialogue, based on constructive engagement and mutual understanding of objectives, is encouraged between institutional investors and the board.

In the part under Communication, the board's duty to present a balanced and understandable assessment of the company's position in reporting to stakeholders is recognised. Here, the quality of information must be based on the principles of openness and substance over form.

The annual report should provide a comprehensive objective assessment of the activities of the company so that all shareowners and relevant stakeholders with a legitimate interest in the company's affairs can obtain a full, honest and fair account of its performance.

The Code also covers a number of the statutory and other requirements that directors should report on in their annual report.

229

In the implementation of the Code, the onus is placed on all boards and individual directors, emphasising that they have a duty and responsibility to ensure that the principles set out in the Code of Corporate Practices and Conduct are observed.

The King II Report makes 27 recommendations requiring statutory amendments or other actions by third parties. Of special significance is that a number of the regulators, including the Financial Services Board, JSE Securities Exchange SA, Registrar of Companies and the Registrar of Banks have already implemented the report or are giving it attention.

Conclusion

The King II Report, together with the various appendices, has already been embraced by affected companies - including those listed on the JSE Securities Exchange, the financial services sector, public sector enterprises and agencies, private companies, and, indeed, the Government itself.

Undoubtedly, compliance with the principles of good governance will lead to increased foreign direct investment and greater institutional shareowner investment through the market.

And, importantly, the international community is increasingly recognising King II as the international benchmark on corporate governance. No doubt this will enhance South Africa's reputation as an emerging market and as a springboard for business in the rest of Africa.

The principles of good governance will lead to increased foreign direct investment and greater institutional shareowner investment through the market.

25

'**South Africa - The Good News**' has focussed on a wide range of positive developments in many aspects of our transformation since 1994. Naturally there are some spectacular successes that are known to most, like Eskom's footprint in Africa, Telkom's expansion of infrastructure and the IDC's contribution to Black Economic Empowerment, but there are a myriad of lesser known initiatives that the public are generally unaware of. For the most part the media does not report them, nor do the tireless developers boast them.

I talk of the Private Sector Miracles that are Changing the Nation.

There are literally thousands of stories that could be told here. The editors, to contain volume, have selected five:

- From Poverty to Paying it Forward
- From Elimination to Entrepreneurship
- The Story of the CIDA City Campus
- The Cato Manor Story
- Starfish - Everyone can make a Difference

These quiet, unobtrusive projects have impacted the lives of many South Africans, particularly from disadvantaged communities, and are a real example of private sector commitment to our transformation.

What really excites me is the underlying determination, inventiveness and entrepreneurial spirit that characterises these initiatives. More and more our diversity is producing remarkable people from all walks of life who are prepared to challenge traditional methods and reject apparent constraints as they contribute to a positive future for us all.

Cyril Ramaphosa

Private Sector Miracles that are Changing the Nation

The Cato Manor Story

Part 1
Les Owen: Director - Owen Adendorff and Associates

The city of Durban nestles against the Indian Ocean and, as you lean on the rail of your cruise ship, the view from the sea is spectacular.

The hotels and expensive apartment blocks have their roots in the sea itself. Behind them lies the magnificent ABSA Stadium, home of the Natal Sharks Rugby Team. To the left of the stadium, the central city buildings seem squashed up against the subtropical foliage of the Berea, Durban's upmarket suburb.

The Berea commands views of the Indian Ocean, the busy harbour and the Bluff peninsula which protects Africa's biggest port from the harsh south-westerly winds. The University of Natal with its Memorial Tower and multi-racial campus stands guard beneath it.

Stand in the Memorial Tower and you will subscribe to the view I have just described. But, turn your back on the Indian Ocean and look inland, behind the upmarket Berea, below the playing fields and car parks of the University, and the contrast will stun you .

In front of you lies the area known as Cato Manor, or in Zulu, umKhumbane. Stretching from the edge of the N3 highway which leads from Durban to Johannesburg, and beneath the opulent Pavilion Shopping Centre, live thousands of South Africa's poorest of the poor. Look below the massive domes of this modern shopping centre and you will see a hillside painted with humanity. Not for them the beach apartment blocks, nor flats in the central business district or a neat, double-storey Berea bungalow ... but, just one room, built out of what can be scavenged. Masonite walls propped up by bits of wood, sheets of corrugated iron tied together with pieces of wire and covered by a tarpaulin. Dotted amongst the shacks are the toilets, holes in the ground guarded by a square metre of flimsy material.

The one-metre spaces between rooms are trampled bare and the area turns into a dust bowl when the south-westerly blows and it becomes a sea of mud when the subtropical storms water the lush Durban vegetation.

How many shacks have been built? How many people live here? Estimates vary between 85 000 and 100 000 people. Some arrived in the late 1980s, but the real migration took place in the mid 90s. There is a multitude of languages spoken in this shanty town: Portuguese, French, Swahili, Xhosa and, of course, isiZulu.

Thandi Memela, a former MK member, speaks all the languages, except French, having learnt them when she underwent her training in the ANC military camps during the umzabalozo, the struggle against apartheid. She is the face of the organisation that is helping to change the conditions in Cato Manor, bringing hope to people whose lives, up to now, have not improved in the New South Africa.

This story concerns Memela and the organisation she represents, the Cato Manor Development Association, and tells of the good things that have happened amongst the shack dwellers behind the Berea.

This is the European Union's most successful project. The intention is to use it as a model throughout the developing world.

History

Named in 1843 by George Cato, Durban's first mayor, who lived and farmed in the area, Cato Manor had a population of about 150 000 people by 1950. In 1955 all were forcibly removed under apartheid's Group Areas Act.

From 1960 to 1980, this vast tract lay uninhabited until the empty land attracted landless people, first from the formal black townships surrounding Durban, then from further afield.

In 1993, as more people moved into the area, a multi-party negotiating forum was set up. This led to the formation of the Cato Manor Development Association (CMDA), with a brief to make sense out of the disorder.

In 1995, it became a Presidential Lead Project of the Reconstruction and Development Programme (RDP), a project that targeted urban areas neglected by the apartheid regime. In 1997, the European Union (EU) agreed to put substantial funding into Cato Manor, applying the EU's guiding principle that such projects should be sustainable and have the potential to be replicated.

By 2002, the European Union had come to the conclusion that this was probably their most successful project worldwide. As a result, they have funded the research and documentation process, ensuring that the details of how and why the project was successful are well-recorded. Their intention is to use Cato Manor as a model for other similar developments throughout the world.

Two Stories

"I wish long life to my enemies so that they may see all my successes." This framed sentence hangs in the centre of Xolani Ngcobo's new home. He moved in two months ago and has plastered the walls, laid a carpet and hung pictures and curtains. It is neat and tidy. The bed is in one corner, a sofa and chair in the other. His food and primus stove are packed neatly behind the door.

Ngcobo was born in 1967 in the Ixopo area, about a three-hour drive south-west of Durban and, in 1998, after he had completed primary school in Ixopo, he joined his father in the high-density Durban suburb of Umlazi where he was sent to finish high school.

His father was a well-to-do business man with four taxis, his own car and a house. In 1990, he died in a hail of bullets during one of the taxi wars. The business and house were taken over by the late father's brother and the young Ngcobo was told to leave and fend for himself.

He survived on his wits, unemployed and homeless until a firm of panel beaters employed him. Life improved and he shared a one-roomed flat with five others. In 1995, the panel beating job came to an end and again he was homeless and unemployed. A friend he had been working with had built himself an umjondolo (hut) at Cato Manor and he offered Ngcobo a room to rent. It was about six square metres - just enough for a single bed, a radio and a primus stove, and the rent was R30 per month.

Next, Ngcobo searched for a piece of vacant land and built his own shack and dug a hole for a toilet. His own umjondolo was bigger and better than his friend's and, although he still had to fetch and carry water from the solitary tap in the neighbourhood, he was master of his own destiny - or so he thought.

One day he was approached by Thandi Memela who told him the CMDA was to build a road between the shacks to provide access for vehicles so that they could build more houses and lay water pipes and electricity cables.

His umjondolo was in the path of the road and, as the owner builder, he had to move. A survey had been done a year before by the CMDA and each shack had received a registration number. All owners would be entitled to a small properly built house, with an inside toilet and a shower. Electricity would follow later but he might have to wait two to four years for a new house.

His good fortune was that he built his house where the new road was to run because this meant that the CMDA would move him - and all other owners on the road - to new homes.

When I arrive, he is watering his garden - something he has not done since he left his father's house 11 years ago. From his garden he has a view of the sea in the south. The green hills of Durban stretch to the west with the Memorial Tower of Natal University to his left on the east. Hills and more hills. I take off my shoes because of the wet earth and walk into his home.

Ngcobo proudly shows me his certificate of handover, proving him to be owner of this bright, new, well-built house. He has a job now in a steakhouse - as kitchen supervisor - and he finishes work at midnight. The taxi drops him on the main road two kilometres away and he walks.

Is he afraid?
"No, there is no crime here. I am safe, even at this time of night."

A sense of doubt enters my mind. Then I look at the windows - no burglar guards, a wooden door with quite an ordinary lock. No perimeter walls.

What are his intentions?
"To build three more rooms onto this one. Then I'll bring my wife and children to live with me. They can go to school here where the education is better.

Is he afraid?
"No, there is no crime here.
I am safe, even at this
time of night."

"The garden will be up and ready by then. My future is bright now. Nothing can ever be as bad again."

He is off to the Durban Metro Offices to apply for electricity to be connected to his house.

What was the worst part of living in the umjondolo? "
"The mud when it rained, and using the little room, especially at night."

Ngcobo introduces me to his neighbour, Bheki Thusi. Thusi is from Eshowe, pushed out because of violence between two chiefs in the area. He came to Durban in 1993 and moved in with his brother who rented rooms in an umLungu's (white man's) yard. Unskilled, he managed to find a job with a signwriting business. There he learnt to signwrite and to do electrical installations. In 1994, the umLungu sold the house. With no place to live he wandered into Cato Manor, found himself a piece of land and built a three-roomed umjondolo with a kitchen, a bedroom and a spare room for "visitors".

Crime was bad then, water had to be fetched and carried. The toilet was a hole in the ground.

Like Ngcobo he was lucky. He was also in the way of the new road. He also had to move into this new brick house.

Already he has replaced the shower with a new, oval-shaped bath. To do this he had to extend the toilet and shower room, and soon, he will add a new room, put in a garden and plaster and paint the inside of the house.

He likes it here, his neighbours are nice people, there is no crime and he has a good job as a signwriter.

The CMDA

Drive through Cato Manor and see the new and the old. About 3500 shack dwellers have already moved into newly-built formal houses. Many have built on more rooms, gardens flourish, and washing hangs on the line. On the other side are those still living in their umjondolo, still sharing toilets, still fetching and carrying water.

For these 3500 people, life has changed and, for the balance, life will change. New roads are everywhere. Community centres, new schools, a newspaper, a community radio station, crèches and shopping centres are all springing up. Order is replacing chaos. Sure, many inhabitants are impatient for change. They have been waiting many years and are now tired of waiting.

But, for many, life is "100 per cent better", to quote Xolani.

How did this happen? Why has change worked so well here when it has failed in many other places?

The answer lies with the CMDA and the people who are that organisation. Speak to Willis Mchunu, chairperson of the board of the CMDA, and you can hear that the determination to succeed is part of his very being.

The original chairperson, Peter Robinson (now deputy chair), recalls the early days of the CMDA back in 1993. He remembers the invasion of desperate people in July of that year. There were about 3000 families in the Cato Crest area, the part of Cato Manor closest to white suburbia. A few months later, 4000 people had arrived to stake their claim, and now, there are about 85 000 inhabitants.

The sheer size of the problem would make ordinary people give up and leave, but Mchunu and Robinson never thought of leaving. They hired Dan Smitt as their CEO and together they set a vision for Cato Manor of a "city within a city". That vision has guided the CMDA in all its activities and the present CEO, Clive Forster, is quite clear on the role of the vision in his life. He used to sit in his office at the University of Natal, look out at Cato Manor and visualise the concept of a "city within a city".

The Vision

The "city within a city" vision had the following as key strategies:

- To build the highest number of houses on the available land
- To increase the range and variety of housing options
- To ensure affordable houses for low and middle income earners
- To develop safe, interesting and environmentally sustainable housing.

To achieve this, their partners are:

- The National Department of Housing
- The KwaZulu-Natal Provincial Government
- The Durban Metro Council
- The cities of Leeds (UK) and Rotterdam
- The European Union.

None of this would have been possible without visionary leadership provided by the board members who include the Cato Manor community leaders.

Clive Forster can see the realisation of that vision. The goals and objectives of the CMDA staff are aligned to that vision. Every day the staff live the vision. The drive to and from their offices goes through Cato Manor, through parts of their vision. It is immediate and tangible. The other important aspect is the level of involvement in the board by local leadership, the idea put forward originally by Willis and Robinson.

New roads are everywhere, community centres, new schools, a newspaper, a community radio station, crèches and shopping centres are springing up. Order is replacing chaos.

236

Public Sector Commitments
June 2000

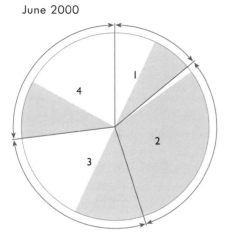

1 Metro/SCLC R58 m, 49% utilised
2 RDP R127 m, 97% utilised
3 PHDE R117 m, 42%utilised
4 EU R113 m, 38% utilised

● Funds utilised
○ Funds still to be utilised

The CMDA has learnt that building houses, roads and community centres is fine - but teaching people to provide for themselves is what is really important.

Current Status Overall Phasing

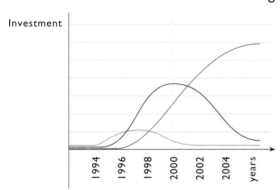

Investment

• Phase 1: Planning and Preparation
• Phase 2: Public Investment
• Phase 3: Private Investment

Annual Investment

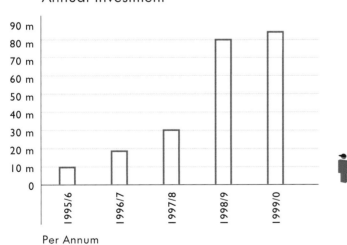

90 m
80 m
70 m
60 m
50 m
40 m
30 m
20 m
10 m
0

1995/6 1996/7 1997/8 1998/9 1999/0

Per Annum

Involved people have a vested interest in ensuring the CMDA succeeds in implementing its vision.

Signs of Success

Finally, is Cato Manor a success story or is it too early to say? What will the place look like in 10, 15 or 20 year's time?

Success is a relative term. To Ngcobo and Thusi, living in their new homes, the story has been a success and it has improved their lives 100 per cent. For many of the other inhabitants they can see how the lives of many of their fellows have improved. Theirs is just a matter of time, according to Clive Forster.

The CMDA has learnt that building houses, putting down roads, sewer pipes, water taps and community centres is fine. But what is really important is teaching people to fish for themselves. The corresponding thrust to develop the "city within a city" is to develop the people who reside in Cato Manor.

Many who live here have very little idea of what it means to live in an urban environment and they have to learn how to be modern day homeowners and what it means to have a "bond". They learn about rights and obligations.

This area lies five kilometres from Africa's biggest and most sophisticated harbour. Yet many people here have little or no experience of such things. They are also five kilometres from City Hall and, geographically, they are part of mainstream Durban. Two worlds juxtaposed incongruously, yet the residents have hope for the future.

The people see progress and they are involved in it. Pride in their community has returned.

I can feel the energy as I drive through the shacks amongst thousands of neatly dressed school children at three in the afternoon when school has ended for the day. From a place of disorder they, themselves, are participating in bringing about order.

There is hope for all of us when we see this miracle happen before our very eyes.

The CMDA newspaper, "Izwi", gives an insight into what Forster means. Here are some of the stories:

"Lucrative Markets for Cato Manor Craft" tells of export opportunities in France and New Zealand.

"Promoting a Business Revival" relates the opening of the Cato Manor Entrepreneurial Support Centre for aspiring manufacturers.

"Business of the Month Competition" with the winners' names being announced on the local Cato Manor radio station inspires other businesses.

"Cato Manor Small Business Fair" invites emerging entrepreneurs to take a stand at the fair to interface with larger businesses and people from outside Cato Manor.

"Spotlight on Community Developments" relates to training programmes run by the CMDA and the registration process as a work seeker.

"Cato Crest Container Park Under Community Management". The community members manage this business park.

And, of course, "Community Safety Still a Priority" tells of the involvement of the people in developing a culture of safety in the community, including plans to build a central safety centre, a family court, a small claims court and a district court.

And, on the back page, "Cato Manor Soccer Tournament Kicks Off" announces that 30 teams have registered for this first tournament.

Shelly Gielink of the CMDA tells of how, when the sports fields were completed, no one used them. She and her staff had to work actively with the residents to reinstall the culture and practice of sports. Now athletics and football are thriving.

Normality returns.

The people see progress and they are involved in it. Pride in their community has returned.

From Elimination to Entrepreneurs

Part 2
Mike O'Connor: Director - Stakeholders SA (Pty) Ltd

Eight months later, some 450 employees have become
shareholders in eight companies.

Despair

"I have been working at this mill for 21 years, my immediate family is my wife and four children, but I support my brother and his kids, since he was retrenched from the mines, and I have supported my parents forever. We were unionised eight years ago, and management has taken our working conditions a bit more seriously. At least now I get decent leave and overtime. But last week we had bad news; the company wants to retrench 617 of us, that means 4500 people will have no food for their stomachs, children will have to leave school, and we will be poor again. The company says it's because of 'operational changes'. I don't understand that, I work just as hard as I always have, I think it is because they are fedup with the union. Now I am desperate, my family is desperate, our lives are finished, where will we get work?"

Such was the dilemma of Jackson Masinga, a chainsaw operator.

Jannie Fourie, the operations manager, had a different dilemma.

"Look, for years we have been in a loss-making situation, our parent company is "hakking us" for debt, our labour force is hellava unionised and we've got too many staff. The union guys can't see the wood for the trees - ag, sorry for the pun - I really don't know what we can do. I know the community will suffer but, shit, we're at sea without a paddle. Tomorrow, I'm talking to some advisors, maybe they can see something I can't."

Quantum Change

Two advisors, one with an industrial relations and business background and the other with an entrepreneurial spirit, have developed a model which they believe can effectively address the above shortcomings, even in loss-making situations. The model is not a window-dressing exercise and will not be implemented unless it makes sustainable financial sense and provides a win-win solution to the parties involved. In essence, the model requires a transfer of ownership to employees and contractual agreement on service levels.

The Insoluble Conundrum

Late in 2001, this international forestry and paper company was about to rationalise its labour force. The subsidiary was making a loss and was unable to service the debt owed to its parent. It was faced with closure.

A combination of factors such as longer than expected low prices for its export product, poor productivity from an ageing work force, an adversarial labour climate, over-manning and the inherited estate management culture from two previous British development business owners, meant drastic action was required. The problem was made worse by a lack of maintenance work and much needed capital investment.

After prolonged negotiations with the affected trade union and discussions with local government, the parent decided against closure but required that 617 employees accept voluntary retrenchment packages. However, there was an unusual dynamic to these negotiations. Many of the retrenchees were offered the opportunity of becoming involved in a process of setting up businesses that could provide a service back to the company.

Win-Win

Eight months later, some 450 former employees have become shareholders in eight different companies, all with three-year contracts to provide competitive and vital services to the mill. The mandate given to the advisers was that:

- All shareholders had to be local citizens
- The businesses had to be profitable and sustainable
- The shareholding should, as far as possible, be held by recently retrenched employees.

Eight registered companies were set up to provide specialist services in harvesting, silviculture, nursery, light transport, research, mechanical services, fire-fighting and, finally, a financial administration company to provide services to these new businesses. A holding company was set up to cater for bulk-buying discounts. All companies comply with required statutory regulations and the combined turnover of these new entities is in the order of R36 million.

These new firms are currently profitable, service levels have improved dramatically and the people involved are excited about their status. The company has reduced its costs and retained its core business.

Experience over the past four years in similar kinds of intervention has illustrated the following benefits:

- Improved productivity and lowering of costs
- Increased responsibility driven by ownership
- Reduction of unnecessary damage to assets and products
- Fast tracking real learning of business skills
- Motivated shareholders with a newly acquired dignity
- Profitable new ventures able to purchase new equipment and to make business acquisitions.

Avoiding Pitfalls

Clearly, ownership is a great motivator. But, the task of transforming the mindsets of employees who have often only worked for one employer (and often engaged in adversarial labour issues) has potential pitfalls. These include nepotism, self-importance, scepticism and power-play in various forms, all very human traits.

Critical success factors required to overcome these are:

- Committed executive management support
- A business environment where a win-win solution can be crafted
- Involvement of representatives from the new entities throughout the process
- Active trade union support, where unionised
- Advisers who are politically neutral, have no association with the past and have a passion for producing a positive outcome.

The Process

After obtaining management support, the advisors presented their ideal model to the union which, initially, gave a neutral response.

Soon afterwards, the retrenchment package was accepted and the Government set up an eight-man committee to oversee the outsourcing process.

At their first meeting with the various stakeholder representatives, the union demonstrated their support of the project to the unsure government representatives and thereafter became vocal supporters of the programme.

The union and the advisors addressed a mass meeting of workers who elected a representative committee. Thereafter, ongoing participative meetings were held as the teams, assisted by the advisors, looked at all aspects of the soon-to-be established businesses.

These included the:
- Nature of the service to be provided
- Equipment required
- Process flows
- Lead times
- Manning levels
- Selection criteria
- Rates of pay
- Contract rates.

Comprehensive business plans were developed and the company sold second-hand equipment to the new entities at discounted rates.

Further support was provided in the form of a bridging loan for working capital to two of the larger companies employing 280 and 130 employees respectively, prior to their obtaining bank loans of R2.4 million each, to pay for the assets they had purchased.

During the entire process, weekly meetings were held with the government committee to keep them abreast of both the progress and any potential problems.

In essence, the model requires a transfer of ownership to employees and contractual agreement on service levels.

The employee shareholders of the new businesses made significant changes to established work patterns. By agreement, these included:

- Employment on a probation period of three months
- When necessary, working weekends and public holidays at standard rates of pay (no overtime pay)
- Flexible work practices
- Performing the same tasks at lower rates of pay with the knowledge that they were working for profits and capital growth
- The opportunity for employees to be replaced by their sons who are required to serve a probation period.

In the larger companies, committees representing various functions in the business concerned were set up to reinforce participation structures and decision-making. These meetings were often held at 06:00 or 17:00, outside working hours.

The results have exceeded expectations. In the production companies, these are easily quantifiable and improvements in productivity have been impressive.

Example of the Harvesting Company

No. of Employees to Harvest Fixed Quantity of Timber

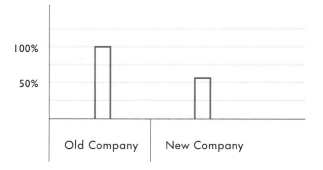

Cost to Harvest One Tonne of Timber

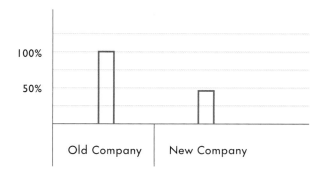

Performance Improvements

While the employee shareholders in the harvesting company are earning less than they were with their previous employer, they are employed, and they are participating in growing a profitable business expected to make a R1 million profit in the first year and which will own assets worth around R4 million.

Other examples include the finance/admin company paying 450 employees in their first month with very few errors (and, at the time, they did not even have an office to work from). They provide monthly financial accounts, and cash flow projections, and the managing director (with two employees) is co-signatory on all of the company's cheques.

The fire-fighting company, operating from five fire stations in 57 000 hectares of forest, is generally perceived to be performing better than before. Response times have improved and the various types of fire-fighting vehicles are no longer seen being driven needlessly around the forests and neighbouring villages.

The incidence of plantation fires has dropped, compared with previous years, and the fire-fighting company is looking at buying a contract transport business where synergies will exist for the sharing of vehicles, service facilities and vehicle allocation out of fire season.

Another success is the nursery which grows six million seedlings a year. In the past, expensive seed trays were often damaged and not recovered from customers.

Today, track is kept of these containers and creative ideas are being considered to ensure their prompt return. Other value-added opportunities are being reviewed to expand growth beyond their existing customers. However, as with most of the new operations, focus is being concentrated on ensuring that the core service is consolidated before expansion takes place.

After four months of operation, the harvesting company has taken over a failed contractor's business, half their current size, and will benefit from economies of scale. This will also enable them to sell some of their older machines and buy more productive replacements.

In reviewing the costs of heavy capital equipment, expensive maintenance and escalating fuel costs, the directors decided to re-introduce an old, tested inexpensive technology - using mules to haul fallen timber to the roadside.

Twenty-four mules were purchased and are rotated on a weekly basis, as well as being regularly assessed by a local vet. They reliably meet production targets and have not experienced any expensive down time in contrast to the mechanical equipment.

Conclusion

South African business is currently seeking solutions to address problems emanating from its apartheid past and the effects of globalisation.

Solutions to the former have been affirmative action targets and the sourcing of empowerment partners in an environment where banks are reluctant to provide necessary finance to purchase equity. The effects of globalisation have often led to the international trend of outsourcing to specialist service providers who, more often than not in South Africa, are white owned.

None of the above provide creative solutions that are broad-based in their application and are truly aimed at the working class who are so vital to our socio-economic realities.

Without the whole-hearted support of the forestry company, none of these exciting opportunities would have been made possible. Clearly they have benefited from the cost savings in this outsourcing venture, but so has the local community. If the accepted estimate is that for one breadwinner there are six to eight dependants, then this "experiment" has kept around 4500 people away from certain deprivation and poverty.

But, most important of all, is the fact that this project is sustainable with a broad-based ownership by people at the bottom of the pile. It is what empowerment should really be about.

Yes, sometimes a calamity does bring people to change, and often the change is deep and profound, creating a better model for the future.

Jackson Masinga now runs the mechanical services business and Jannie Fourie has reduced his operating costs by 53 per cent.

From Poverty to Paying it Forward

Part 3
Nicolette De Bruyn: Acting MD of Africa Foundation

Richard's Early Life

Richard Mabaso grew up in the rural village of Lepesi in Mpumalanga Province and, like many in his community, Richard's early life was defined by the poverty of his family.

When he was a small child, his father left home to find work in the city and did not return. His mother, struggling to feed, clothe and educate her children on her income as a domestic worker, only came home once a month, leaving Richard to look after his three siblings.

In Richard's final year of school, she lost her job and the family's meagre income dried up completely. Richard, barely a man, became entirely responsible for the welfare of his family but, by taking every odd job he could find, he was able to build a brick house for his family.

However, the long hours packing supermarket bags and laying bricks took its toll and his school results plummeted. The following year, his mother found another job and, determined to succeed, Richard went back to school and passed with flying colours.

If you want to change the world you must change man.
If you want to change man you must make him want to change.
Dame Ester Gress, Poet Laureate of Denmark

Community Support - a New Era

Richards's prospects of continuing his academic career would have been slim if it wasn't for the fact that the village of Lepesi is located on the border of the Mthethomusha Game Reserve where Conservation Corporation Africa runs the Bongani Mountain Lodge.

The lodge operators had long ago recognised that if they wished to protect the seriously threatened ecosystems, the endangered species, and the precious biodiversity of the wilderness areas that are South Africa's great treasure, they would need the support of the people most closely involved - the communities living in and around the conservation areas.

Traditionally, a game reserve's electric fences demarcate the haves and the have-nots. Well-heeled tourists absorbing the benefits of the wilderness experience are sealed off from the local rural people.

The old policies that barred indigenous people from land designated for conservation, and imposed borders and fences where, previously, great beasts roamed free, have been continued until very recently. It was a situation bound to breed resentment and suspicion.

In South Africa's changing social climate, enlightened environmentalists, like the Bongani Lodge management, now see that, for conservation to succeed, the needs of people and animals must be better balanced. The most significant means of achieving this will come from ensuring that local people benefit directly from protected areas.

In 1992, the Africa Foundation was established as a non-profit organisation whose task it was to raise funds and implement projects within the adjacent communities.

For the past 10 years, the Foundation has partnered with lodges, such as Bongani, to empower individuals in, and adjacent to, conservation areas, and so create enlightened neighbours who are ready to recognise each other's needs and values. It is the Foundation's task to transform the imbalances in the conservation landscape into mutually beneficial partnerships, based on shared goals and parity in benefits. Individuals like Richard are given the opportunity to succeed and, through this, ensure that conservation efforts also succeed.

Throughout the country, these rural communities who had, for so long, been denied even the opportunity to visit the neighbouring conservation area, are now invited to participate in identifying projects that would best meet their primary needs. From the start, and almost without exception, education and capacity building were the communities' first concern. They needed to address the legacy of Bantu Education, rural neglect and under or unqualified teachers.

> It is the Africa Foundation's task to transform imbalances into mutually beneficial partnerships.

Education - the Lighting of a Fire

If people, particularly those who have been so marginalised, are to take environmental issues on as their personal concern, there is no doubt that education is vital. For this reason, the Africa Foundation initiated a comprehensive programme available to all conservation communities, of which the first step is opening children's eyes through learning rooted in the local community - the place where history, nature and society intersect.

It is possible to provide evidence of the success of the programme by listing tangible achievements such as the building of 64 classrooms, establishing 19 pre-schools and funding the environmental awareness training of thousands of learners and teachers. Through these and other means, the Foundation and its partners have assisted an estimated 50 000 learners from pre-primary to high school. But these are all just worthy claims without the evidence of real change provided by the example of individuals.

And there are so many good news stories: a poacher who is now a world-class pastry chef, numerous boys who have gone from tending cows to game-ranging, and brilliant women who have succeeded in the boardrooms of South Africa's business. But without the space to laud them all, the Foundation chose two tertiary scholarship candidates, Richard Mabaso and Thuthukani Ngwenya, who are evidence that, if you want to change the world, you change the "man" by giving him good reason to change.

Ubuntu - "I am who I am because of who we are." Ubuntu is one of the major contributing factors to our peaceful transition.

The power of education is seen first on an individual level, but each student's success has proved to have a powerful ripple effect throughout the community, proving that education is indeed the lighting of a fire. There are so many shining lights worthy of acknowledgement, people that have discovered depths of dormant capabilities and opted for a life of committed contribution to their less fortunate fellow community members.

Moët et Chandon - Helping Us to Help Ourselves

Richard Mabaso was a recruit in the Africa Foundation's first intake on the Siya Kwamukela Internship Programme. Sponsored by French champagne house, Moët et Chandon, and implemented by the Africa Foundation, Siya Kwamukela, meaning "warm welcome" in Zulu, selects students from rural communities to participate in a two-year hospitality training course within a five-star safari lodge environment. The intention is to provide the highest standard of hospitality training for Africans from rural communities, equipping them with the necessary skills to secure good positions in the neighbouring ecotourism developments.

Self-reliance was the key emphasis of Richard's efforts. On his days off from the lodge he rounded up his friends and trekked to surrounding villages where they marketed themselves as a garden service.

Richard explains: "I decided that I needed to make a plan and help my friends who now could not even find work to survive. So, I have now started a community project, which is called Masitakheni (let's build/help ourselves) Project Group. We are now doing well with different kinds of things such as knitting, woodwork, art, printing, preparing marula nuts and recycling cans and bottles. Our main aim as a group is to work to create many job opportunities in the community and for South Africa to become one of the best countries for tourism."

It is inspiring to see this 19-year-old trainee working so hard to be a success and share his good fortune with the community in which he was raised. This is very consistent with the African concept of Ubuntu: "I am who I am because of who we are."

Ubuntu is not unique to Africa and is shared by many peoples of the world who have been beset by oppression and poverty, but it is one of the major contributing factors to our peaceful transition.

The truly astounding thing is that he is not unique. So many of the selected candidates are rejecting a passive, dependent life, and opting for an interdependent mode of existence, a life connected to the well-being of their entire community.

Creating Future Leaders

The Community Leaders Education Fund (CLEF), of which Thuthukani Ngwenya is a recipient, was first considered in 1994 when it became evident that the opportunities for gaining a tertiary education were severely limited for black rural South Africans. The aim of the Fund was, and still is, to develop natural, educated leaders who can serve as an inspiration to their rural communities. In the beginning it was not simply a case of offering the scholarship and awaiting applications. The potential candidates had little idea of what career options existed and had received little or no guidance at schooling - naturally so, as few career paths had been open to skilled blacks during the apartheid years. In the first years, it was the task of the Fund and its partners to help the students to understand what was being offered.

Now, with R1 372 800 awarded in scholarship funds to date, the CLEF programme has found an effective way to ensure that school learners do not remain ignorant or uninspired about their future careers.

One of the main criteria of the bursary programme is for all current and past students to participate in the CLEF Club through which they are expected to share and apply their newfound skills and knowledge within their communities. The CLEF Club brings together fellow students from the same community in a forum to share ideas and initiate youth development projects. A key requirement is that they spend time at local high schools informing pupils about career options, tertiary courses, how to apply for bursary grants and handle interview sessions.

The Africa Foundation identifies between 15 and 30 students per annum and has a 96 per cent success rate. This is a most remarkable achievement considering that the students come from the poorest of households.

Thuthukani is one such success. He knows about hardship first-hand; he was the eighth child in a family of twelve - born to a father who had another family to support as well. While growing up, supper was the only meal of the day and in the middle of the freezing Newcastle winter, he had to go to school in tattered shoes. (It seems that, in so many examples, hardship teaches African people calm and humility. Maybe it is part of the Ubuntu cultural characteristic, or maybe just part of their humanity.)

Thuthukani says his difficult childhood taught him to accept his circumstances and to work hard. "I could have chosen to go to the streets and beg for food or rob people for money - but I chose to accept that what I was facing was meant to be and that, one day, my perseverance will bear fruit. The way I understand life is that the reason we live is to face whatever forces we come across until our dying day. By so doing we fulfil the meaning of life."

After several attempts to further his education and help support his family, Thuthukani applied for a CLEF scholarship, through Africa Foundation partner CC Africa's Phinda Private Game Reserve. He enrolled for a Social Science Degree in Industrial Psychology and Legal Studies. Though he struggled at times throughout his studies - even saving his meal allowance to help support his family - he graduated in 1999. Soon afterwards, he got a job with Hewlett Packard. "From here, no one knows where I will end up, but I'm on the highway, driving in the fast lane, unstoppable."

And so he certainly appears to be - after becoming a valued member of the human resources team at Hewlett Packard, where he helped to spot other youngsters in need of development and further education for their training programme, he has now joined respected recruitment firm Lumka and Associates.

Thuthukani commented on his involvement with the Mduku Community: "As per the CLEF spirit, I am committed to share the skills and the knowledge I have gained. Since the days when I was at university, I would go around with Mr Isaac Tembe (Regional Field Manager in KwaZulu-Natal) to assist him with all the projects he was managing.

"Our main aim as a group is to work to create jobs, and for South Africa to become one of the best countries for tourism." Richard Mabaso

The power of education is seen first
on an individual level
- but there is a ripple effect
throughout the community.

"I visited our local high schools to assist the teachers in English and history. I taught English to Standard Six pupils and history to the Standard Nine class. The schools I visited were Mduku and Makhasa High Schools.

"I have maintained close contact with CLEF Head Office since moving to Johannesburg in year 2000. As a founder member of the Community Youth Empowerment Organisation, we have approached the CLEF Head Office to assist with career guidance in Mpumalanga and KwaZulu-Natal. Other than that, I am still committed to assist my community in any way I can and I believe that, by assisting the youth, we are laying a strong foundation for the future of my community."

The Budding of the Seeds of Change
Richard and Thuthukani, and all the others like them, are the reason why South Africa's splendid natural heritage will endure. "We operate on the belief that a single person can change the world," says de Bruyn, "and after a decade of operations we have seen indisputable evidence of this. South Africa was able to survive its most difficult times because exceptional individuals brought a message of hope and courage to those who were struggling."

Now, as Southern African conservation enters a brave new era, there is, more than ever, a need for these pioneers. The groundbreaking "Peace Parks" straddle borders, open ancient migratory routes and will affect the lives of approximately 40 million rural people.

Seeds of change are beginning to bud in South Africa. In time we will be able to say that, never again will a fence be erected without consulting the people who have lived for generations on the land; never again will conservation aims take priority over the basic needs of people. And when that happens no man or woman will ever again question the role of conservation but rather be grateful that they live in a land so rich in nature's blessings.

We operate on the belief
that a single person can change the world.

Taddy Blecher tells the story of how he set up one of the world's most unusual universities ... in the heart of Johannesburg.

"I have an abiding belief in the infinite potential of every individual. It's not the gold in the ground that will make this country great. It's the tremendous talent of our youth, the minds of our people. So much unnecessary suffering can be eliminated with the right kind of development. I believe that South Africans give up too easily by emigrating. I decided that if I was going to stay, I would make a difference."

The Cida Story

Part 4
Taddy Blecher: Director - CIDA City Campus

No Hope
In the hub of Johannesburg's city centre, positioned between the old stock exchange and the vibrant informal economy of street traders, a South African miracle is set to explode global ideas on education, private sector commitment and African innovation.

The inequalities and injustices of apartheid South Africa's social and education policies - many of which were supported by the private sector - are well-known. Their legacy is one of poorly trained teachers, under-resourced schools and large numbers of disillusioned matriculants from impoverished communities for whom the university experience is unimaginable.

Today CIDA City Campus, with the support of South African business, is undoing this legacy and providing a homegrown solution to the mass-scale tertiary education needs of South Africa (and, potentially, other developing countries).

CIDA Hope
Established in 1999, CIDA (Community and Individual Development Association) City Campus is South Africa - and indeed Africa's - first free, non-profit university for previously disadvantaged students. With the use of cutting-edge technology and innovative learning and operational strategies, CIDA provides an accredited four-year Bachelor of Business Administration (BBA) Degree to approximately 1000 students per year, at five per cent of the cost of an average South African university (see graphs below).

Cost of Highter Education Provision for four-year Business Degree

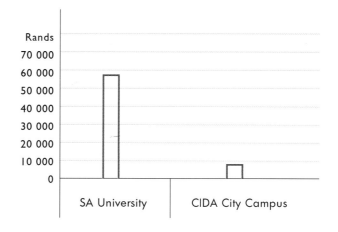

The Cost of University Education to the Average African Family

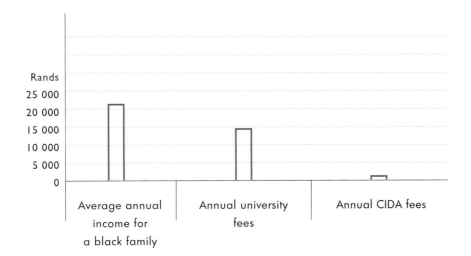

Rands

25 000	
20 000	
15 000	
10 000	
5 000	
0	

Average annual income for a black family

Annual university fees

Annual CIDA fees

Investing in the creation and development of a new generation of skilled optimistic young people is Africa's highest priority.

All students are on scholarships funded by the CIDA Trust or by company and individual mentors who, in turn, receive tax exemptions as well as exposure to CIDA's considerable and influential network of patrons.

As with most innovations, CIDA was born out of necessity. By profession, I am an actuary and management consultant and, while working with high school students in Alexandra, I saw the need for accessible and affordable tertiary education.

Although students were working hard to pass matric, the cost of going to university was well out of their reach and most young black people who have finished high school are still unlikely to escape the poverty spiral. Consequently, South Africa had little hope of enjoying true economic democracy.

I assembled a team whose only resources were commitment and a borrowed fax machine and we established a free university with the aim of providing a high-quality, holistic and relevant education. With no venue, we optimistically accepted applications from hundreds of desperate students. Investec Bank recognised the potential of the project and donated their former headquarters, an R86 million building in the city centre.

This lent authenticity and security to the project and other companies such as First National Bank and African Bank joined in. The Government awarded us full university accreditation, and CIDA was launched.

CIDA's knowledge - sharing strategy - It takes a child to raise a village.

Strategies for Hope
Innovation, technological excellence and self-empowerment are the strategies CIDA employs. The private sector funds the CIDA Trust and is involved in management, curriculum development and teaching at the university.

Field experts from companies like PricewaterhouseCoopers and Internet Solutions donate time and expertise as lecturers. In this way, students are exposed to skilled professionals who not only teach but also share their experience of how the theories of business are applied in practice.

CIDA students are trained in 14 schools of excellence:
African Leadership
Accounting
Finance and Banking
Insurance
Marketing
Strategy
Management
Entrepreneurship and Innovation
Operations Management
Communications
Resource Management
Investments
Asset Management
Information Technology.

Students may also take a variety of professional qualifications such as those offered by Microsoft, Pastel Bookkeeping and the South African Institute of Management. This exemplifies CIDA's aim to produce graduates who are thoroughly prepared for the South African business environment. Advanced multi-media facilities and maximum levels of student participation have created a unique system of learning that allows CIDA to offer a professional and practical education at a cost that is lower to both student and educator.

Strategies are also employed to address the imbalances and weaknesses of the students' high school training. Students have three times more class contact hours than average South African students and are offered remedial courses in Maths, Accounting and English. There is also a strong practical component and the CIDA BBA degree is not awarded unless students have completed a set amount of after-hours work.

Hope and Service
Partnerships with the private sector provide opportunities for part-time jobs and students are also responsible for the day-to-day running of the campus, which serves as practical work experience in areas such as computer support and administration.

Self-management and creative intelligence skills are part of the CIDA curriculum and all students learn to play chess, meditate, and mentor their younger peers.

CIDA provides an accredited Bachelor of Business Administraion degree at 5 per cent of the cost of a normal university.

They also have access to counselling services and more than 50 extra-curricular sports and activities ranging from dancing to poetry. They also manage their own radio station and soccer team.

In this way, CIDA has created an environment that supports the holistic development of each student so that he or she may take up a confident, productive and socially conscious place in modern South African life.

Hope and Knowledge

To this end, CIDA's vision has extended even further to launch a powerful knowledge-sharing strategy called ExtraNet. With the belief that, "It Takes a Child to Raise a Village", each student returns home in the holidays and presents prepared workshops on:

- HIV/Aids awareness
- Financial responsibility
- The basics of small business creation.

It is estimated that, each year, one million people from the most impoverished areas in South Africa are being reached by these crucial messages: in their own language and from a kinsman or woman.

The impact that ExtraNet can have on job creation, disease prevention and the elevation of individual and collective self-worth is unimaginable. It is undoubtedly part of what inspired President Thabo Mbeki, in his 2001 budget speech to Parliament, to thank CIDA City Campus for its innovation in helping to end the marginalisation of the majority of South Africans.

Hope and Ubuntu

The university has been visited and commended by a number of top thinkers including Edward de Bono, Tom Peters, Suze Orman, Ben Zander and, soon, John Kehoe.

Mrs Zanele Mbeki, The Lord Mayor of London, Iman and local business leaders have also come to address, inspire and applaud the approximately 3500 students, whom they recognise as a generation of South African pioneers with unprecedented courage, integrity and promise.

The recognition received from such role models, as well as regular contact with professionals through lectures and mentorship programmes, has resulted in a high level of optimism, self-confidence and energy among students.

This alone is a valuable achievement when one considers that most students come from homes that live below the poverty line and where neither parent has graduated from high school.

Students work in teams to take care of their own campus and this engenders a strong work ethic and respect for resources and community or Ubuntu values.

Taddy Blecher (CEO) was the recipient of the World Economic Forum's 2002 Global Leader of Tomorrow Award.

Conclusion

Prior to 1994, South Africa owned a generation of disenfranchised, disempowered and, often, poorly educated young black people for whom hopelessness and desperation were almost unavoidable. The correlation between this and subsequent levels of unemployment, poverty, crime, corruption and HIV infection is, unfortunately, clear and predictable.

It stands to reason that investing in the creation and development of a new generation of educated, skilled, self-aware and optimistic young people is Africa's highest long-term priority.

The founders of CIDA, together with dedicated staff and committed students, have created a partnership with South Africa's private sector in true African style where one hand washes another.

This symbiosis is generating energy, creativity, resources and knowledge to fulfil one of our country's most ambitious human development strategies.

We warmly invite you to visit the CIDA website, http://www.cida.co.za, or, even better, visit us at our Commissioner Street campus. You will experience the dynamism and hope of our students and witness in action CIDA's belief that the future of South Africa lies in discovering and developing its human gold.

The Statistics
- Only three per cent of people in sub-Saharan Africa have a post high school qualification.
- There is a 90 per cent correlation between a nation's level of tertiary education and its wealth (Source: Monitor Company Analysis of World Bank figures).
- Only 15 per cent of students in South African universities and technicons graduate.

CIDA Successes
- Pass rate of more than 75 per cent each year
- Winner of World Economic Forum's 2002 Global Leader of Tomorrow Award (Taddy Blecher, CEO)
- Hailed by many leading educators and corporations as a considerable breakthrough in education: "In my many years of tertiary education I have never come across a higher level of commitment, innovation and creativity being applied to a programme of adult learning, and the excellent use of available resources to match, than at CIDA City Campus" (Professor Nick Binedell, Director of the Gordon Institute of Business Science)
- Partnerships with the South African Institute of Chartered Accountants, South African Institute of Financial Markets, the South African Institute of Bankers and the Insurance Institute.

An old man had a habit of taking early morning walks along the shore. One day, as he looked down the beach, he saw a human figure moving like a dancer. As he came closer, he saw that it was a young woman and she was not dancing, but reaching down to the sand, picking up starfish and very gently throwing them into the ocean.

"Young lady, why are you throwing starfish into the ocean?"

"The sun is up and the tide is going out, and if I do not throw them in they will die."

"But young lady, do you not realise that there is miles and miles of beach and starfish all along it? You cannot possibly make a difference."

The young woman listened politely, paused and then bent down, picked up another starfish and threw it in the sea, past the breaking waves, saying:

"It made a difference for that one!"

Starfish -Everyone Can Make a Difference

Part 5
Written by Tracey Webster

Whilst sitting at my banking desk in London, my thoughts found their way back to the land of milk and honey.

"I want to be part of Starfish because I am hugely excited about the potential to change lives: the lives of children affected by Aids and the lives of all of us in the Starfish community who would otherwise miss the transformational experience of helping offer these children hope and a future. It's an extraordinary adventure."
- Meyrick Douglas, UK

The Starfish story describes how the parable of the woman on the beach brought about a change in ordinary people's thinking, opening up a new way of responding to seemingly impossible challenges that surround us all - everyday.

It is the story of how, in little more than a year, from unlikely beginnings in a London coffee shop, the idea took root in the imagination of South Africans across the globe.

It is the story of how this idea has generated a new sense of optimism for one of our county's greatest challenges, providing a vehicle for every individual to become involved, and, in the process, raise enough money initially to support 3000 children, while further inspiring a vision to reach five per cent of the children orphaned by HIV/Aids in South Africa by 2005. (Editor's note: It is estimated that there will be two million Aids orphans by 2010.)

One Such Starfish
"The evolution of Starfish comes at a time when all South Africans are searching for an opportunity to make a positive difference in tackling HIV/Aids in our country. The vision and passion of those involved in the organisation has captured my attention and compelled me to be a part of turning the tide. This is without a doubt the most exciting and important humanitarian project I have ever witnessed."
- David Becker, UK

The Starfish parable has many dimensions, from the children in the rural valleys of KwaZulu-Natal, whose lives have been touched by the support of strangers around the world; to South Africans in far-flung places like Hong Kong and California who have been able to reconnect with their country.

Now, a few words on how I became involved with the organisation.

"While sitting at my banking desk in London in June 2001, my thoughts found their way to the land I had left four years earlier, but which had never left me. In the midst of this reflection, an e-mail appeared on my screen, inviting me to a midnight theatre event in the West End. But, this was no ordinary invitation: it was a Starfish invitation.

"The following words struck me:
'It is so easy to become overwhelmed by the magnitude of the Aids orphan crisis in South Africa, but it is Starfish's hope that we should not feel powerless. It's about each one of us looking within ourselves and then taking action - picking up our own starfish. There is hope, real hope, but hope demands action.'"

Someone once said: "All people dream, but not equally. Dreamers of the day are dangerous because they act out their dreams with open eyes and make things possible."

"Let us be dreamers of the day!"

In these few words, I found expression to my longing, shared by so many others, to contribute as an individual to my country's future. A longing that had never been diminished by the extended geographic separation."

The Beginnings

"I have been waiting a long time to meet people like you. Young South Africans of the next generation who are able to put the past behind them and start building a new future together. You are the hope of history."
- Dennis Goldberg, a Rivonia trialist, speaking to Starfish in December 2001.

Much of the initial inspiration for Starfish had come from a single girl called Patricia, resident of the Ethembeni Children's Home in Johannesburg, who had stolen the hearts of two young professionals, Anthony Farr and Mark Tindall, during various outings to the Johannesburg Zoo and Gold Reef City.

Anthony and Mark later found themselves in London, where the desire to do something to change the circumstances of the thousands of children like Patricia, would not leave them. Yet, as individuals how could they make an impact?

It was the words of Robert Kennedy, from a speech made in Cape Town, that helped show the way:

"Each time a man stands up for an ideal, or acts to improve the lot of others or strikes out against injustice, he sends forth a tiny ripple of hope, and crossing each other from a million different centres of energy and daring, these ripples build a current that can sweep down the mightiest walls of oppression and resistance."
- Robert Kennedy, Cape Town, 1966

Anthony and Mark teamed up with Kate Macdonald, another South African living in London, and the first ripples of the Starfish journey were formed.

The Growing Current

"What really attracted me to Starfish was that it offered the ability to raise money for children orphaned by Aids, not by simply giving money, but by doing fun, communal activities with like-minded South Africans."
- Dalton Odendaal, UK

The initial philosophy was simple: by means of unusual events, social gatherings and publications, Starfish began to develop a community of South Africans, heightened in their awareness of the problems created by the HIV/Aids pandemic and determined to overcome them.

The central motivation was to be a catalyst of inspiration, convincing all that they had a contribution to make in the rapidly growing Starfish movement. As a result, events were selected on the basis of being interesting, accessible and doable. Events were further designed to emphasise the global connectivity of the South African community, bringing together people around the world for a common cause. Since June 2001, Starfish has hosted nine events which, when combined with corporate and individual contributions, have raised in the region of R6 million.

C T G A
A C G
G C T
T C A

"Each time a man stands up for an ideal, or acts to improve the lot of others or strikes out against injustice, he sends forth a tiny ripple of hope, and crossing each other from a million different centres of energy and daring, these ripples build a current that can sweep down the mightiest walls of oppression and resistance."
Robert Kennedy, Cape Town, 1966

The Thousand Dinners of Hope

"It was one of those evenings when you return home knowing that you have been part of something extraordinary."
- Edith Venter, SA

The event that perhaps best epitomises the Starfish philosophy was the Thousand Dinners of Hope initiative. It coincided with the launch of Starfish in South Africa, brought home by myself and Anthony Farr who had returned, volunteering full-time, to plant the movement firmly into African soil.

The initiative was held on Freedom Day, 27 April 2002, providing a new way for South Africans across the world to celebrate the extraordinary freedom we enjoy as South Africans, while at the same time investing into the freedom of the future generations.

The event was conceived to mobilise the global network of South Africans and friends of South Africa. The concept was stark in its simplicity - inviting people to host a dinner in their own homes.

The host would make the contribution of providing the food while the guests would, in turn, be encouraged to make a donation, as if enjoying a meal at a restaurant. People were able to sign up on the Starfish website, which updated a graphic representation of participation in the global event.

Prior to the evening, a documentary video was dispatched to all dinner venues, showing the impact that the funding was having on the lives of the children supported by Starfish, and informing people of the vision, while allowing Starfish to acknowledge individuals for their contribution to the evening.

The manner in which the event came together was a remarkable example of the power of collaboration between individuals and businesses for a common cause. In the space of a few short months, an ad agency offered to make a sixty-second Starfish TV commercial for free and this was flighted, at no cost, by Cinemark, M-Net and e tv as part of a national awareness campaign.

No less than nine companies were involved in producing the Starfish documentary shown at the dinners.

Meanwhile, large corporates challenged their staff to host dinners: churches challenged their congregations and schoolteachers challenged their learners' parents.

There were dinners from Mossel Bay, to Matubatuba, from Putney to Perth. Pieter Dirk Uys celebrated a dinner at his theatre, Evita se Perron, in Darling near Cape Town and there were queues outside Nando's in Wimbledon, London, from 11 in the morning until 10 at night as patrons joined the event by eating chicken for the children. By the end of Freedom Day 2002, a total of 2200 people had sat down to dinner in 10 different countries around the world and raised close to R500 000.

The Starfish Model

"Fate conspired to make possible a wonderful opportunity to leave Australia to study at Oxford as a Rhodes Scholar, where I met a number of South Africans who not only inspired me about their country, but also reminded me of the gratitude I owe that part of the world on account of the scholarship. Starfish has given me a way to give back to a country in return for all that it has given me."
- Peter Barnett, Australian in the UK

Starfish, in recognising our universal responsibility as keepers of our brothers and sisters, aims to establish a caring community, which refuses to relegate caring to the realm of large organisations staffed by people "whose job it is to care". This responsibility can be separated into two elements, namely the raising and spending of funds.

The fund-raising is driven by a small core team of permanent employees supported by a volunteer leadership and a wide network of motivated individuals and corporate partners. To date, Starfish has enjoyed support from more than 60 corporate partners, ranging from the largest listed company in South Africa to small owner-managed enterprises.

The power behind this model is that it:
- Inspires the growth of a large, caring community which gives time, talents, energy and financial resources to providing for children affected by Aids
- Minimises Starfish administration and marketing expenses
- Enables Starfish to keep its commitment to apply 100 per cent of donations received by individuals to target projects, with no deduction for expenses
- ensures access to the best skills in all areas, including legal, financial, marketing and administration.

The project funding is achieved by Starfish defining itself as a vehicle that brings life, hope and opportunity to children in HIV/Aids-ravaged communities.

In order to achieve this, Starfish has committed itself to community-based initiatives at two levels. The first provides funds for crisis-management programmes that take care of the immediate needs of nutrition, education, health and shelter. The second level, known as community upliftment, is built around establishing, with the assistance of delivery partners, a network of Star Centres to create a platform from which to assist affected communities in turning the tide on Aids.

A Star Centre is a community resource centre focussed on improving the community's capacity for responding to the orphan crisis created by the HIV/Aids pandemic.

Each Star Centre, while reflecting the unique characteristics of the participating community and delivery partner, will look to provide the following services:

- Education
  Crèche and pre-school services, either within the centre itself or by linking up with existing resources, to ensure that older children's education is not interrupted by having to care for younger siblings. Homework support and life skills will also be offered.

- Food Security
  Provision of meals and instruction in survival gardening in order to assist children in supporting themselves and in obtaining their nutritional requirements.

- Recreation
  Promotion of activities such as sport, music, drama and art as an outlet for the children. These activities will be supported by an annual Starfish Event of Hope.

- Income Generation
  Implementing income-generating projects to assist the capacity of the children and care givers to support themselves.

- Community Services
  The resource centre will act as a platform for further services such as the facilitation of the registration of government grants and the provision of basic medical care.

It made a difference to that one!

"Many thanks for the wonderful work that Starfish has done in the Kwa-Ncgolosi Valley. Everywhere I go, I meet people who are almost in tears when the children come home with new shoes and new uniforms. Unbelievable! Transformation is taking place in the valley."
- Eric Shezi, Rural Outreach Administrator

"Who are these people? We've never seen this before - people who care!"
- Headmaster of Hlahlindlela High School, commenting on change at a school following Starfish support.

The Starfish story ends where it began because the inspiration behind Starfish will always lie in the impact it has on the lives of South Africa's children:

- Mkusi left school following the death of his parents. Starfish was able to get him back into school and it was this change of circumstances that generated one piece of paper that sums up the entire Starfish dream: his school report for the end of 2001. Mkusi had finished top of his Grade v class of 56 pupils.

- A ragged group of around 20 children looked on with interest as they were instructed in a program called, Microsoft's Magic Bus Tour of Bugs on Starfish's newly-acquired computer, acquired against all odds by the children of Noah's First Resource Centre near Wartburg, KwaZulu-Natal. And, so, they began their journey across the digital divide and the first of many new champions was born as one of the children, Samkela, typed his name on the keyboard, one letter at a time.

- Debbie Wells, a social worker, was rather confused when asking 11-year-old Mdondo in Mophela Valley for his shoe size while providing uniforms for the Starfish funded Gcinosapho Rural Outreach Programme. He seemed genuinely stumped by the question. It was only after further questioning that Debbie realised the problem: Mdondo had never worn shoes.

It is so easy to become overwhelmed by the magnitude of the Aids orphan crisis, but it is Starfish's hope that we should not feel powerless.

Anyone who did biology at school and had to learn about osmosis will know that trying to develop a thriving South Africa, to the exclusions of our neighbours, will not work. There is ample evidence in the world's financial markets to prove that NEPAD is Africa's best chance of proving to the rest of the world that we are serious about reform. It attempts to re-engineer the commercial, social and political relationships between African states to their mutual benefit. If it works, it will rival our own miraculous transition.

26

NEPAD

Changing the Perspective on Africa

Editorial comment: Brett Bowes and Steuart Pennington

NEPAD has been developed by five countries: South Africa, Nigeria, Senegal, Algeria and Egypt, whose representatives criss-crossed the continent in 2001, working to formulate the programme.

Greeted with cynicism by the media and a fair degree of criticism from local political parties, NEPAD (New Partnership for Africa's Development) is slowly but surely beginning to be accepted as the best opportunity in many years to shift Africa's development onto a new path. What is often not understood is that, since 1994, South African businesses have moved into some 40 different African countries, with about 400 substantial projects. Trade agreements have been signed just as quickly. "Clearly our companies believe there is money to be made in Africa, and that they will increasingly engage if economic growth across the continent can be accelerated and sustained. This is what NEPAD aims to achieve," says Stephen Gelb in the publication, **Brand South Africa.**

"Investors outside Africa take a far less rosy view of the continent, directing about one per cent of global foreign direct investment flows towards it, with South Africa not seen as some sort of special case. For these investors, Africa's lack of development is South Africa's problem, so the success of NEPAD is very much in our interest," he concludes.

"Your truth is not what the facts are, your truth is what you perceive them to be."

Greeted with criticism, it's now being accepted as the best opportunity in many years to shift Africa onto a new path.

President Thabo Mbeki understands this, as do many of his African counterparts. This has to be a good move for Africa.

NEPAD's Objectives

"NEPAD aims to increase Africa's (and South Africa's) integration into global markets while also mitigating global risks originating in the continent. It intends to overcome the weakness and inability of individual African governments to promote development in their countries by facilitating collective action on a continental scale, thereby adjusting perceptions of Africa as a whole.

NEPAD rests on a three-pronged strategy:
· Pre-conditions for development
· Prioritising sectors and
· Mobilising resources."

As Gelb says, the pre-conditions are at the heart of the development agenda.

"For states still mired in internal conflict, establishing peace and security for citizens is obviously the absolute priority. In more stable countries, better political governance required the enhancement of democratic representation and the ability of citizens to exercise their rights and obligations, and the establishment for the respect of human rights and the rule of law in the criminal justice system."

"Better economic governance means reducing corruption, increasing transparency and accountability in the collection and the use of public finance, enhancing financial regulation, and promoting sound accounting and auditing practices in the private sector," he says.

With the advent of the African Union, it would appear that there is serious momentum among thinking African leaders to build Africa into an organisation rather like that of the European Union.

It must be remembered that the EU was created, not out of a sense of good neighbourliness or a requirement to reduce the tensions that started the Second World War, but rather out of the necessity to establish a powerful economic block that could rival the United States of America.

On 25 September 2002, **Business Day** wrote: "The meeting of the Commonwealth Troika in Nigeria on Monday was noteworthy for the absence of tougher action against Zimbabwe, despite the further deterioration of the situation in the country since the March Presidential Election. The unfortunate message that came out at the meeting is that South Africa and Nigeria are prepared to sacrifice their own interests and the continent's promising economic recovery plan, NEPAD. How else can one explain the fact that both Pretoria and Abuja keep repeating Mugabe's propaganda that the problem in Zimbabwe is about land rather than one of democracy and governance?

What is of major concern is the failure of South Africa to change its position on Zimbabwe and admit that the problem is about a stolen election and illegitimate land grabs and not emancipation from the evils of colonialism that pervaded the land 20 years ago. A failure to adopt this position creates the perception that the governance provisions of NEPAD cannot face up to a test that really counts."

Niall Fitzgerald, Chairman of Unilever Worldwide, and a member of the Presidents International Investment Council, says: "Government has been told that this (Zimbabwe) is a very urgent issue, it is strangling the NEPAD process ... the bad neighbour syndrome is an inhibitor to people investing" (**Business Day**, 15 October, 2002).

Clearly Nigeria and South Africa are still pushing for quiet diplomacy whereas other members of the Commonwealth are pushing for Zimbabwe's expulsion.

In the big scheme of things, Mugabe's rule of dictatorial terror will be relatively short-lived and, hopefully, the approach of quiet diplomacy will work because either Mugabe will weaken or he will be overthrown. For South Africa and Nigeria to propose the expulsion of Mugabe from the Commonwealth and even the African Union could polarise the African continent and jeopardise both the AU and NEPAD.

In a way, President Mbeki is in a Catch 22. For some, this was perceived as stumbling at the first hurdle. Fortunately, the recent decision to remove Mugabe as the next deputy president of SADC does send a strong signal that his time and credibility are drawing to a close.

Big Business and NEPAD
There is a perception that big business has no direct role to play in the initiative.

Geoff Cowley, senior advisor on Africa at the World Economic Forum, points out that business engagement in the initiative is crucial at policy, implementation and investment levels (**Business Day,** 10 October). "In fact, the biggest challenge now is to get business involved at the top level," he said, "particularly, gaining market access should be a combined effort by business and government, while finance is an area business can drive. And if business and government co-operated in the area of infrastructure development, this would happen quicker."

Essentially the tone of his talk at an American Chamber of Business meeting in Johannesburg was that NEPAD could not afford to fail; that Africa must not be marginalised any longer, and that the involvement of business in NEPAD would give it impetus and, to an extent, legitimacy.

NEPAD aims to increase South Africa's integration into global markets whilst mitigating global risks originating in the continent.

The big challenge is how to get business involved.

Priority Sectors

"Progress in the priority sectors will reverse Africa's marginalisation and lay the basis for sustainable long-term development. Progress in health, education and infrastructure, especially, depends on improvement in governance and regional collaboration," says Gelb.

Clearly within Africa there is much to be done, but as some quite devastatingly disadvantaged countries have shown (Mozambique being the best example), fast turnarounds attract international help.

Mobilising Resources

Mobilising is necessary to pay for the strategy's first two prongs (infrastructure and human development), and especially the second. The raising of finance itself depends on progress in these two areas. In the short term, additional resources will largely involve more debt relief and aid. Industrialised countries have already indicated that better governance will help to increase flows.

Over the longer term, improved governance together with progress in sectors like infrastructure, education and health, will cut costs of doing business in Africa and cut investor risk. More private finance - domestic savings and foreign investment - should follow.

The Peer Review Mechanism

NEPAD will establish an African peer review mechanism so that states which cannot improve governance by acting on their own will receive support from other African countries. The peer review process will operate like a club. Membership will be voluntary but countries will have to play by the club's rules, which means firm commitments to address governance problems over time.

Clearly, the peer review mechanism will be the make or break of NEPAD. In many sectors of the world, Africa is viewed as a collection of states as opposed to a collection of independent countries. It is true that the behaviour of Zimbabwe, the war in the Congo and the attempted coup on the Ivory Coast continue to create the impression, certainly in the developed world, that Africa is a basket case.

If the peer review mechanism is rigorous and is seen to be taking action against those countries that do not uphold the basic tenets of democracy, the confidence of the developed world in Africa will increase. Failure to make the peer review mechanism work will result in a continued perception that Africa is unable to pull itself up by its boot straps.

Hopefully, as the AU starts to put flesh on NEPAD's bones, many of the issues cited above will become clearer. We trust that the meeting scheduled by the UN Economic Commission for Africa late in October 2002, will do just this.

Conclusion

Clearly, a great deal of lobbying and consultation is still required to give NEPAD a real chance of making a difference to Africa; and the African Union needs to settle down as well. But the initiative is crucial, from the point of view of both development and legitimacy. As a continent we really only have one shot at this and, if we fail, our credibility will disappear.

We have to change the "truth" of Africa.

There is no doubt as to the economic, social and political upside if NEPAD achieves its objectives. The sceptics already have their knives out - but they had them out in 1994 when South Africa transformed. We should have greater faith after witnessing our own miracle. NEPAD is a bold initiative of five governments, but it needs the power of private enterprise and the citizens of its most powerful nations to drive it. There is no downside. We cannot sit back and blame government if NEPAD fails, if we as business have failed in our duty to make our contribution.

Dr Wiseman Nkuhlu, Chairman: NEPAD Secretariat.
The following 11 questions define the initiative:

1. What is NEPAD?
The New Partnership for Africa's Development (NEPAD) is a vision and strategic framework for Africa's renewal.

2. What are the origins of NEPAD?
The NEPAD strategic framework document was prepared by the leaders of the five initiating states (Algeria, Egypt, Nigeria, Senegal, South Africa), in response to a mandate given to them by the Summit of the Organisation of African Unity (OAU). The 37th Summit of the OAU in July 2001 formally adopted the strategic framework document.

3. Why the need for NEPAD?
NEPAD is designed to address the current challenges facing the African continent. Issues such as the escalating poverty levels and underdevelopment of African countries and the continued marginalisation of Africa needed a new radical intervention, spearheaded by African leaders, that would bring forth a new vision that would guarantee Africa's renewal.

4. What is the NEPAD programme of action?
It is a detailed action plan derived from the NEPAD strategic framework document.

The NEPAD programme of action is a holistic, comprehensive and integrated, sustainable development initiative for the revival of Africa.

> As some quite devastatingly disadvantaged countries have shown (Mozambique being the best example), fast turnarounds attract international help.

5. What are NEPAD's primary objectives?
- To eradicate poverty
- To place African countries, both individually and collectively, on a path of sustainable growth and development
- To halt the marginalisation of Africa in the globalisation process
- To accelerate the empowerment of women and
- To fully integrate Africa into the global economy.

6. What are the principles of NEPAD?
- African ownership and leadership, as well as broad and deep participation by all sectors of society
- Anchoring the redevelopment of the continent on the resources and resourcefulness of the African people
- Partnership between and amongst African peoples
- Acceleration of regional and continental integration
- Building the competitiveness of African countries and the continent
- Forging of a new partnership with the industrialised world by, amongst other things, ensuring that it changes

the unequal relationship between Africa and the developed world and

- Commitment to ensuring that all partnerships with NEPAD are linked to the Millennium Development Goals and other agreed development goals and targets.

7. What are the elements of strategic focus of NEPAD?

- To reduce the risk profile of doing business in Africa
- To create the conditions conducive for investment, high economic growth and sustainable development
- To increase Africa's competitiveness in the world economy
- To transform the unequal and donor/recipient relationship with the developed countries and multilateral institutions to a new partnership that is based on mutual responsibility and respect and
- To increase investment on the continent in order to ensure social and economic development.

8. What are NEPAD's priorities?

a. Establishing the conditions for development by ensuring:
   - Peace and security
   - Democracy, political, economic and corporate governance, with a focus on public financial management
   - Regional co-operation and integration; and
   - Capacity building.

b. Policy reforms and increased investment in the following priority sectors:
   - Agriculture
   - Human development with a focus on health, education, science and technology and skills development
   - Building and improving infrastructure, including Information and Communication Technology (ICT), Energy, Transport, Water and Sanitation
   - Promoting diversification of production and exports, including promotion of agro-industries, manufacturing, mining, mineral beneficiation and tourism
   - Accelerating intra-Africa trade and improving access to markets of developed countries; and
   - The environment.

c. Mobilising resources:
   - Increasing domestic savings and investments

- Improved management of public revenue and expenditure
- Increasing capital flows through further debt reduction and increased ODA flow sand and
- Improving Africa's share in global trade.

9. What are the immediate desired outcomes of NEPAD?

- Africa becomes more effective in conflict prevention and the establishment of enduring peace on the continent.
- Africa adopts and implements principles of good economic and political governance and democracy and the protection of human rights become further entrenched in every African country.
- Africa develops and implements effective poverty eradication programmes and accelerates the pace of achieving set African development goals, particularly human development goals.
- Africa achieves increased levels of capital flows and increased investments to the continent, both domestic and foreign.
- Increased levels of ODA to the continent are achieved and its effective utilisation maximised.
- Africa becomes more effective in terms of policy development on an international level thus ensuring that the continent's needs are taken into account, for instance, in WTO negotiations.
- Regional integration is further accelerated and higher levels of sustainable economic growth in Africa are achieved.
- Genuine partnerships are established between Africa and the developed countries based on mutual respect and accountability.

10. What are the elements of the current focus of NEPAD?

- Operationalising the African peer review mechanism
- Co-ordinating and facilitating implementation of projects and programmes
- Further developing programmes of action and specific interventions for
   - Market access, industrialisation, increasing intra-Africa trade and diversification of production and exports
   - Science and Technology, and the establishment of Regional Centres of Excellence and
   - Gender mainstreaming
- Political, economic and corporate governance
- Education

- Agriculture
- Infrastructure
- Health
- Broadening ownership and participation by all sectors of African society

Clearly the effectiveness of the peer review mechanism will be the make or break of NEPAD.

11. What does the NEPAD structure look like?

NEPAD is a programme of the African Union designed to meet its development objectives. The highest authority of the NEPAD implementation process is the Heads of State and Government Summit of the recently launched African Union, formerly known as the OAU.

The Heads of State and Government Implementation Committee (HSIC) comprises three states per AU region as mandated by the OAU Summit of July 2001 and ratified by the AU Summit of July 2002. The HSIC reports to the AU Summit on an annual basis.

The Steering Committee of NEPAD comprises the Personal Representatives of the NEPAD Heads of State and Government. This Committee instructs the Secretariat of NEPAD to coordinate and implement projects and processes that have been identified by the HSIC as being of priority. The Secretariat is the coordinating and liaison arm of the NEPAD Steering Committee.

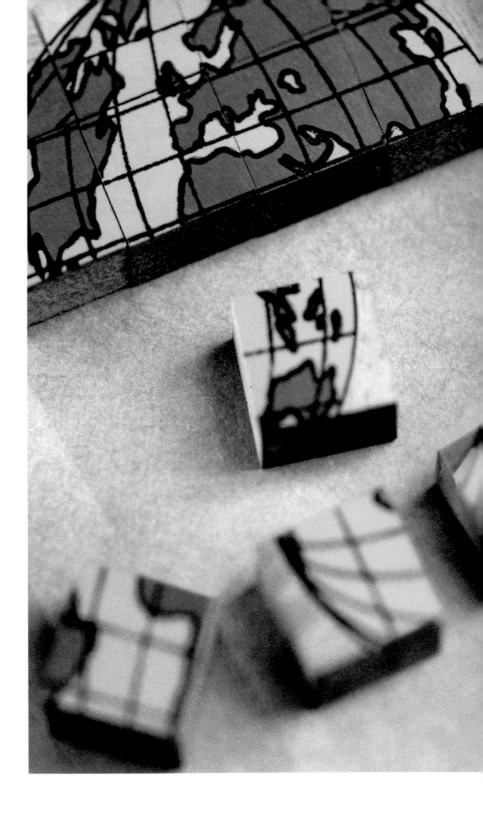

As a continent we only really have one shot at this. We have to change the "truth" of Africa.

27

Its important to think about how high we pitch our vision. We need to examine not only our economic and social structures, but also the way we think of ourselves, and sell ourselves. We were a pariah state in the late 1980s. The vision was survival, and it was inwardly focused. Our historical tendency was to avoid attention. But our new-found freedom demands that we shout our competitive advantage from the rooftops. To do this we need a compelling vision which inspires all of us to make our contribution. And we need evidence of progress so we can sell our country with confidence.

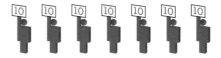

The South African Vision

Do we have competitive advantage?

Brett Bowes and Steuart Pennington

Vision - Illusive or Attainable

In concluding this book, we thought it would be useful to raise the debate on the South African Vision and whether we are becoming better at being one nation?

Vision has been described as, "a lofty ideal of a future positioning or state of being. A place where you would like to be."

It is often said that vision should be somewhat dreamlike and, if nothing else, create "stretch" in the mind of the audience. Strategy is what needs to be done to get there.

Joel Barker describes a good vision as having the following characteristics:

- Its is leadership initiated (leadership agreement on direction)
- It is shared and supported (understood by all constituencies)
- It is comprehensive and detailed (backed up by clear goals and measures)

- It is positive and inspiring (encouraging motivation and passion)

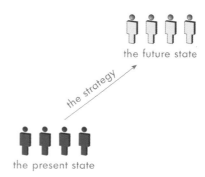

In South Africa's context, there can be little question that the ANC vision of "a better life for all", is leadership initiated. Those who have had the opportunity to see it may say that the vision is comprehensive and detailed with clear goals and measures.

As far as shared and supported is concerned, i.e. understood by all constituencies, the ANC is anxious about

No one would disagree that when it comes to delivery, the ANC is, for the most part, doing a good job.

the level of buy-in, as reflected in the resolutions raised at their September Congress regarding inadequate communication, and by recent criticism by members of the President's International Marketing Council.

Positive and inspiring probably applies to many of the constituencies who have had the vision shared with them, and seen some of the benefit.

Unfortunately, many are unaware of the vision and the great strides that have made in making it a reality.

For many, "a better life for all" is a positioning statement developed by the ANC to send a clear message to the electorate on the priority of delivery to the poor. For others it is more embracing, designed to appeal to all citizens, sending the message that ALL South Africans will ultimately benefit from the changes that sweep our land. But it does belong to the ANC, and consequently is used to criticise and oppose much of the way the ANC governs.

This is the South African Paradox.

Having read the chapters of this book, no one would disagree that, when it comes to delivery, the ANC is, for the most part, doing a good job.

Yes, we may have lost our way temporarily on Aids, Zimbabwe and crime, but the building blocks of a great nation are in place. The global community acknowledges that. So why don't we all subscribe to a compelling vision, a rallying point that will garner all South Africans to feel especially proud of their country, their flag, and their people?

Although the Government has, in a short eight years, done a remarkable job reinventing our country and its policies, in our view it has a poor record of sharing and communicating its vision and its progress. Consequently its ability to engender a positive perspective among its constituents is hampered:
· Valuable people still leave our shores.
· Confidence levels trail reality.
· Investment does not meet expectations.

The inspiration behind this book was driven by Government's poor record of presenting comprehensively the evidence of its remarkable achievements. Maybe an independent review is required to kick-start the process? In the business world, the implementation of vision integrates communication into every facet - otherwise key constituencies are left behind. Although the business strategy may be sound, the organisation will seem frail, and may fail, if perceptions do not support reality.

We have developed the following framework to better examine the Government's competence in the area of strategy.

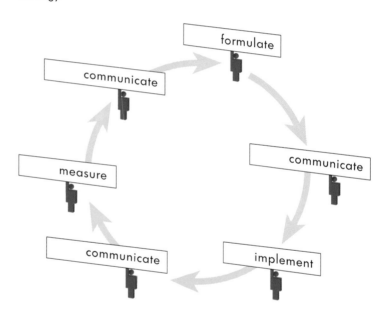

The TerraNova Strategic Model

Unfortunately, in a fast changing world, perceptions, rather than facts, become the reality of many. The management of perceptions to reflect the true reality is the key challenge for the Government as it travels through this period of rapid transition.

Key target markets for communication are:
1 The population (both corporate and private)
2 Foreign investors and tourists
3 Regional and international governments and trade blocks

Formulation of Strategy

This is a continuous process. It is important that the organisation (government or business) has a view of how the future will unfold, and then selects the most competitive options. It further requires the construction of a world-class plan for rapid implementation. The pace of change requires this.

South Africa obviously has a strong strategy underlying its achievements over the past eight years. It is also a competitive strategy underpinned by wise choices. It is acknowledged that there are criticisms in the area of health, crime and foreign affairs.

Rating 7.5/10

Communication of Formulation

In business, it is recognised that a few people lead and the majority implement and operate. These people need a clear message from the leadership, a message that is simple, gives clear direction, and creates confidence.

Planning and acting need to happen simultaneously, sometimes described as "Planact". Fast and accurate communication is crucial, both to those responsible for implementation and to those who are the target market of the implementation process. Fortune Magazine concluded, after an extensive survey, that most chief executives and companies fail, not because their strategies are weak, but because their communication and implementation process is flawed (Fortune: June 1999)

The communication should be:
- Simple
- Inspiring
- Easy to remember
- Accompanied by clear facts and measures

South Africa's abiding weakness in the strategic process is communication. As a nation we are only aware of our strategy through the evidence of its implementation, and not through simple and inspirational communication. Important target markets are only able to judge the quality of strategy on the basis of the evidence of change. Consequently, they are unaware of the intended direction and, often, there is a lot of misdirected criticism.

Rating 2/10

Implementation of Strategy

Effective implementation demands the understanding, capacity and organisational will to turn a plan into reality by those who are responsible for implementation.

Clear milestones are needed with a rigorous performance-management system and a culture of zero tolerance for non-performers. All stakeholders are better off under these circumstances and milestones should be published so that stakeholders can live their lives with more certainty.

South Africa has done a remarkable job on the implementation of strategy and there is every reason to expect that it will continue to do so. President Mbeki's resolve and his choice of ministers and Directors General is the major reason for this performance. We would suspect that where there has been poor delivery, the strategy itself has as often as not been deficient.

Rating 8/10

Communication of Implementation

In business, there is always a gap between leading and lagging measures and the greater the gap the more the likelihood of implementation failure.

The narrower the gap between the strategy and the result, the better.

The South African Government is fortunate to have a strong mandate and the time and strength it requires to implement its policies resolutely.

There must still, however, be regular and rapid communication with all stakeholders, informing them about the rate of progress against the published targets. This will:

- Build certainty about government plans
- Build confidence within its various constituencies and target markets
- Speed the process of implementation itself
- Cause debate (and rapid reformulation of policy) where circumstances change
- Give credit where it is due

Most South Africans know less than they should about our implementation successes (and failures). There is ample evidence of sound progress, helped partly by what we see

Although strategy may be sound, organisations (and governments) will seem frail, and may fail, if perceptions do not support reality.

and experience and partly by what we read. Our vibrant press and many NGOs see to that. Notwithstanding this, the government has not developed clear benchmarks against which to compare our progress and often fail to keep key target markets abreast even of their successes.

Rating 4/10

Measurement of Implementation

Because the circumstances and the pace of change are never predictable, the measurement of implementation against agreed objectives is the key to continuous progress. Clearly some conditions for the achievement of objectives will be volatile, and for others reasonably constant.

It is therefore inevitable that not every objective will be achieved on time and in full. Organisations that are able to manage this unpredictability are the most likely to succeed. There is no place for defensiveness, inflexibility or dogma.

South Africa has a well-developed system of statistically relevant and reliable measurement. Many independent organisations and NGOs, using different methodologies, ensure that the important measures have integrity.

Rating 9/10

Communication of Measurement

Regular and open communication on success and failure, and of the adjustments demanded by the changing environment, builds confidence with all stakeholders. Governments, multilateral agencies, multinational corporations, local business and civil society can all operate with more certainty where strategy is clear and progress is measured and communicated.

This openness reduces risk, and experience shows that willingness to do business is directly related to the level of confidence and understanding of stakeholders.

If South Africa has clear measurement, and if the government is vocal about its successes, the country will improve its reputation and its attractiveness. In addition, an open acceptance of failure, with consequent corrective action, will also increase confidence.

It is our view that, because the communication of strategy formulation and strategy implementation, respectively, is so poor, that whatever communication of measurement there is exists in limbo. Inevitably, this means that success is neither celebrated nor recognised to the extent that it should be.

Rating 4.5/10

In spite of an excellent record of strategy formulation and implementation the Government has let itself down by not sharing widely its vision or its considerable successes.

So we pose the question what is the South African Vision? Is it to become the world's most competitive emerging market? Is it to address the social backlogs that we inherited from our apartheid past? Is it to build a more egalitarian society? Is it to become the hub of the sub-continent? Is it to be "Alive with Possibilities?" Or is it all of the above and more?

Brand South Africa - Alive with Possibilities
In a recent publication, **Brand South Africa**, the lessons on branding campaign strategies derived from other countries are explained in detail. It is pointed out that a brand should comprise a "phew!" factor, and in South Africa's case "reflect the reality and provide the perception of a nation brimming with promise and self-confidence."

The slogan, "South Africa - Alive with Possibilities" has been chosen by the President's International Marketing Council.

According to **Brand South Africa**: "Brands need to be managed carefully as they focus on different target audiences, eg. other governments, multi-national and local business, overseas populations from a tourist point of view, and, of course, our own people."

The critical challenge facing the Government is to ensure that the strategy, and the positioning statement **Alive with Possibilities**, are aligned. After all, a brand is a promise and, if the promise is broken, so is the brand. Promoting and sustaining a brand is part of building a reputation. If we want to have the reputation of being **Alive with Possibilities**, then we have to deliver and delivery means the strong adherence to the entire strategic process and the building of reputation.

So how is South Africa doing on the alignment of vision, the strategic process and the building of a reputation? Are we becoming better at being one nation? Are we becoming more competitive?

The scores above are applied to our model below:

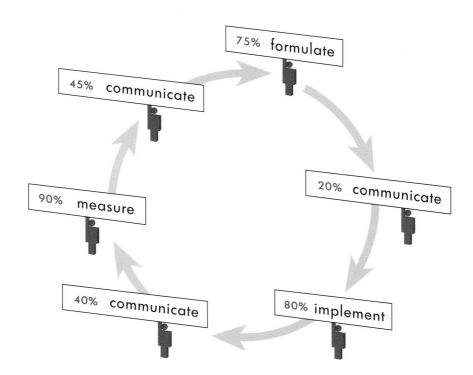

South Africa's poor communication ability has resulted in confidence problems amongst its main stakeholders.

there can be better communication with the international community on the processes taking place in the country so that people, as they go around selling SA, are able to respond." How true!

Most would acknowledge that there is an unfair contest between bad news and good news. In our view, in a transforming society, the media have an important nation-building role to play. Diversity is not always a source of positive multiculturalism, it can be divisive if openness and debate are not valued.

Conclusion

We would conclude that the South African government does have a visionary strategy. It has also, as evidenced by the chapters of this book, achieved much in the way of implementation over the past eight years.

Its measurement systems are in place and excellent. Every department we dealt with had an absolute handle on where they had come from and where they were going to.

In fact, it is our opinion that there are no parallel examples in history where two powerful factions who seemed headed for inevitable conflict were able to, firstly, create the miracle that is the new South Africa and then, secondly, deliver such remarkable transformation so rapidly.

Saki Macozoma's words quoted above are profound. It is our view that, as a nation, we have failed to communicate effectively. Fortunately, this is the easiest element of the strategic process to correct. The international and local business communities now require that the Government significantly improve its communication. The creation of the President's International Marketing Council is a positive step in this regard. The management of Brand South Africa and the Proudly South African campaign need to be led by Government with the full support of the media and the business community. Business and the media need to understand and use the power they wield and their ability to change perceptions locally and abroad.

We hope that this book will be useful to all parties to enable them to achieve their aligned but different objectives. We hope that many South Africans armed with this good news will do their bit to change the perceptions of our beloved land for the better, forever.

As most will acknowledge - there is an unfair contest between good and bad news. The media bear an awesome responsibility going forward.

The government is clear about where it wants to go, an enormous amount of successful implementation has already taken place and, increasingly, every department is being measured.

Why then is the reputation of South Africa and the government not receiving the credit it deserves? Is it because, as a nation, we are so used to bad news, that we can't hear the good?

As we went to print, Government and the Big Business Working Group, which consists of SA's top industrialists and financiers, met to discuss issues of confidence and investment in SA in a bid to clear the way for the Growth and Development Summit early next year.

Saki Macozoma, New Africa Investments Limited CEO said: "The major issue, is how to build confidence in the SA economy and SA society. We have to find ways in which

Is this the promised land?

Jovial Rantao, Deputy Editor of The Star and Editor of The Sunday Independent

Jovial wrote this essay in answer to the question, "Are we becoming better a being one nation?"

The Legacy

South Africa, eight years after the dawn of democracy. Eight years after the elimination (in a peaceful manner) of apartheid, a most evil system. What has changed? Has anything changed?

Yes, a lot has changed since 26 April, 1994, on the eve of this country's first democratic elections, when a series of bomb explosions echoed through the country, the work of those who did not want to see South Africa becoming the country of all those who live in it. The death and mayhem that came with the heinous acts of the terrorists did not deter South Africans, both black and white, to turn out in their numbers and exercise, together as one nation, their right to vote for the government of their choice.

Soon after his inauguration as president, Nelson Mandela spoke of the rainbow nation, his desire for South Africa to become a country rich in diversity, a country as beautiful and bright as the rainbow itself. Eight years down the line, have our communities, forced to live separately by apartheid laws, started to move towards a nation where blacks and white live side by side, in peace?

The Dawn

The apartheid gulf was too huge to close in just under a decade, but a start has been made. Picture this scene - It's 12 noon on a Saturday. The sky is a dazzle of blue. A cool breeze wafts across, providing a much-needed relief to the smoke-filled, heavily polluted atmosphere. A taxi grinds to a halt, the side door slides open, passengers alight and the door closes with a thud. The taxi hooter goes off, the driver sticks his finger out, indicating his next destination. More passengers hop on, he drives off.

As the minibus goes up Roodepoort Road, a major road that runs through Soweto, a young white man in his twenties crosses the road. He is alone, doesn't look panic stricken and, with a loaf of bread in his hand, he saunters on. He smiles and greets a young woman walking past him. The young white man's presence did not attract undue attention.

He did not stick out.

Eight years ago, a white man in Soweto would have been the centre of attraction.

The scene along Roodepoort Road on this particular day mirrors similar ones right across South Africa's world famous city. In Mofolo Village, for instance, a young white woman was so integrated into that community that no one questioned why, every day, she was perched on a pavement, selling fruit and vegetables to sustain herself and her family. She moved into the neighbourhood months ago, after she fell in love and eventually married a Soweto lad. The scene in Roodepoort Road indicates a very important development which is that, albeit slowly, South African communities are beginning to be integrated.

The success of the integration of Soweto and other black areas is a small step in the process that would begin to reverse a trend where integration of residential areas has occurred largely in the former whites-only areas, where young, upwardly-mobile blacks have moved in.

Many schools in these areas have been totally integrated. Some of them now have a perfect racial mix while others have moved from being whites-only institutions to being totally black.

Back to Roodepoort Road. As the young white man finally crosses the road and continues to walk up Mooki Street, a white minibus taxi drives past him. There was one striking feature about the taxi. On the back windscreen was a huge flag, used both as a windshield and a decoration.

The flag was green in colour and had, emblazoned on it, the picture of a Springbok and next to it a rugby ball. A minibus taxi, the symbol of black economic empowerment, proudly carrying a flag advertising a game that once symbolised the evil system that oppressed and suppressed black people.

Yes, this was the scene in Roodepoort Road and I am sure elsewhere in the country.

A lot has changed since 26 April 1994.

Rugby was a sport played by policemen, soldiers and security operatives...all that has changed. Eight years on Rugby is a sport all South Africans identify with.

Again, this scene would have been impossible a mere eight years ago. Rugby was the sport of people who believed or were made to believe that black people were inferior. It was a sport played by policemen, soldiers and security operatives responsible for the murder of scores of black people during the apartheid era. Rugby, then, represented everything that black people in South Africa stood against.

That has all changed. Eight years on, rugby has become a sport that all South Africans identify with. Perhaps it started at Ellis Park in 1995 when then President Nelson Mandela handed Francois Pienaar, (the then national rugby captain) the World Cup trophy after South Africa had sensationally defeated the All Blacks. That moment, and the success in the development of the sport in all communities in the country, changed for the better, the attitude of the majority in this country towards rugby.

Black youngsters in many schools across the country now share the rugby field as well as the passion for the game with many of their white colleagues. Their dream is one and one only. To play very well, score points and to represent their school, their club, their province and ultimately their country.

My 18 year-old nephew developed the love of rugby five years ago when he was enrolled at Mondeor High School, a formerly whites-only school. Since his introduction to the sport, the youngster has become obsessed with it. He eats, sleeps, walks and talks rugby. His heroes include a number of white South African rugby players.

My nephew has now been included in a developmental programme by the Blue-Bulls, the Pretoria-based rugby outfit, known over the decades for its love for the sport and for having produced a number of white rugby stars.

Although teething problems are visible, the Blue Bulls programme to integrate their players has gone quite well. The success has predictably led to tension, particularly from white parents who feel that the chances of their children have been reduced by the inclusion of black players in the side. Like all new things, the integration was bound to bring tension, but the overwhelming aspect of it is the support that the majority of the people in that part of the South Africa gives to the team.

Rugby is not the only sport that has made some progress in transforming itself. Other major sporting codes such as cricket have made strides. So, if the progress made in the sporting fraternity is an indication of any sort, some positive things are happening and, soon, when team South Africa plays, it will have the support of each and every member of this family.

Rugby was once the symbol of apartheid. This much was evidenced by the number of old South Africa flags which were hoisted by many supporters at rugby games. That has changed. As a national symbol, the eight year-old South African flag has become the pride of all. Every citizen of this country now identifies with the flag. And what an emotional moment it is when athletic stars such as Mboneni Mulaudzi and Hestrie Cloete run the lap of honour in international meetings, draped in the South African flag.

Some storm clouds still exist, he old flag has not totally disappeared. Nor has the number, albeit few, of those who hanker for the past. However, the majority is streets away, adding new blocks in the building of our new country. Some progress, not enough though, has been made in the business sector. The face of this crucial part of our country has changed to some extent in the last eight years. There are more black-controlled companies than there ever were in the history of South Africa. However, that is not enough.

The problem with the transformation of business in South Africa is that it has tended to benefit a handful. We see the same faces signing lucrative deals all over the show. They're in mining, services, banking and other sectors.

The delay in black economic empowerment has led to government indicating quite strongly that if business does not move quickly to up the pace of change, government would step in. The recent accord through the Mining Charter between Government and our mining houses is a

major step forward. The procurement and ownership knock ons will transform our land because of its relative importance to GDP.

At a formal level, the South African Chamber of Commerce (white) and the National Federated Chamber of Commerce (black), where, at the time of writing this article, still trying to find each other, in a desperate attempt to form a unified body that would represent business in this country.

While a lot of has changed for the better, there are those who want to reverse the clock. There have been ugly incidents of farm evictions of black tenants by white farmers, the racial killings of white farmers in remote areas. However, in general, most South Africans cherish the vision of the new South Africa.

So, change has occurred in the business sector but much more still needs to be done.

For some the day is brighter
Have the lives of ordinary people changed? My 81 year-old grandmother says, "Yes!"

She might not have all the things she wants in her life. but it has certainly changed for the better. She should know. She lived through what is probably the most repressive period in the history of this country. She lived long enough to witness the birth of freedom in her lifetime.

How has her life changed? Many years ago, she, and many villagers, were forced to walk at least a kilometre to the nearest stream to fetch water. Today, they walk a couple of metres to a communal tap that offers, clean and potable water.

Have the lives of ordinary people changed? My 81 year old grandmother says "Yes!".

For many years electricity was a dream to her. Today, she has power in her house. A telephone line has been installed. And better still, for my stylish granny, cellphone reception masts have been installed and she insists on a cellphone as her next gift.

Roads leading to her house, which used to be so bad that people would have to park a distance away, have been spruced up. The delivery by government on its election promises for housing and education have been slow, but

We have magnificent highways, warm, friendly and vibrant rainbow people, the worlds most progressive constitution, kreepy kraulies, Mrs Balls chutney, biltong and the worlds best looking population.

- Eskom is the largest producer of coal-fired electricity in the world, and South Africans pay the least for electricity in the world.
- South African Breweries is the second-largest brewer in the world.
- Mercedes Benz C-Class, the BMW 3-Series and VW Golf/Jetta vehicles for the most discerning markets in the world are produced in South Africa.
- The Cape Peninsula has more species of plants per hectare than any other area of the world.
- We have the world's fifth most productive labour force, measured in dollar terms

In addition we have magnificent highways; warm, friendly and vibrant rainbow people (if you have any doubts ask the thousands who attended the World Summit of Sustainable Development); the world's most progressive constitution; Kreepy Kraulies (a South African invention); Mrs Ball's chutney; biltong; and the world's best-looking population.

For some it never rains

There are problems. For instance, it is hard to believe that in South Africa, in the year 2002, you have children dying of poverty. Crime remains a cause of serious concern. The ranks of the unemployed are too high. Since 1994 South Africa has slashed tariffs on many imports, cut taxes, kept a lid on social spending and inflation, reduced the public workforce and began selling off state-owned utilities such as water, electricity and telephone services to investors.

``We believe,'' said one senior U.S. official, ``that South Africa has definitely taken very positive steps toward alleviating poverty.''

But the measures so far have produced only a trickle of new investments, and the economy has shed at least 500 000 jobs since1994.

The HIV/Aids pandemic continues to destroy our society. But these are challenges that we can face and defeat by being positive. The Treatment Action Campaign, for instance, did not sit in a corner and sulk over the non-availability of drugs for people living with Aids, it made use of the constitution and won. They found a positive way of dealing with the problem. Now, thousands of people living with Aids have hope.

a solid start has been made. There can be no debate that the little that is there was not there during the reign of a government that did not care about all who lived in South Africa.

For many the sun does shine

Here are some of the reasons why we have to be positive:

- Our country, almost alone among emerging market economies, escaped virtually unscathed from the latest bout of investor panic sweeping the developing world's fragile economies.
- The South African banking sector has been consistently ranked in the top 10 in terms of competitiveness.
- When Nelson Mandela was inaugurated president in 1994, South Africa was insolvent. Today, the government's deficit is negligible.

- 15 years ago, in 1986 - when a state of emergency was declared, white men did two years compulsory military service, 64 184 black people were removed from 'white areas', and 3989 people were detained without trial and our economic growth rate was 0.7 per cent. Today it is three per cent. Back then, 64 countries had sports boycotts against SA!
- South African wines win international awards every year and we have the longest wine route in the world.

- Nelson Mandela, an international icon of forgiveness, tolerance, and humanity, is the world's favourite son.
- The Kruger Park has the most innovative management of a national park anywhere in the world - and it is the world's most profitable game reserve

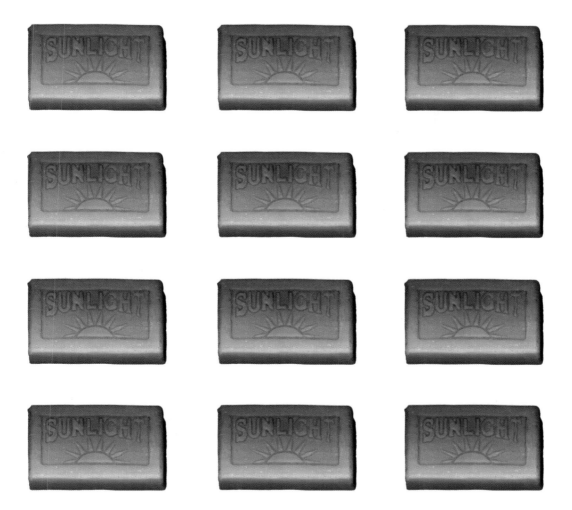

There is no doubt that huge changes have occurred in the past eight years. However, huge as these changes might have been, they are not enough.

The gaps that still exist remain obstacles in the formation of a truly integrated South Africa society. As Malekgapuru Makgoba, one of South Africa's talented sons once observed, we are the only country in the world that think we can participate in the soccer World Cup for the first time and go on and win the trophy.

But despite the weather we are getting better at being one nation. We're perhaps the only country that wants to be perfect after only eight years of democracy. But who can blame us. Our history was so bad that we're trying very hard to run away from it. We are some distance away from advertising it but we're moving inexorably and for the most part in unison in the right direction. Of course it will take some time before ALL South Africans can genuinely proclaim that they have reached the promised land.

Comment from the editors
Could this essay have been written just five years ago? We think not. The balance, the belief, the passion, and the sense of common destiny is nothing short of a miracle.

Proof of the Good News.

The real beneficiaries of the dramatic change we have witnessed in South Africa are our children. The people who graduate today were only 10 years old in 1994. They are growing up increasingly wide-eyed at the opportunities that await them. Significantly, they are largely uncorrupted by apartheid memories, untainted by racial issues and proud to be South African. They are our future.

Epilogue

The Lives Of Our Future Leaders

Dr. Olive Shisana: Executive Director: Human Science Research Council

"I feel honoured to stand in front of you here today at such an important event in the lives of our future leaders. Graduation is a time for us to take a moment and recognise those who have achieved academically.

It is a time for graduates to begin new lives as professionals. It is also a time to ponder the gaps in our society that you are best equipped to address. It is on this latter point that I want to focus today.

South Africa is a rich country in many ways. Our country has a lot of resources, i.e., human, financial and physical. We are a microcosm of the world, having diversity in terms of our race, culture and ethnic backgrounds.

We have in our country a range of different socio-economic worlds, from the richest to the poorest. We are a country with the brightest minds that have contributed significantly to development in the world. This presents us with opportunities and challenges. The question to ask is "How can we harness our diversity, skills, knowledge and other resources to make South Africa a better place than it is today?" Perhaps it is a good idea at this time to reflect on what some of our compatriots have accomplished thus far.

Achievements of our people

Heart transplants are done as a matter of routine today. The pioneer of this life-saving procedure is the late Dr Chris Barnard, a South African. We are the only country to produce two Nobel Peace Prize winners who lived in the same street. These are none other than the Honourable former President, Nelson Mandela and Archbishop Desmond Tutu who shared Bhacela street in Soweto. What a feat! Imagine what it will take for another country to have two of its citizens living in the same street accomplish this.

Mark Shuttleworth, although living in London, is the first African, might I say South African, to go into space. Just in case we have forgotten how he made his money, he developed an Internet technology that enables the processing of payments using encryption and it is used worldwide today.

When we talk about leading brain surgeons, one of our own, Dr Mokgokong, is on that list. Amongst our great artists who have entertained and educated the world are the likes of Miriam Makeba, Hugh Masekela and Abdullah Ebrahim.

Our expertise is highly sought internationally. Our chartered accountants, nurses and doctors are hot items overseas. We contribute significantly to international organisations, for example, Dr Mamphela Ramphele, at the World Bank and Vivian Taylor at the Commission on Human Security. I am afraid that if I go on you may not be able to receive your certificates today. Let us now look at economic matters.

Economy

The accomplishments we have just discussed are possible because, as a country, we are not poor. Did you know that South Africa has the largest economy in Africa? Did you know that the size of Gauteng's economy is bigger than every African state except Egypt? Did you even know that only six African countries have an economy larger than that of the Eastern Cape?

Even more interesting is the fact that our country is home to the 20th largest economy out of 230 countries in the world (using GDP measured in US dollar purchasing-power parity).

We are not poor because we have strong mining, agricultural, tourism, catering, manufacturing, educational and health sectors. We have a very large country for a population of 43 million, large enough to give each person a piece of land and remain with plenty more to conduct our economic activities in all sectors. We have enough land (and productive land for that matter) to settle all our people to prevent homelessness. We have enough food to feed all South Africans and still export to other parts of the world. And what about infrastructure, you may ask.

Infrastructure

We have 377 public hospitals, 3387 clinics, and 285 private health care facilities throughout the country, with a doctor-to-patient ratio of 2.9 doctors per 10 000 patients and a nurse to population ratio of 32 nurses per 10 000 patients. Despite this health facility and human resource infrastructure, we still are unable to ensure access to health care for those who need it most, the poor.

We are able to communicate among ourselves and with the rest of the world much more easily than most of our neighbours. Did you know we are the ninth-largest Internet user in the world? And think about it, we are even ahead of the United States in terms of using the cell phone as a common mode of communication.

We are the cheapest electricity supplier in the world, and generate a large percentage of all of Africa's energy. Did you ever look at the picture of the whole world at night? You will see that the lights are shining in the metropolitan areas of Europe and the North America, while much of our continent is dark. The concentration of our lights in Johannesburg, Cape Town and Durban approaches those of the metropolitan areas of the Eastern part of the USA and Western Europe. Look at the night pictures of the world and you will see this.

We have enough airports and planes to transport our people and non-nationals to all corners of the globe. Our airline, South African Airways, has an excellent safety record and it is listed as the best airline to Africa. Just go to the Johannesburg International Airport, in the domestic or even international section, on any Friday, and simply watch human movement and you will marvel at the sheer number of people scrambling to catch a plane. And, did you know that the commercial air route between Cape Town and Johannesburg is the 11th busiest "city pair" in the world?

Not everyone travels by plane. So, what about the roads? Our road infrastructure allows us to traverse this nation in a relatively short period of time, and to enjoy the beauty of our country. From Cape Town to Musina, from Durban to Upington, from Johannesburg to Nelspruit we can travel on good roads while marveling at the beauty of our country. Visitors and tourists are impressed by this infrastructure.

What I have just described is enough to make you feel proud as a South African. But you may be asking yourself a fundamental question: How does this South Africa compare with my South Africa? Right here, in your surroundings, for example, do I see evidence of plenty, of resources and infrastructure in this rich South Africa? Once you start asking that question you are bound to ask: Why are my relatives not employed?

There are even more fundamental questions to be asked. Why are the human development indicators for this country so poor? We rank very low on the human development index, lower than other African countries that have lower GNP per capita compared to ours, like Zimbabwe and Botswana; and lower than other middle-income countries that have equal GNP to ours, like Malaysia or Brazil. We are the country with the largest number of people living with HIV/Aids in Africa and in the world: 12.5 per cent of the 40 million people living with HIV/AIDS in the world reside here in South Africa. We are the country with the largest number of Aids deaths in the world at 360 000 per year, according to the Joint Programme of the United Nations HIV/Aids Programme (UNAIDS).

Why do we have these problems? The answer lies partly in the history of this country and partly in the economic and social development path we have chosen. Apartheid has left us with a legacy of many of these problems. But I will not spend much time discussing the past because we now have the political, economic and moral power to change for the better. I believe we must look at the path we have chosen as a model for our own development. Some lessons from elsewhere may be useful here.

A world-renowned business thinker, Gary Hamel, in his book, **Leading the Revolution**, recounts an interesting observation. Four finance ministers, four Oxford economists, four corporate CEOs, and four London trash collectors were asked in 1984 to predict, 10 years hence, the dollar/pound exchange rate, the rate of inflation among the Organisation of Economic Cooperation and Development (OECD) countries, the price of oil etc.

When 1994 came, none of the predictions were correct. Most interestingly, the finance ministers made the least accurate predictions. In fact, the CEOs and the trash collectors made the best predictions, even though they were still wrong, leading Gary Hamel to suggest: "When it comes to predicting the future, humility is a virtue."

We in South Africa have chosen a macroeconomic model in the name of Growth, Employment and Redistribution (GEAR). By adopting the GEAR model, some may argue that we opted for a short-term solution to stabilise the economy. We may have sacrificed economic growth, job creation and redistribution of the existing wealth. In fact, we lost jobs.

We imposed on ourselves a structural adjustment programme, so we could pay the debt. We now can say the economy is stable. Perhaps we need a new economic model that will take South Africa out of poverty. We need to grow the economy and redistribute the wealth. We need to give a basic income grant to the needy and, more importantly, we need to generate jobs.

We now have the political, economic and moral power to change for the better.

Some suggestions:
1. Celebrate that you are a South African
2. Do not wait to be employed - create a job for yourself.
3. Enhance your compassion
4. Use your constitutional right to speak up
5. Think Think Think
6. Be guided by principles.

So, as you graduate today, there is no queue for filling applications for employment. You can decide to wait for development to trickle down to you or you can claim a spot in the queue for creative solutions.

It is indeed a very good thing to party after the graduation ceremony. You have worked very hard and you deserve it.

And, the first thing you must do after the party is to consult a trash collector. You don't have to go to London. I strongly believe that we have our own talented trash collectors.

This country needs creative graduates to address the many challenges that are facing us. It is through our own creativity that we will be able to create opportunities and improve our lives and those of our compatriots. And there are vehicles to harness our creativity.

Whilst you engage the trash collectors you may want to consider the economic empowerment plan being championed by Mr. Cyril Ramaphosa, the Chancellor of this university. You may also take into account that the Government is currently engaging the mining industry to ensure participation by blacks in this industry. Ask yourself: What opportunities are there in these initiatives?

We have chosen a policy to return the land expropriated from the rightful owners, who became victims only because of the colour of their pigmentation. The process is very slow, while grinding poverty continues to determine the fate of those dispossessed of their land rights. We should not underestimate the importance of land ownership in regard to development.

In his famous book, **Mystery of Capital**, Hernandez de Soto illustrates how ownership of land and property are powerful instruments to unlocking capital for development. We have heard recently how South African banks have been reluctant to lend to blacks because of lack of collateral and the uncertainty of loan repayments. Land ownership can serve as collateral for business loans and as capital towards a business venture such as farming or building a conference centre.

An even greater challenge is HIV/Aids. Let us think for a moment. About 50 per cent of our hospital medical wards are said to be occupied by people afflicted with the disease; and approximately five million people are living

with HIV/Aids here in South Africa. The cabinet's statement, made in April this year, suggesting that there is a place for antiretrovirals (ARVs) in the management of HIV/Aids patients, is encouraging.

Middle-income countries like ours, such as Brazil and Thailand, now treat this condition as a chronic disease and provide life-prolonging antiretroviral drugs, yet we are not able to.

Our Southern African Development Community partners are beginning to say it is more cost-effective to treat people living with HIV/Aids than not, given the large burden of Aids in their countries. South Africa needs to take a bold move to produce low-cost ARVs for its ailing population. We have the law that supports this move; the international community is on our side, as is the political and economic power to produce ARVs for our people and our neighbours. Compulsory licensing and parallel importation are options that are available to us.

The call for increased access to these drugs is not limited to the public sector. The recent call by the Pan-African HIV/Aids Treatment Access Movement to mobilise for a "Global Day of Action Against Coca-Cola", the largest private employer in Africa, and other multinationals, on 17 October 2002, to demand ARV treatment for all HIV-positive workers and their families, demonstrates the impatience the public has for the private sector not playing its part. However, there are sterling efforts that must be recommended such as the plan by Anglo-American and De Beers and BMW to give ARVs to their staff living with Aids. More companies are considering this route.

Given the paradox of living in a wealthy country, but being unable to access this wealth to improve your life and your community, what options do you have? Here are a few suggestions you might find useful.

First, celebrate the fact that you are a South African. There are countries that are worse-off than we are.

Second, do not wait to be employed by someone: create a job for yourself and for others. You have the knowledge, the skill and probably you have a flair for entrepreneurship.

Be an inventor of ideas or products. Let us grow the pie. Be a master of your own destiny. Take a leaf from Donald Trump, the American tycoon, who once said and I quote: "I like thinking big. To me it's very simple: if you are going to be thinking anyway, you might as well think big. Most people think small, because most people are afraid of success, afraid of making decisions, afraid of winning!"

And, might I add, afraid of making mistakes.

In your desire to acquire wealth, start examining the existing wealth and think laterally. See gaps in the different sectors of the economy and find your niche. You might wish to spend time, as Gary Hamel once said, "not speculating on what might happen, but to imagining what you can make happen."

Third, enhance your compassion. If you have none, acquire some as a matter of urgency.

For, as you reach new heights, compassion will help you realise how your development is intertwined with the development of society. It will enable you to wear the moccasins of the poor, unemployed and uneducated who may not be as fortunate as you are.

Fourth, take decisive action upon graduation to use your constitutional right and speak up. Become an advocate and contribute to better policies. Get involved in ensuring that we have policies that will make development move as smoothly as our traffic does on our wonderful highways.

For example, you may develop your advocacy skills so that, by coupling them with your technical know-how, you can present convincing arguments to the Treasury for an alternative model for economic development. Read, read and read. Add **Mystery of Capital** to your reading list...

Fifth, think, think and think. When you think you, will ask questions and by asking questions you will be on the way to solutions.

Sixth, be guided by principles and, as someone once said, "never let your principles die before you do".

As we congregate here, Zackie Achmat is refusing to take antiretroviral therapy unless the government extends the availability of these drugs to some public health facilities. So, as you go out there and land yourself an income-generating opportunit,y and your insurance allows you access to antiretrovirals, think about those who have no access to these life-prolonging medications.

Ensure that you are not contributing to the next HIV infection, by protecting yourself from becoming infected. Inform yourself on the debate on HIV/Aids. Do your best to facilitate access to treatment for those living with HIV/Aids. In doing so you may actually be saving your own life. HIV/Aids does not discriminate on the basis of colour; it has no respect for your education, financial status or power.

Last but not least, make sure the world is a better place because you have touched it.

Thank you for your attention."

Speech delivered at the Graduation Ceremony at the University of Venda on 7th September 2002 and presented to: The Chancellor, Mr C Ramaphosa; Vice-Chancellor, Prof GM Nkondo; Chairperson, Prof B. Pityana; Distinguished guests; Graduates.

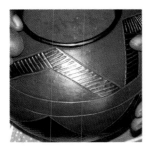   

You can wait for development to trickle down to you, or you can claim a spot in the queue for creative solutions.

"Ex Africa semper aliquid novi."

Pliny the Elder - Roman Historian AD 23 - 79

"Africa always offers something new"

Nkosi sikelel' iAfrika

south africa
THE GOOD NEWS

Credits

Prologue Change in Africa
Flag on Cover - African Collection/Gallo Images; Mandela with Child - Independent Newspapers/Trace Images;

1 Benchmarking Progress in South Africa since 1994
Welcome Mat - Cross Colours Ink; Dancing Feet - Guy Stubbs/Touchlife Images; Constitution Wall - The Star; Schoolboy & Dragonfly - The Star; Women in front of house - The Star; Hands doing Beadwork - Doreen Hemp, Susan Sellschop & Desklink Publishing; Hands weaving Basket - Doreen Hemp, Susan Sellschop & Desklink Publishing;

2 The State of the Economy
Mbeki - AP Photo/Themba Hadebe;

3 Political Leadership
Tap, running water - Guy Stubbs/Touchlife Images; Mandela in Crowd - The Star; Women with Key - The Star; 2 school kids - The Star; Teddy - The Star; Mbeki - PictureNet Africa - Photographer Shaun Harris; Ethnic Woman - Copyright, South African Tourism; Mbeki - Trace Images/Louise Grubb; African boy - Guy Stubbs/Touchlife Images;

4 Government and Opposition
Martinus v Schalkwyk - Independent Newspapers/Trace Images; Egg Cartoon - Minderd Vosloo; Mbeki with African Drum Player - PictureNet Africa - Photographer Henner Frankenfeld; Tony Leon - PictureNet Africa - Photographer Johann van Tonder; Mandela in Parliament - Sunday Times; Mandela & de Klerk - Sunday Times; Black women with Flag - The African collection/Gallo Images; DP Bus with boy & tyre - PictureNet Afirca - Photographer Peter Bauermeister;

5 Financial Stability
Pebbles - Gallo Images; Pebbles - Gallo Images; 2 Boys playing - Gallo Images;

6 Freedom of Speech and the Media
Flying papers - Gallo Images; Religious Man - The Star; Vrye Weekblad - The Star;

7 International Trade
Man in grass - Gallo Images; Employment Ad in Newspaper - Gallo Images; Welcome to SA - AP Photo/Obed Silwa; Woman picking - PictureNet Africa - Photographer Don Boroughs; Gifts in Chair - Gallo Images; Ship at Harbour - PictureNet Africa - Photographer Margaret Waller; Men loading at Harbour - PictureNet Africa - Photographer Margaret Waller; Logs in Water - PictureNet Africa - Photographer Lisa Trocchi; Cape Town - Hetty Zantman/Touchlife Images; Hands with Wheat - Hetty Zantman/Touchlife Images; Cape Town Harbour - Wayne Keet/Touchlife Images; Kids with Candles - Guy Stubbs/Touchlife Images; Man with Wooden Giraffe - Brenda Shelley/Touchlife Images;

8 The Constitution and Constitutional Court
Woman Voting (red box) - The Star; Women with Election Form - The Star; Election Aerial - The Star; Doctor & patient - Guy Stubbs/Touchlife Images; Nurse & Mothers - Guy Stubbs/Touchlife Images

9 Housing Infrastructure
Concrete Houses - Guy Stubbs/Touchlife Images; Bricks & Window Frame - Brenda Shelley/Touchlife Images; Truck & Labourers - Guy Stubbs/Touchlife Images; Builder - Guy Stubbs/Touchlife Images; New House Owner - Guy Stubbs/Touchlife Images; Agriculture - Guy Stubbs/Touchlife Images; Running Water - Guy Stubbs/Touchlife Images; Cleaning Ladies - Guy Stubbs/Touchlife Images; JHB with Shacks in Foreground - The Star; Children with Angel Poster - The Star; Shacks only - The Star; Kettle Image - "Pictures taken from the book SHACK CHIC, Photographer Craig Fraser; White Investors - The Star; Cleaning Ladies in Soweto - The Star;

10 Education
3 Pics on 1st page of Children - The Star; Black Schoolgirl - The Star; Childs Drawing of Flower Flag - Lydia Gates; Boy eating an Orange - Shack Chic "Pictures taken from the Book SHACK CHIC, Photographer Craig Fraser; Girl & Tyre -The Star; 2 School Girls -The Star; Guy with Computer -The Star; Small Kid jumping - The Star; Teacher & Class - Guy Stubbs/Touchlife Images;

11 Agriculture and Transformation
Bakkie with Veggies - Shack Chic "Pictures taken from the Book SHACK CHIC, Photographer Craig Fraser; Windmill - Des Kleineibst/Touchlife Images; Man in Field - Guy Stubbs/Touchlife Images;

12 Tourism
Umbrellas - The Star; Zebra - Malcolm Dare/Touchlife Images; Ethnic Women - Guy Stubbs/Touchlife Images; Beach - Jean-Paul Liveaux/Touchlife Images; Hands with Wirework - Doreen Hemp, Susan Sellschop & Desklink Publishing; Hands with African Pot - Doreen Hemp, Susan Sellschop & Desklink Publishing; Ethnic Man - Guy Stubbs/Touchlife;

13 Environmental Management
Hand with Globe - Gallo Images; Curios - Copyright, SA Tourism; Kids carrying Water Drums - Copyright, SA Tourism; African Girl - Copyright, SA Tourism; Kudu - Copyright, SA Tourism; Bird in Oil - The Star; Cleaners at Dam - The Star; Boy on Stairs - The Star; Dead Bird - The Star; Cleaners - The Star; Recycling Cans - The Star;

14 Tax Collection
Man picking up Coin - Gallo Images; Paper Figures - Gallo Images; 4 Hands Holding - Gallo Images; Paper floating into Computer - Gallo Images; Birthday Cake - Gallo Images; Mbeki with Hand Raised - PictureNet Africa - Photographer Greg Marinovich; Man with ANC Hat - PictureNet Africa - Photographer Nadine Hutton; Man with ANC Flag - PictureNet Africa - Photographer Shaun Harris;

15 Sport
95 Rugby World Cup - Pienaar & Mandela - The Star; Little Boy with Flag - AP Photo/Themba Hadebe; Soccer Players - Picture Net/Photocopier Henner Frankenfeld; Silhouette of Man Jumping - Picture Net/Photocopier Shaun Harris; Baby Jake - AP Photo/Dave Caulkin; Ernie Els - AP Photo/Jon Hrusa; Bob Skinstad - AP Photo/Jon Hrusa; Sibisiso Zuma - AP Photo/Themba Hadebe; Little Boy Playing Soccer - Picture Net/Photocopier Henner Frankenfeld;

16 War Against Crime
Revolver - Gallo Images; Policeman with Folded Arms - Guy Stubbs/ Touchlife Images; Stop Street - Shahn Rowe/Touchlife Images;

17 Black Economic Empowerment
Pillows in Sand - Gallo Images; Street Sign with Buildings - Gallo Images; Cyril Ramaphosa - PictureNet/Photographer Shaun Harris; Bafana Bafana - PictureNet/Photographer Adil Bradlow; Clothes on Washline - Guy Stubbs/Touchlife Images ; Black Business Man - Robert Koene/Touchlife Images; Men at Work Sign - Agent Sprong/Touchlife Images; Business Man in front of Township - Guy Stubbs/Touchlife Images; Mechanics - Guy Stubbs/Touchlife Images;

18 Chameleons, Colour and Culture
Woman with Detail - Brenda Shelley/Touchlife Images; Trumpet - Bruno Bossi/Touchlife Images; Black woman - Gallo Images; Sculpture Hands - Gallo Images; Black Guy - Gallo Images; Paint - Gallo Images; Painted Face - Flag - Dave Rogers/Touchline Photo; Museum Africa- Copyright, SA Tourism; Theatre - Copyright SA Tourism; Black Man Drawing - Copyright, SA Tourism; Small details - The Star;

19 Medical Facilities
Medical - Gallo Images; Medical - Gallo Images; Fire - Jean-Paul Lieveaux/Touchlife Images; Hands - Guy Stubbs/Touchlife Images; Johannesburg - Jean-Paul Lieveaux/Touchlife Images;

20 Aids
Red visual - 2 figures - Jean-Paul Liveaux/Touchlife Images; Nurse - Guy Stubbs/Touchlife Images; Baby reaching out - The Star; Robot - The Star; Candles with Children - The Star;

21 Global Connectedness
Globe on Table - Gallo Images; Tunnel with Light - Gallo Images; Globe with Cable around it - Gallo Images; Boys at Telkom booth - PictureNet Africa - Photographer Brendon-Jon; Multichoice in Tanzania - PictureNet Africa - Photographer Bruce Conradie; Ponti building in JHB - PictureNet Africa - Photographer Eddie Mtsweni; MTN Umbrella's on Beach - PictureNet Africa - Photographer Shaun Harris; Mark Shuttleworth - AP Photo/Misha Japaridze; Power Lines - PictureNet Africa - Photographer Shaun Harris; Eskom Sign - PictureNet Africa - Photographer Shaun Harris; Sasol - PictureNet Africa - Photographer Henner Frankenfeld; Women Making Clothes - PictureNet Africa - Photographer Don Boroughs; Man on Cellphone in Field - PictureNet Africa - Photographer Henner Frankenfeld; Fixing Power Lines in Township - PictureNet Africa - Photographer Shaun Harris; Fixing Power Lines - PictureNet Africa - Photographer Shaun Harris; Kids Working on Computers - PictureNet Africa - Photographer Henner Frankenfeld; Vodaworld - PictureNet Africa - Photographer Shaun Harris; Woman Talking on Cellphone - PictureNet Africa - Photographer Joao Silva; Telkom logo - PictureNet Africa - Photographer Shaun Harris; Pile of old Phones - PictureNet Africa - Photographer Johann van Tonder; Man talking on Phone at Booth - PictureNet Africa - Photographer Shaun Harris; Shop in Township with Vodacom sign - PictureNet Africa - Photographer Suzy Bernstein; Coast Scene - PictureNet Africa -

Photographer Fred Hasner; Children & Computers - PictureNet Africa - Photographer Shaun Harris;

22 Exports & Labour Productivity
Plant photographs - BMW - SA; 3 Hands Holding each Other - Gallo Images;

23 Transport Infrastructure
Eye & plane - Shahn Rowe/Touchlife Images; Train - Wayen Keet/ Touchlife Images; Aeroplane - Image Bank; Road Concrete - Gallo Images; Roads - Photo Access; Taxi - The Star; Metro Train - The Star; Bus Station - The Star;

24 Corporate Governance
Bottle with Coins - Gallo Images; Newspaper Crown - Gallo Images; Pot with R-Sign - Gallo Images; Growth - Gallo Images;

25 Private Sector
Growth - Gallo Images; Person in City - Gerda Genis/Touchlife Images; Hope Building - Oliver Pelipo/Touchlife Images; Black Boy - Guy Stubbs/Touchlife Images; Nature reserve - Guy Stubbs/Touchlife Images; Class room - Guy Stubbs/Touchlife Images; School Boy & Girl - Merwelene v.d. Merwe/Touchlife Images; Boy on Beach - Jean-Paul Lieveaux/Touchlife Images; Ships - Peter Maltbie/Touchlife Images; Woman & candle - Guy Stubbs/Touchlife Images; Street at Night - Guy Stubbs/Touchlife Images; Workers - Guy Stubbs/Touchlife Images; Woman & House - Guy Stubbs/Touchlife Images; Sea & Starfish - Gallo Images; Starfish - Gallo Images; Girl & Doll - Jean-Paul Lieveaux/ Touchlife Images; Discussion - Gallo Images; Papers in Circle - Gallo Images; Globe & Hands - Gallo Images; Ethnic Environment - Gallo Images; Green Robot - Gallo Images; Mandela - Sunday Times;

26 NEPAD
Iris - Gallo Images; Maze - Gallo Images; Globe Puzzle - Gallo Images; Mbeki - AP Photo/Saurabh Das; Mugabe - AP Photo/Obed Silwa; Placing Brick - AP Photo/Mohammed Rawas; African Flags - AP Photo /Obed Silwa;

27 The South African Vision
Men with "10" Signs - Gallo Images; Hands & Glass Ball - Gallo Images; Woman in Front of TV - Gallo Images; ANC Poster - PictureNet Africa - Photographer Nadine Hutton; Coca Cola - PictureNet Africa - Photographer Suzy Bernstein; Mandela with dove - AP Photo/Themba Hadebe; Rugby Player - PictureNet Africa - Photographer Adil Bradlow; Mbeki in Rugby Jersey - PictureNet Africa - Photographer Shaun Harris; Wine Vats - PictureNet Africa - Photographer Henner Frankenfeld; Kruger Nat Park - Heads - PictureNet Africa - Photographer Shaun Harris; Eskom - PictureNet Africa - Photographer Shaun Harris;

Epilogue
Graduates - Gallo Images; Hands - Gallo Images; Candles - Gallo Images.